HYDROLITH

SURREALIST RESEARCH & INVESTIGATIONS

Hydrolith: Surrealist Research and Investigations.

Cover image by Ribitch.

Cymatic photo by Collin Cunningham on page 32 appears via
Creative Commons *Attribution-Share Alike 3.0 Unported* license.
Microfossil images by Hannes Grobe, pages 1, 38, 72, 232, 235 and back cover,
via Creative Commons *Attribution 3.0 Unported* license.
Ice images on pages 19, 25, 30, 118 and 217 are in the public domain, and were photographed
by the Electron and Confocal Microscopy Laboratory,
Agricultural Research Service, USDA.

ISBN: 978-0-578-05039-3

Additional copies of this book can be ordered from LuLu:
http://www.lulu.com

Oyster Moon Press is a non-profit, surrealist publishing co-op that
originated in Berkeley, California.

OYSTER
MOON
PRESS
www.oystermoonpress.com

Table of Contents

HYDROLITH
OR, WATER STONE OF THE WISE

THAT IS, A CHYMICAL WORK, IN WHICH THE WAY IS SHEWN, THE MATTER NAMED, AND THE PROCESS DESCRIBED

NAMELY, THE METHOD OF OBTAINING THE UNIVERSAL TINCTURE

Hydrolith brings together a selection of recent work from the international Surrealist movement. It aims to provide a partial "snapshot" of contemporary Surrealism for an English-speaking audience, and includes work originally produced in English – some especially written for this volume – and work originally produced in French, Greek, Romanian, Spanish, Swedish and Turkish which is being presented in English for the first time.

The scope of contributions is almost as wide as that of the Surrealist adventure itself, but we have chosen to highlight three themes in particular. First, sound and auditory expression, including both noise and music, which has been a lively and contested area of Surrealist investigation since the appearance of Paul Nougé's "Music is Dangerous" in 1928. Second, the exploration of space and place – a persistent preoccupation of the international movement during the past 15-20 years, with a new wave of Surrealist interest in psychogeography arguably having been sparked by the Stockholm Surrealist Group's investigations of atoposes ("worthless places") in the mid-1990s. Third, myth, which has been a Surrealist obsession since the movement's inception. The project of mythopoesis continues to dominate much Surrealist research and creation today.

The six editors of *Hydrolith* are spread geographically across Europe and North America, and although some of us have been able to get together for brief periods in twos or threes, most of our editorial work has been conducted long-distance by use of email and the internet. This has brought with it the obvious advantages (speed of communication, ease of contact with Surrealist friends worldwide, relatively cheap publishing software and print packages) as well as the disadvantages (the danger that fast and easy communication can be superficial, the paradox that faster communication can mean slower decision-making, the misunderstandings that can arise in the absence of more personal and non-verbal contact). Despite the limitations of this way of working, we envision the *Hydrolith* project as a way to continue Surrealist research across national borders, not just for the purposes of sharing and collaboration, but also as a means to connect with old and new friends and comrades who share our fury at the great capitalist machine which threatens all life on the planet.

The aim of the international Surrealist movement is to change life and transform the world. As Surrealists and revolutionaries, with our individual voices and actions as well as with this collective publication, we repeatedly take aim at the global economic and social system which crushes the life and freedom of humans and non-humans alike. We are acutely aware that the world is in a potentially cataclysmic state of crisis – for us, Surrealism is essential in our response to the crisis. While the 20th century might come to be viewed as the "golden years" of capitalism, with its saccharine illusion of endless expansion and "progress" without consequences, the beginning of the 21st century has forced all but the most wilfully ignorant to acknowledge the realities of global pollution and toxicity, biological extinction, and new levels of urban insanity and death which mark the pinnacle of miserabilism to date. But in the face of all this, we proudly retain our revolutionary optimism, and defiantly continue to pin all our hopes on poetry and the Marvellous. We offer *Hydrolith* as an expression of our desires, in the spirit of love, poetry, pleasure and revolt.

Eric Bragg, Merl Fluin, Mattias Forshage, Ribitch, Shibek & Nikos Stabakis
Berkeley, London, Stockholm, Portland & Athens

Spring 2010

Untitled drawing by Schlechter Duvall (1922-2009)

The Lizard's Cry

Bertrand Schmitt

It would not be too risky to hazard the guess that music, a forbidden topic in surrealism until further notice, represents on the contrary all the excess, all the vibratory bedazzlement, the supreme flight of a surrealist wing still scarcely agitated.

Pierre Naville "Of sounds and noises"

May a failed encounter be repeated? The surrealists' reservations on the matter of music are so striking that even today we wonder why it met with such mistrust, indeed hostility, given that surrealist activity otherwise sought to embrace all domains of thought and sensibility. Of course there were certain rapprochements, whether avowed or not, between the surrealists and music. There was the manifest interest of certain individuals (Soupault, Naville, Leiris, Zežek, or more recently Petr Král, Alain Jouffroy, François-René Simon, Ludvík Šváb, Hal Rammel, Aurélien Dauguet, Johannes Bergmark, Alexandre Pierrepont...), but very few theoretical texts have attempted to evaluate all that music might have to offer to the surrealist quest. Even less considered was the possibility of encounters or collaborations with musicians. However, at a time when music is omnipresent, indeed intrusive, it seems urgent to undertake a profound study that might disengage from the poverty and standardisation of the musical field that which remains extraordinarily vibrant, and which, in spite of the stupefying mass mediatisation, maintains a direct, vital, essential approach vis-à-vis a form of concrete imagination.

1. Language of music, music of language

A man is like a tree, the music is the healing force of the universe.

Albert Ayler

I am not interested in revisiting the anecdotal reasons that have partially explained the surrealists' dislike for music (even if, on this point, the personal views of André Breton seem to have been decisive) but rather, to start with, in attempting to shed light on certain essential characteristics that have deferred the inevitable rapprochement.

In fact this mistrust towards musical expression is not a trait of the surrealists alone. It is even striking to note that numerous poets were impervious to musical accents. That is because, in essence, the language of words and that of music are fundamentally different. The language of words is first and foremost a matter of conceptualisation. It is an expression differentiated from the real, which uses the medium of words to transmit concepts, and hence images. The morphemes employed for speaking, before being simple sounds, are already visualisations. Also, the articulation of phonemes with one another obeys a syntax that is ideological rather than purely auditory. Thus, it is not at all necessary to hear in order to master language, and a deaf person can interiorise the real phenomena expressed by the language of words with the same acuity, the same pregnancy, as one who can hear. Whether spoken or written, language is *formulated.* It is largely an abstraction, an incessant metaphor of real phenomena by signifiers. Speech thus appears like thought looking out (or in a mirror) towards the exterior.

It is all very different when it comes to music (at least "pure music," which is not associated with words). What motivates this expression is a non-differentiated and fundamentally concrete rapport with things. This is what Pierre Naville expresses when he writes: "There is in the combination of pure sonorities something irreducible, that no semiotics can manage to reduce to the rules of language formed by words." One may think that surrealism, which aimed to be a research into "the real functioning of thought," has embraced the two articulated forms of thought: the language of words and that of images (both of which are *articulated* around a representation of the real), yet has left behind music, which could not speak to it. This difficulty to enjoy music has also been confessed by Freud in his study on Michelangelo's Moses[1].

By choosing to operate within the sphere of formulated thought, surrealism put aside music and the essentially emotional world to which it offers access. However, between the two poles, namely the language of words and that of music, there have been detected numerous bridges, and it is particularly the surrealist researches and findings on language that have rendered these connections manifest. In fact, by means of automatic writing and the questions raised by psychic automatism, surrealist expression has reached the "beyond" of language. There, what is expressed no longer belongs solely to the order of the concept, meaning the abstraction of speech, but also to a form of concrete imagination, which no longer concerns sense alone, that is the signified, but the very material quality of words. This verbal material attained substance via the byway of verbal slippage, of semantic and auditory games, of prosodies, rhythms and resonances of speech, as they are produced in the most liberated expression. There thus appeared transparently that astonishing verbal availability that is as much the outcome of the image (hence of the concept) as of the purely material (even physical) jubilation of words and sounds. Certain passages of *The Magnetic Fields* are therefore actual verbal improvisations, whose speed is given by the fluidity of assonances and auditory collages. For our thought, entirely wrapped within the envelope of language-concept, does not for all that cease to be an "archaic," "primitive" expression, where sound remains a primal, almost animistic echo, along with the universe of external phenomena. In fact, the morphology of our thought, and hence of our language, was constituted during the early years of our existence, with the aid of auditory-concrete games, whereby crying, stammering, stuttering, rhythmic repetitions of the same syllables, have formed a quasi-"solid" matter upon which the conceptual edifice was elevated. It is actually a return to that "primal" and concrete music of language that was researched in certain bruitist dada poems, in Kurt Schwitters' *Ur Sonata*, and subsequently in the Lettrist experimentations. The hardly convincing results in these cases, however, point towards an impasse. And if language once materialised on the basis of a concrete and musical form, it nevertheless surpassed swiftly this isolated aspect in order to acquire, via the concept (that is, by passing from the auditory to the visual), a different power peculiar to it.

The fact remains that, brimming over pure abstraction, there subsist some kinds of sonorous rust, pointing towards a form of imaginary-concrete. It is these concrete aspects of language that render poetry the most energetic form of thought (and thus the harder to translate, the most resistant to conceptualisation. The alchemy of the verb is a mixture of the abstract and concrete powers of language, in other words of the images and the physical sensation of the sounds which also forms the poem's "musicality.")

Music, for its part, has trouble accommodating the abstractions and structures peculiar to language. Thus in the West we have seen an evolution of musical form, from free, open, concrete and instinctive structures to codified forms of scored music. Besides, this evolution has followed that of thought and language (from certain magical and animistic modes to scholastic, classical, then positivist thought). This movement has led western music towards closed and defined forms of classical music, whose structure struggles to repeat the syntactic structures of linguistic forms (the "partition" of musical tempos, the articulation of parts into sequences, the transcription of the execution in the form of a reproducible code...) By doing this, western music has lost that which constituted the vital kernel of all musical expression, namely its immediately concrete and indeterminate form (since these two aspects are interlinked). This evolution has led straight to an impasse and a grave crisis. A crisis that actually corresponds (but is that so astonishing?) to the general crisis in sensibility, manifested, at the end of the 19th and the beginning of the 20th centuries, by the appearance of the avant-gardes. Thus, at the moment when dada, futurism, poetism and then surrealism questioned, each in its own fashion, certain sterile ideologies of western thought, music was tearing the veil that used to cover it and attempting a return to primal forms, closer to immediate emotional expression. Of course, this questioning was neither generalised nor effected by established musicians. And, facing emotional barrenness, some even attempted to push even further the formal abstraction of scored music, to the point of sclerosis under the dictatorial yoke of serial, dodecaphonic and repetitive music.

2. Musical body, music of bodies

> *Liberating music implies not only making it exit the ghetto of fixed form, but also accepting sound as an autonomous organism: composing thus resides less in the act of domesticating than in imitating nature in its modus operandi.*
>
> John Cage

This questioning of music's conceptual and ideological language has taken different and equally radical forms, whose foremost aim was to "reincarnate," to give back flesh, blood and breath to an anaemic music. By turning away from classical western thought and towards eastern thought (John Cage studied Zen philosophy for two years, La Monte Young went to study in India...) and African rhythms, by returning to certain "traditional" or "ethnic" kinds of music, these musical forms searched for a new vital impetus.

One constant desire of these musicians was also to go back to the original unity, that of sound and noise, in other words to reject the ideologisation of music through the sign (notation), privileging instead the raw expression of reality and its phenomena. Music was thus restored to its magical and incantatory power, that of a direct influx of nature. Sounds have deserted metaphorical language in order to find again analogical language, which is that of our own corporeal perception. In fact, if neurologists are to be believed, our perception of music does not pass through the articulation of language or of the image, but rather through direct physical perception (vibrations, variations, pulsations...) Music is thus a language of the body before being a language of the spirit. What it puts into play is a non-mediated resonance of our body with the external phenomena and objects. By returning to this conception, music found once more its primary goal, that of engaging in a dialogue with nature. This dialogue may include everything from the simplest mimicry (whistling in order to reproduce sound of the wind...) to the magical or animistic conception (appropriating the qualities of an animal by reproducing its song...), or to a vaster analogical conception which turns music into a correspondence between the individual microcosm and the universal macrocosm. What, then, is so surprising in the fact that the amplified pulsations of quasars uncannily resemble heartbeats? Each moment, what is at stake in music is an exteriorisation of this energetic rhythm that traverses all things (from the tiniest quark to the biggest novas) and is the rhythm of life itself. Consequently, there can no longer be abstract music, given that each kind of music is "the music of the spheres" as well as that monotonous beating of arterial pressure in the hollow of our ear.

The magic peculiar to music would thus be to offer us access to a physical and emotional mode of participation in the universe. Henceforth, there is no longer a valid reason to keep thinking that this approach contradicts that offered by the image or by language, nor to regard it as secondary. On the contrary, music allows us to embrace forms of the concrete imaginary that words or images do not manage to make us attain. Besides, the sonic expression appeals to deeper layers of our perception, which have not been totally colonised by the "dictatorship of seeing" or reduced to conceptualised perception alone. Just as touch allows the resurgence of certain "primal" sensations that derive from our animal mind as from our individual mental morphology, sound and noise also bring about raw affects, capable of carrying along new images, new sensations. Music thus does not lead to a meaning, it opens towards an enigma. It permits access to a prehensile world through imagination rather than comprehension. However, the imagination at work here is a concrete one. The futurist Luigi Russolo was conscious of this when he wrote his *Art of Noises*. It was in the same spirit that Pierre Schaeffer wrote his *Treatise of Musical Objects* and developed his *musique concrète*, in the heart of the workshop of the Office of French Radio-Television (O.R.T.F). They have thereby shown that there is no difference between sound and noise other than a cultural and aesthetic one (that of wanting to turn musical expression into a codified language based on the ideological schema of speech).

3. The echo of chance

We can turn towards towards works of suprarational orders, by which I do not mean irrational.

Karlheinz Stockhausen

All these experimentations have highlighted the incredible evocative and creative power of raw reality thanks to the direct resonance it attains over our perception. They have also shown to what point this resonance is evanescent, instantaneous, fleeting. It leaves but the mark of its passage (as remarked by Pierre Naville again, the note is only a momentary trace whereas the word is a permanent mark of meaning). The nature of music is thus above all about being ephemeral, punctual, factual, which contradicts all theories of musical scoring and notation. Hence also the indeterminate and open nature adopted by music, once it is liberated from the conceptualisation of language. Raw sound, like all physical expressions of the real, actually seems to be governed by aleatory principles rather than by immutable rules. Sensitive to the tiniest variation (atmospheric pressure, hygrometry, temperature, resonance of the materials...), it is unpredictable both in its emission and in its reception. Being restored to the primitive entity, namely that of sound, has allowed musicians to take into account all the fluctuations, all the hazards involved in its execution. Henceforth, all music ought to integrate the caprices of chance (that is, to let the sound develop and evolve like a living entity about to borrow unpredictable forms). Each executed morsel can only be so once, since upon each execution an unsuspected multitude of uncontrollable and aleatory parameters surface and recreate a new morsel. Based on these observations there appeared the principles of aleatory music, or of factual music. By introducing less and less controllable parameters to the open structures (for example different possibilities of play for each performer, each one choosing to play whichever sequence whenever s/he desires…), these structures have little by little come to leave the lion's share to chance and occurrence. This is what John Cage proposed, by refusing to consider music as a domestication of sound, or power over it, but rather seeing it as a manner of letting a situation, a living process, be and evolve by itself, by integrating the role of chance that this induces. For his part, Karlheinz Stockhausen introduced concrete elements (voices, noises...) that intervened in an aleatory fashion during the execution. He was also opposed to the traditional form of the linear development of musical themes and defended the idea of a lyricism of immediacy and immanence, in order to bring into question the "eternal" (hence ideal) status of music.

This new conception of music, beyond principles of determination (whether musical score or the mathematical sequences of serial music), has allowed the sonic material to express itself beyond all constraints other than physical ones, and has rendered audible all the inexhaustible and unsuspected faculties it possesses… This new questioning over musical language is characterised by the musicologist André Boucourechliev as "total abandon of dualist forms of thought, conception of a relativity and multiplicity of structural rapports, rejection of a priori hierarchic concepts, rejection of certainty in favour of probability, abandonment of closed and immutable forms in favour of open structures and forms".

4. The blue notes of a black revolt

The oppression of the political system is also to be found in the aesthetic system.

Cecil Taylor

However, despite the interest they aroused, those different "revolutions" within music have remained mere formal controversies. They unfolded like battles between castes, musicians' disputes, affairs of specialists, of those possessing musical knowledge. At no time did they actually overturn the way of hearing and the musical sensibility of each and everyone. They did not, after all, constitute anything but an evolution in the interior of the musical sphere and did not bring about a wider questioning of sensibility. On this account, they are inexorably condemned to remain within the cultural and aesthetic plane of Art, where after all they evolve with no particular problems. Dialectically, they represent but one of those rebounding movements which permit the regeneration of an ideology that has run its course. If the tendencies apparent in these evolutions (questioning of the ideological and conceptual structure of music, return to concrete forms, appearance of the aleatory, instantaneous and ephemeral character of works....) problematise essentially the mortifying and alienating character of western music, it is nevertheless not in "classical contemporary" music that one has to look for an actual mutation, but in jazz.

Jazz is a real musical "revolution," both in form and in essence. Having emerged at the beginning of the 20th century, it has been linked from the start with the effervescence of sensations and ideas that agitated the period between the two world wars. Yet jazz was not only the emanation or the result of a mode or an era's climate. To start with, it was in a visceral fashion the raw and collective expression of a people struggling to forge its own mythology. Thus it was very soon established as a radical questioning of the intellectualised and codified conception of western classical music. But whereas contemporary music tended to borrow from other cultures (Indian, African....) in order to reverse them within a still-Cartesian discourse, jazz has invented its own culture and let it deviate according to the inventiveness and sensibility of its interpreter. Nor is it surprising that jazz was born in the African-American community: an uprooted people with ancestral traditions, a demoted people in the country where "everything seems possible," a people of liberated slaves yet also a community that suffered humiliation and persecution. Jazz thus appeared to be at once a resourceful and inventive music, a cry of exaltation, of jubilation, but also of revolt. It is thus that it sought incessantly to escape from the temptations of recuperation or integration. A raw and physical music, jazz has been described from its very beginnings as the music of "negroes," the music of "savages," a veritable return to the body in an American society of Calvinist and puritan tradition. And if a certain classicism was installed around the '30s, jazz soon manifested itself in other ways, flirting with all kinds of limit-experiences (including those of alcohol and drugs), mixing love, death and life in a never-ending quest for pleasure (or suffering).

This radicalness of jazz, nevertheless, was not a purism, and even in its more advanced experimentations jazz has remained a "live" music, a living music, made for and (partially) by hearing, sharing, the moment of performance. And even if jazz is an eminently personal and subjective expression that invokes, more than any other kind of music, the soloist (that is, individual expression), it is also a collective music. In this, it incarnates a certain utopia, that of an organic fusion of different strong individualities (and the best moments in jazz are those that let us half-perceive that magic of real harmony which is no longer the function of a partition, that is, of a specialisation, nor of a division of labour among the performers). The jam session thus realises this "community" of sensibility, whereby what is collectively shared and attributed to everyone is no longer the lot of a common referent (language) but that of a raw and concrete emanation of the imaginary.

Jazz has also found this collective expression to be the emanation of a community. It is thus that jazz posed naturally as the expression of black revolt in the '60s and '70s, as it had already been the music of contestation for the Beat generation (even if the latter remained after all a rather "existential" contestation, confined to a certain artistic and intellectual milieu). Jazz, and more particularly the "New Thing" or free jazz, have been directly link to the struggle for Black Power. Cries of raw energy and incarnations of a certain refusal, these forged, via the experimentations of the Art Ensemble of Chicago or Albert Ayler, the hymns and arms of a fighting era. It was by this same movement that May '68 saw the flowering of an incredible musical explosion. This latter, appropriating the energy and radicalness of free jazz or improvised music, went beyond the jazzists' milieu to join popular music (mixing jazz, freak-rock, psychedelia, with the experimentations of contemporary music; creating a big movement that goes from Bernard Lubat to Colette Magny, from Henry Cow to Frank Zappa, from Can to Soft Machine, from King Crimson to Gong...). Thus, jazz touched the white European community, giving free rein to a plethora of inventions and radical vindications, while remaining outside the hammering effected by the media and the commercial record industry.

For beyond mass movements, jazz remains the emanation of an intimately personal revolt. It is the revolt of a John Coltrane attacking all the commonplaces of his time, that of a Charlie Mingus, enraged rebel, fighting the authorities, and also that of a Charles Gayle, fighting every day, on the limit of marginalisation, to live the accents of his music. This intimate character is linked to the subjective and unique nature of the music, whose expression, while collective, is above all the vindication of an interior singularity.

5. Psychic automatisms and improvisation

Has music ever been anything but an automatic wave?

Georges Ribemont-Dessaignes, "Déjà-jadis"

It is through its character, at once concrete and subjective, individual and collective, that musical expression most profoundly meets surrealist research. The (often disappointed) faith that Breton accorded to researches on the pure automatism of thought finds in musical improvisation an incarnated form. Actually, in improvisation the instrument even loses its implemental function, in order to become instead a physical extension and permit the quasi-magical augmentation of organic capacities (those of breath, bodily rhythm, speed...). Playing an instrument no longer serves to reproduce a mental construction (the composition) but is, rather, the amplification of internal desires and urges, which comes to include even the slightest physical details (fatigue, reflexes...). Musical improvisation thus poses as the unique and momentary space of an encounter between psychic and gestural automatism (as this may appear in dance as well). One must also have seen a musician play at that crucial moment in order to feel along with him/her all that this represents, in terms of danger but also of physical pleasure. For the performer, the uninterrupted and unpredicted eruption of the interior flux no longer strays along the direction of images and visualisation but takes the path of concrete and physical perception. The slightest sound becomes sensation. The note is no longer the fundamental unity of a codified language, but the raw, real and immediate expression of the body. What the performer expresses, then, is those internal agitations rather than an aesthetic or ideological discourse.

"First sight at a womb, I wish I were a worm in it", photograph by Ayşe Özkan

Music here joins the function of the magical trance in its desire to exteriorise certain internal urges via bodily language. It is therefore the space of a liberation of the libido and allows the overcoming of oppression (which also explains its importance in our societies, in which it plays the game of an outlet, whereby it equilibrates, regulates, even interrupts, the inherent savagery of the body. However, this recuperation by the system is not due to the music itself, but rather to the *society of the spectacle*.)

The liberation procured by raw music is also a result of excess. Musical improvisation, with the frenzy and violence peculiar to it, is a passage from quantity to quality. The tiniest improvisation by Coltrane might thus wander for more than 20 minutes before finding its centre of gravity. Similarly, Cecil Taylor avowed his desire to multiply the notes excessively in order to attain an original and dense magma from which there might emerge the most profound emotional expression. We find here the same dynamics of lyrical accumulation that is at work in *The Chants of Maldoror,* in the poetry of Jean-Pierre Duprey or in the novels of Sade. It is this emotional and erotic agitation that André Breton anticipated when he wrote: "[It] seems to me that it is in the expression of the passion of love that both music and poetry are most likely to reach this supreme point of incandescence."[2] A savage and excessive form of desire that finds its incarnation in a poetics of the body, musical improvisation joins the most primitive kinds of music: those of trances and ecstasies, or even more those of the rites of possession. What it expresses is this love, this energy (whether creative or destructive) that links the individual in its utmost intimacy with the immanence of the phenomena that surround it. There is, then, nothing astonishing about witnessing virtual metamorphoses in the course of playing.

I will thus long remember that concert we went to, Alexandre Pierrepont, Michel Zimbacca and I. There, and while he was accompanying the saxophonist Tim Berne in a deafening sonic quest, we saw the guitarist Marc Ducret being transformed, down to his tiniest gesture, into a reptile. We then heard what none of us could have suspected, and that Marc Ducret alone, at that very moment, was in a position to make us share: the lizard's cry.

.... to be continued.

Prague, January 1998.

Translated by Nikos Stabakis

Notes

1) "I wished to approach (the works of art) in my own manner, that is, to show myself in what way they attain an effect. In a case when I cannot do that, with music for example, I am almost incapable of enjoyment. A rationalist or maybe analytical disposition objects inside me, refusing to let me be taken in without knowing at the same time why I am and who it is that takes me."

2) André Breton *Le silence est d'or*, in La clé des champs [English translation: Louise Varèse, in: Franklin Rosemont (ed.) *What is Surrealism? Selected Writings of André Breton* New York: Pathfinder, 1978, p. 268.]

Surrealist Music?

Mattias Forshage

Nowadays it seems music is one of the central aspects of surrealist creativity, in spite of those traditionalists who still believe that surrealism just is not applicable in relation to music. While some want to tie any idea of surrealist music closely to certain strands of black music, or to free improvisation, many others look for various superficial or profound connections with all kinds of phenomena within the field of music. This text is more or less within the latter perspective, trying to modestly look for fruitful co-incidences of perspective wherever they might appear, but also suggesting the possibility of an overall methodological view of addressing the surrealist possibilities in the entire sphere.

Even if the semantic discussion of the adjective "surrealist" is not very interesting in itself, it might need to be addressed so as to get clear on what we are talking about at all. Obviously, we cannot develop a general perspective if we stick to the most narrow and rigorous senses of the word "surrealist" (as referring to things created by one or more explicit surrealists for a consciously surrealist purpose and in accordance with an in some sense surrealist method), and any real curiosity about the possibilities of the field will also create the need to go beyond a slightly broader but still rigorously historical sense (as referring to things created by someone or someones who have been associated with, or in some other way have positioned themselves as consciously sympathetic towards, the surrealist movement, with a purpose in some sense surrealist). It will be necessary to address some general objective sense (that clearly showing themes or spirit parallel to, influenced by and/or relevant to that of surrealism). On the other hand, if we reach out to the subjective-objective definition (as referring to things that have a surrealist, poetically fruitful mode of action, suggestion, frame of association, for a given listener at a given occasion), which will certainly be one of the interesting perspectives, it will nevertheless be very difficult to delimit the relevant discussion, and we will end up amassing interesting anecdotes about how various pieces of music have under particular circumstances provoked fruitful poetic coincidences and openings, which is not the purpose here.

It seemed that Nougé's "Music is dangerous" and Breton's "Silence is golden" suggested a way of addressing the world of sounds from the viewpoint of poetry which long remained largely uninvestigated within surrealism. The fact that many people pointed out very interesting similarities in sensibility with much black music didn't change this. Then Davey Williams and his friends in Alabama from the '70s onwards, and even more tirelessly Johannes Bergmark in Stockholm and elsewhere from the '80s, pointed out the extent of coincidence between the perspectives of surrealism and free improvisation.

My own perspective on surrealism and music is largely built upon this solid ground laid down by Johannes Bergmark's agitation, theoretical investigation, historical charting and practical experimentation, which all of us Stockholm surrealists more or less took part in somehow. He has elsewhere emphasised how any early simplifications or formalisms in his own views of music were corrected by his reading of Christopher Small's writings, with the concept of *musicking* stressing the processual and ritual character of music. Later, I personally found that Chris Cutler's book *File under Popular* corrected and magnificently clarified my own views in a perhaps analogous way, making impossible a formalistic perspective on what constitutes radical experimenting by developing a strictly historical context.

Cutler teaches us to ask ourselves what constitutes a literally progressive music in a particular historical situation, what constitutes progressive or regressive choices in relation to the possibilities of the field, its markers, its market, its technologies, etc. To stick to an established idiom is rarely very radical in this sense, but also not regressive in itself, it all depends on the configuration of the field – the point is, through conscious experimentation, radical subjectivity and intersubjectivity, and through conscious attitudes opposing the market of the specific field as well as society in general, to stay in motion and be able to discover something. In this sense this perspective doubtlessly constitutes a kind of avant-gardism, even if it also is in the nature of things that in many situations one of the most radical possibilities is to close one's eyes to current fashions and conflicts which seem superficial and spectacular, and instead relate back to "outdated" forms to the extent they are perceived as relevant to radical subjectivity at that time and place.

For anyone who operates within the specialised forums (which there often is a point in avoiding, but also a different point in participating in, in order to find comrades, find the "gold of time", find effective subversive strategies, see the field of possibilities, see history), much will concern choices and attitudes in relation to those specific alternatives which are currently in motion concerning genre conventions, style markers, techniques and technologies, alliances and channels. But of course a radical music can't be "calculated" based on such concerns and expected to have very much to say – it remains the inner criteria, the poetic spirit, which decide. And purely iconoclastic breaks with convention, like the cultivation of purely statistical freedom, is of course never interesting in itself, but only to the extent it manages to tear an aperture towards the genuinely unknown.

For that reason, I suspect that a certain focus on reasoning about how well-known surrealist techniques can be applied in music may have been a hampering factor. For those who make music or want to make music, techniques may of course still inspire or force inspiration, or not. I mean, based on a basic formula where exteriorising an inner model ≈ invoking the hidden sounds ≈ awakening the songs of the shadows ≈ listening to the unknown, and applying a poetic criterion, it is still possible to do anything (or nothing). That remains the main thing, and all that is needed. Trying desperately to come up with musical equivalents of automatism, paranoia-criticism, exquisite corpses, questions-and-answers, collage, frottage, decalcomania, simulation of madness states, one inside another, détournement, parallel stories, news from nowhere, time-travellers' potlatch, etc. etc., might eventually be worth it whenever it actually leads to discoveries, but in most cases I suspect it remains a formalistic therapy for curatorial nerds or overenthusiastic dogmatists.

The discussion about surrealism and music also seems to demand a discussion of use value and market value. This good old distinction has been defended by Marxists and muddled by post-structuralists for a long time (and sometimes it is difficult to tell which is the most mystifying). Here I would like to invoke it as a universal analytical distinction between two logically polarised functional aspects, and not as discrete entities.

It is easy to problematise the simple opposition between the two by bringing in the category of the *symbolic*. First, market value in itself has originated as a kind of secondary symbolisation of use value by way of a universal equivalent starting to live a life of its own, and second, symbolic dimensions can mediate between the two categories (and muddle them) in any direction. Via the symbolic it turns out that nothing is what it seems to be and simple dichotomies become very difficult to uphold. But nevertheless it is still possible to make simple analytical distinctions. The symbolic order, too, has its aspects of use value (in the case of music we see the people-uniting, identity-creating, emotion-expressing, message-communicating aspects in this category) and of market value (that which is called the "personality market" and "cultural capital": the performer's name and "cred", competition and power aspects).

Much of what is interesting about music will always take place within the domain of this symbolic use value (the ritual function of music, physical expressivity etc.) – of course it is difficult to draw the line. But use value and market value both primarily concern utilitarian aspects however you twist and turn the question. Surrealism is usually much more interested in the non-utilitarian aspects. But even that is a kind of use value. It is a use value insofar as it is an immediate, in principle unmediated and autonomous (yes yes, we have all heard the objections against considering anything unmediated and autonomous), concrete social and individual usage, but only with other criteria than practical utilitarianism in the narrow sense. It would be possible to tie the formula *l'art pour l'art* to such a non-utilitarian use value, but in practice it is usually connected with focusing on cultural capital or symbolic market value: on the social meaning of the gesture of being able to be a proponent of such a disinterestedness. Well, along the same lines Marcuse (and German philosophers before him) called this "the aesthetic dimension". But then again, today we prefer to add a disclaimer to the word aesthetic, because it, along with *l'art pour l'art*, has been put to work carrying many connotations of both the upper-class arrogance of cultural capital and the more or less purely formal concerns within each art form.

Pure joy, emotional movement, elementary communication (elementary in the sense of being an expression of elementary sociality, rather than a specific mediation of a message or a game with roles and hierarchies) would be non-utilitarian use value, but what is most central from the viewpoint of surrealism is astonishment and everything connected to it: the domains of falling in love, unruly curiosity, imagination, disinterested playing and ceaseless experimentation, everything having to do with the poetic and with the qualitative sense of the unknown.

Perhaps the distinction between historical and ahistorical interest can be put in these terms: the value of different cases of music from the historical viewpoint very much concerns how music situates itself in the social sphere, i.e. its symbolic use value, while from an ahistorical viewpoint everything worth listening to is unique, an exception, i.e. a non-utilitarian use value.

One of the most stubbornly (and possibly vainly) dialectical things about surrealism has always been the notion of a sublation (*Aufhebung*) of this distinction between historical and ahistorical. The way history moves would assure us that that which is most historically relevant would be identical with that which has the most sovereign lack of concern for – and which hence almost magically negates – the given. In a sense, this is a step backwards, but nowadays we are often reasonable enough to see that there is still a need to separate the two aspects analytically in this search for the gold of time. Even more significantly we tend to lack Hegel's historical optimism, and see that the most dynamic possibilities often are on the losing side in the struggles of history, and that the progressive isn't necessarily a harbinger of developments to come but instead very often fails or gets repressed or remains an unintelligible exception until it one day perhaps will find its true usage.

If it is possible to use the word "progressive" as the encompassing adjective for whatever makes single cases of music interesting to bring up in this connection, this does not necessarily imply a belief in progress or in novelty in itself. "Progressive" would refer to that which relates in a relevant way to its situation, and even more relates actively to the unknown and indulges in real experimentation – as opposed to that which is based on habit, established formulae, and lazy or cowardly retrospection, which could be called regressive (while it still may retain in a particular historical situation a progressive function in the area of pure or symbolic use value!). A lot of what is unconventional, and a lot of experimentation, may of course be purely formal exercises based just as much on established formulae as the banal, and in that sense relating just as little to the unknown.

Drawing by Patrick Hourihan

So, the only real meaning of, and the only (necessarily partly elusive) true criteria for, which parts of music we would want to "claim for surrealism" are the poetic attitude, the inner model, the genuine urge to experiment, the invocation of the unknown. And then there are a number of supportive external criteria.

These are usually more or less formal or technical details, or material-social circumstances, which are very often not interesting in themselves and which do not guarantee any relevance, but which are used heuristically as indications of something interesting and in order to quickly discern the specific contradictions in a given field.

To begin with, collectivity is more useful as a starting point than individuality. Collective experimentation is beyond the control of the individual, and will for that reason reach further towards the unknown. Collectivity sets aside many of the regressive and market-like jerkings of self-assertion, self-legitimation and resentment which are a great part of the individual personality. But nevertheless it is also necessary in an artistic context to see that a distinct poetic vision very often comes out of a single person's cultivation of radical subjectivity, while collectivity regarding poetic vision sometimes also involves banalising compromise. Since the vision of the individual in that sense may remain more distinct, it may also under certain circumstances be truer and more potentially collective since it will remain recognisable for the individuals it speaks to.

Whatever we don't know is in principle more interesting that what we know. Creation must always be investigative. Therefore it is obviously necessary to utilise improvisation, design aleatory methods, cultivate disorder in the senses and follow hunches. Mediumism is a valid ideal, which is to say that the musician is not the creator of music but only a tool for it, just as alien to and curious about the result as any listener. But even if the unknown is statistically more interesting than the already known – and to stay clear of all mysticism it can be a good thing to insist that the definition of the "unknown" is the simple epistemological negative, that which is not known – we do give it a particular place in our methodology because it assumes a qualitative sense, by being not known, creates a more or less fear-inducing or intoxicating curiosity and profusely generates meaning in its meeting with the imaginative and associative faculties, that which compels us to investigation but never is exhausted by it.

Non-conformism is a valid principle on many levels and not least on the musical. Divergence is not a guarantee for a relevant activity, but sticking to a norm or an established formula, designing one's activity to fill a certain available function within the current social order, is almost a guarantee for not having anything interesting to come up with.

There is no point in retaining borders between art forms and genres. A surrealist interest in music will quickly come to situations where it cannot really remain, and would not have any interest in remaining, distinct from dance, poetry reading, game playing, ritual, more or less scientific investigation, creation of atmosphere, creation of situations, etc. In that sense it is always sliding towards the *Gesamtkunstwerk*. Perhaps it should be noted that this involves unities which are difficult to classify, and that it is about manifesting a shared poetic core in different forms of expression, or perhaps about an honest experimental confrontation, while the more formalistic "crossovers" which are common in official artistic connections, regardless of how they may more or less by chance sometimes offer such real meetings, usually are content with placing things side by side without bothering with inner coherence or real sense of meeting. This is probably also where what might be called general aesthetics comes in, that is scenography, costumes, design of posters and record sleeves, etc.; which is sometimes part of the striving for such a *Gesamtkunstwerk* and an integrated part of the creative process and artistic whole which the musicians themselves are involved in and experimenting with, but usually is instead either pure marketing by professionals, or a conventional minimum on the whole.

It is often important to bring in various external more or less meaning-bearing elements. To lift things out of their usual context and give them new connections is the principle of the poetic image and the collage, and of course remains relevant in music, be it real cut-up/sampled sound fragments or allusions/references or lyrics (because to the extent that the lyrics do not grow out of the musical idea/improvisation in parallel with other parts of the music, they are in fact always such elements brought in from outside). Concerning general themes, spheres of reference and subject matter of lyrics, surrealists of course traditionally take an interest in marginal phenomena and dreaming, madness, falling in love, revolt, chance phenomena, mythologies, horror, eroticism etc. Several of these are conventional subjects within particular genres of popular music in an entirely conventional and banal way. Among them, however, dreaming seems to retain a particular integrity and usually remains interesting as a theme, even in many otherwise entirely predictable connections. Concerning actual sound elements and atmospheres it is often interesting to bring in concrete elements of natural environments and animals, as well as elements from the musics and everyday life of foreign cultures. Concerning allusions/references it is important to make a distinction between on the one hand snobbish exercises in erudition, artistic derivatives, formal paraphrases, and winks to the initiated (all of them lacking any interest as such), and on the other hand creating a tradition for oneself, selecting and highlighting heroes, artists' bodies of works, precursors or any phenomena worth acknowledging and building up alternative traditions around. The very same thing, such as Pa Ubu, or Dalí's rainy taxi, or surrealism on the whole, can be related to in one way or another (obviously, so far, many more musicians have been interested in surrealism than surrealists in music, and the superficiality of the reference is only partly determined by its advertising purpose; there is also an element of simple ignorance and lack of communication). It is also on this level that the musicians' explicit political stands should be considered, ranging in aim and function from pure advertising slogans and concessions for radical market segments to genuine attempts to educate and instigate. The political stands may be more or less coherent with the musical and artistic project on the whole in various ways, ranging from simple propaganda set to music to integrated revolutionary projects.

But then we get back to the social aspects. Non-conformism is the only general red thread. In a sense, music as such (but even more every occasion where music is presented) entails a choice, either sticking to social norms, not questioning the current social order, or challenging, questioning, and expressing outsiderness. What will be efficient in this sense, what will be self-delusion etc., is a never-ending discussion, and at this point I will merely repeat that the question is always relevant.

To start with there is a need to try to avoid any simple reification of music. For anyone who cares about the poetic core of music and its imaginative and social explosive power, it is necessary to emphasise the process over the work, "musicking over music". A recorded musical work is a more or less interesting residue of the musical creating and not its goal. Of course it may still be essential as a vehicle for different types of communication, for inspiration, dialogue, distribution of ideas, good old amazement, but in those cases too it is actually the process and not the work which is the main thing. The canon of cultural history and the market are the two large purchasers of creative products, trying to reduce them to things and commodities, which in itself doesn't necessary kill them but displaces the focus of attention away from any real potential and real content. Wherever it is possible to plainly leave outside, minimise, belittle and betray these two monsters it should be done. Music which is progressive in some substantial sense usually does establish its own new channels. It may be called autonomy (with the Marxists, anarchists and post-structuralists) or DIY ("do it yourself" with the punks); it is all about establishing self-controlled independent forums and meeting points, and self-controlled independent channels for concerts, records, etc. This takes place in the form of popular networking or pure outsiderness (*"art brut"*). The market and cultural history are always at work, and usually absorb all initiatives sooner or later, but the elements can be re-circulated in inventive and popular ways after that, and this tug of war is of course one of the most fundamental arenas for the struggle over the historical importance of music. Other important means in this fight are the appropriation and subversive use of new technologies, new forums, contemporary contradictions, contemporary popular movements, etc. Some of those who are most eagerly radical will of course spend most of their time trying to analyse the field and logically deduce strategies which might be the most appropriate to what is perceived as the very cutting edge of current novelties, or the short-term historical focus of the present social situation – and in nine cases out of ten such efforts will be wasted and will have forgotten the fundamentals in the process. A methodological approach and a concern for the core questions, which surrealism embraces, would in contrast see the need to choose strategies which are creative and meaningful whatever the outcome, which will be able to communicate poetic content and create interesting things regardless of purely tactical concerns, and regardless of whether the assessment of the situation is correct or mistaken.

The communicative aspect is of course central. This can be concluded equally well from the emphasis on the poetic or on the collective or on the processual or from the belittling of the work as a thing or of the individual as creator. But since it concerns poetic communication, which is communicating that which we do not yet know, this communication must have the form of play or ritual. We agree that it is important to try to disintegrate the traditional distinction or even contradiction between the creator and the audience. But often it has been attacked in

The Wolf Plays the Owl, assemblage by Dominique Paul

hasty and ridiculous ways. If we start out from the ambition that the musician would be sufficiently sensitive, attentive and curious him- or herself to be a fascinated observer of his or her own musicking, then it becomes much easier to see how everybody who is present in the situation can become co-creators, all concretely contributing to the ambiance, atmosphere, the field of possibilities, the situation where the music takes form, with the musician as its medium and not as its producer. A concert is always a ritual, but unfortunately one where the distribution of roles is strictly predetermined and the form entirely conventional. This is superseded and the meaning of musical communication approached wherever it succeeds in evoking a more distinctly ritual atmosphere, of its being something actually happening specifically there and then and which everybody is involved in. If the musicians at that point have the crucial openness towards each other's and their own musicking, and together with the concert arrangers have succeeded in creating good conditions in general for a rich and open presence, then that classic contradiction is so to speak already resolved on the theoretical level. At that point it will also become much easier for individuals to transgress or play with the distribution of roles in inventive or spontaneous ways, without having to go by way of the sad substitutes of formalistic obstructions, leftist-school-teacher-like dashing, or just compulsory voluntarism.

And after all these thoughts about the circumstances of the music, I cannot avoid returning to a more substantial aspect again, namely the immanence of poetry, that which is sometimes referred to as the first principle of alchemy and which has always been one of the most fervently defended positions of surrealism, and which is particularly relevant in relation to the musical. Music in a surrealist sense, which could perhaps be defined as poetry related to the auditory sense, is always available – as a creative strategy in everyday life, where its elements are freely available surrounding us. Regardless of whether one collects these elements for different types of manipulation and explicitly musical usage, or listens to them on the spot where they occur, in fact many of the most meaningful, most interesting and most purely pleasurable examples of music of all categories are in fact things that surround us as beautiful voices, strange words, whispers, all kinds of small and big noises, rhythms from machines, clicking of trees, of houses and furniture, the roaring and squeaking of gadgets, running water and waves, birds and insects, wind and rain and thunder, etc etc. It is not merely a coincidence that a consistent special interest in the field of surrealism and music has been the invention of new musical instruments and a systematic investigation of the auditory world of everyday objects, to lend an ear to all these household objects, natural objects, toys, to listen to their own sounds, to their reactions to our squeezing and scraping them, drumming on them or playing them with a bow. The Philosopher's Stone is available everywhere and we trample it on a daily basis.

EMOTIONAL ENTRAPMENT OF SOUND AND THE PLEASURES OF NOISE

SHIBEK

Some very interesting and diverse sounds can be found within the 'noise' music which has blossomed in the last three decades. In this article I'll examine some links between surrealism and sound and noise experimentalism, and look at the noise phenomena culturally. An appreciation of noise in its strongest parallels with surrealism might move us towards a provocative renewal of hearing and sensibility, and provide points of departure for understanding desire-based personal languages. Placing this within the history of sound also reveals many directions of interest and possibility.

What is 'noise' and how is it part of, or different from, 'music'? While noise appears in formal music and in free jazz and improvisation during peak moments and in emotional crescendos, much of the modern noise milieu takes these moments as a point of departure. And yet noise is not always played at high volume or at maximum intensity. Noise is free to roam between softer ambient sounds and explosive chaos, or to synthesize these approaches. Automatism, trance, and inventive discovery all play a strong role in noise, and many noise performers are directly inspired by the Surrealist Movement or by different aspects of surrealism appearing in popular culture. There are hybrid forms of music that mingle noise with ambient electronic, free jazz or industrial styles, as well as extreme minimal noise currents which avoid traditional instruments and composition altogether. Since noise is often a certain type of free improvisation, some discussion of free improvisation is warranted. And several of the more creative 'alternative' bands have made a place for improvised noise within songs or at live shows. But here I will concentrate on experimental sounds coming from, or parallel to the Surrealist Movement, as well as on various acts from the more extreme, or 'harsh', end of the spectrum.

Modern noise has its precedents in atonal classical music, Futurist intonarumori noise machines, Dadaist bruitism, *musique concrète*, free jazz, minimalism, butoh dance soundtracks, and dozens of outsider musicians and renegades such as Antonin Artaud and Harry Partch. The synthesis of free improvisation and noise, especially when carried out collectively, is a meeting point which draws from, and appeals to, a deeper range of emotional resources. This is where surrealism appears most readily among the noise milieu.

Experimental noise and sound collage erupted in the late 1970's and early 1980's from those like Throbbing Gristle, Merzbow, Nurse With Wound, The Haters, Whitehouse, The New Blockaders, Maurizio Bianchi, Negativland, and their contemporaries. Acts from Britian, Italy and France played prominent roles. New dimensions of sonic and tactile experiences were opened. The Haters, for example, wore suits and wrestling masks while creating sound out of, or alongside, destructive situations. There was damage to clubs in the process. Granted, there is a lot of influence from Dada, *musique concrète* and nihilism, but sound sculpting in these contexts might still have something poetic to offer.

One of the early noise pioneers with links to surrealism was Japan's Masami Akita, also known as Merzbow, who made furiously abrasive noise, drones and feedback from unorthodox sound sources like broken machinery, tape decks, old instruments and objects. His limited edition handmade recordings were packaged along with pornographic imagery, to further emphasize Akita's preference for 'the unconscious of sound' or 'the lowest form of sound' and to agitate against Japanese cultural norms by reflecting its repressed content.[1] If this seemed to some a monotonous attack, and nothing more than a piercing and destructive maelstrom, it was necessary to attune to another kind of listening where the dynamics and undercurrents of the noise could challenge the ear's organizational habits as shaped by consumerist entertainment. Akita claimed that noise helps people access the unconscious, and called his method of noise composition a form of automatism. He spoke of people finding that the noise put them into a trance, and said this was a good way to understand what he was trying to do.[2] His connections to surrealism can be seen in his participation in a 1984 surrealist mail-art project, his creation of soundtracks for an international surrealist exhibition in Sjöbo, Sweden, and a collage which appeared in *Arsenal: Surrealist Subversions #4*.

In the 1970's and 1980's sound explorers like Davey Williams and LaDonna Smith, Hal Rammel, Mal Occhio, and Johannes Bergmark emerged from within or in close relation to the Surrealist Movement. While none of these creators could be called 'noise' *per se*, they each have their own relationship to noise.

Williams and Smith began collaborating as early as 1973 and took part in the dada-surrealist inspired group Raudelunas in Tuscaloosa, Alabama. The Transmuseq record label emerged from this multi-media collective and released its first album, TRANS, in 1976. The Trans Duo and their many collaborators are based in free improvisation which borrows from many styles. Their sonic play with viola, voice, guitar, and other instruments remains compelling, and induces a variety of moods. Both players made connections with the Surrealist Movement. Their poetic and theoretical writings and creations can be found in their out-of-print surrealist journal *Glass Veal*, as well as in *The Improvisor* magazine (now a website), the French journal *Discours* (where Williams' important 'Group Improvisation' essay from 1979 appeared), and in *Arsenal: Surrealist Subversions #4*. They also provided soundtracks for the previously mentioned surrealist exhibition in Sjöbo. In the liner notes to 1993's *Transmutating* CD, they speak of trying to make music that emulates or utilizes natural processes, where unpredictable conversations between players can occur. Sound improvising is likened to the activity of a flock of birds, and seen as a kind of 'electrical statement' that allows for 'floating barrels in a river of varying degrees of placidity and action, up to gale force conditions'.[3] The members of Trans Duo have evolved in different directions over time but remain active as important explorers of surrealist-oriented sound in the U.S. On top of this, Smith organized the Birmingham Improv Festival, where Johannes Bergmark and many others have performed, in 1996 and 2004.

Hal Rammel is a musician, instrument-builder and participant in surrealism in Chicago and Wisconsin. He built his first instruments in the 1970's and later began collaborations with Steve-Nelson-Raney, LaDonna Smith, Davey Williams, Johannes Bergmark, Nihilist Spasm Band, and others. He also plays the musical saw and designed, among other instruments, an Amplified Palette, which consists of numerous reed and twig-like appendages rising from a surface amplified by contact mics. These are played by plucking, bowing, rubbing and drumming motions and they create a miniature universe of soothing and frantic pitch and texture. While some of his sounds are more subtle, they are no less 'noise' to orthodox ears; might it be a question of scale? Some of his collaborations, on the other hand, delve into full-tilt comedic mania. His yard sculpture, which emits sound in response to the force of the wind, also gives us ideas. His essay 'Beyond Music: A Brief Historical Survey of Music and Surrealism' was printed in 1996.[4] Other writings and graphics by Rammel appear in *Arsenal: Surrealist Subversions #4*, *Experimental Musical Instruments* magazine, and elsewhere. His *Song of an Aeropteryx,* which features the musical saw along with his artwork, was reprinted by the Transmuseq label. Rammel himself runs the independent label Penumbra Records.

From 1980 to 1982, Mal Occhio from San Francisco and Los Angeles produced densely atmospheric combinations of sound from creatively misused instruments, modified electronics, and industrial drumming along with echoing samples. In the spirit of psychic automatism, surrealists Thom Burns, Steve Lock, Byron Baker, and Jhim Pattison sought to use sound as a canvas for their desires. As Thom Burns wrote:

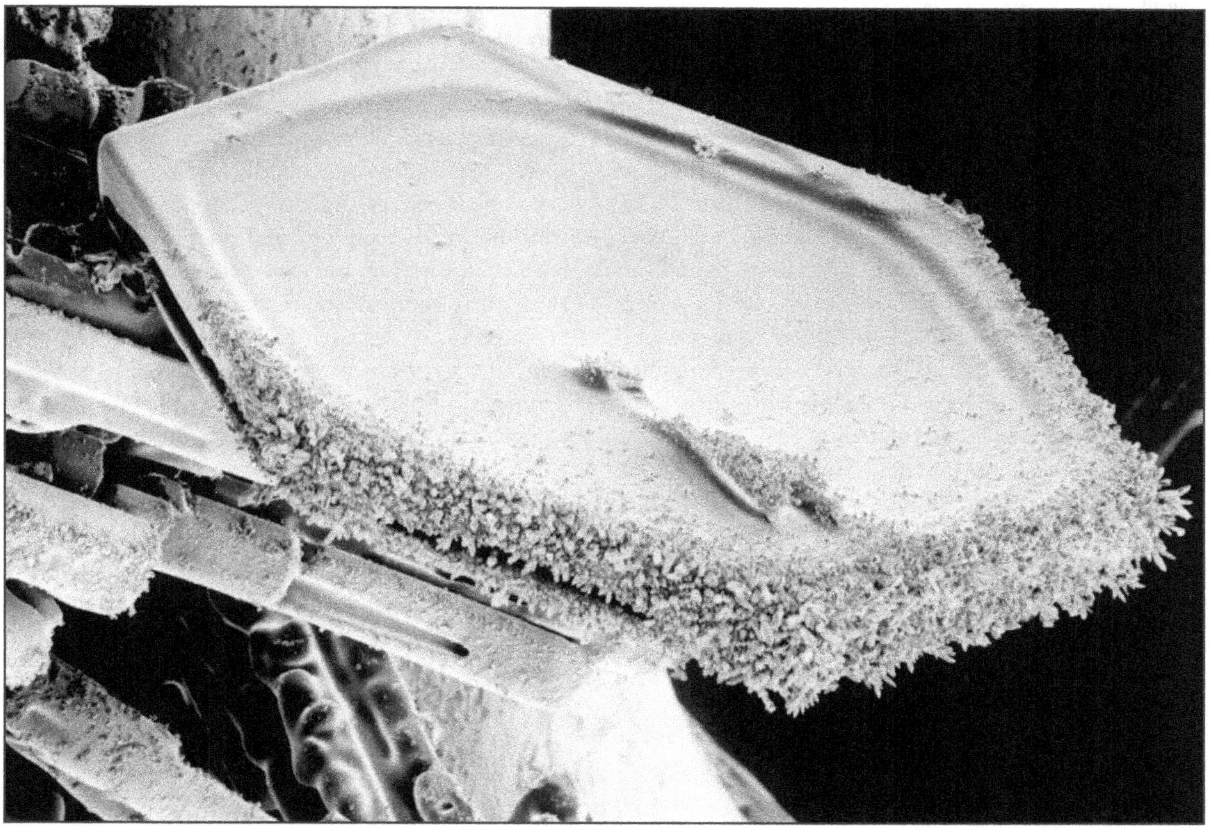

> "The group agreed to rely, as much as possible, on found objects and invented instruments...If it was necessary to use traditional instruments like the cello and electric guitar (which were never played normally), it was only a temporary expedient until an alternative was cooked up. The result was music of both comic surprise and darkness. The performances sometimes broadcast a malevolent tonality that went way beyond the expectations of the group and sometimes a Marx Brothers style chaos in which they felt right at home...it was their intention to go with the spirit of chance and surprise wherever it took them."[5]

Other occasional participants included surrealists like Raman Rao, Brooke Rothwell, Alice Farley, and Laurence Weisberg. Every member of Mal Occhio took part in the 1983 *Harvest of Evil* exhibition in Colombus, Ohio. In more recent times Mal Occhio played at Weisberg's memorial gathering. There are no available public recordings, but a future release is possible.

Johannes Bergmark has been an active surrealist improvisor since the mid 1980's. He instigated sound experiments within the Surrealist Group in Stockholm, an activity that came to be known as Orchestra of the Great Invisibles or Ensemble of Free Psychic Automatism. Inspired by people like Hugh Davies and Hal Rammel, Bergmark built his own instruments and has played them on various CD's and in solo and collaborative shows across the world. Using invented instruments along with the saw, electronics, and voice, Bergmark seeks 'the hidden sounds' and 'wild music' so he can be 'played by his instruments'.[6] The Whalefish is a large amplified surface bursting with disparate objects of sonic potential, the Singing Coffin is a full-body experience, and the Stringed Stirrups allow for a very theatrical exploration of sound arising from the pressures of gravity upon piano wires which hold a harness Bergmark wears while swinging from a roof beam. In his electronics and voice compositions, and in the haunting *Saw Octet*[7] we find something that moves in spaces of hypnotism and carnal humor. Najo Team is a more recent project realized by Bergmark and Tippi to explore improvisation, unorthodox instruments and sound sources. Amplified objects, constructions, and electronics mix with circuit-bent toys, self-made electronics, and aquarium equipment.[8]

Others manifesting a surrealist and pro-noise outlook within sound include Six Heads, Criadero En Seres, and Qkcofse. William Davison in Toronto has been playing experimental music since the 1980's, but in 2000 he and Sherri Lyn Higgins, James Bailey, Linda Feesey, Colin Hinz and Pete Mosher formed Six Heads to focus on a more surrealist orientation. They pursue 'exploration of audio surrealism via improvisation, sound collage, experimental instruments and approaches'.[9] Davison maintains Disembraining Songs, a Recordist/surrealist label. To confirm that noise does not always require electricity, Six Heads sponsored a 'noise picnic' in Toronto where the public was invited to bring acoustic and battery powered devices and join in.

In Buenos Aires, Mariela Arzadun and Leandro Ramírez collaborate in the experimental group Criadero En Seres, formed in 2003. They have written, 'The Criadero En Seres project...is a praxis, an investigation, a surrealist game, a dialogue with abstract spontaneous languages'.[10] Processed guitars, keyboards and horns move from warbling insectoid noises to cacophonous free jazz. Their live film soundtracks offer much to the senses. Arzadun and Ramírez pursue solo sound projects, have numerous recordings, and take part in the Río de la Plata Surrealist Group.

From Portland, Oregon, my project Qkcofse features extreme noise, hypnotic ambient sounds and undefined experimentation. Live and pre-recorded layers mix according to chance factors. In the spirit of black humor these lo-fi noise aerobics are created with prepared guitars, voice and percussion along with miscellaneous instruments like detuned scanners, box flutes, and objects. The name comes from the phrases 'Quantities of Excitation' and 'Kandinsky-Clerambault Syndrome'. Sample recordings have been hand-made in limited editions; collaborations and shows happen occasionally.

The profoundly inventive zeal of so many completely unknown, dedicated sound artists has left its mark on the underground, and to a lesser degree upon mainstream society. The new generations of underground sound use low-budget do-it-yourself methods to distribute small circulation handmade recordings, often with adventurous artwork and poetic song titles. Within our reach is a fantastical canvas of obsessive sound textures propelled by the creative subversion of conventional definitions of music and 'entertainment', where anything can be a sound source, from toys to guitars to circuit bent devices, thrift store antiques, wind and reed instruments, field recordings, and even the human voice. This wide open spectrum can create an emotional entrapment of sound that compels our becoming. Masami Akita's erotic appreciation of feedback as a sensuous trance reveals one way that a person can respond to something thought of as 'painful'. Dance, including butoh, is sometimes enacted alongside noise sets. Those like Arachnid Arcade, Ecomorti, Rubber-O-Cement, Crank Sturgeon, Caroliner Rainbow and Smegma use costumes and puppets to enhance their live shows. Rubber-O-Cement's costume seems in many respects like a mobile surrealist object. Others like irr.app.(ext.), Sparkle Girl, Anakrid, Hal McGee, Dead Air Fresheners, and Soup Purse have displayed surrealist elements or influences within their noise practice. Matt Waldron from irr.app.(ext.) in San Francisco is a co-creator of the Oneiric Ambiguity Collective, which formed to explore collaborative storytelling and exquisite corpse drawings as well as sound. Sparkle Girl from Seattle have given away mass amounts of noise recordings and cite the Surrealist Movement as an influence. Some of Anakrid's music is based around an attractive and sinister blend of atmospheric and harsh sounds. Hal McGee is one of America's electronic noise pioneers. Dead Air Fresheners present a colorful mix of free jazz and eclectic noise, while Portland's Soup Purse speaks of being a 'shaman of technology' as he coaxes sound from an 8-bit sampler made from coins and wires as well as from processed keyboards, radio samples, and measuring tape.[11]

There are problems in the noise scene. Occasionally lyrics and vocals can be crudely shocking, misogynist or misanthropic in a way that reflects the tantrums of young men. The extreme nature of the sound encourages this, but vocals and lyrics can hinder the otherwise more ambiguous phenomena. This doesn't mean that there aren't women dealing with equally challenging or controversial themes within noise, however, although they appear less frequently. Most who create noise are on the side of adventure, but there are no uniform politics to the noise scene. Many fans appreciate the sensory overload and experimentation as an end in itself, without necessarily identifying with or caring about performers' views. Among other varieties, one can find anarchist, leftist, fascist, occultist, Christian, gay, goth, and quasi-surrealist noise acts, for example. Some have tried to claim noise as a racial domain, but participation within noise by those from various ethnic backgrounds proves this incorrect. It is easy to notice the large number of noise artists who walk too closely in the shadow of Whitehouse and Merzbow, but they cannot drown the mischievous exuberance of collaboration present in the more intelligent and engaging noise events. Improvisational or semi-improvisational conducted noise ensembles show how the isolated ego is mixed just like a sound source in an intimate dialogue and hurled towards an unexpected result.

What is the appeal of noise, one might ask? Is it a form of 'thrill-seeking', an attempt at the anarchical reinvention of music, a fetishistic synthesis of pleasure and pain as a listening experience, or perhaps all of these? We should acknowledge the role of the passions in forms of 'extreme' cultural undergrounds and understand where greater liberation and new poetic connections lie. Thus we might find within noise our desire to hear what we desire and not what is offered in other sound experiences we are forced to endure.

Alongside the 'coarse' moments of noise, there's a radical beauty formed from collisions between sound and chance. Many noise performers are just as surprised by the sounds they create as listeners might be. This convulsive gem may not always shine, as alchemically the volatile chaos is among the first steps of cognitive awareness. Consider

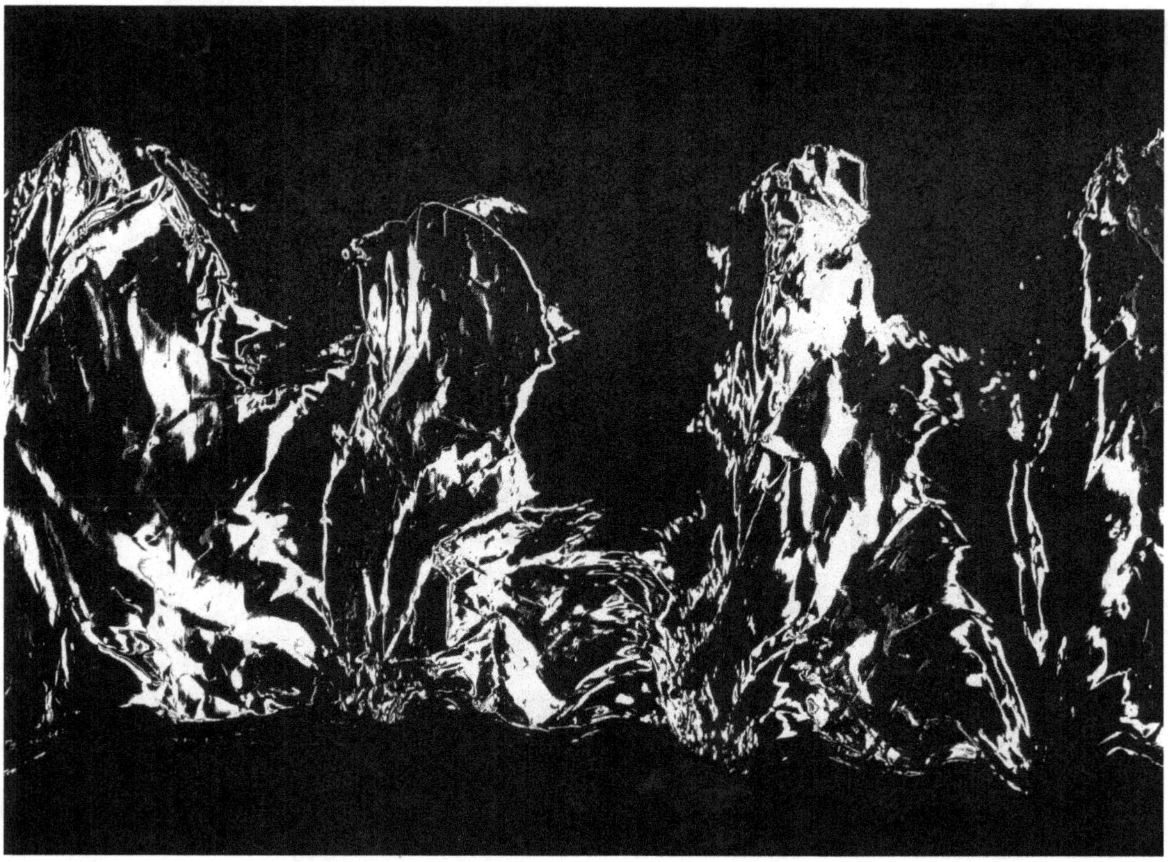

Across the Desert, interpretive image by Shibek

that 'wall noise', or what has been called the 'militant wall', can promote paranoiac listening (apophonia or delirium of interpretation), bodily vibration and heightened senses through the pure overwhelming cacophony. The poetic hunger and enervating humor of the sound searching is the core emotional drive that might communicate in a kind of soundtrack to ungraspable dramas. The exceptions that arise within a noise context are interesting whether or not one considers them 'noise' or 'music', or some variation of these. Thus noise can be seen as a great outside or hidden tradition within the history of music. It remains to be seen what the future holds.

There are too many performers and innovators to mention in this article, so my sense of history and the present will no doubt be incomplete. I hope to share my enthusiasm for objective surrealism as it appears in noise. At its best, noise performers can inspire us to seize the ability to create the kind of sounds we want to hear. Regardless of musical training, we can develop sound from salvaged and collected elements that are entirely acoustic, or we can mix electric and acoustic equipment in a search for our own peculiar gratifications which can be shared with others who take similar risks. A 'swing' can be developed from an inspired approach to what is typically thought of as 'junk' or 'debris'. The important thing is that players remain true to their own skills and intuitions, which, as a member of Smegma notes, can come full circle to meet each other in these difficult listening contexts.[12] It is the fulfillment of desire and the desire to desire that motivates some of this resolutely non-commercial sound exploration. Surrealists around the world have taken steps in these domains.[13]

Thanks to Masami Akita, who spoke of 'the pleasures of noise' which inspired my title, and to Mattias Forshage, Johannes Bergmark, Thom Burns, and the *Hydrolith* editors.

Endnotes:

1) http://www.musicianguide.com/biographies/1609002811/Merzbow/html
2) Ibid.
3) *Transmutating* CD by Davey Williams and LaDonna Smith. Transmuseq, 1993. Also see http://www.theimprovisor.com
4) *Sounding Off: Music as Subversion, Resistance, Revolution.* Edited by Ron Sakolsky and Fred Wei-Han Ho. Autonomedia, 1996.
5) Mal Occhio 1980-82. Unreleased CD.
6) These are titles to Bergmark's writings which appeared in Stockholm publications like *Kalla Handen* and *Stora Saltet* as well as on his website.
7) From a compilation CD passed out during Bergmark's West Coast U.S. tour of 2005.
8) http://www.bergmark.org/najoteam/music.html
9) http://www.recordism.com
10) http://criaderoenseres.com.ar/web/
11) *People Who Do Noise* documentary by Adam Cornelius, 2008.
12) Ibid.
13) More recently, Eric Bragg has released *Chelator*, a CD of humorous and intriguing collaged sound samples from various sources. There are rumors of other groups conducting private noise experiments as well.

Tomb Haunter, photograph by Paul Cowdell

Is Music Abstract?

Johannes Bergmark

This is an excerpt from a text that I, for the purpose of this publication, recently dusted off after having abandoned for many years.

The ambition back then was to write a critical history of surrealism and music. The task eventually seemed too big for me, but a lot of work had been done that was never published, so I intend to make the full text, in spite of everything, available in a publication especially devoted to the subject of surrealism and music, including the efforts of other surrealists interested in different aspects of the topic.

With this excerpt I hope to stimulate discussion and inspire new points of view on the question of surrealism, music and sound.

J.B., Szczecin and Stockholm, 2009-2010

Music is not verbal. Song texts and librettos have nothing to do with the contents of music, but are another dimension, as Breton and Souris said in different ways. Many texts by surrealists have been set to music, by surrealists as well as by others, and many surrealist film-makers have used music in different ways. This is of course interesting, but can probably best be regarded not as a clue but as a sidetrack: in such cases either music has been treated not as music but as a collage element for poetry or play, or else the music is the main thing and a poem is merely an element for the singer to illustrate by means of music. Not a very interesting method for surrealism.

Music is physical – not as a physical object, but as a set of physical processes (with sound as a central phenomenon) which are nonetheless always connected to the physical objects from which they originate, ultimately the human body (or through it, the "spirit"). This is a concrete side of music.

The structures of the physical processes correspond to the structures of spiritual processes. The volatile stratum of music consists of an interaction between the concrete and the abstract. The central essence of music is neither feelings, ideas, sounds, notes, instruments, musicians nor listeners, but this stratum.

From a surrealist perspective, music does not need to be seen as a phenomenon essentially separate from others. In the Second Manifesto, the experience of the disappearance of contradictions is described as the state that surrealists try to identify and investigate – regardless of the object of this state. Some examples are given, but not in music (nor actually in terms of art at all). An agreement (an experience of unity) between sound movements (physical, material vibrations through the body) and spiritual movements (experience of "abstract" forms, structures and relations), a passionate and marvellous state, can be a domain to be interested in, in music as well as elsewhere. One example is what many traditions call a creation or an experience of trance, which, in certain cases one can say that surrealists (as well as others of course) have been doing, e.g. through improvised music of different kinds.

But the musically active surrealists have also dealt with international and local games where they have made interpretations in the form of sounds, interpretations of poetry, words, pictures or objects. This collective urge for experiment or playfulness, where chance also plays a part, has also always been a surrealist character trait that does not stand in opposition to the passion for free creativity, but rather experiments in order to find new routes to the same type of intersection between desire and reality.

Maybe it was Nougé and Duchamp – two non-musicians – who came up with the most valuable contributions to the view on music in surrealism. It is interesting that both authors take up and criticize the roles of the artist, object and spectator. Nougé discusses the "veritable optical illusion" of the stage ritual, Duchamp the "dirt of the ear drum" and the "brainities" – which he also explores through his compositions, better understood as "descriptive models" which do not need to be performed. Typically, both use glass as a material for their thought-provoking objects.

Nougé states something basic for the understanding and discussion of music: "we are not judging something, but taking part in something."[1] He emphasizes the parallelism of what happens on stage and what happens "in the spirit", in other words, empathy.

Mind the Gap, image by Kathleen Fox

Thus in this case he takes the same position as radical musicologist Christopher Small, who describes the musical situation as a collective ritual recreation of an ideal society, consisting of musicians as well as listeners. Surrealists have in a similar fashion described their "art" as windows, passages to a free world, a manifested utopia.

The musical ritual

Even though surrealists sometimes take inspiration from primitive rituals, ritual is for some surrealists a controversial word in which they see repression. Christopher Small (who is not a surrealist) uses the word as an (anthropologically or sociologically) value-neutral tool for his analysis of the position of music in our society and others, and links it to the ideals and ideologies of the participants, which of course can be repressive as well as liberating. Since Small's critique has significance for me and some (but not all) other musically active surrealists (Hal Rammel pointed him out to me), I think he should be mentioned here.

Surrealism has attacked the artistic ritual and the art concept itself, as a pale reflection of the miserable conditions of poetry, or of the repression of magic (in a poetic sense), or the objectification of the spirit. When we talk about the stage ritual (which surrealists have done very little of: theatre, performance art and dance are as marginal as music), e.g. a concert, the artificial, organized and predetermined behaviour is of course in some sense a repression – but there are reasons for arguing that even this form should be able to be used and potentially be exploded by its contents for instigating or marvellous purposes, with the same caution, of course, as surrealists hitherto have used exhibitions, galleries, publications, film and different parts of the media (radio, newspapers...). The difference in form is most of all only formal (e.g. concerning time and place, the aspect of forced silence and response), and might depend on the traditional prejudices that have established themselves within certain parts of the surrealist movement and made it somewhat slow to choose new forms of expression – a situation which may be exacerbated by the fact that it may be mainly artists and poets who come into contact with the concept of surrealism, at least to a greater extent than musicians do.

For my part, art and poetry are of lesser interest in my view of myself as a surrealist. I would rather develop the ways in which I connect my musical activity and my interest in the "stage" with surrealism.

The concept of ritual, as I understand it, is of central importance here. I am not sure whether it would be justified to see ritual as something solely repressive, or even as a temporary "compromise form" to be accepted while we wait for poetry to be "generalized", i.e. to disappear as a marginalized and oppressed domain of the marvellous, as it is today. This would, in that case, be parallel to the view that the victory of the working class will herald its destruction as a class, and that the workers' state will be a stage on the way to the abolition of the state. I agree, but there is still a lack of understanding of the complexity of the ritual and its inherent powers.

Not only Christopher Small, but also, and earlier, Paul Nougé revealed that the stage is an "optical illusion": the visitors are themselves participants in it, and (according to Small's viewpoint) create, together with the musicians, their ideal image of human relations. I agree of course, but this potentially utopian element does not explain it all, either.

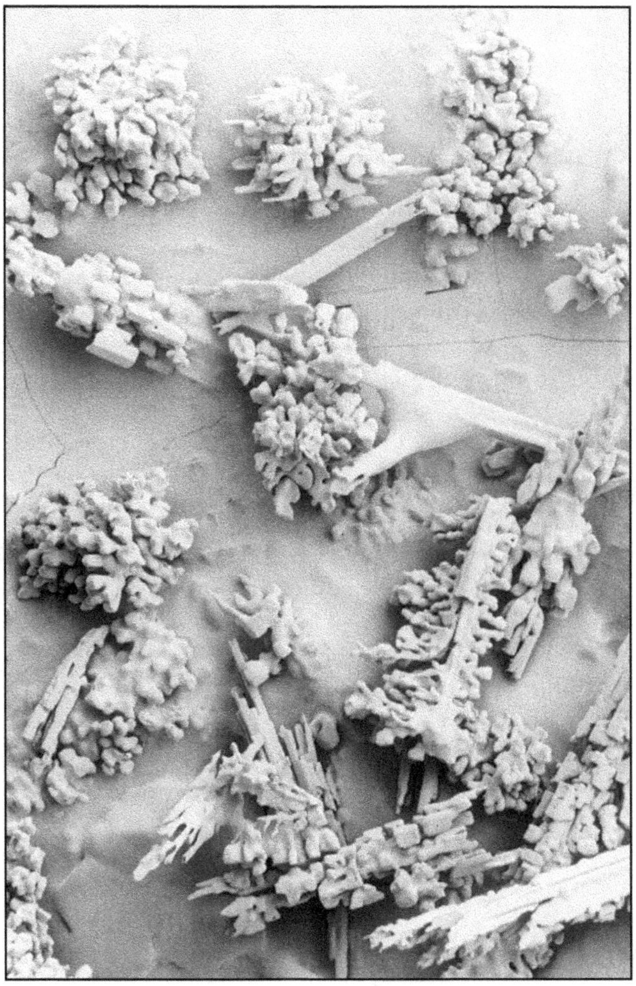

Abolish the ritual?

All organization in society demands force or repression, not least in primitive societies – but the economic and political organization of the psychosocial structure of our time is repressive in ways and to degrees that go far beyond what is socially motivated.[2] This "surplus repression" is of course to be found in stage rituals as much as anywhere else, e.g. in their commercialization.

But it would be laughable, embarrassing, if one were to dismiss the possibility of using stage rituals purely because of the existence of a certain structural repression, and to stop analyzing the other parts included in the structure. It would be like rejecting mankind because of capitalism. One part of the repression that belongs to the necessary structure of the stage ritual is the part which causes the sublimation and the "empathy" without which it is impossible. It might be easy to think of the importance of a performance's starting moment, when "illusion" breaks with everyday life, but in reality, since it is a continuous but limited process of birth, every moment is of the same ritual kind, from the first to the last, including the breathing space before and after. The ritual element means that one gets into another state, where a different set of rules of judgement and criteria for life apply. One is shown the new rules, but liberated from the old ones. It is, in other words, an experiment with behaviour, with the way to lead one's life, the way to communicate.

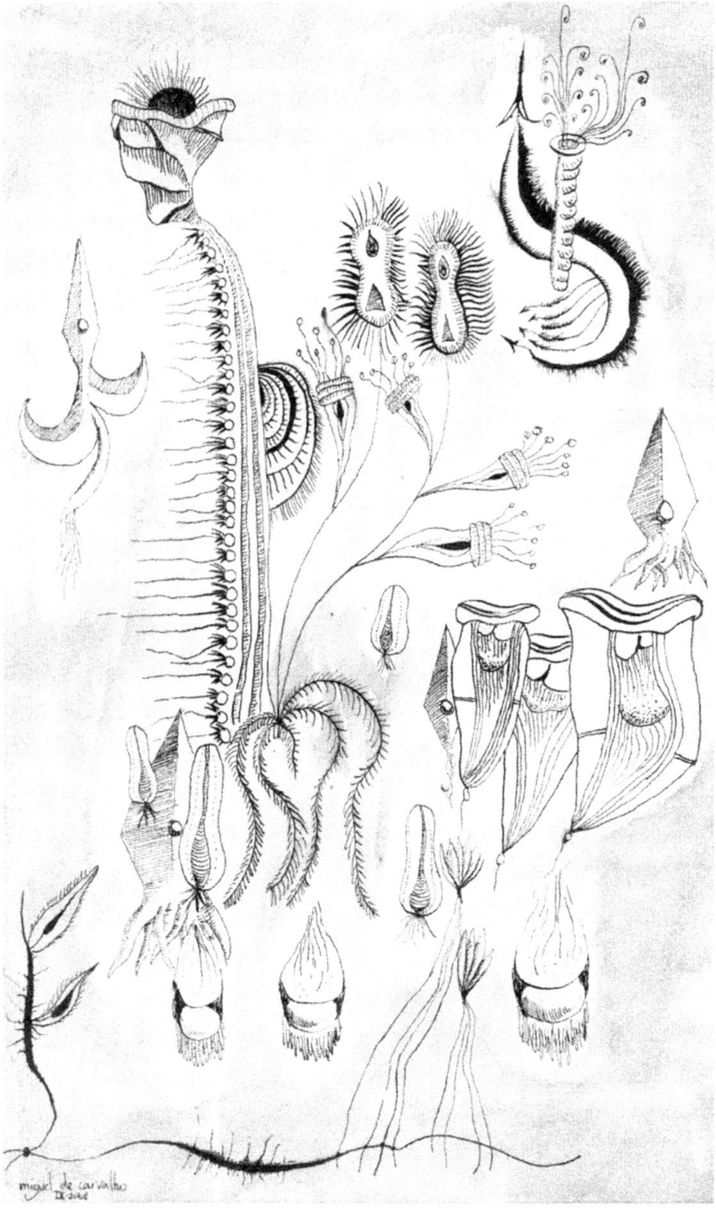

Drawing by Miguel de Carvalho

It is not possible to abolish the ritual element in the ritual of art. Making theatre in the street, for example, doesn't make it any the less theatre, or at least it demands a statement from the visitors, but there is only an either/or, no grey area. To "involve the audience" always means to activate the embarrassment and the demands involved when a person in the audience takes the step over the border into illusion. Maybe it can feel liberating for some, but the border in itself is only manifested more evidently. It is at best pedagogical, but probably not even a good pedagogy. Instead it belongs most of all to the speculative means that the very stage ritual itself sometimes uses. The abolition of the ritual is not carried through by such easy formal means.

Art seems to be running along the same lines from time to time. At such moments it belongs to contemporary art's arsenal of effective tricks to stage "events in real life", e.g. crimes, in order to once again pose the meaningless question "is this art?" The artists do not escape ritual in their activity, no matter whether the form used is exhibitions, installations or happenings. Squabbling about where the line is to be drawn only serves one opinion-merchant or another on the personality market.

The human act

It is actually incomprehensible that so few care to pose Nougé's central question: What are the human consequences of our actions? Artists especially seem to be among the last to realize that their artistic actions are also rightly human actions. One has to reveal what artistic and stage ritual is – but also to point out and, yes, defend the fact that it *is* a ritual, a domain of its own with its own laws, like the "laws" that operate inside a picture frame, an exhibition room, the covers of a poetry book, or on the white cinema screen, or like the laws of play. The reason for this is, in a way, moral: it is in order to defend, as far as possible, inside this ritual border, the enormous potential for freedom that the human spirit could express there – maybe to a greater degree than anywhere else. Because if we fail to use this ritual to the full extent, freedom cannot expand anywhere else either. And there is surely a connection in moral attitude between this "virtual", artistic freedom and the freedom we desire for life as a totality.

The reason why all this is not made clear in the statements of artists is of course because artists have not unmasked the illusion of freedom in the public spectacle – they have not despaired, or at least not enough, over the miserable conditions in which poetry lives in our so-called everyday life, with the money economy, wage slavery and nationalism. That is why they mistake their conditions on the personality market for their task as artists. This is not surprising. Of course it is like this, at least in a society which has a personality market and which is not in a state of war or insurrection.

We have stated two things: the necessity of an understanding of the essence of the stage (or generally artistic) ritual, and the total demand for freedom of the spirit. Starting from Nougé, we have suggested another important thing: the moral responsibility of the musician to rethink his actions, even as a musician. In a stage ritual, a performance, there is the possibility to express one's wishes, desires and ways of thinking or relating. One can also show one's greed, one's thought about oneself or the audience, and one can lie. One can play or obey. One can, in short, use freedom for one's own purposes. One has the possibility to be an example and inspire.

This aspect has been a hook for some influential surrealists, but maybe especially for politically engaged artists. If one felt the need to interpret music as signs, verbally or in pictures, it would be utterly unpredictable, confusing and fuzzy. But that is just one of the meaningless wrong tracks from which surrealism still suffers, and other possibilities exist.

Physical confrontation

Music, whether you see it from the stage or from the audience, is to a large extent a meeting and a relationship between body and matter. Thus the basic concepts of physics, together with the parallel apprehension of them from the spirit, are essential concepts in music: the place of the human being in time and space, i.e. the parallel movement of matter and spirit that is the central stratum of music.

Simple examples of parallels that can appear through music are the wish for calm and a cosy daily life, and the confident predictability that is to be found in the cyclical dance music and popular music of all times. Business as usual, and we enjoy it.

This is in itself not only a value judgement. Christopher Small points out three relational activities that always take place in the musical ritual: confirmation, celebration and exploration. These things take place at the same time but to varying degrees and with varying focus. Since a musical ritual is the establishment of an intricate network involving a large collection of relations, there are many levels that can be analyzed from this perspective,

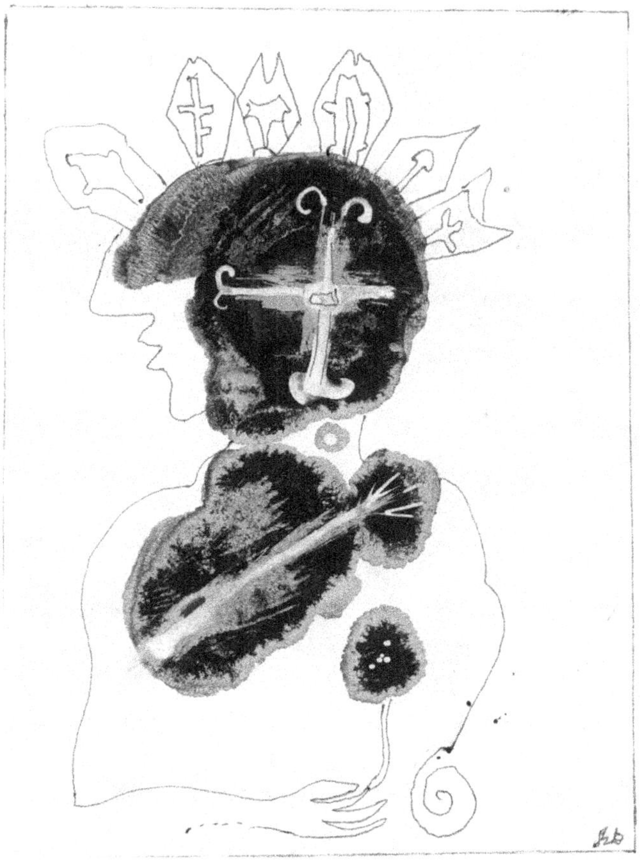

Drawing by Schlechter Duvall

and I think that an understanding of these functions is necessary for surrealists to be able to see their position in music more clearly.

Another example: the enlightened, reasonable belief in progress and the belief in the individualist power of creation corresponds to the classical/Romantic form, with its functional harmonic development and its drama with melodic themes ending in triumph.

The whole 20th century, with its theory of relativity, its wars and crises, its confusion, its chaos and its chaos theory, have all been obviously mirrored in music, right down to today's ironic personality market, dejection and postmodernism. Mirrored, yes, but often perhaps as if in moving water, with an indirectness that does not illustrate but works back and forth like an echo in a forest, a reflection from hundreds of directions and in hundreds of ways, and gives a confusing impression when interpreted. Music as expression and impression is delusive, but as the expression of and establisher of relations, poetic, social or otherwise, it is much clearer.

Nougé is thus entirely correct in that for surrealism in music, as in art and poetry, it is a question not of formal criteria but of a moral standpoint, a desire that is about life and death. Should that mean that a so-called surrealist musician expresses this desire totally, uncensored and uncompromisingly, in his music?

I had a similar idea when I first engaged in surrealism in 1985, immediately equating automatism and "free improvisation". It was not quite that simple, of course. I became an "automatist" in my musical practice and theory, a believer in automatism.

"Free music" today?

Among contemporary composers and musicians, improvisation, intuition, freedom and the unconscious are of course known concepts. Many are composing in a relatively open way, and freedom can nowadays be used by more and more classically trained musicians. Some can even improvise freely, which was almost unthinkable some years ago. Even the electronic music culture has become more and more "musicianly" and improvisatory.

Improvisation is of course ancient. It has existed and still exists in almost all genres, as something as necessary as it is self-evident. "Free improvisation" as a genre of its own, however, is only about 40 years old in Europe, and in America has grown gradually from jazz above all.

Some free improvisers had or have an interest in surrealism, which is not to say that free improvisation is always the same as automatism. Automatism is a special, uncontrolled state (the concept comes from spiritualism, where it is used, however, with a totally different point of departure) that is perceived as self-generating. It can express itself through all kinds of human activities, and though it surely often occurs in free musical improvisation, it probably also often occurs in other kinds of improvisation with musicians who have "grown together" with their style, and maybe also in certain "notation-bound" performances, as well as in composing. The "musicianly", in all genres, may also lie on the borders of automatism, i.e. the unity between the physicality of the body and the sounds. The person "victimized" by it is not a surrealist just because of that. It is inevitably also a question of how to take responsibility and relate to what you do, even if what you do is not controlled behaviour. A surrealist can do very thought-out things just as well as he can use chance and whim, including in music, if he relates to it with a surrealist attitude. Chance music, concrete music, yes even mathematical music or serial music – yes of course surrealists can have interest in that.

This statement is not as important as it seems. "Why not?" is not a very inspiring answer. "Why?" is a much more interesting question.

That is why it is hard for me to tolerate musicians who radiate ideals of cleverness, self-regard, reconciliation of serious contradictions instead of taking them deeper, or discordance with their task.

When we talk about the expression of the musician at the performance, it is interesting to state the importance of the whole of the scenic expression, conscious or unconscious. All parts contribute to the ritual or mythic contents, and make more apparent not only their relatedness to dance, theatre, architecture and the plastic arts, but also their relation to the money market, work market and personality market, which can be revealing for the unconscious message of an artist.

That said, we must of course also observe that most of the music we hear around us today is mechanized. That fact does not mean that the ritual is taken away. Background music, which is what most mechanized music is intended to be, is meant to ritualize the activities for which it is piped out – in most cases in a reassuring way, with cyclical and brainwashing pop music which mostly seeks to cradle us in the everyday market stomp of personality illusions. Musical environments create spaces that, among other

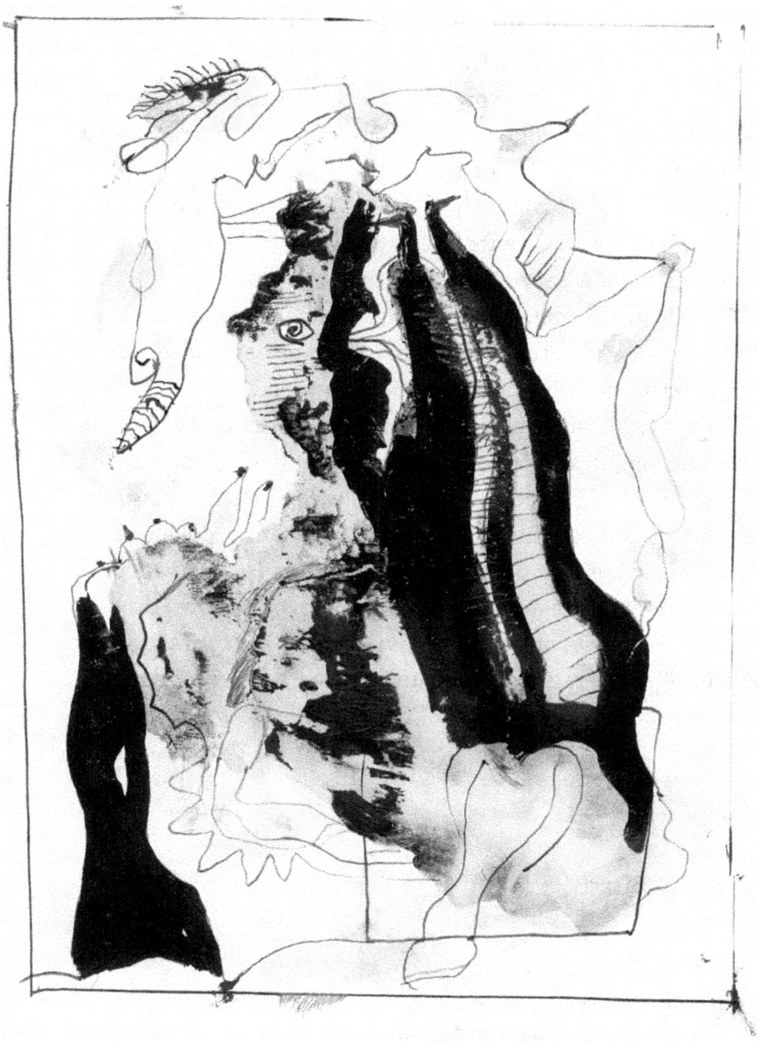

Drawing by Schlechter Duvall

things, define social relations and illusions in relation to the ego.

Then we have taken one step further: the ritual, independently of the physical presence or absence of a musician, contains not only an expression but also, to the same degree, a network of relations – many of them remaining unconscious behind the illusion of music as expression alone. The relations are on many levels: economic, social, ideological, physical, poetic etc. – and all of these are relevant to a full analysis of music, as well as of other arts.

Free improvisation

In improvisation I experience an urge for beauty momentary in unique newborn details, where it is the circumstance and play of contrasts that give them their value whether they are small, big, comical, ugly, beautiful or strange. There is a similarity between this process and surrealism's poetic concept of beauty or poetic objects (as Pierre Reverdy defined it: "the greater and truer the distance between two juxtaposed realities, the stronger will be the image and the greater its emotive power and poetic reality"[3]) and convulsive beauty ("convulsive beauty will be veiled-erotic, fixed-explosive, magic-circumstantial, or it will not be"[4]).

An important and even unique trait in free improvisation is the collective development of a language that takes place at the same time as it is practised and improvised. Everything happens in public. Among surrealists, more than others, this has already been applied, but usually in graphic and written expressions, in games and experiments.

I chose free improvisation as my musical method in 1985 (to be complemented, eventually, with electro-acoustic music, sound poetry and text-sound composition), and it has become my natural language, spurred into development by poetic methods and new means of expression. It has become a meeting place with matter, with my body and spirit, and with other people. And it has become a continuously desired field of experiments for a liberating utopia: this is the way we would like to live, even if it were not music, even if it were not a "ritual".

Davey Williams has written that "free improvisation is not an action resulting from freedom, it is an action directed towards freedom." This clarifies the concept of "free improvisation" as well as the concept of freedom. Freedom is not a state, it is an act. You take liberties, you do not "have" any freedom (the "democratic" illusion), you are not free, but rather unfree. With this reservation in mind, one can very well use the concept of freedom about much free musical improvisation, without any prejudice. In practical terms free improvisation can often be inhibited by the democratic illusion's concept of freedom, while being encouraged by audacity and violence in an interdynamic way to create convincing, durable solutions, immediately and without afterthought. Of course, this requires training in a world where this kind of behaviour isn't encouraged.

I often experience it like this: in every moment, concentrated in a sound-emitting point, a silent or maybe "hypothetical" explosion is taking place in all directions at the same time. Unknown but undoubted forces decide which splinter from this explosion will be manifested in sound, or rather, in musical objects (silence is also such an object) and comprise the new explosive centre. This chain of manifested points can form dense or thin, interconnected or split forms that billow or are hurled through the air. (There are other musicians who associate to colours.) Such is the poetic flood of improvised music for me, in this way the analogical chains are formed, from the "fixed explosion". And in this violent freedom, which is often strangely relaxed, it is not unusual for the music to create itself without my having any time to reflect on it. The control is often quite inexact, the events often go more quickly than thought or muscles manage to define. One plays in a way that lets the means, sound-tools, come to speak and to claim their right, so that they are perceived to create the music just as much as the human factor (as has also been noted by Davey Williams). A palpable "meeting between man and nature"? What more can be demanded from a surrealist perspective? What more can be wished for, in terms of a revolutionary musical utopia?

I conclude in this spirit of free improvisation, but above all with an urgent request to reflect on the human possibilities to orchestrate every human striving for freedom, beauty and adventure, with an obsession for, in and through sounds, as well as through a similar exaltation of the other senses. However I do not have any grand expectations that I will convince free improvisers or concrete musicians, for example, to suddenly show mutual enthusiasm with surrealists. It is evident that many creative people, to quote *Silence is Golden*, defend the "necessary prejudices" of their art form. It is also evident that everyone has to go through his own process of divination, training and refinement of his method. But I hope it will be a little less common for contemporary surrealists to tiptoe through the early surrealists' polemical exaggerations and insufficient statements. And maybe also fewer people will repeat the phrase that "the surrealists were against music", and a few more will say, "some surrealists do music as well."

Notes:

1 Paul Nougé. *Music Is Dangerous*, published as *Radical America, Surrealist Research & Development Monograph Series* no. 6, Cambridge, MA 1972 (after: *View magazine*, Dec 1946 and Spring 1947, also in Marcel Mariën (ed.) 1979 *L'Activité Surréaliste en Belgique (1924-1950)*, introduction and facsimiles of publications, Editions Lebeer-Hossmann, Brussels., after *La Conférence de Charleroi*, lecture 1929; first published 1946, also in *Histoire de ne pas rire*, Les Lévres Nues, Brussels 1956, also in Mariën 1979).

2 See the work of the civilization critic Herbert Marcuse and the anthropologist Hans Peter Duerr.

3 André Breton *What Is Surrealism? Selected Writings*, edited and introduced by Franklin Rosemont, Monad Press, New York. 1978, part 2, p.282 (Rising Sign 1947).

4 André Breton *Mad Love (L'Amour fou)*, University of Nebraska Press, Lincoln/London, 1987, p.19 (1937).

Download: an Incursion into Electronic Alchemy

Eric Bragg

Perhaps contrary to surrealist sentiment about the immediate past is the idea that surrealism in music is not necessarily limited to blues and jazz, but should theoretically be encountered by way of many different musical approaches and traditions. Likewise, the creation of noise, such as that from machines, should not be narrowly sequestered away from the realm of music, and instead, the two – noise and music – should actually overlap, potentially creating a marvelous interface where the alchemy of poetic sound could arise from the most accidental overlay and/or juxtaposition of noises, notes and voices.

At least within certain traditionalist sentiment, ever since the creation of the first Moog synthesizer, there has been a prejudice, perhaps due to technophobia[1], in favor of more traditional, hand-made instruments whose notes and noises are produced by way of their materials of composition, and their moving, vibrating or resonating parts. For a long while, the synthesizer had to evolve quite a bit in order to surpass whatever hollow, tinny sound some people have attributed to it. And in the transition from analog to digital recording and production, the sound quality has improved in its depth and complexity, multiplying the potential for experimenters to make use of these improvements.

One group of contemporary musicians that has taken advantage of this technology, and even gone so far as to make surrealist use of it under certain circumstances, goes by the name of *Download*. Described by the mainstream with various adjectives such as "experimental," "industrial," "noise," "ambient," "electronica," and at certain moments comprised of Phil Western, Mark Spybey, Dwayne Goettel and cEvin Key, *Download*'s sonic creations have ranged from harsh, layered cacophonies of industrial noise to more melodic, improvisational compositions that seem almost danceable. The purpose of this text is to use *Download*'s music as a choice illustration to demonstrate why such experimentation is important and why it should continue, of course under surrealist auspices.

■

While not intended as a thorough analysis or ultimate classification of *Download*'s music, the following notes should at least provide one with a few interpretational insights about the experimental nature of their music, and why it should be of interest to surrealists. These notes are organized into themes or qualities:

Percussive Force – The use of percussion is a strong, active element in this music. In other kinds of electronic music, the beat is often used as a passive stopwatch or rigid metronome, so as to herd the synthesizer motifs along their predetermined courses, but with *Download*, the percussion often figures strongly as an aggressive *diadochokinesia*, almost like the fervid rattle of the sidewinder, evoking the presence of something that is alive. Under these circumstances, the beat not only pushes the other elements of the composite sound, but responds to them and interacts with them. A great example of this furious drivability can be found in "Sigesang" from the *Furnace* album. The sound becomes frenzied, reaching a crescendo, and represents one of their most intensive percussive efforts ever. "Fill Her" from the *Charlie's Family* album, "30065 Morningview Dr." from *Inception*, and "Manmade" from *III Steps Forward* are also excellent examples. Percussion is thus like the movement of a being, or perhaps a physical journey or transitional movement, rather than an accompaniment. It is active, rather than passive, and integrated (rather than separated from the rest), therefore proving invaluable to the evolution of the sonic environment.

Likewise, percussion is not only established with obvious drumbeats, but with sampled noises from machines and other non-drum sources. Often the percussion has many elements that are derived from everyday life – from the tapping of small objects to the heaving, repetitive din of industrial machinery. Wonderful examples of this industrial flavor can be found in the noise-jams "Interlude" and "Tweeter Blower" from the *Charlie's Family* album. This music reminds the listener that if she walks through an urban area where there are so many industrial sounds, it is easy enough to follow the interactive rhythms of the machines as they become musical in nature, as a springboard for the imagination – perhaps even as a musical daydream. Percussion doesn't have to limit itself to being an intentionally orchestrated noise made by a group of people with sticks and skins, but can provide a means for spontaneously interacting with the surrounding elements. In this respect, percussion within many *Download* tracks has this interactive quality – that of creatively using sounds from the environment in percussive ways, rather than being stuck with drums and drum machines.

Gothic Element & Umor – *Download* has its dark moments, incarnating at times very rich veins of black humor which reflect a "gothic" sensibility[2]. One of the best examples is "Trick or Treat," from the *Charlie's Family* album. This song radiates a gothic darkness, crowned with a healthy dose of black humor, by way of a sinister blend of synth and percussion, punctuated in the middle with a sample of a doorbell rung during Halloween, followed by children's voices shouting "trick or treat," most likely hewn from the same source as the cantos of Maldoror. The track is pure evil. This vein of Umor continues throughout other pieces, such as "Yes" from the same album, "Separate" from *The Eyes of Stanley Pain*, and "Dakota" from *III Steps Forward.*

Aside from adding a sometimes "creepy" flavor to the music, this gothic dimension is elaborated by way of certain integrated voice samples, often in unexpected ways, and which perhaps are a continuation of similar experimentation carried on by cEvin Key from his Skinny Puppy projects. While collage has been made from the written word, collage from human voice hasn't been explored quite as much. The difference is that not only does the spoken word convey linguistic meaning, but it also has an emotive component that the written word lacks. Therefore, the spoken word also carries meaning, as well as emotion, including whatever poetic effects (i.e. irony, humor, etc.) from the interaction between the two. In addition, when samples of human speech are integrated with noise and music – such as through the use of voices taken from television shows, movies, radio etc. – the opportunities for poetic play are enriched. Such is the case with some of *Download*'s tracks, where snippets of voice from certain horror B-movies and other melodramatic sources have been incorporated. The point where the pure horror of suburbia intersects with the ridiculous has been reached on more than one occasion, all through the use of a decontextualized, off-hollywood voice, often dripping with second-hand emotion and crocodile tears. One might listen to their "Yes" song, for a particularly good illustration. In this way, the human voice can be used as a poetic device, especially when decontextualized and then integrated with other varieties of sound and noise. Additionally, this approach supports Breton's assertion that the task of the musician is to "unify, reunify hearing" by way of finding common ground between poetry and music[3].

Continuity & Collage – In contrast to popular varieties of western music done according to traditionally accepted conventions of rhythm and melody, *Download* manages to release itself from the predictable patterns of the western song, often distinguishable by its beginning, middle and end, and which often follows a predetermined formula[4]. Their tracks have components that seem unrelated, which

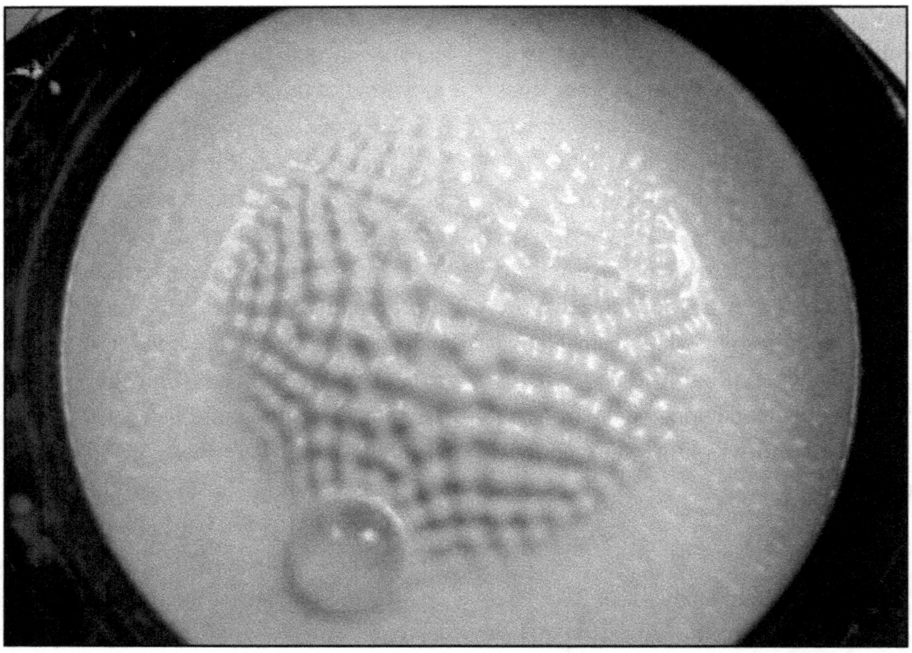

Cornstarch and water solution under the influence of sine wave vibration, photo by Collin Cunningham

are pasted together (sometimes seamlessly) in a mutually reinforcing way, or at other times in stark contrast to each other, yet which all produce the same effect experienced with visual collages. In fact, much of their music is collage-like, and is composed analogously in the way visual collages are: through the overlay and juxtaposition of various, unrelated elements. Traditionally, such discontinuities might be perceived as non-sensical, irrational and/or aesthetically displeasing, but as we know from the chance meeting of the sewing machine and umbrella on the dissection table, the coupling of seemingly unrelated passages has strong potential for poetic magnetism.

Some great examples of this process are found on the *Inception* album. Among others, the tracks "Weed Acid Techno" and "Recovered" both offer experiences in the form of music/noise jams: these can be considered evolving or "multi-paned" sonic environments, to the extent that melodic sequences within them smoothly transition into discordant or unrelated parts that nonetheless poetically resonate as a whole – the shift from musical sense to nonsense and then back to sense again, when each work is weighed in its entirety, as a complete unit. The beginning of a piece sounds quite different from its ending, and represents a meandering journey through various unrelated passages of melody and noise, yet integrated by way of percussion and rhythm, manifesting the entire experience perhaps as a *sonic dérive*. In this sense, it should be clear that chance plays a large role in these strange sonic journeys.

In other situations, disparate tracks of music, voice and noise are mutually overlaid, integrated, and at times reinforce each other, ever so magically. A great example of this activity is "Energy Plan" from the *Microscopic* album. Among a continuum of interconnected soundscapes, at one point the repetitive shuffle of marching soldiers gradually falls into synch with the throbbing drone of the percussion, in a doppleresque pattern.

Organic-Electronic – As music that is primarily "electronic" and which often sounds machine-like or even like a broken machine (although more traditional devices such as drums and stringed instruments are indeed used as well), *Download* is able to achieve a sound that is "organic," to the extent that it has its share of spastic, quirky, chaotic, even "dysfunctional" moments that remind the listener that it is people who create electronic music, not computers or machines. Noise and music do indeed overlap, and at times become indivisible, evoking the true randomness of nature and erasing the artificial boundary that is often erected between the two, ultimately allowing their sounds to become a "correspondence between the individual microcosm and the universal macrocosm," in the words of Bertrand Schmitt[5]; the drone of the universal machine melds with the deliberateness of the indvidual melody. The result is an experience rich in sound-poetics and experimental complexity, and is often the product of chance and accident. While the electronic pop and dance music of mainstream culture has the tendency to breed monotony and repetitive, machinelike movement for the listener, *Download* succeeds in using electronic means to create sonic environments that reflect the imperfection – the beautiful and ugly, side by side – of the human condition, and which can only stimulate (rather than euthanize) the listener. In fact, reflection leads to transformation.

Also, the question is answered affirmatively about whether manipulated sounds, notes, and melodies can achieve the same potency of effect as can be done with traditional "instruments"[6]. When music was still music (before the advent of "noise"), instruments were more easily defined: pieces of wood or metal, with strings or other parts that held tension, so as to create resonating sound. But with the availability of analog and digital synthesizers, and then with various editing and mixing capabilities offered by computer software and other gear, it becomes possible to create a spectrum of sonic possibilities that can rival (yet also cooperatively integrate with) the dynamic range of any traditional instrument. Additionally, the ability to merge the sounds of objects, machines and voice samples with musical notes by way of computer software also surpasses the traditional conception that music can only be made with instruments, and once again confirms that alchemical connection of music with nature (noise). Therefore, the concept of the "instrument" should cover more than just the object of metal or wood that emits a sound, and should now also include those methods of sound and noise made through artificial means, not excluding the intervention of computers and other electronic equipment, and thus the processes and interactions associated with these elements. As a result, *Download* is at times able to reach the threshold of this state of "instrumentless" music[7]. It should be noted that the sounds produced by these artificial instruments and those produced by their organic counterparts should not be considered mutually exclusive, as some purists might insist. There isn't any reason why traditional instruments can't be used effectively in the presence of other, more synthetic means; and of course they already are.

Automatism & Improvisation – Many of their songs have an ongoing, spontaneous quality, such that the idea was to create the elements of a "jam" session, rather than some conscious or deliberate construction. In some cases it's very obvious that certain note arrangements and rhythms, in whatever way they appear disharmonious, incongruous, etc., exist as an alternative to the common formulas prescribed for pop and dance music, thus identifying these particular "anomalous" musical phrases as the result of automatism, intuition, accident, chance, etc. In particular, these automatic traits are manifested by way of the previously described merging and juxtaposition, as well as shifts in melody or rhythm (like the introduction of discordant notes or voices) which might initially seem off-key or out of place but which resonate in new and unpredictable ways, and which ultimately make poetic sense. This automatic quality is one of the key features of *Download* music, and is present as a strong current that runs through many of their works, especially their albums from the 90s.

And in their own words, the musicians characterize their activities as being automatic, in much the same way surrealists would describe their own work: as Phil Western says, "the person using the computer and the machines is... feeling his way through the process [of which] accidents are a very regular part...and I would even say that they are an indicator of a healthy relationship with the muse. One finds, for no apparent reason, that quality accidents will happen seemingly free of any will or effort on behalf of the person creating." Or according to Mark Spybey:

> The spontaneous act is at the heart of my approach to music making because it creates the possibility of the accident occurring. I believe accidents are important events that often create new possibilities. I also think that there is a link between being spontaneous and being able to tap into powerful emotions because the very essence of the spontaneous act cuts out the middleman so to speak, the rational and revisionist parts of us that really don't want to expose our vulnerabilities[8].

While automatic techniques figure strongly in these musicians' approaches, there is also an improvisational element at the collective level, which was actually the main approach for *Furnace*, their first album. As Spybey says, the album...

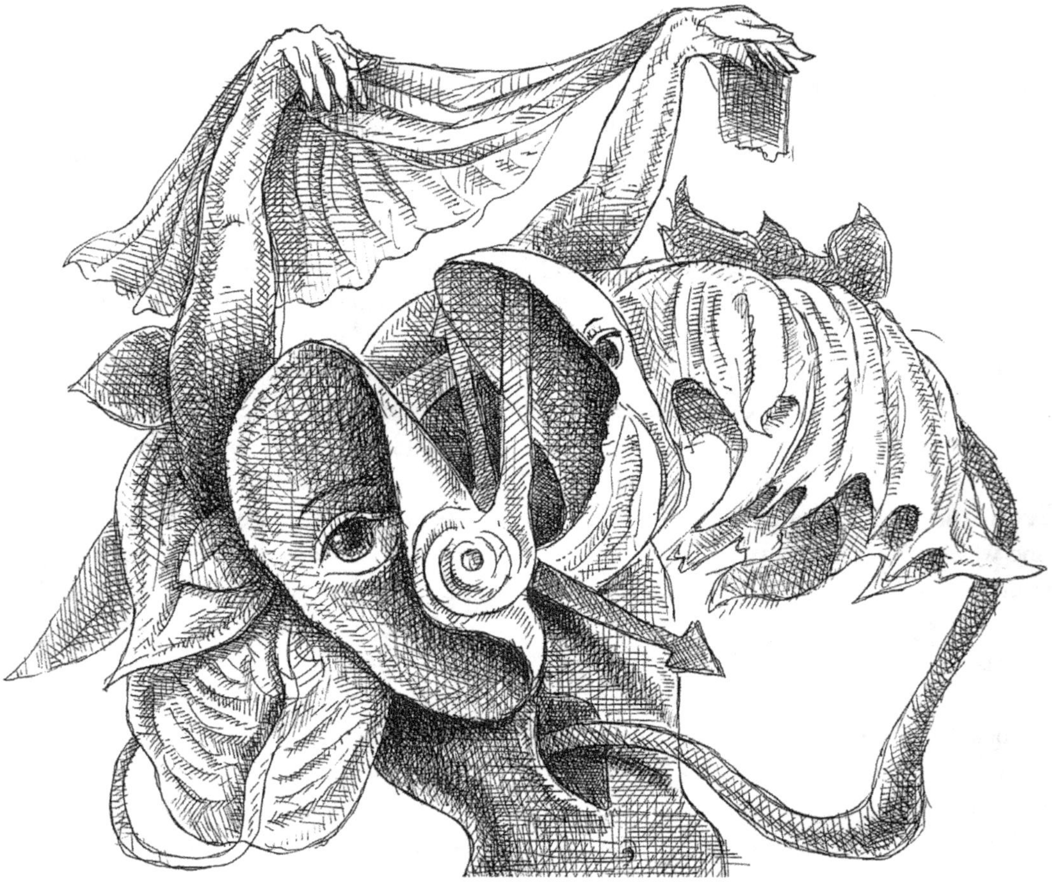

Drawing by Patrick Hourihan

...was based on a series of late night improvisations. We rarely spoke about what we might do, save for making a decision about programming our effects so that the delays were all in time with the beat. That was a stroke of genius. I think we really tried hard to listen to each other; it was strange because we couldn't really see each other and we worked through headphones. I think the results were exhilarating.

And then Western provides us with even more details:

With *Furnace*, we all had our own individual setups, which were synchronized in the studio, so all of us were receiving the same master clock, except we all also had performance devices, such as synthesizers or samplers, which were not receiving clock, but were sending sound to the master recording anyway. These were numerous in number – Kevin [Key] had an array of analog synthesizers, I focused a lot of energy on effects processing, Dwayne [Goettel] had the minimoog but it was Mark [Spybey] who was the most performance based of all of us, and who had the most improvisational sound. Mark had a large selection of noisemaking devices, including toys and other such things which he recorded using contact microphones, which gave everything a unique sound.

In these regards, *Furnace* should be considered a masterpiece of the electronic fusion between music and noise, and an ideal place for the uninitiated to first become acquainted with *Download*'s music.

While some may be disappointed to learn that their subsequent albums[9] were not done live, in the way *Furnace* was, the fact that these folks still relied on collaboration, albeit in a more "studio-oriented" manner (i.e. sharing and collaborating on tracks offline), should in no way invalidate their later music, which has just as much to offer. Although live, improvisational music is certainly prized by surrealists, other forms of collaborative music done through automatic techniques also have their merits. In this respect, *Download* has produced a variety of sonic environments, both through live improv and collaborative file-sharing in the studio. These approaches have yielded powerful, pioneering results through tapping into a vein of *electronic, collective alchemy.*

One should note that while it is impossible to posit any one band or group of musicians as *the* paradigm of contemporary, innovative music, *Download* should be considered an important contributor, to the extent that they have been able to 1) redefine the musical instrument (in terms of facilitating electronic expression's coming into its own), 2) assist in the dismantling of the awkward barrier between noise and music (thereby restoring the connection between listeners and their environment – ultimately, nature), and 3) elaborate a body of work that represents a poetic, alchemical evolution and which remains completely outside of the traditional formulas of consciously directed, commercially driven pop music. In all of these respects, they are pioneers. Their music represents an *alchemy of sound*, and if anything, *Download* demonstrates for us that electronics exist so that we can make surrealist use of them. The next question to ask, of course, is how to push these experiments even further.

■

So far, this text has only provided a pseudo-analytical case-study of *Download*'s music, for the purpose of characterizing it. Obviously such music can better reveal its energy and potential in an intact state. Perhaps the following thoughts might help explain the appeal of their poetics from the surrealist perspective, as well as help clarify a direction for further surrealist exploration:

In the surrealist sense, we can learn from *Download*'s approach to music and recognize it as another method of apprehending reality: environmental sounds (noises from the environment) are used by the poet to build a new, composite sonic space. In this sense, and for those who take this approach, noise/sound/music is a means of experiencing reality, in and of itself, so the sound poet is charged with the task of creating or transforming a new reality with the ambient sounds he has encountered: for example, the recording of a broken, hiccupping machine might be merged with sounds of moving air or liquid, which then segues into composite noises made from human speech, then transitioned into something else, and so on and so forth. These cyclic movements of sound run their courses, evolving just like visual or any other kinds of imagery evolve – this is a sonic daydream, after all, most likely started when the noises of the everyday world enter the ears, and when subsequently the mind begins to play with them. Likewise, during a more passive state, such as when one is on a train or in some urban place quietly listening to the din of perpetually humming and clicking machinery, it becomes possible to discern rhythms within these sounds, perhaps inspiring the urge to alter them, punctuating them with other encountered noises. During such moments of passivity, or even during the times where the listener might be falling asleep, these interacting noises in the imagination begin to congeal, and take on a direction of evolution such as our imaginations would determine, creating the rudiments of music that come directly from the surroundings, not from any preconceived ideas about what someone might want to play or hear.

And for the sake of improvisation, it should be recognized that some of the most fascinating discoveries come through the poetic intervention of chance and accident, as Spybey and Western have solidly indicated. Along these lines, we might expect the elaboration of such noise-poetry to occur in a way analogous the process of the *dérive*, such that the experimenter might drift from place to place, sampling various sounds according to whim or chance, ultimately using them to make a composite movement of noise integrated with music which could unveil the nature of a particular neighborhood or location, and ultimately change it as a result. There are many such games yet to be played.

Perhaps a significant difference between this kind of ambient music and other improvisational approaches like jazz emerges when viewed in this way: while the latter requires the musician to have his means of sound creation within his own hands (his instrument), and of course the will to improvise with or without the collaboration of other musicians, the former approach emphasizes a direct dependence of the musician on his sonic environment: to allow himself to become a mirror off which the numerous, ambient sounds reflect, albeit in distorted, altered, and ultimately transformed reflections. In this sense, the poet's environment becomes a part of the "instrument"[10]. Therefore the goal of the activity is not necessarily to "play notes," but essentially to become a mirror or channeling medium for the sounds and noises that occur around us. And that some of those channeled experiences will evolve into music is inescapable.

In this manner, the music is not apprehended with the well-known voice of, say, a guitar, but instead is created from scratch using those seemingly random, ambient sounds, thus allowing the imagination – which includes subconscious influences and manipulations – to do its work: to take these noises and enhance their tonal qualities, leading them to create a new form of music that can clearly show its roots, origins, its constitutive raw material. In this way, music acquires the potential to be made from sources other than the instruments that some of us are so strongly attached to, although there is no mutual exclusivity implied here: musical instruments and synthetic sources of music-making (such as I have suggested here – i.e. through the use of sound manipulation and alchemy) might generate music through different processes and means, but certainly one can only expect there to be fruitful cooperation and even interdependence between the two. But gone are the days of the traditional instrument being the sole maker of music.

In light of these ideas, we should take the luminous music of *Download* for what it is: as a pioneering step towards the alchemy of sound: of using artificial means to manipulate noises that come from the world around us, and to create a music that can be more easily accessed through the world of noise. From *Download*, we learn that as long as the rhythmic and chaotic sounds that come from everyday life can be internalized – from the random conversations of passersby, to the din of heavy machinery, to the random and sporadic collisions that happen spontaneously – then we can count on our imaginations to play with these noises in the most poetic of ways, allowing the sounds to interact amongst themselves, provided we make ourselves receptive to them. How often have we gone about our daily routines that are so often replete with the kind of repetitive drudgery found within urban areas, being forced to experience and re-experience the daily mess that calls itself modern life? We know that within that repetitive drudgery is the component of sound. The din of the machine can be just as intrusive and disruptive as the machine itself. Over time, such noise is drilled into our heads and it only makes surrational sense that the "stunning revenge" that the imagination should take on the world around it, which Breton spoke of in the first manifesto, should use sound as one of its weapons. Accordingly, the routine, repetitive noises that so often stultify and annoy are transformed, and subsequently affect the reality of those who listen to them, becoming yet one more species of poetry that refuses to remain confined to any cage of tradition.

Silence is not golden; it is the calm before the storm.

Special thanks to Mark Spybey and Phil Western for their interviews and correspondence, which were invaluable for the elaboration of this text.

Notes:

1) *Download*'s music also serves as an illustration to combat surrealist technophobia: the idea that any work made through electronic means, such as with a computer, could only be inferior to something made with more organic, material tools, such as paintbrushes or musical instruments built from wood or metal, for example. The idea is that a tool is a tool, whether it be organic or electronic, and should only be seen as a means for expression, not as an end in itself or a fool-proof method of expression that doesn't require an imagination to propel it. As most would agree, imagination should always be the driving force of music, whether the music is made through organic or electronic means. Fetishizing, or conversely shunning, any particular means or method of expression is simply reactionary and ultimately revealing of aesthetic preoccupations.

2) The term "gothic" is used here in a way analogous to the gothic novels of the 18th century, not the angst-ridden, nihilistic, wearing-of-black-clothing kind of "goth" that is prevalent among middle-class youth today.
3) André Breton, *Silence is Golden*. 1946.
4) And instead of the traditional lyrics that one would expect from pop-culture songs, there are instead certain choice moments, such as can be found on their early albums, where a person can be heard speaking and vociferating in the same way as one might expect to find in a surrealist automatic text.
5) Bertrand Schmitt, "The Lizard's Cry" (1998). Translated by Nikos Stabakis from the French and published elsewhere in this volume. In the second part of the text, he explains that "sounds have deserted metaphorical language in order to find again analogical language, which is that of our own corporal perception," and thus notes the potential of music to put "into play… [the] non-mediated resonance of our body with the external phenomena and objects."
6) Once again, there is that issue of technophobia to address.
7) By way of analogy, what do we really care if a visual collage is made of elements cut from drawings, photographs, painted surfaces, etc., as long as the final image opens the door to the marvelous? Are collages made from photographs any better than those made from clippings from printed newspapers, for example? If music (or noise) is created with traditional instruments versus artificial ones, aren't we more interested in the final result rather than the means which led to that final result?
8) Spybey also goes on to say: "Improvisation is at the heart of how I work. I have become more comfortable with the idea that a studio can be a creative tool if you like but I find that most studios are just stagnant places that ironically seem designed to stifle creativity. I always strive to capture the first take when working by myself. It seems to work but I'm not afraid to change what I do. I try to remove obstacles from my way. Technique can be an obstacle. Technical proficiency can be an obstacle. I can't play anything well but I can make sounds that work, at least to my ears."

And even more: "Musicians need to work off other musicians. It takes great skill and tremendous courage to just let go. To actually be yourself and recognize that the sounds you create are not permanent markers, they are disposable. You don't live or die in improvisation, you just exist but you have to prepare for the possibility that what you do might not make any sense at all to you, your collaborators or the audience. It's risky. It's blissful when it works, distracting and often ugly when it doesn't but you just have to do it."
9) Discography: *Furnace*, 1995. *Microscopic*, 1995. *The Eyes of Stanley Pain*, 1996. *Sidewinder*, 1996. *Charlie's Family*, 1996. *III*, 1997. *Effector*, 2000. *Inception: the subconscious jams 1994-1995*, 2002. *III Steps Forward*, 2002. *Fixer*, 2007. *Helicopter*, 2009.
10) The concept of the "instrument" should be expanded not only to include noise-making objects, but also the *processes* of capturing disparate sounds from one's immediate environment.

THE DOUBLE

a poem by
Raúl Henao

There is a card player seated on the edge of
  my bed

until I decide to open the window.

With the cold night-air first his hat
   disappears,

part of his coat, his striped shirt, his shoes

In this state of undress he chooses to depart

angrily down the staircase.

Below I can hear the latchkey being turned

in the old lock of the building,

the dogs bark momentarily, a sound like a car

pulling-up and the door closes with a bang.

At that moment I remember having seen the
        card player

on a previous occasion,

and pausing only to adjust my dressing gown

I rush down the stairs

The street-door is slightly ajar and opposite

a car waits in the darkness

pressing my face to the window

I see myself in the back-seat of the taxi

as it sets-off on its journey unknown.

Translated by Philip West.

DELTA BLUES

Black cat bone across my collar like a 44 long barrel
that reaches down my side like a stiff erection
Delta screams, the moan of the Delta down
The crossroads where 61 and 49 meet upon the hips of the dead
Their backs are bent with the blues
The blues with its swivel haunches of a mad dog
Blood on the tracks and on the eyelids of the catfish bottoms
Crossing the Yellow Dog exciting a fever of the oncoming Peavine
Muddy foot prints across the highway
The crossroads, where at midnight the moon sings harmony on a perch
The bones of fallen guitar players who have slept beneath the moon
Waiting for the devil to tune their guitars
A whole host of finger picking skeleton horses
who play the Georgia skin game on the back of a black snake bone.
Delta heartbeat, the deep down of black mud
King Cotton with his smile of hanged men
Who swing from shadow trees where the Mississippi moon
Hides amongst the cattails and mosquito moss
The plow stands rusting in the field
like an old corpse
The Delta smells of blood and mud
The Delta smells of the blues and the rhythm of slavery
The Delta cries out with the tears of the black mud
And death whistles in the graveyard of the hateful
Where the human voice of a slide guitar wails like a dead man.
The Delta with scars across its back
The open wounds of whips and rope
Where the penitentiary gate swings shut on forced labor
and King Cotton with bristled breast crows across the river
Mojo bags are hung from magnolia trees like dew drops hung from a Mississippi moon
Harmonica's moan broke and hungry, ragged and dirty
The hoodoo woman has left her door open till the flood waters recede
When she will gather up the mud in her hands
To form little figures of saints and husbands, pickers and ramrods
The Delta with its skin colored in the blues
Whiskey brown and Mississippi mud black
White cotton stained red with blood
The rising flood waters cannot wash it away
But can bury it deep in the rich bottom land soil
From West Memphis to New Orleans
The sound of the jook and the rollicking barrelhouse
The sound of the night wringing its hands of the day
The sound of the mule dying in the sun
It is carried by the whistle of the B & O
On the steel veins of the Southern
Or the watery backbone of a river that holds the secrets
Of the Delta, whose flesh, is our flesh,
Whose tears are our tears sewn to our cuffs not to be forgotten
These blues, like a steel guitar ring in the night
Sounding the voice of the Delta
Like a scream in the American fabric
The Delta carries its pride along with its shame
Inside a battered guitar case
That is thrown across the shoulders of a bluesman
Who has wandered from the root
And the waters of his birth...
The Delta

Ribitch
01/23/06

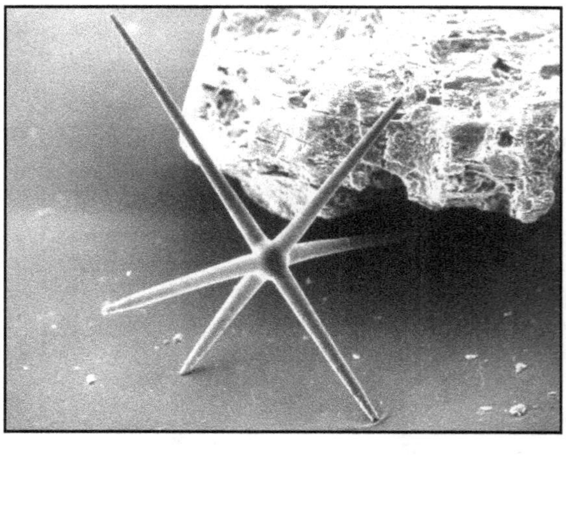

HIS WIFE JUDITH

Emma Lundenmark

Laurent had just finished cleaning the whole of his great house and sat down at the table in the sitting room. Everything was sparkling clean and at last he could let his head drop to his hands and doze off for a little while. His brother had come for a visit and was walking quietly about the room with a regal air. He was perturbed to see that everything had been cleared away. The lion's head that he himself had given to Laurent after a long voyage, the carpet of purest wool and the little toy theatre. It was no more than ten years ago that they used to put on little plays for the rest of the family. The two of them had delighted in those great tragedies. They always ended with somebody dying just at the moment when the curtain fell. Those had been their private games and not a living soul could disturb them. The fair queens always fell madly in love. The gentle knights were invincible. The fact that the monster always won in the end was not important. They only knew that that was how the story always went.

Laurent's brother Valejos wandered out of the sitting room with its shiny walls and into the kitchen. There was no trace of anything left to suggest that this was where food was prepared. Even the cooking smells in the tapestries had gone. The clock struck seven and the pendulum rumbled loudly as it swung back and forth. Outside the window the wind blew listlessly in the pollarded elms. Suddenly Valejos felt that he was not alone in the room. Something moved at the far end of the wall. Something which could not be clearly distinguished from the tapestry but which was moving towards him all the same. A weak cracked voice came from the shadows.

"Can I get you anything, sir?"

It must be the manservant. Valejos had forgotten he even existed, he had seen no sign of him since arriving at the castle the previous evening. But elusive as he was, Laurent was very proud of him. He had the appearance of a yellow paper angel but was able to go about his duties just the same. Valejos walked up to him and took his hand. It was a firm handshake even if his skin was rough and his hand rather cold.

"Pour me a drink and have one yourself."

For a moment the manservant disappeared again before he became visible in front of the drinks cabinet. They sat out on the verandah, Laurent would sleep for several hours now anyway, as he usually did whenever he managed to tire himself out. Valejos learned that they had just come home from a long journey. They had headed off across the gardens then wandered far into the forest. Since then Laurent's wife Judith had never been the same, she lay in bed and did not want to be disturbed except at night to take her medicine. Valejos had not even seen her yet but the manservant said simply that that was how Laurent wanted it. The manservant was an old man who never smiled. According to Laurent it was because he had never had anything to smile about. He never said more than was strictly necessary and he sat silently at the table and gazed at his master's brother. He did not touch his glass. The later the hour became, the thinner and more unreal he appeared. Valejos forgot him again and let his thoughts wander.

He had travelled the whole world by both air and sea and was only staying with Laurent on his way home from the Far East. Even though he had enjoyed it very much when he was young, he now found travelling more and more troublesome and he envied his brother's quiet life. He was also baffled at how they could have got lost. The grounds were not large even if they had gone far into the deepest forest. He and Laurent had once got lost when they were children. His memory of it was rather vague but he remembered that they had tried to run after a beautiful deer. They did so intending to call their father who would then come and shoot it but they had gone much too far. They had hidden behind a bush and watched as she drank from the stream. The large antlers jutted out far over the water and Valejos had taken it into his head to push her in. He talked Laurent into doing it, but when the boy had run forwards the deer had kicked out and he had fled into the bushes. He was crying and looked so afraid. When Valejos approached him he saw a large wound in Laurent's side and blood pouring onto the ground. He tried to drag him home but they had only gone round in circles. Then they had come across the deer again. She had suddenly rushed up out of the trees and grabbed Laurent in her mouth. She laid him across her back and ran away on quick hooves across the tundra. Valejos had looked for them for several hours, but then had trudged home alone when night came. Laurent turned up in the gardens a few days later but could never say what had happened while he had been away.

Valejos had also dozed off for a while and when he awoke the manservant had disappeared. It was dark outside and he wanted to go and lie down. He went back into the sitting room and his brother was still asleep at the table. Valejos stood nearer. He wanted to stroke his hair and wake him but he looked as if he was sleeping much too deeply. His face looked so much younger than his own. Younger and more beautiful even though he was so very pale. He had always been pale. His complexion as light as the coldest lake. Right up to that day when his blood had flowed it had appeared almost blue. It was that that distinguished the two brothers. Valejos's thoughts were interrupted as the manservant reappeared without a sound at his side. He was carrying a tray with a bottle of tablets which he placed in Valejos's hand. It was Judith's medicine and Laurent would certainly appreciate it if his brother would take it to her.

He found her upstairs in one of the larger bedrooms. The moonlight lit up her face as Valejos stepped quietly into the room. She was sleeping deeply and he was in no hurry to wake her. He sat beside her on the edge of the bed for a few moments and then lay down and stretched out behind her back. She had only a thin white chemise over her shoulders and he looked for a long time at her pale gaunt skin. Eventually he too fell asleep and began to dream. That night he dreamt in a stream of images of Laurent as a child. One face dissolved into another in a continuous eddy. The yellow paper angel was also there and dived into Judith's back. He soon realised that everything was coming from there. Judith's back had opened like a book and he was lying behind her and leafing through the pages. It was like a series of animated images of her, going around the room, up to the mirror, over to the wardrobe and out of the window, then coming in and returning into her own back, over and over again.

She had felt him open the book as she slept. She had felt his hand on her back for a while and was amazed that he could keep all the pages fluttering with just one hand. That was when she decided that she could get dressed. In the past she would usually get dressed around this time but the sleeping tablets had stopped her from doing so for several years. So she lifted herself up in the moonlight and carefully folded one garment after another, her white fabric, face and skin. Everything in a pile on the chair by the bed before she returned to her proper self. That was what made Valejos cry out when he awoke with his nose buried deep in her fur. As each image passed into the next he had begun to understand what was happening. The beautiful face had hovered close to his own and then been slowly transformed. First the eyes, then the muzzle, while he felt her cloven hooves holding onto him, but when he was fully awake it was he who was holding onto the deer.

He threw one leg across her and gripped her throat between his hands. She bellowed and broke loose and her antlers ripped his flesh. Valejos tore the knife from his pocket and drove it deep into her heart. Slowly the life ran out of her and over Valejos. He staggered from the room and down to the sitting room. He could find neither Laurent nor the manservant anywhere and he continued out of the door, zigzagging across the gardens and away towards the forest. Nobody answered his cries for help, and he staggered on in confusion, further and further away across the grounds.

Translated by Merl Fluin and Emma Lundenmark

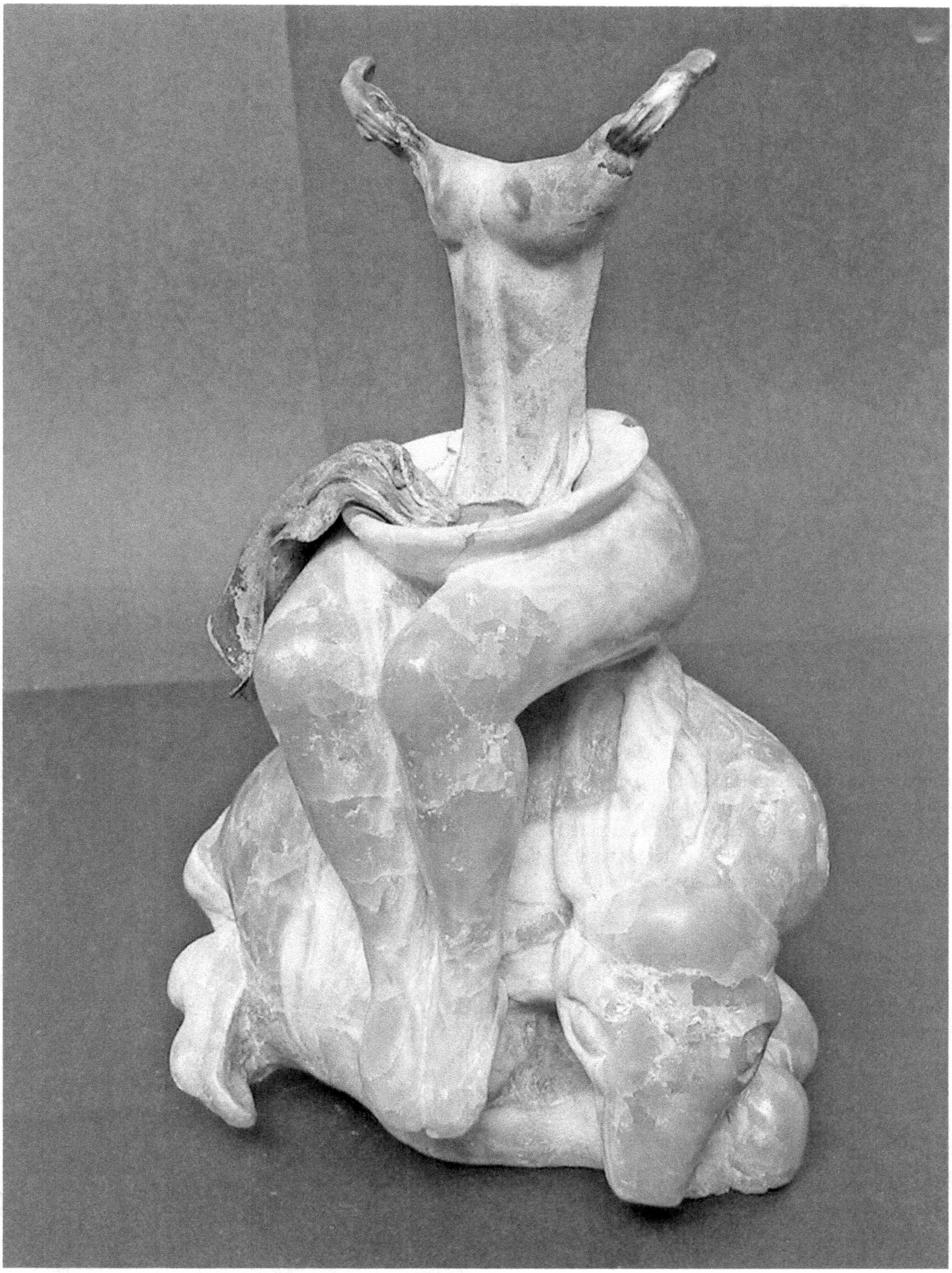

Washerwoman, sculpture by Robert Green

RONNIE BURK

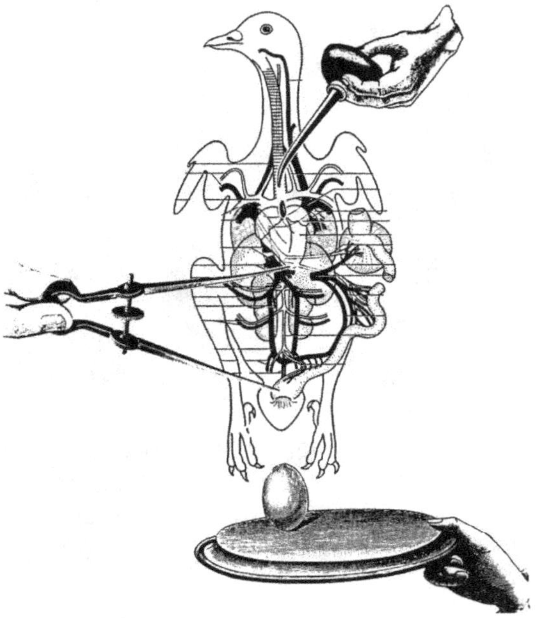

Corpses

Leaving behind
treasured sorrows
old age
madness
my wrinkled skin
my bony frame
my haunted
life
beaten between the wings of
a dragonfly

Once upon a time
I was an Indian
Hunched over
Carrying a bundle of sticks
Down a mountain
Dried sperm
Roasted flesh
That's all I remember

Arcimboldo

to Philip Lamantia

My brother with the face of a cracked china doll. His vest of turnip greens and rutabagas conceal the vegetable eye of William Blake in pilgrim shoes. Molten forests of stone evacuate the premises overridden with glass houses filled with copulating octopi. While his ship of purple water leaves the clouds to read the meaning of a lattice of sticks in the matted trees of his wooden hair.

My brother with the face of a cracked china doll. His mirror argues for sideshows. Although his father deserved the whipping he got. Zeus as George Washington in a mausoleum sunk in cement.

Let's bury our boy under a hill of bone. Better yet try the mating dance of the twin butterfly fluttering about his yellow stamen.

Veined the wax hoya flower dipped in porcelain water makes for a clear double. But the bloody egg runs down the side of his mouth rosy and luscious as an overturned bowl of lichees soaking in cherry cream.

Fever

To suck the diamond
Spinning
Behind the tongue
Of a corpse
A flower sweats
Dying of its own
Grief

Twelve pills
The sleeping
Machine's
Chrome to touch
This side of you

Hangnail is the serpent
Raped of wisdom and
The lotus of sleep
Returns the damage

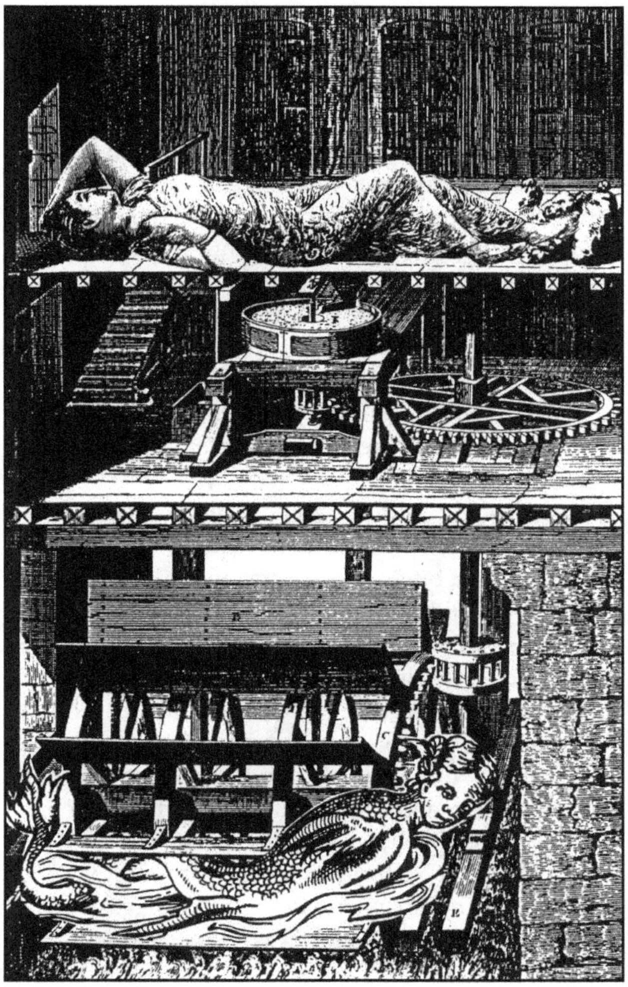

My Death

My death has a baboon's head
alligator teeth
eat the flames
of his evil spells
pierced lovers embrace
wheels of naked bodies
vedic pills
burning tigers of your solar mansions
narcotic splendors
on a desolate landscape of fired bauxite
My death sits shimmering
a black hole of reconnaissance
tied up with white
altar scarves
smoking mule-faced
cigars

Ronnie Burk (1955-2003) was a surrealist poet, collage artist and ACT-UP activist who lived in San Francisco and New York. He self-published several chapbooks, including *Man-Of-War* and *Basilisk*. Other writings appeared in U.S. surrealist publications and in the small press.

The Pact

Josie Malinowski

Far from the wayside I called out and waited for the reply, which came across the icicle bridge, cycling along, peddling furiously as though there was no time to spare, and thus it came to me, panting all the while, to deliver the verdict, to deliver my sentence.

I wailed as I waited; the damned creature – for damned it was, its punishment being messenger to the judiciary – withholding its information, torturing me as it was tortured, a mexican wave of agony flowing from each being in turn as we awaited and suffered the price of our folly.

"Get on with it," I muttered and spat on its feet in my consternation. It looked in disgust at the filthy act I'd just committed, forgetting that actually, in limbo, the act of spitting on a messenger's shoes is considered flattering and all I was trying to do was get it to hurry. But the stupid thing still lived with its head stuck far up the arse of reality as it was, rather than fantasy as it is now, the damned fool – damned, as I said, being literal.

"Come, come," I said, bashing it over the shoulder with the bicycle pump I held in my fist. "Come, name a price, then," I said, realising it may be a fool but it knew its own price and wouldn't sway from it, neither by my cajoling nor threatening it.

"Forty hours of service," it hissed. "Forty hours you deliver my messages for me."

"Ludicrous!" I declared. "I've never heard such tyranny. Never!"

The being shrugged and began to slope away.

"But you're duty-bound to deliver your messages! Honour bound, bound by fire and hell!"

"What more can they do?" it asked, its eyes blazing with the hatred of the sea. I shrank into my hat, feeling suddenly like a pipe being smoked by a fat walrus, as if they come any other way.

"I agree," I said, shaking its crackled hand, and as I did so, a roar like that of a heifer in childbirth sounded about my ears and I fell to the floor. "Mother of fire! What–" but I wasn't allowed to finish my sentence, because the messenger-creature began cackling mercilessly, a sound so chilling my feet froze, and it grew in size higher and higher and wider and wider until it was the exact size of the house I lived in before all of this happened. I shrank even further into my shoes and in a voice that definitely wasn't mine I asked it what was going on.

"Good luck, my friend, my saviour, my foolish little catamite!"

Without another word it was gone and around my neck was a chain of red metal, heavier than my hair, and the second I looked at that chain it was being dragged along by an invisible bastard, so that my neck, and thus, I, was also dragged along, like a chariot, only I wasn't Roman and this wasn't Rome, and I couldn't see my horse, and it wasn't a horse but a terrible thing made entirely of evil thoughts, so in that sense, it wasn't like a being a chariot after all.

It chucked me in a pond of red urine where not an hour earlier all the catacomb guardians had come for their weekly Bladder Liberty Group, which I'm sure can only be imagined in the minds of deranged saints. But the product was there for my human eyes to water at, and into this pool of putrid fester I lived on rush-weeds and the tears of the indigo frogs who'd been banished to the pool for daring to attack their king, for seventeen years of human reckoning.

On the first day of the eighteenth year a manic man, shorter than a zebra, with a face covered in crinkles like nobody had ever ironed him, came unto me and told me my initiation was over and I'd passed the test.

"Test?" I asked, choking on a pea I'd found under a rock. "Nobody told me about a test."

"But you've passed, aren't you pleased?"

I shrugged. "I don't really care either way."

"Listen here," the small man said. "I've gotta sit on your head for a bit now. You don't mind, do you?"

"Why should I mind?" I replied. I hauled myself out of the pool and prostrated myself before the man. He looked at me incredulously and sat on my head. I felt myself suffocating and thought about the trees behind me who'd always been a good friend to me and how actually I didn't want to die, lest they develop depression or wage war on the frogs. I threw the man off and pierced his heart with my iron fork.

"Death! Ever victorious!" I cried, as the man bled profusely. He beckoned me in with his finger. He said:

"Good work, mate. That was the second test," and

died.

"Puny men, I detest," I said. I puffed up my chest and felt my nipples harden with the eroticism of the kill, or the chill of the breeze, I don't know which. It'd never been cold down there by the pond so I knew some balance of power had shifted, and I assumed myself to be queen. "Ha!" I said, and waited.

Three days passed without incident and I wondered why my subjects had not yet come to serve me jelly on elephant's feet, as is traditional. I hummed and ummed and even erred for five minutes and then, on the fourth day, I saw an opening in the infinitesimal clouds, through which a few pebbles landed in my palms. They fought each other in my hand until all but one had fallen to the floor. The remaining pebble said:

"You have passed the test."

"What bloody test?" I shouted.

"It's time for your forty hours to commence."

"What bloody forty hours?"

"Of service, silly wench, promised to my father eighteen years ago."

"Shit," I said, and the pebble teleported me back to the place of message-taking where I was given a notepad and told to go. The forty hours passed uncomfortably, as there was some sort of requisite stating that messengers must be burnt with ice every three minutes and immersed in a mild acidic solution every five, but pass they did, and then the original messenger came back, sloping unhappily after his long respite.

Daral, painting by [Radvan] Rıdvan

"Well then, clever little pact-man, what have you to say to me, what be my message?"

"You're wanted upstairs. You've got five minutes or you'll be demoted."

"Five minutes from now?"

"From when the message was given to me."

Cursing his idiocy, I poked his eyes out with his own pebble-child and feasted on his carcass, for I was tired of rush-weeds and indigo frogs, and he tasted of barbequed fish.

The Daughters of Fishwives

Barrio pesquero, Santander harbour, 18th of July 2009, 00.48 – 01.48

(Eugenio Castro, Vicente Gutiérrez Escudero, Bruno Jacobs, Noé Ortega Quijano)

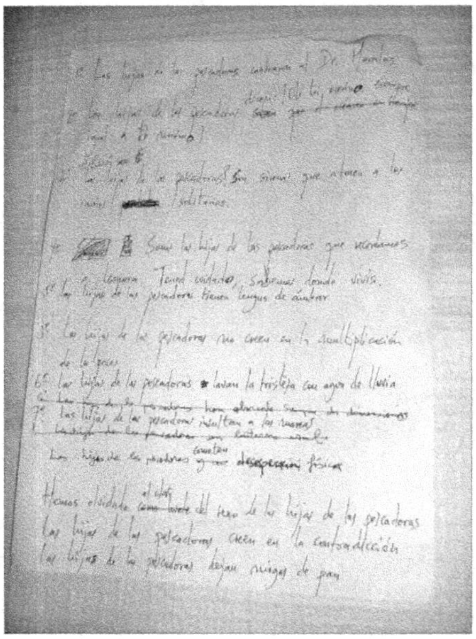

Noé with the list of sentences

The daughters of fishwives have a tongue of amber

Vicente writing

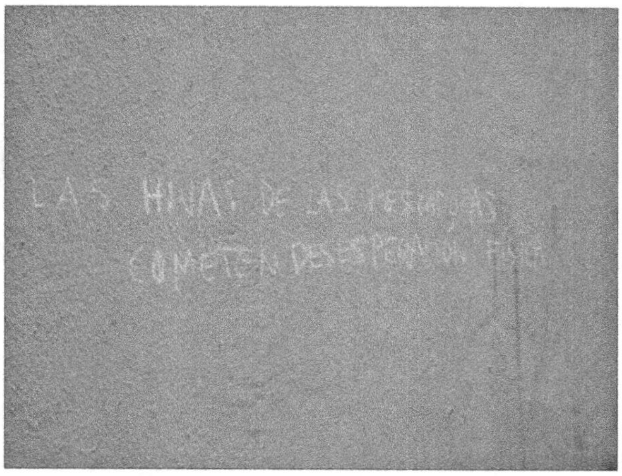

The daughters of fishwives commit physical desperation

The daughters of fishwives castrated Dr. Morales (*)

(*) Dr. Morales was the head of the Morales sanatorium in Santander where Leonora Carrington was incarcerated in 1940. See her book *Down Below*.

The daughters of fishwives leave crumbs of bread

The daughters of fishwives say: oh you, ocean, always equal to yourself!

Vicente, Eugenio and Bruno quoting Lautréamont (see left)

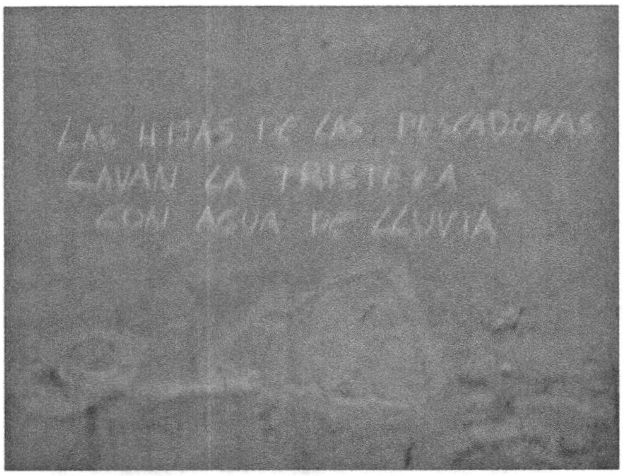

The daughters of fishwives wash away sadness with rainwater

The daughters of fishwives poison their swerve with snow

Eugenio writing

The fishwives' daughters are the sirens who attract solitary children

Ah, the pleated skirts of the fishwives' daughters

The daughters of fishwives sell honey with blindfolded eyes

We have forgotten the smell of the sex of the fishwives' daughters

The daughters of fishwives dance upon thimbles

The daughters of fishwives believe in contradiction

The daughters of fishwives dream with transparent eyelids

We are daughters of the fishwives who remember Leonora.
Watch out, Morales, we know where you live!

The daughters of fishwives summon the tides

The daughters of fishwives do not believe in the multiplication of fish

SURREALIST FERRY DEMANDS

1) COASTAL FERRIES REDESIGNED TO RESEMBLE GIANT ORCAS, SALMON, CRABS, OYSTERS, CLAMS, HERRING AND OTHER SEA CREATURES.
2) WINGED BOATS CREATED TO SIMULATE THE FLIGHT OF EAGLES, WILD GEESE, HERONS, SEA-GULLS AND OYSTERCATCHERS.
3) REPLACEMENT OF ALL BC PROVINCIAL AND CORPORATE FERRY FLAGS WITH THE JOLLY ROGER.
4) ALL BC FERRY AUTHORITIES MUST WALK THE PLANK.
5) FREE FARES FOR ALL.
6) AN END TO WAGE SLAVERY FOR ALL FERRY WORKERS.
7) THE TOTAL EROTICIZATION OF FERRY WORK.
8) ABSOLUTE SEXUAL FREEDOM ON ALL FERRIES.
9) FREE CONDOMS IN ALL FERRY LOUNGES.
10) FREE BC BUD IN ALL CAFETERIAS.
11) FREE ALL-NIGHT SUMMER DANCE PARTIES TO BE HELD ON EVERY FERRY DECK.
12) UNSCHEDULED FERRIES RANDOMLY GLIDING INTO STRANGE AND UNEXPECTED HARBORS.

WE VIEW THESE IMMEDIATE DEMANDS AS THE INDISPENSABLE FIRST STEP TOWARD A PLEASURABLE LIFE FOR ALL FERRY-GOERS.

INNER ISLAND SURREALIST GROUP

* The above proclamation envisions ferries as floating autonomous zones. It was written out of sheer exasperation at the underlying miserabilism and lack of imagination evident in the plethora of polite pleas for mercy addressed by aggrieved ferry passengers and union bureaucrats to the corporate management and government officials associated with BC Ferries. Instead of crumbs from the cafeteria table, we desire a lavish feast. The ferries that ply the watery highway between Vancouver Island and the marvelous necklace of Gulf Islands that are widely scattered throughout the Salish Sea in British Columbia can be re-imagined. Now is the time to rock the boat and chart a course toward freedom!

Originally published in *Swift Winds* (2009) by Ron Sakolsky.

RISING ABYSS

Joël Gayraud

Prague after the flood. The waters have submerged the quays, invaded the streets, the avenues, the squares. The sky reflected in the waters has taken on the colours of muddy silver.

The heart of the city has been extinguished. Not a glimmer of light tonight in the sidelong alleyways, strewn with debris vomited up from the cellars: piles of wet coal, crippled furniture, paraphernalia which has been left to rot for years on end in the vague belief that it might come in handy one day and which has finally relapsed into uselessness. And all the things we saw during the day in the doorways of the devastated shops: drowned refrigerators, piles of macerated paperwork, heaps of shoes enthusiastically looted – and the bust of the Golem lying stunned on the pavement.

This is a state of exception, with no war and no enemy. At every crossroads, tanks and other armoured vehicles risibly stand guard. What use are cannons and machine guns against the rising abyss?

A city set free from electricity reveals unexpected perspectives, vanishing points that stretch away endlessly, like shadows, until they disappear altogether. The night-dwellers have disappeared too. In the blind recesses of the mediaeval city, we come across only three tipsy tramps and a soldier who is half asleep. Not a sound either: no motors, no music, nothing save for the occasional droning of a generator which powers the pumps that ceaselessly suck up the sludgy floodwater from underground.

Suddenly, from amidst the shadows, the postern of Charles Bridge rises up, a fantastical black cut-out against the golden fog. And from the other side of the Vltava, the illuminated bulk of Hradčany contemplates the disaster.

Tomorrow we will go through the woods to the starry castle.

Translated by Merl Fluin

The Daily News

Manhattan Scenes

Allan Graubard

64TH STREET WHARF, HUDSON RIVER

The rotted twisting iron and wood
wharf
in the river

No metaphor
can match
the resonance of its ruin

Even a visual gong
burned
by the sun
in these
very temporal eternities

Collage by David Nadeau

FOR CARMEN FIRAN

She said she came from a surrealist country. At first I didn't believe her. Then I caught the wing under her left eye, the moon-burned crisp under her right eye. And I realized that not only did she come from that country but she'd never left it or, more precisely, it had never left her. And now, of course, I can't leave it or her and only wonder when, in this grand absence, where neither she nor I actually live but believe we do – when, in fact, we don't – it will leave me.

Ah, what's the use? I've asked that too many times to believe it can mean more than it does or less than it might, given her attraction, right there, at the café table across from me, a beautiful woman, exhausted, no doubt, by her effort to understand the ins and outs of this place she isn't in but comes from, and that, try as she might to prevent it, comes through her, touching, more, *infecting,* me and all those beside me. That fellow, no him, her, the other one walking in, smiling, with a knapsack of viscera stitched with gold braid. And the bar tender too coy for her own good, as if she expected from him something he's not ready to give.

Perhaps it's all there and I can't see it or sense it as she does, this woman from a surrealist country – the reticence, the give and take, the all too baroque feints and parries and lunges that boil up between us like so many cresting waves. Because her country, unlike my country, is a place where things happen, yes, things that shouldn't happen as they do, and no one says a word about them or they talk about them as if they didn't happen, which they did. Don't mistake me, they did. And their silence, which is as much a kind of consent as a kind of avoidance, makes it possible to live, to live like that, with all that duplicity; neither believing nor not believing in what's happening around them, neither talking about it openly nor wishing they could talk about it intimately. But doing so, just the same, and accepting it; priding themselves on their capacity to accept it.

In her country, you see, a gesture, any gesture, whether personal or political, takes on a significance or insignificance it simply does not have here, where she is, but feels she isn't, most of the time. And her being here, not there, sustains in her a similar disproportion, also most of the time. Despite her exile, because of her exile, exile confounds her with exile. She lives in exile, exiled even from that exile when it suits her, when she uses her exile to make a point about it or the fact that there's no point in making a point about it any longer because it's there, most of the time. And the topsy-turvy of it all, this exceptional somersaulting, from one scene to the next, makes it possible for her to find, where she is, an undercurrent (for us) which she knows, which she feels poignantly, and as something perfectly apparent and common and, yes, virulent. A preternatural bug that attacks when we don't expect it and have the least capacity to refuse it.

So when she told me she came from a surrealist country – and wouldn't accept anything less – for that's what she meant, *there* and *here,* I believed her.

February 18, 2008

THE CLOUDS OF NEW YORK

The clouds of New York float imperial
in the caravan blue
each with its elephantine eyes
sprinkled with phantasts

10 years old, the boating pond in Central Park
where Alice rules over wet radishes
topped with blue jays
shaking from their feathers morning's last
febrile list

and why not stupefied grace notes
shimmering
from an intimate sigh 30 years hence
export henbane with its salty circus kiss
the shallow stamp of a mottled branch
in the mouth of an hour alone

Or the fleet, shadowy, limp
over the river's sodden groin
brushed with algae
this warm ruinous winter

Clouds
moniker for the wind of the Hesperides
in your face my face facing faces
never seen again

Yet above
Incandescent
on those canticle banks
that crest and foam

But oh the forgotten Tridents
    that whistle Vampira
the reeds with white shards peeling from
sinister oaths
the transit broadlooms for spinning moist

the reef gray gorse
    that falls from a scar
    so tiny and livid on the yellowing moon

And we
Concubine twins jealous on Corfu
        – a stenciled bench 11th and 31st

distress our guerdon
    between this war and the next

shave cuneiform nests with rusty coal lit eyes

  as the clouds of New York float imperial

and mica snare drum udders drip tungsten
kestrels
            one mortal twist
          by twist
              of the sky

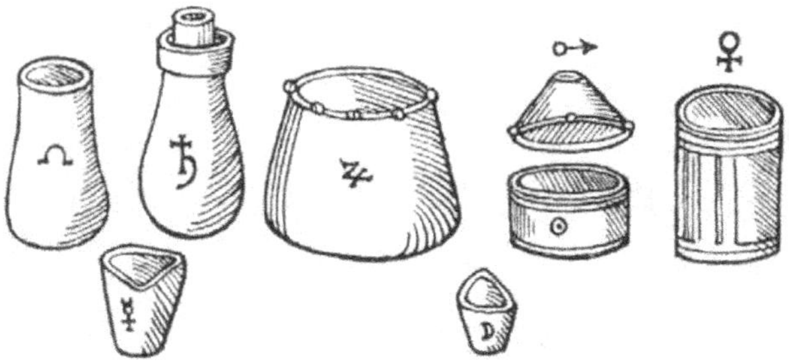

○ ○ ○

It's one of those throw back cafés where you can sip coffee for hours. There's a jukebox with blues from the '50s and '60s, ancient times now a half century later, the ashen celluloid glimmer of abrupt convections and spetzle kisses born by a few dusty photos framed above the bar. And whatever you do or want to do in the stunned slow motion waltz that seeps from the damp magazines hanging on the rack behind you, does no good. Because you can't leave. You can't bring yourself to admit that you'd rather be here than anywhere else; that it doesn't matter a damn whether or not you'll make anything more of it tomorrow when you've caught your breath and the streets roll out, one into another in an endless vertigo of s feints and parries, lunges and twists, here where the via Sebastiani hits the via Cecilio at the edge of the park whose drunks and whores grind fate down to boredom in a bloody handkerchief or a sharp needle stolen on the sly.

So the café is it, this axial shallow hinged to a termite wall with its dank stains and fetid vests. Just you and your fellow tuberculars sucking on nicotine straws and crusty garrotes; languishing out where trumpets mewl in cottonmouth and espresso piss dangles its mambo key in thick sucking prawns and distant storm Tobagos.

It's one of those wet thankless afternoons of green illusions, elephant-eared fronds dropping buckets of water on the drowned.

Poems by

Mattias Forshage

Tesseract 2

(an introduction to a novel)

Failing, upon awakening, to recall name, place, occupation, relations etc upon awakening
a stain of new geometry with new epistemological problems grew as mercury,
a privileged position to start asking questions
(An amoeba is nothing but a morphology, the particular morphology of not
having a determined bodyshape, and of walking and eating
by throwing out pseudopodia, constantly changing)
But here it seems we are walking like battleships through ontological layers
tearing them to fleshy pieces, or more likely not, as we pass,
layered much like danish pastry but most of them not immediately accessible
if not by stretching out as a ghost
and then the very boundaries between layers may facilitate such fast transportation
reducing friction to almost nothing
(If history is perpetually bifurcating, geometry might be too)
So that is why I have to invent such an elaborated character gallery
love's labor in a straitjacket
employ as help sciences dream geography, general methodology,
pansexual phenomenology and poetic epistemology,
rejuvenate art and the death star
to reinvent friction and reinvent awakening

Thinking, Geographically Anchored in Riddarfjärden

For the way to these wonders stood wide open,
stood wide open and torn,
stood like cleavers and madwort around the legs by the shortcut
by the unauthorised and dirtied passage,
this nonplace with pamphlets hidden in its smell.
The expedition does not write these novels
but stand hidden in the shrubs waving their arms.
One only misses their silence;
misses the nightingale, the rats, the runaway cricket
and the snot-slippery quay edge
To wander is to become seduced
one breaks the water surface and believes oneself to be the dawn
having stood before the door during all these funerals
but no one threatens a bay
if the drinkableness of clarity is endless
and still this eye of the storm was a mere blood droplet!
It was born from the same sea
panted forth from carried away breathing like any lost aerosol
sandpapered the senses where it poured forth
like a strongly concentrated tear
burnt itself into the skin of the vainly comforting friend
and was now the undeniable centerpoint of the whole city
From here all carousels started out
and no one reached here

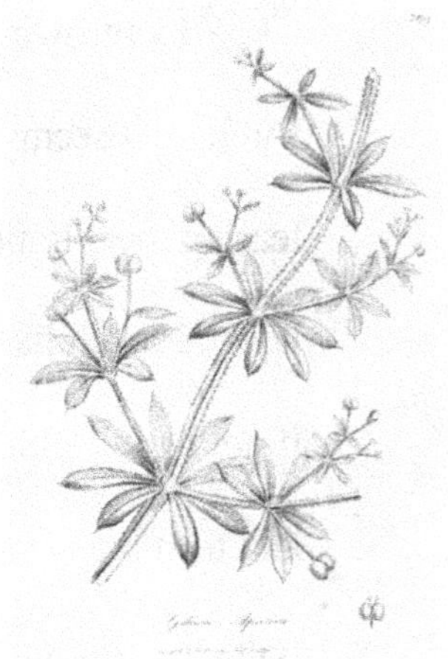

710. Asperugo procumbens L.
Madwort; B.

a pulsating starfish
if the city had assumed life
if the possibilities ran by in serpentine deathdance in the streets
if the feet are burning
if the branch cracks
It can continue dripping
for at least there will always reign the desired naval battles
in clouds of smoke and haunting winter gulls
in an unspeakable calm yes like reconciliated
in shivering participation in this spectacle radiant with colours
The one and the other and some quickly healing wounds
when dawn quickly emphasises every absent answer
But the expedition fraternises with the vegetation
emotional life is bobbing up and down in the bay
species of thousand weeds sprout
Everything is what it seems to be

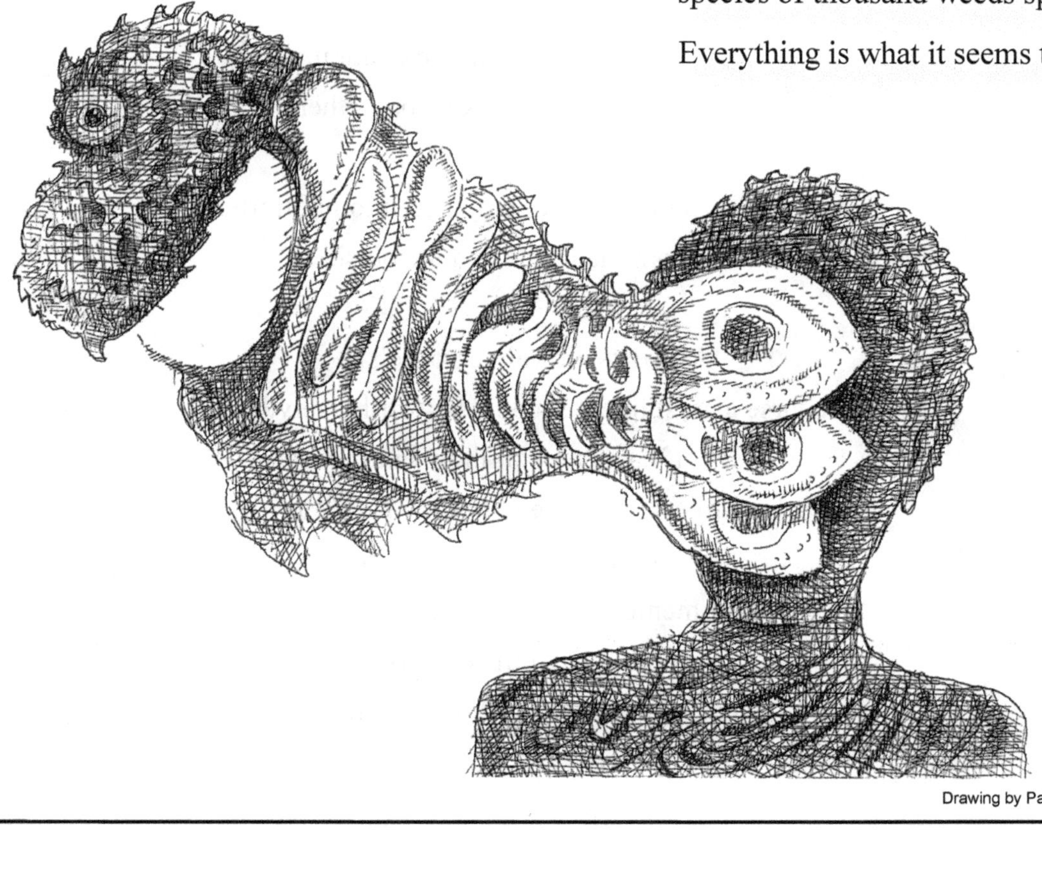

Drawing by Patrick Hourihan

Exodus

Vagrant's poem August 2002

Well it circled
and I caught myself in negotiations about that blood
that swimming
It is a mere dollhouse world from the truth
and everything one needs is scattered on those plains
calcareous glittering detached from its crow chest
and the note apparatus will not reveal them
Carbonate stone and shadow it is then
an air where there is no place for this heavy rest
which wants to see me as scraps
rather well concealed against the rock surfaces
the caressing and experienced stone surfaces
One fruit is the other

Thirst is not worse than intoxication,
death is a trademark among others

The skin is being rolled as a dough of joint efforts
from the inside and the outside

All boats are vain carousels
of course a crust like this could be worth everything
the lack of nakedness of those enthusiasts
The streets of this neighborhood all lead
to the same explored attics
The large memory blanks of the large banquet
The upsetting fumblings of the expensive expedition
I expect everything from the big erasing

THE RIGHT PLACE

Game proposed by Guy Girard and Marie-Dominique Massoni, May 24, 2006

The Tour Saint-Jacques, at the centre of Paris, is for surrealists one of the highest places of this city. Sole vestige of the Saint-Jacques-le-Majeur church, known as la Boucherie, whose bell-tower it was, built from 1508 to 1522, it replaced a building called l'Hôtel de la Rose, on the south side of it. To start with, in fact, during the Carolingian era (9th-10th centuries), it was a chapel dedicated to St Anne, expanded through construction work from 1146 to 1148. Two centuries later, newer works doubled its surface. Some of these were funded by the alchemist Nicolas Flamel, whose little shop which he kept as a scribe, under the sign of the Fleur-de-lys, was adjacent to that church, where he was to be buried. Before discovering the secret of the Great Work, he participated in the Compostelle pilgrimage, one of whose points of departure was, precisely, Saint-Jacques de la Boucherie. In 1648, Blaise Pascal repeated in this tower the Torricelli experiment, which formed the origin of the barometer's invention. The church was destroyed in 1797, and in early 19th century the tower was reconverted into a hunting bullets factory, before being bought in 1836 by the City of Paris. The latter restored it, notably by enveloping it with a 14 steps-high octagonal base, with a square replacing the houses that had been built on the ruins of the old church. The works revealed a Gallo-Roman column representing the god Mercury. In 1855, on the nearby rue de la Vieille-Lanterne, Gérard de Nerval hanged himself. There then came the terrible repression of the Commune, and the square served as a mass grave for the victims of the Bloody Week. Further renovation works took place from 1906 to 1912, then from 1932 to 1937, and again in 1968, which concealed the Tower under a mask of scaffoldings which, according to Breton, "contribute to turn it more and more into the world's great monument to the unrevealed" *(l'Amour fou)*. For some years now (and until late 2009, as promised by municipal officials), further scaffoldings once again surround it, as it threatens – like capitalism? – to collapse onto itself. For quite a while, nobody had seen any builders around. It seemed frozen in a metal mask. Then suddenly, in spring 2006, we saw it "wrapped" in a white fabric which makes it resemble a grain silo, a glass tower, sugar icing, or else, we wondered, what? Then we decided to carry out an investigation among our surrealist friends. In our eyes, it seemed to stand like a trivial enigma in the very heart of Paris, especially at dusk, just before nightfall, "between dog and wolf".

We thus sent the following photos and questions to our friends around the world:

Where is this building?

When was it built?

For what purpose?

Who may have lived there?

What can you make of it and do in it?

What would it be if it was:

- *an animal?*
- *a vegetable?*
- *a mineral?*
- *a poem?*
- *a language?*
- *a mask?*
- *a mental state?*
- *a symbol ?*

Certain rumours talk of secret ceremonies, at night. What is that all about? What are the rituals? What is the procedure?

We received almost 50 responses. We made a preliminary assessment seeking to present a contribution on the theme of masks and rituals proposed to our investigation by our Czech friends.

Certain friends, recognizing the magic place behind its tarpaulin mask, could not play or were annoyed. Some made a "shock at white color"[1], fixating upon it to expand on associations linked to sugar, salt, snow, ice (and indeed icing sugar or barley sugar). But essentially this implicated few answers linked to ingestion (or denying it, in the case of Jan Švankmajer), excepting feasts included in the rituals themselves, yet in which no one swallows the place itself.

MASK:

The blank parallelepiped evokes a death mask (8 responses move along these lines), that of Lautréamont, of Frankenstein. It is sometimes double, like the one uniting William Blake and Elisabeth Vigée-Lebrun, unless it is that of Pierrot in a mad grimace, it is a "mud mask" for Sarah Metcalf or "a fencer's icing sugar helmet" for Eugénie Morin, death mask of a hospital incinerator, according to Gareth Brown.

It is the bearer of menace (or protective) when it becomes "eyeshade of an ivory helmet [*heaume*]" (Stephen Clark), "integral helmet [*casque*]" (Anne Pellegrini), unless it is that of an "anti-riot brigade" (Merl). Obviously, it evokes carnival and its dominos.

Metal and humidity are linked by the purest analogy (in hermeticism everything that flows is analogical to water). For some it is a question of snow, argyle, mud, water; it is even associated to the diving-suit of captain Nemo[2] (Joël Gayraud). Miguel de Carvalho attributes the mask to a nocturnal sailor, as for him the "walkers with foam gloves descend and breathe in the water's interior". Dan Stanciu discovered that the place had been inhabited by "a handful of searchers for washable water".

WHAT IS MORE OR LESS REMINISCENT OF THE TOWER'S HISTORY:

The original chapel was dedicated to St Anne, black earth, the material favored by alchemists. Curiously, in reading the answers, we found ourselves associating some of those to the liberal arts, as though the latter had inscribed in the former each degree of their ladder. Negation of aristotelism? If the liberal arts have, over the course of centuries, structured understanding and applied a formal framework to knowledge, why is it that long after the autumn of the Middle Ages we find so much pleasure in detecting today these ancient categories? Might imagination, in order to become comprehensible, resume and divert all the ancient order which denies it? For Dan Stanciu, the place is situated "at the confines of celestial grammar". We have also linked grammar to invented languages (the volapük, of course, but also the spidery), to languages of blindness or silence (Braille, sign language), to secret codes (grammar of the word or of the gesture). The dialectic (which, if well practised, should be conducted only in spidery language) brings us back to Sarah Metcalf's net that can catch a passing comet, and from there to the painting of Veronese: *Dialectics (or industry).*

VERONESE'S DIALECTICS:

Rhetoric is less present, yet Jan Richter proposes to us "rituals of planning", Stephen Clark proposes to write a poem concerning "the comic relations between broccoli and the brain", and Paul Cross a haiku "woven in stirred sugar". Arithmetic gives us the "vegetative growth of the number 8" for Dominique Paul, while Alfredo Fernandes evokes the repetition of mathematical formulas aiming to "reduce living to abstraction". František Dryje sets in competition 1000 elevators divided in 33 teams. Let's split up, then! The subversion of geometry delights us in Dan Stanciu's response: "All these nocturnal visitors are cubomaniacs or even squarely obtuse. Each one of them arrives equipped with an Arab lamp and accompanied by a nutritive triangle". Music (from a racket to a requiem, from a national hymn to a children's song, from electro-acoustic experimentations to lunar music) is very often present. Luke Dominey notes the "development of selective audition". At the top of the elevator of liberal arts, astronomy or astrology are dominant, be it in the form of the world's navel, of a comet's passing, of the multiple aspects of the moon or "upon a hellish height, under a multitude of black suns, in a parallel meridian of France" (Dominique Paul). The astrologists' predictions are published and verified; "in case of error the person responsible for the column may die", as Jean-Pierre Guillon attests.

After touching jestingly on aristotelism, we have woven certain links between the myths born by the legendary history of the Tower and its whereabouts, on the one hand, and the responses of our friends, on the other.

The rituals revealed to us consist of putting into practice certain creation myths. The subtrerranean cult evoked by our friend Kathleen Fox recalls the Black Virgins, how can one forget the chapel dedicated to St Anne or the mythical link between Paris and Isis (Bar-Isis: boat of d'Isis), how can one forget Nerval? The "black square", visible on the photos, becomes for her a table of orientation on which is emprinted the image of the moon, recalling the link between femininity and the moon. The tower is also, according to Gabriela Trujillo: "the sanctuary of the lunar cult", where one can hear a moony music. Nikos Stabakis proposes to "transport it to New York to imprison therein the Statue of Liberty (the window would reveal her sex)". But the responses have also recalled Hecate and her power over sailors. The emblem of the Paris water merchants ("boatmen") on the Middle Ages was a boat, which we find even today in the city's armoury, with the motto *Fluctuat nec mergitur*: it sails without flowing.

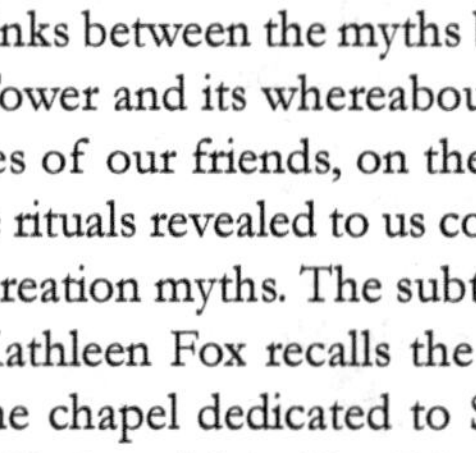

Armoury of the City of Paris: "Gules on the ship equipped with silver, sailing on waves of the same, a chief azure with scattered golden fleur-de-lys, representing ancient France".

Sometimes, the rituals demonstrated prepare interventions on the exterior world in order to empoison it. When led by women, in connection with lunar cycles, they set in action the dignified charms of Hecate and Medea, from the luxuriance and exaltation of the senses to the death of certain males. The tower thus lies at no fixed place and may emerge anywhere, before disappearing into transparency. Many responses of that type were given by women. Terrifying powers of Black Virgins, of those women "living in a labyrinth of caverns beneath the construction" (Kathleen Fox), of lunar cycles, of the primordial female: the female may become threatening, murderous, including the case in which the statues of eroticism poison themselves after having apparently embraced the sleeping masons (Eugénie Morin).

What risk, then, do the stone-cutters run, those who, at this moment, are seen to be working behind the shop window at a carving workshop? Should they fear Sébastien, the mysterious Portuguese king evoked by Dominique Paul, who lived there, so she tells us, after "leaving Aggartha, under the identity of a false political prisoner supposedly dumb"? Might the boulevard Sébastopol, to the west of the square, be a testament of his passing?

Apart from links with the tower's legends, we discovered that our friends lead us to its surroundings, from the square des Innocents to the Seine.

DYSTOPIA:

Water is the dominant element, yet it is often putrid, and may flow in nauseous streams, feeding pipes. A marvelous rainbow-colored fountain, whose flow renders the building transparent, leaves upon the tower's disappearance "a putrefying black mucus-like substance" (Kathleen Fox).

The place where Jan Richter situates the building is the "la Défense" district in Paris. It condenses fairly nicely numerous responses, both in the latter's "repulsive" aspect and in the attributes conferred to the "mask". For Bruno Montpied, who has a passion for "art brut", this place arouses conflicts, both because one must prove one's competence to be admitted there and because this labyrinthine world seems to be that of permanent chicanes. Those who succeed in entering "pass their time modifying the questions posed in the corners of the labyrinth and are destined to lead the searchers to the tower's entry. As there is no referee to decide between the questioners and the answerers, there emerge numerous controversies, sometimes leading to bloody battles. This place has paradoxically led the individuals who felt concerned by the subject it illustrated to interminable divisions and battles instead of bringing them happiness".

There are also those who have seen the appearance of a tooth, of bones, of ivory, and that "skeletal" aspect is of course combined with the mortiferous aspects sensed by many players. Might the skeletons be performing the dance of death? Two steps from the Tower there was the Cimetière des Innocents, where one could see a Danse macabre and a Massacre of the Innocents (according to commission of Nicolas Flamel's), painted on a fresco. Today, we see a fountain near which silent "women in black" demonstrate their refusal of wars.

Le Cimetiére des Innocents in 1785

The mental states evoked: catatonia, schizophrenia, hebephrenia, depression, paranoïa, or "a painful compression of the cranial box leading to a whirling and nauseous dive that deprives one of thought by excess of sensory consciousness" (Dominique Paul), account for the toxicity peculiar to the place and emphasize its negative reception.

The usage of poisons secreted by decomposition, which we have already evoked, may lead to practices such as necromancy (Nikos Stabakis). Diverse forms of putrefaction are to be found in the responses. Let us recall that in the Middle Ages this district was truly pestilential: faecal materials, urine, croppings and bits of fat, as well as streams of blood flowing from the butcher's blocks to the gutters infested the place, without taking into account the rats and pigs. "In the Turkish barley sugar there can only be the process of fermentation", as Jan Švankmajer concludes!

Another form of threat, more invisible and more actual: the building, according to Allan Graubard, had been conceived to "collect and diffuse nightmares by electric compression". For many, the surveillance exerted by the powers that be, whether outside or inside the tower, purports to colonise the brains. Philip Kane points out that government rituals are practised there in order to capture the dreams of the working classes, and that the latter shall be used for the leisure of the rich (since the bourgeoisie is incapable of dreaming), as well as for exploiting more efficiently the proletarians at work. These rituals are secret, as they must, yet our friend has sent us a photo taken by an activist overseeing the place from a balloon:

Philip Kane: aerial photograph

But power is intoxicated without realizing it. Jill Fenton evokes subversive rituals in which we may see the spawn developing in the turds of "vile and giant" surveillance dogs. "As the spawn travel in the gutters, microorganisms, that normally live there, welcome them and energetically speed them on their way to the water supplies of the government social security buildings. [...] The rituals of the microorganisms and the spawn substantially contribute to eradicating wealth and monetary values and introducing an openness to love".

A terrible silence, or the birth of another world? The calculated chaos of certain rituals derives from the refusal of speech and its substitution by the Braille or sign language, as long as sound is made out of anything bar words (Stephen Clark).

Eugenio Castro affirms that this "is neither a castle of subversion", nor "the Clear Tower" dear to anarchists, but "their total negation". Most of the responses along these lines come from the Czech Republic and Great Britain, making us ponder the evolution of our society since the end of the iron curtain. Also, it is not surprising that eight of our friends propose to destroy the building. Nevertheless, quite a few responses tend toward the utilization of possibilities for transformation for playful and subversive purposes. In fact, the rituals aim, predominantly, to avert, sabotage or destroy the system of social surveillance, of control imposed by power.

UTOPIA?

Many responses referred to the seditious side of the rituals, to their defensive aspect as well as the threat that they may make hang over the capitalist society. A new emergence of the mediaeval "jacques"[1], this time in the very heart of the city, or else of butchers armed with cutlasses?

Not far from the gutters, Allan Graubard points out that at night, "beggars living in the sewers slip into the interior to spend a few pleasant hours. Not in order to redo what they were doing and what they were before being beggars—one a banker, another an engineer—they dress up with whatever bric-à-brac they may have found by some ruse. And when this whole menagerie is ready, they start singing and clapping hands, all of them making new variations on old tunes—a tribe of Mardi-Gras Indians in exile. At dawn, they leave dragging their feet, happy to have once more found themselves in the rhythm, the rhythm, the rhythm they love". How not to associate this response to Terry Gilliam's Fisher King?

For Stephen Clark it is the living place of a silent community, who has made the pact of silence and whose rites "concern the re-actualisation of an event whose consequences were tragic and remain actual"; it is also a matter of its "forming a sort of myth of creation".

Eros is present, but not much, and somewhat poorly: three times by way of orgasmic orgies, bacchanalia of skeletons or under cover of Masonic rites, in the context of Mozart's requiem, or under the aegis of Rabelais and Fourier. For Dominic Tétrault, there are set in motion "rituals of a new eroticization. The participants must climb a ladder up to the open part and throw objects toward the exterior. The noise of the objects smashed on the ground results in stimulating reactions from those who hear the noises while being unable to establish the destructive state of the objects' impact on the bruised surface. [...] The speculations between throwers and listeners must be resolved in a prolonged series of breathing and rubbing on the wall of the building. The vibrations produced by the banging of shovels and brooms are amplified by sound recorded via contact microphones and the sonic layers are woven together and superimposed on one another into a gigantic buzzing that shall accompany the ascension of the next thrower. Mike Peters wants to turn it into a sort of orgone accumulator (cf. W. Reich).

For Dominique Paul: "At nightfall, they place mattresses on the ground, have people lie on them, then cover them with a further layer of mattresses, on which they place more people. They then cover the whole with grated blankets and let ferment all night.

"At dawn, they unpack the semi-unconscious fallen bodies, and then the savage animals of the surrounding country—birds, warrens and other rodents—enter by the barred windows and brush delicately against the soft skins, provoking an ecstasy rare among these languid men and women.

"It seems to be an ancient, weird sexual ritual, rediscovered in the old magical books of this subterranean world which may be accessed via the tower caves. It was precisely the obscure Portuguese king who'd restored the custom".

Sometimes there are evoked the charms of shivery pleasures, of an alchemical union: "the couples about to be initiated must be placed in the position of the philosophal couple", writes Michaël Löwy; Michel Zimbacca imagines "reality dreaming of itself as hermaphrodite". Paul Cross makes of it "the interior church of the Ice Virgins licking the New World into existence. Love for *Sapphic Christabels*". For Dan Stanciu, the elegance derives from strange rustlings, like "the caresses of limas".

Gabriela Trujillo recalls: "certain rites took place for centuries in this place amid the rare lunar people who remained in this world. Due to its strong magnetism, this place upsets compasses and even defies gravity. On the evenings of new moons, the faithful ones flocked to participate in rites of flying lessons to the rhythm of an ocarina. The photograph is hardly eloquent, but the dimensions of this column of air allow each of the participants to reveal an aerial nature, a cloudy heart or indeed to become a butterfly. A dream-place, quite obviously".

The building's mobility, its capacity to take flight or disappear into transparency, if potentially charged with negativity for Kathleen Fox, presents in her account sensorial and sensual marvels. As in a land of plenty, "the time of celebration now begins, music plays, there's a greeting of old friends and new lovers, the fountain liquid is drunk, fruit and bread/cake are plucked from the trees, a feast of the senses begins". And for those not afraid to take off: "They spin webs and threads. Cords [...] can be tied around the construction fixed to a net that can catch a passing comet. The velocity of the comet then lifts the construction back into orbit", writes Sarah Metcalf.

For Michel Zimbacca : "They bring shed tears to extract the salt, exhaled sighs to put breaths back together, gathered shudders to galvanize applicants, overwhelming joys to lighten up the whole and reassemble the energy required for the ritualisation of multiple kicks in the arse to all that lies kneeling, prostrate, flattened or frozen upon command".

A utopian place or a call for "a civilisation that has yet to appear" (Eugénie Morin)? It seems to us that, if this was not quite the case, this great white building, situated a couple of steps away from the rue des Lavandières-Sainte-Opportune and the rue de la Lingerie, might be compared, not to André Breton's "great white refrigerator"[4] but to a gigantic machine for washing the miasmas of this time. On the subject of this "abolished tower"[5], shall we then whiten Latona and tear up the books?

Paris, 11 September 2006

The following people participated in the game "The Right Place", proposed by Guy Girard and Marie-Dominique Massoni:

Mariano Auladen, Jean Benoît, Anny Bonnin, Gareth Brown, Donald Campbell, Miguel de Carvalho, Eugenio Castro, Michel Caubel, Claude-Lucien Cauët, Stephen Clark, Paul Cross, Jan Daňhel, Aurélien Dauguet, Luke Dominey, František Dryje, Jakub Effenberger, Jill Fenton, Alfredo Fernandes, Merl Fluin, Kathleen Fox, Joël Gayraud, Guy Girard, Allan Graubard, Jean-Pierre Guillon, Josef Janda, Philip Kane, Andrew Lass, Michaël Löwy, Přemysl Martinec, Sarah Metcalf, Bruno Montpied, Eugénie Morin, David Nadeau, Dominique Paul, Anne Pellegrini, Mike Peters, Kateřina Piňosová, Jan Richter, Bruno Solarik, Nikos Stabakis, Dan Stanciu, Wedgwood Steventon, Martin Stejskal, Jan Švankmajer, Dominic Tétrault, Gabriela Trujillo, Nick Wing, Michel Zimbacca

Translated by Nikos Stabakis

Originally published at http://surrealisme.ouvaton.org/

Endnotes:

1. Cf. Rorschach test.
2. Cf. *Twenty Thousand Leagues under the Sea* by Jules Verne.
3. "Jacques Bonhomme" was the nickname attributed to peasants, hence "les jacques". Peasant revolts since the Hundred Years War were likewise called "jacqueries".
4. "The great white refrigerator in the night of times // Distributing shudders to the city // Sings for itself alone".
André Breton, "Le soleil en laisse", preceded by the poem "Tournesol", in *Clair de terre*.
5. "I am the sombre one, – the widowed, inconsolable one, // The Prince of Aquitaine with the abolished Tower: // My sole *Star* is dead, – and my starry lute Bears the *Black Sun* of *Melancholy*". — Gérard de Nerval, " El Desdichado ".
6. *La Tour Saint-Jacques*, review dedicated to occultism, alchemy, spirituality, etc., which published texts by Eugène Canseliet, René Alleau, René Nelli, Jean Richer.

Photo left: by Marie Baudet

Photo below: Robert Amadou, who founded the review *La Tour Saint-Jacques*[6], in 1955, died in Paris, on March 14, 2006. The works started in March 2006. Presumably he never saw the wrapped-up Tower...

Old Night Equinox

Apio

(September 23, 2002)

Darkness has its magic. It opens gates of the imagination that would otherwise remain closed... At times, I feel that the deadening of imagination in modern society is due in part to the violent destruction of the night by artificial lights. For in the dark, the stark definition of all things breaks down, the rigid lines, the stiff separations disappear anarchy breaks forth, the opening of all possibilities - the marvelous appears in the world.

At noon, I left the dusky coffee house to go in search of the night. Not having a watch or other measured timepiece, I cannot give precise times hereafter. In fact, the "time" of this exercise was as measureless for me as the time of dreams—and this may be the first opening of my day to the night, bringing the passional time of dreams into this search. But even before I began my search, I was sitting in the coffeehouse, the dusky atmosphere of which blended day and night. The level of light is not unlike that to which I would read late at night as a child, a low watt bulb squeezing light through a narrow crack in my closet door. This to prevent my parents from knowing that I read late into the night. When my mother found out, she scolded me telling me I would go blind. Yet it is this same half-light, which leaves colors, shapes and boundaries somewhat indistinct, that seems to permeate most coffee houses where so many choose to write.

I left the dusk of this coffee house to begin my search for the night and found myself in the brilliance of the noon sun. I headed toward Tower Grove park and was greeted by a bed of flowers in which I found every shade of night-blue from the gentle indigoes that begin to spread as the sun sets to the deepest midnight blues that draw the eyes in, inducing a dreamlike state. I wandered further into the park where the blackness found in holes and notches in the trees drew me in. Some were shallow and as I approached, the midnight that I saw from a distance slowly lightened to a pre-dawn grey, revealing but not dispelling the mysteries within. Others, in their depth, retained the black of midnight, the pitch-black that enshrouds the unknown. Who knows what strange eyes may gleam their phosphorescent light from the depths of these dark caverns of night? I was moved by this adventure to leave the well-paved paths, and though it hadn't rained for days, at times I found my footsteps sinking into dark, softer soil. Here too the night was drawing me into its mystery, the soft indistinct boundary between the black soil and the daylight sky.

I wandered into the midst of a grove of trees with wide spreading branches creating a dusky atmosphere through which the daylight filtered. In the haziness of shadows, the darkness that fades into the light rather than separating itself abruptly, one can see as well the haziness of the distinction between night and day—and also perhaps between reason and passion which for revolutionaries must become one. Nearby a pair of dense, low bushes create a deeper night, not quite black, but a darkness difficult to penetrate, a place that one can imagine is full of the beasts of dreams.

And yet my encounter with such a beast itself showed the haziness of these distinctions. I wandered into a large patch of brilliant daylight and even found a bit of night there. A yellow butterfly flew up from the grass and flitted in its dreamy dance with air and sun and life. And what is there of night in this? Here I find one of my own nights, a night from my childhood in which I dreamed. In this dream, I found myself being chased by two men who sought to kill me. One was an old man in a wheel chair—in this chair he could move with great speed and I knew he was very rich and powerful. The other was his aide, a tall long-legged man who could run like the wind. Finally, they had me cornered in a coliseum that was underground and yet open to the sun. It was like one of the building of an acropolis in ancient Greece. I had no place to turn, so I had no choice but to turn the power of dream upon my would-be assassins. With a simple wave of the hand, I transformed them into harmless and delightful yellow butterflies. Today, as I sought the night, one of them returned to me in the bright noon sun to remind me of the dream of that night more than 35 years ago.

Looking ahead, I saw a particularly dark area. I walked toward it. It was a small grove of oak and cherry trees. The oak seems to me to hold the night to a greater extent than many other trees. The shade here is darker and that is what attracted me. As I approached the grove, I noticed that the shadows of the oak leaves were particularly dark, looking black and sharply outlined from a distance. As I approached they maintained an intense darkness, though it lightened somewhat to a dark grey, but the sharpness disappeared as the apparent boundary between dark and light changed into a gradation. Still one is left to wonder if this capacity to hold the night throughout the day is an aspect of the mystery of the oak that has led some cultures to consider it as particularly magical.

I left the grove, guessing that it might be nearing one.

Passing under another grove of trees, a spot of intense blackness on the ground strikes my eyes. I approach to find a muddied magazine called *Outlook*. I know nothing of this magazine and it was too muddy to open and investigate, but the cover was black with what appeared to be a multi-colored comet (blue, indigo, purple, dark lavender and green) shooting through this midnight sky. A few steps later I found a pair of reading glasses missing one earpiece. What *outlook* might they offer? What colorful comets flying through the night? Who had brought them here on what adventures? I took them with me. Shortly I came upon a fallen yellow ginkgo leaf that immediately became for me the second yellow butterfly of my dream. Right next to it I found an eye of the night, the eyeball a dark, dark brown—nearly black—and the iris and pupil a light grey, nearly white. It was, of course, some kind of chestnut, but for me it was the eye of the night—the eye through which one sees the world of dreams.

As I wandered home, my mind remained in the state of reverie this exercise provoked. I continued to see the night everywhere in the cracks of the day.

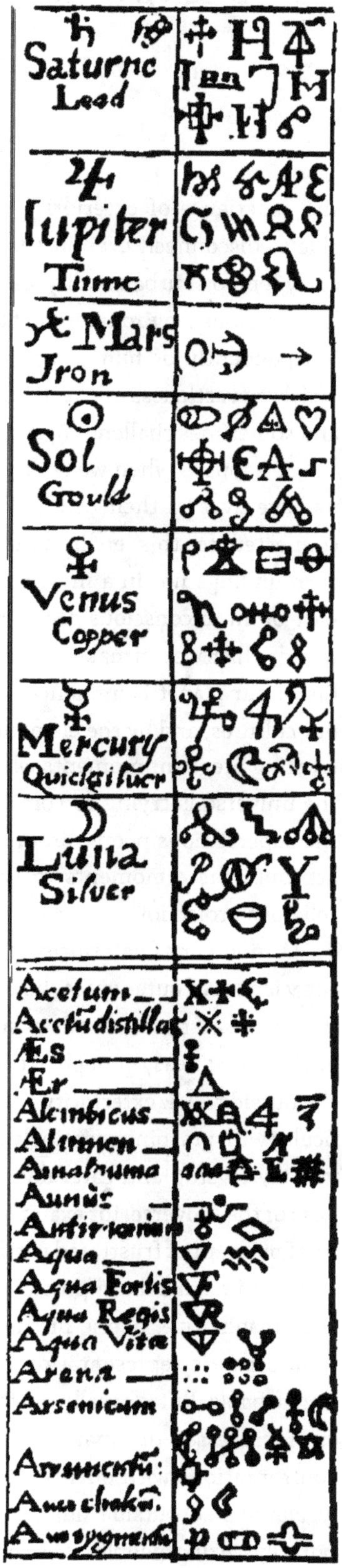

This is one response to an 'Old Night Equinox' proposal from Don LaCoss. Intended as a 'scavenger hunt for night in the full light of day,' it was inspired by 'Old Night,' a game exploring shadow and darkness by day, which came from Gypsy Sherred and was developed by Stephen Clark and the Surrealist Group in Leeds. Eight responses were compiled in the pamphlet 'Old Night.' The entirety of 'Old Night Equinox' remains unpublished.

Hairy Granny, drawing by Theoni Tambaki

The Experience of Exteriority around the Salton Sea

Eric Bragg

The experience of exteriority begins when a person is able to disconnect, even just for a little while, from the crazy tempo of urban reality, instead coming into contact with various environmental forces which often occur independently of human activity but not always, and which nevertheless make their perception a powerful and sometimes challenging experience.

It happens when we realize that the objects around us have lives of their own[1], and that we are somehow connected to this environment and the rest of the surroundings not in a mystical or religious way, but as part of an unconscious *poetic method* of relating to the world, which we can make as subversive as we like: that the life of our planet is influenced by our imaginations and our cultures, and by the elements as well, synergistically creating pregnant moments when we feel as if somehow the universe is trying to communicate with us, even if the superstitious people around us have been taught to attribute these moments to Fate or Luck or whatever religious projection.

A moment of exteriority is like oxygen rushing into the vacuum of outer space, however violent or damaging it can be at times. From a surrealist interest in the analogon[2], it's easy enough to consider our experiences of the outside – i.e. exteriority – in light of the psyche's difficulty with grasping seemingly infinite things, like when you try to stop and carefully imagine the infinite vastness of the universe, for example. Such an infinitesimally brief moment of frustrated vertigo is often the case when trying to imagine the impossible, the infinite, so therefore this imaginative, poetic hiccup is the analogon, or the mind's poetic representation of something cognitively ungraspable. But it's really much more than just a hiccup; such processes of 'analogonization' occur during our confrontations with environmental forces independently manifested outside human control, sometimes temporarily curing people of a core blindness brought on by industrialized civilization, or perhaps momentarily giving us a poetic 'sixth sense' that is enough to get us to reconsider *everything*, while also simultaneously letting us feel the life-pulse of the world.

We can understand from a materialist perspective that our environment, whether it exists within a metropolis, a suburb or something more rural, is a *material* force to be reckoned with, often driven by economic factors. Of particular interest are those material forces and trends which are *not* under the control of the capitalist apparatus: because the influence and transformation that often come from these material events effectively play with the human psyche, then as a result, the psyche plays with them, by way of our senses allowing us to powerfully experience certain moments and places which disrupt the lethal monotony of alienated life. But these special events are not so prevalent in the urban landscape, since the mandates of capitalism often apply here, but fortunately not all of the time. And hence the problem persists: the thoroughly modern, disconnected human (with all resulting manner of insanity) destroying his or her own environment and having become completely unaware that, ecologically speaking, our species has reached the threshold of its carrying capacity (and perhaps in some places it already has been surpassed) and that afterwards reaching an unbearable state of crisis would be inevitable.

One way of considering this crisis, in terms of the struggle between the rationalist imperatives and tendencies of humanity against everything else that occupies the earth (i.e. the 'environment'), is that there is a constant mutual process of *invasion* which might be interpreted as a form of 'feedback' exchanged between humans and the world around us. In light of Julio Monteverde's text 'Beyond the Walls of the City'[3], it is possible to consider the boundaries of a city or town not only as a means for repelling fellow humans, but more importantly for creating a psychological barrier that helps these city-dwellers differentiate their own inhabited space from whatever remains outside of it. It is this latter concept which is often religiously and/or ideologically maintained in the urban psyche and which is perturbed when this sometimes invisible and silent boundary is influenced, modified or even thoroughly disrupted by external influences. These events powerfully affect consciousness and the rest of life, are capable of instantly reminding those who experience them of their own organic nature and of mortality, and can spontaneously induce people to reevaluate their relationship with the world[4], undoing in a terrifying moment our repressions and other forms of social conditioning. No matter how painful they might be, these punctuated and stochastic events remind us that we are alive, and thus occupy a significant place in the human psyche, even if perhaps remaining in the shadows until those seemingly fateful moments arrive on the cusp of a drought or a tidal wave or an earthquake or whatever manner of convulsive natural act forces us to change our behaviors. In this sense, everything that is non-human has this invasive potential, and as such exists as a force of exteriority which helps define the human psyche and has always influenced our evolution beyond the ability to consciously and collectively remember.

In order to provide a telling illustration, this text will focus on the Salton Sea, an environmentally sickly location in southern California[5]. This region once was intended as a place of agriculture and fishing, but due to human intervention was overcome by forces of nature which may seem contradictory but serve as a colorful example of environmental feedback. By way of history[6], there is plenty of geological evidence to indicate that the Salton Basin was routinely flooded for several previous centuries, with subsequent desiccation. But the

definitive event in 1905 which led to the formation of the Salton Sea was a mishap resulting from a series of irrigation canals dug from the Colorado River so as to promote agriculture in the basin. Similar to other disastrous outcomes from human intervention, the following events occurred here: the mass flooding of the Salton Basin as well as the altered course of the Colorado River. For more than the next half century, the newly-formed gigantic lake served as a fishery and established refuge for several species of wild birds. By the middle of the twentieth century, the area was converted to a state park and for subsequent decades attracted many tourists. Even during those times of prosperity, it was expected that eventually enough of the lake would evaporate to create dangerously high levels of salinity, which indeed occurred. By the 1970's, the area was hit for two consecutive years by powerful tropical storms that caused mass flooding and destruction, raising the level of the Salton Sea significantly, yet paradoxically doing nothing to stop the trend towards increasingly toxic salinity. During the 80's and 90's, the salinity continued to increase, resulting in extinction of local wildlife, as well as concern about the safety of consuming fish, such as the possibility of excessive selenium intake. Into the twenty-first century, the U.S. government has implemented ambitious programs to reduce the salinity and to nurture the area as a wildlife refuge, hopefully producing a healthier ecosystem, but the signs of devastation are still visible.

The documentation presented here was obtained during July 2007, during record temperatures (on one day it reached 115°F), with me spending a few days traveling around the perimeter of the lake, camera in hand, looking for physical indications of recent history. The extreme environment certainly influenced my perceptions of these shoreline areas, creating an almost unbearable atmosphere of heat and the inescapable odors of saline and the numerous dead fish on the beaches. For a place that was once a hotspot for tourists, it now seemed dead and physically oppressive.

Located on the eastern shore, furthest away from the Pacific Ocean, Bombay Beach most likely received the lion's share of surging water when those two big tropical storms blew in during the 1970's, pushing water from the western side of the lake towards the east. The part of town directly on the shore was irreparably inundated, leaving behind many ruins of buildings and vehicles, prompting the construction of a protective levee. Of the once devastated area, all that could be seen were the partially buried wrecks of corroded vehicles and skeletal houses, including an enigmatic dog house with the shape of a crescent moon cut through the wood. Covering this area were not only the beaches, but also a thick, whitish salt layer that extended inland up to the protective levee. Underneath this coverage of salt, apparently deposited through years of desiccation, was a layer of thick, black, grimy mud, quite unlike the dirt of the surrounding region[7]. In Bombay Beach, the city limits are not as clearly defined as they apparently once had been, providing concrete evidence of this invasion *from outside*. Overall, it is very clear that the place is decaying, even for the remaining inhabited dwellings on the 'safe' side of the levee, due to poverty, desolation and neglect.

Other paradoxes have resulted from this flooding, which point to a crumbling boundary between humans and nature, leading to formations of 'no-man's-lands' such as the agricultural or irrigation site near Niland, further south of Bombay Beach and also on the eastern side of the lake. This particular area had the rusted hulk of an ancient truck, with various damaged, cracked buildings (with floors covered in cracked mud) that were associated with the operation that once existed there. And next to these was a centralized system of troughs and concrete tanks which might have served as a way to irrigate or treat water for the surrounding open fields. One might be tempted to think that these stormsurges put a damper on whatever irrigation/agricultural activities that used to take place there, given the archaic-looking nature of the buildings and the vehicle. And on the road next to this site was a rusted sign that read: *No Tresspassing, Property of Imperial Irrigation District*. We know that imperialistic irrigation was curtailed here by at least two natural acts of large-scale 'irrigation'.

Possibly as a result of the flooding, as well as of toxic salinity, there are many other abandoned structures, including homes, gas stations, cafes, motels, etc., that sparsely litter the shoreline on the eastern half of the lake. The caustic humor of the place remains, such as the ruined mechanic garage, devastated by fire but still proudly bearing a sign that reads 'we take better care of your car.' One could only imagine what the exodus from this place might have been like: dreams and structures destroyed during a few fateful moments, followed by years of the landscape reasserting itself, gradually erasing the traces of human control and occupation. Just off the southern shore, dead trees project from the water, and are still rooted to places that were not always submerged. These trees now serve as nesting areas for aquatic birds, while the occasional inflatable sex doll is found on the nearby beach, only beginning to show bleaching from the sun. And in the north shore area there persist two abandoned motels inhabited only by birds and whatever other animals that also need to find shelter from the blistering sun (just like humans there do). In the fancier motel, the remnants of the restaurant and bar area have become a home to various cackling, squeaking birds, which due to the acoustic echo of the room created a sinister presentation, since the birds themselves were not visible, but hiding out in the ceiling and ventilation ducts. Yet they still made quite a din. Near the other motel there was once a metal play area for children, consisting of a slide and swingset, but which by now has become halfway covered with sand, making it look outlandish. And both of these motels have had their swimming pools emptied of water and later filled with debris and graffiti. While these particular structures show no direct evidence of flood-damage, they still seem to be at least 30 or more years old, suggesting that the march of progress for this place stopped not long after the 1970's.

The hydrology of the Salton sea appears to be contradictory, at least in a poetic way, to the extent that there is plenty of evidence of water activity (such as the previously described examples of flooding), but also of desiccation, given the high temperatures, the presence of desert-looking areas, as well as places with caked,

encrusted salt formations; however this situation is easily attributed to the arid landscape being physically, geologically ill-equipped to deal with those infrequent but voluminous precipitation events. Also, and unlike the eastern part of the lake, the western side does not show a rise in water level, but rather the opposite: the south and southwest have their share of bleached, rickety piers far inland from where the water level is now; places that used to be covered by several feet of water are now dried beds of cracked mud, with debris such as half-submerged, algae-encrusted automobile tires. It may be that Salton City, the only heavily populated place on the lake's periphery, has the closest appearance to normality, since the interface between land and water reveals no such telling signals of disruption or historical environmental events. If this place was once considered a recreational paradise, there is nothing there now that could maintain that appearance.

But the damage due to flooding and desiccation are only part of the picture: toxic levels of salinity (25% higher than that of ocean water) and increasingly fatal levels of nutrient accumulation from agricultural runoff[8] appear to have stressed the ecosystem, to the point where aquatic birds and the fish have been dying for quite some time — the latter routinely wash up on the shores. Despite the arid conditions, hydrological runoff is thought to have prevented the lake from drying out, although the evaporation leads to increasing concentrations of salt and these nitrogenous fertilizer compounds. The visitor is unlikely to find beaches there that lack these stinking fish carcasses, not to mention the fact that the shores of the lake are in many spots completely covered with bleached fishbones (most noticeably the vertebrae) that make everything appear strangely white and sterile. It might be said that the Salton Sea represents an invasion in and of itself, created by the diversion of the Colorado River and subsequent water pollution; that without prior human intervention, it is very unlikely that there would be such a large, dying body of water there today.

Under these conditions, one might be tempted to think that the Salton Sea area has a mind of its own, in terms of its perceived indifference or hostility to the expansionist, colonial efforts of human beings. And when considering the issue in terms of exteriority, it is quite certain that it *does* have a mind of its own, to the extent that those who are or have been there can perceive a power that seems unconquerable, as well as from the signs left behind by the forces of nature which still operate there. In the past and even for many people now, whether the topic at hand is the Salton Sea or somewhere else, this form of poetic projection has also been elaborated under religious auspices: that a god or whatever theocratic power is responsible for these devastating movements of nature – perhaps that it is trying to punish us or provide some didactic message. Or in other cases, Nature itself (with a capital N) is apostrophized, as if it existed as an abstract conscious or unconscious will that capriciously exercises its power over us in a perpetual tug-of-war. But in truth, these variations of perception point back towards human subjectivity, as an unconsciously and involuntarily elaborated poetic response that can be especially stimulated and/or exacerbated by the seemingly incalculable size and strength of whatever surrounds and affects us – hence, the experience of exteriority.

In light of the global economic-environmental crisis currently underway, with the (to understate it) unpleasant changes in climactic conditions, increasing pollution and the exhaustion of natural resources, all due to the recent centuries of guilt-free exploitation and the never-questioned, reproductive swarming mentality of humanity, people all over the world are finding themselves reminded of the precariousness of overpopulation and the toxicity that comes from senseless consumption, just for the sake of generating and maintaining capital for that small, sickly minority that still is to be found 'hiding under a rock', leering at their surroundings with selfishness and impunity. And there is no doubt that these 'revelations' will continue with increasingly intense and fatal consequences until genuinely practical measures are taken to change our behaviors. Whether we bother or not to remember the briny desert of the Salton Sea, or the hot and haunted ruins of Chernobyl, or the results of the Kill-a-Sparrow campaign in China from the late 1950's, or the ongoing Amazonian deforestation, or the numerous petroleum spills that have washed up on the shores of several continents, our psyches are more than willing to remind us of the ironic and concomitant smallness and vastness of this planet which coexist poetically within the seat of what we call 'mind'. God and Nature are and have always been indefinitely on vacation, but what remains are just our non-human neighbors and us.

Notes:

1) Eugenio Castro, Surreality and Exteriority, translated by Terry Berne, Eric Bragg, and Bruno Jacobs, *The Exteriority Crisis: from the city limits and beyond*, Oyster Moon Press, Berkeley, 2008, pp. 155-8.
2) André Breton, The Breadth of René Magritte (1964), reprinted in *Secret Affinities: words and images by René Magritte*, translated by W.G. Ryan, Rice University exhibition catalog, 1976, pp. 29-31.
3) Julio Monteverde, Beyond the Walls of the City, translated by Eric Bragg and Bruno Jacobs, *The Exteriority Crisis*, p. 96.
4) Or as Noé Ortega has aptly expressed it: "That sensation of vulnerability, of finding oneself in front of an uncontrollable and unknown reality of colossal proportions fertilizes the relationship between the mind and the world and makes it appear to us in all its depth, so far-removed from the superficial, decorative and inoffensive aspect that the society of well-being tries to sell us." Noé Ortega Quijano, The Magnetized Land, translated by Eric Bragg and Bruno Jacobs, *The Exteriority Crisis*, p. 93.
5) http://tinyurl.com/c8ba44, a wikimapia representation of the entire area.
6) http://www.saltonsea.ca.gov/histchron.htm, Salton Sea Authority, historical chronology.
7) And I only found out about the mud after accidentally learning that some parts of the salt coverage could not support my weight. The jagged edges of broken salt cut my leg as I fell through, so after finishing up with the photos, I found some shade and cleaned off. A vast, hidden layer of black mud, imbued with the dregs of recent history, neatly entombed beneath a layer of white, caked salt, and nourished with freshly drawn blood: this is the stuff of latent environmental alchemy! It was at that point when I became aware of a commotion and the loud sirens from fire trucks that were dispatched there to deal with a house fire created by the hot, arid conditions of that mid-summer day: Bombay Beach is a place where fire and floods coexist quite well.
8) http://www.saltonsea.ca.gov/ss101.htm, website of the Salton Sea Authority.

LINES OF THOUGHT, LINES OF EXPLORATION

Frank Antonsen

Originally published in *EAR de Jour - Far from Equilibrium*, July 1998

Any object will trace a line of evolution, connecting it forever backwards with its own past. Any subject opens up an infinity of lines of desire escaping into its future. Thus, lines are the basic means of exploration of space as well as time.

Nothing, considered as a point, induces a line by its own evolution (its history), thus becoming something. The dialectic of *something* and *nothing*.

A collection of objects weaves a tapestry of space behind them, whereas subjects weave an infinity of possible tapestries of space ahead of them.

This woven (and interwoven) space is the difference between "nowhere" and "now here".

In this manner, the instantaneous end point of a line of history of a point (nothing) is an object, and any object is the end point of a line, a history (in the making). This is how spacetime and matter appear in modern quantum gravity. By adding desire (subjectivity) we also get a description of the poetic capacity of life. It is, by the way, also a theme in ancient myths, where the *Norns* of Norse mythology and the *Moira* of Ancient Greece weave the destinies of men, and the tying of knots in various rituals of magic and voodoo. But it is a modern, atheistic version thereof.

The subject is not distinct from its objectified tapestry of its past nor from its subjective tapestry of possible futures. But the object of the past becoming the subject of the present is the intersection, and the matrix, of the spacetime continuum. On the other hand, the objective elements in the past condition the subject of the present and the desires for the future. Hence, the relationship between the object of the past, the subject of the present, the objective (and reified and experienced) past, the subjective (and desired and, perhaps, feared) future all stand in a dialectical relationship to each other.

These tapestries and threads also constitute the subjective element of the objectively given, as well as the objective element of the subjective reality.

•

In connecting the interior world of the subject with the (more or less) objective world around it, the eye traces out lines of exploration, scanning the environment, filtering the information. These lines of sight are closely related to lines of thought, and the lines of thought, furthermore, construct skeletons and scaffolds in the exterior world as points of contact and of reference. Our eye carries out a perpetual *dérive* of our environs; our thoughts (including dreams and day dreams) carry out a continuous *dérive* of the interior landscape of past experiences and future projections. Both of these *dérives* can be made material or physical through carrying out an actual, physical *dérive* of one's surroundings. The actual walking or driving around will interweave the three *dérives* making them into reflections of a common underlying *dérive* – the *dérive of the dérive*.

It is also through actual physical contact with the exterior world that the subject relates to other subjects. Sometimes, the tapestries of two subjects can become entangled, leading to a more complex tapestry. *Desire* is a very strong element in this, and, moreover, desire can arise – or, rather, materialise – through precisely such an entanglement. In *love*, and in particular in actual lovemaking, tapestries can merge, thereby weaving ever more complex and beautiful tapestries for the future and the present – even reaching backwards in time and reorganising the past by changing the view of the past, the present and the future.

It is also such encounters that give the sparks from which objective chance can fly.

•

The interweaving of more and more tapestries is the birthplace of revolutions.

The body is the intersection of all these lines or threads. It is simultaneously the cloth woven by them and the weaver that does the weaving.

(...to be continued)

Towards the Solidification and Relativisation of Atopos Theory

Erik Bohman & Mattias Forshage

Surrealists as urbanists

Nothing could fool us into thinking that the city is a familiar place. Urbanity is a system of the dynamism of cramping things together, and its most interesting parts will remain those which grow in its interspaces, bud off from its inner limbs, retain its difficultly charted characteristics. There are, of course, all-too-familiar patterns and all-too-obvious conscious motives, of those who want to control the others and of those who just want to be left alone. But the unknown always remains a distinct possibility in urbanity's collaging of people, physical and mental environments and thus of social relations in general. And where the unknown emerges, there is always the potentiality of poetry.

Early surrealist investigations into urban flow led to the development of concepts such as objective chance. But most of the arsenal of methods, games and perspectives was never systematised into a particular theory. It was to a large extent up to the surrealists' prodigal children the situationists to cast it in pseudo-academic terms with the theory of the dérive and the theory of psychogeography. These were later recuperated into surrealism, and the surrealists' own investigations of urban environments were refuelled. In this new wave of exploration, additional new perspectives and concepts emerged.

One concept which gained some distribution in the previous decade was that of worthless places (*atopoi* or *atoposes*, literally meaning non-places—*atopoi* being the greek plural which the Leeds surrealist group insisted on, *atoposes* the ridicule-anglification first utilised by the Stockholm group who introduced the term). It was used in print first in the "Geografi" issue of *Stora Saltet* (1995). A brief summary of the subject by MF from the "Upphittat" (found objects) *Stora Saltet* was subsequently published in english in *Manticore* (as "The poetry of worthlessness", easily found on the web), in spanish in *Salamandra* and in czech in *Analogon*. Recently another piece, putting the concept to concrete work, was printed as "Explorations of absence" by the Leeds surrealists in *Phosphor* #1 (2008). (In the meantime we had found some Plato quote including the term, and not too distantly Roland Barthes had called love an atopos; only recently however it was pointed out to us that in greek it is the common word for something absurd in the mathematical-logical sense. There has also been some internal debate whether the concept was closely related to Foucault's idea of *heterotopia*, but its affiliations on a purely theoretical level is not of particular importance for a concept we now address as an analytical tool.)

Drawing by Desmond Morris

Other surrealist groups pursued their geographical investigations in other directions. The Paris group maintained focus on objective chance and analogical geography in the "Géographie passionelle" issue of *S.U.RR.*, the Madrid group together with individuals elsewhere developed the concept of "exteriority" for epiphanic experiences of sensory presence at certain border locations. Some of these groups were never particularly interested in, or impressed with, the concept of worthless places. This is of course conditioned by differences in direction and local traditions, but a certain role could also be assigned to differences in conspicuousness and function of the locally available such sites.

In this text, we would like to sketch some of these differences in conditions while restating the basic background of organising urban space, and restating, perhaps even forwarding, some principles and perspectives for surrealist investigations into urban geography.

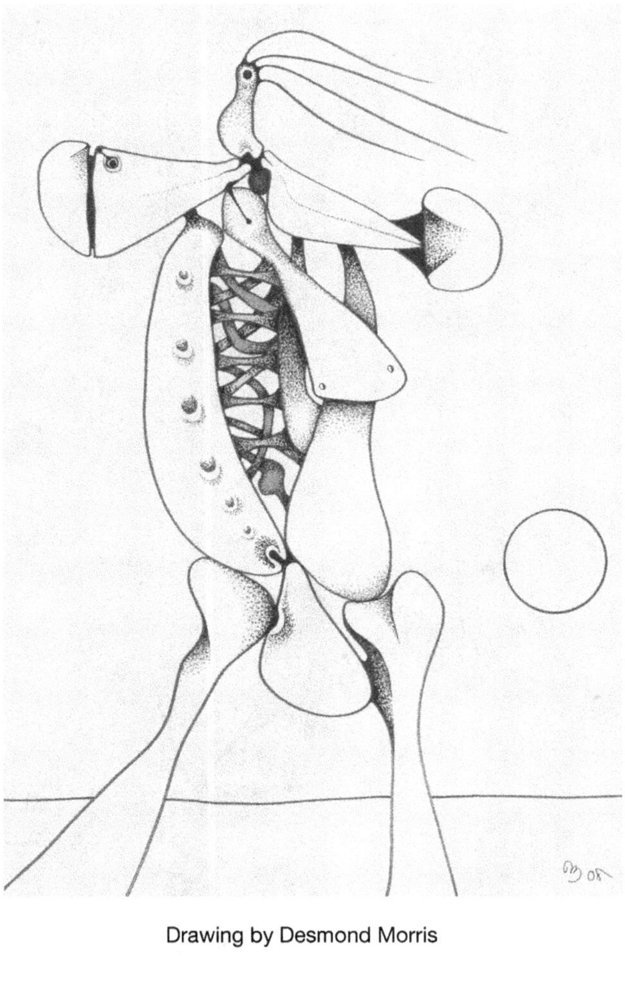

Drawing by Desmond Morris

Recognition of worthless places

The emergence of worthless places in urban environments depends on several conditions. Their recognition typically focuses on either of three approaches.

a) that of poetic phenomenology—keeping up the vigilance towards spots conveying a distinct feeling of being out of control and having a distinct diffuse potential (if such a seeming contradiction is excused), of having a hidden history, a hidden usage or a hidden future in the realm of collectivisation and realisation of desires. This is straightforward to apply, but not in a strictly intersubjective way.

b) that focusing on usage (in terms of sociology, ethnology or behavioral ecology)—tracing spots which are generally used in a non-regulated way for activities not at all intended by owners, city planners, entrepreneurs, architects—which people individually or collectively snatch and exploit for various needs. This is obviously the most difficult criterion to apply, since we have no particular interest in acknowledging thousands of semi-secluded spots where males sometimes urinate... we want perhaps to be able to distinguish between using the same spot for a wellbehaved rendezvous or consumption of drinks and entertainments offered on one hand, and on the other hand a non-regulated nothing-buying hangout... and we would possibly like to be able to somehow define non-usage, abandoning to spontaneous decay, as a special category of unintended usage...

c) that of economic history, which allows for the most rigorous definitions—recognising spots of non-productivity in economic terms in the middle of a generally high-productive city-planned area. Being a formal and not a qualitative distinction, this criterion has the advantage of pointing out unexpected and inconspicuous places. On the other hand, it will also cover phenomena which don't interest us in themselves. Still, the determination will then sometimes require vast knowledge in local history and economy, and in practice, even with this criterion, the most *obvious* instances are *diagnostically* spotted via one or several of the following:

1. poetic suggestions in accordance with the first approach above,

2. artifacts giving a clear indication of popular usage: such as displaced chairs and sofas, toys, abandoned clothes, notes and drawings, porn magazines, condoms,

bottles and beercans, abundance of cigarette butts or garbage in general, etc,

3. an abundant flora of fast-growing, easy-dispersing, more or less globalised, ruderal plants, indicating that no one manages or tidies the spot.

It should be remembered that within surrealism, such a concept with a rigorous definition is a mere tool for poetic investigation and not something interesting in itself. The gap towards academic cultural geography is still wide. The point here is not refining the concepts, comparing it with other concepts, and debating its merits and failures; the real question is to what extent it actually sharpens our vigilance for the active contradictions and poetic possibilities in the urban environment.

There is a certain correlation between the explanatory power of a concept and how discriminately it is applied. Therefore we here stress certain objective characteristics of atopoi, insisting that the concept will not be obviously applicable to the same extent on a global scale, and that local factors will make it more or less interesting.

Value production in urban settings — In the lapses of accumulation

The decisive regularities conditioning the distribution of sites of value in the capitalist city give us a methodological starting point from which we can approach the question of the spatial distribution of worthlessness. Here the object is not one of exploration, for which such a method would prove all too general and lacking in inspiration. Rather, it lets us avoid a couple of not-so-productive interpretations of atopoi and their relationship to the capitalist city, culture or whatever might strike the fancy of anyone prone to thinking in abstracts and unmediated totalities. We are prepared to posit the existence of a certain break between the patterns of distribution (or production by chance) sketched herein and the unlikely but constantly reoccurring product. This break is not to be understood along the lines of those pairs of opposites that pretend to say something very profound while hiding difference, particularity or reserving room for them squarely on one side of the opposition. The critique of civilization that proceeds from the *a priori* positioning of "culture" and "nature" teaches us nothing and substitutes experience with moralist still-lifes. Not in opposites but in living contradiction do we hope to find those sparks of wonder that illuminate the fragility of the present order of things.

The capitalist city is by and large determined by the processes of accumulation and the contradictions inherent in these processes. These imply a tendency towards general urbanisation while effecting local processes of de- and re-urbanisation and a (more or less) dynamic redistribution of people and sites of value according to the needs and limits of accumulation. The ability of capital to impose an urban dynamic governed by its voracious appetite for surplus value is checked by the continual struggle waged in a variety of forms between those who are its agents and those who suffer its consequences. The immense number of contradictions arising from the conditions of the modern city are breeding grounds of the marvellous.

The capitalist city is a structure made out of a number of heterogenous elements. Its development is not a one way street, neither does it develop in a frictionless manner. The tendencies and countertendencies that give rise and direction to the deployment of urban spaces can only result in an uneven development. Just as the global economy simultaneously accumulates massive material wealth and an even more glaring (spiritual, material) poverty, so does the city.

The atopos might be defined negatively as a place that doesn't lend itself to a) production of commodities, b) circulation of commodities, c) reproduction of labour power or d) the reproduction of those apparatuses necessary to secure the conditions of accumulation on the level of society (police, state initiatives, etc). A purely negative definition thus far—as a place devoid of value, a lapse in the circuits of accumulation. Such a definition stops short of the aims of surrealist investigation and leaves the place itself a blank, since the same concepts that let us grasp the patterns of distribution have nothing or very little to say about it. We can go one step further: the definition will rather give us hints as to where and under what conditions one can expect the emergence of atopoi.

The creative destruction through which city development unfolds has an almost inevitable tendency to produce temporal lapses just at those places where economic growth is most apparent, such as in the process of *gentrification*.

Typically in a modern city there will be a dynamism of worthless places which can be decribed in foucauldian-autonomous terms: on the one hand gentrification and various urban development schemes; the infinite struggles to increase profit, utilising any old and new means of disciplining, exclusion and appropriation; on the other hand popular usage, countering and competing with gentrification by way of various non-regulated non-commercial useless usages. This should preferably be studied empirically, but it can be assumed that there are always struggles occurring. Places will fall out of order and be reintegrated at a certain pace, which will be different in different cities and different parts of the cities at different times. Acknowledging worthless places a little too publicly will usually lead to their reintegration (if not for direct exploitation then for the ideological exploitation resulting from open recognition of their eventual picturesque qualities). Few largescale triumphs for the popular side are possible within the given socioeconomic order (and will probably often count as steps in a social revolution), but the struggle is perpetual and will produce a variety, at any given moment, of worthless places for leisure and play, indicating the impossibility of total control, inspiring surrealist usage of urbanity and the dreaming of yet unknown senses of urban life.

We recommend caution to some of our enthusiastic friends of the ultraradical variety some caution: city planning cannot be monolithic and is usually not pursuing a hidden agenda. City planning is the chaotic outcome, suboptimal from all viewpoints, of compromises between various concerns and interests; fulfilling a function that is—among other things—disciplinary on the whole largely because this is the involuntary sum of the competitive commercial, political and popular interests. A lot will be about facilitating work and work transports, and offering occasions for entertainment and isolation, based on the joint interests of the capitalists of reproducing labor power and of the people of having at least some fun and getting left in peace to at least some extent. There are always conflicts of usage but also conflicts of planning, and thus small and large spots which fail to conform to intentions or where intentions fail to resolve themselves—the city is a dynamic arena and this has always been obvious to its surrealist users. There are not so few good intentions in some of the political planning, which is then always implemented in a coopted and coopting way but which may simultaneously allow for independent popular possibilities. In fact, various philanthropic and social-liberal ambitions are at least as historically important in city planning as the all-too-often cited examples of purely repressive concerns. Hausmann's avenues and the metaphor of Bentham's Pantopticon should at least be accompanied by the various utopian-socialist, early-ecologist, radical-egalitarian, mystic-esoteric etc traces. Sometimes these could challenge the limitations of philanthropic liberalism when taken literally.

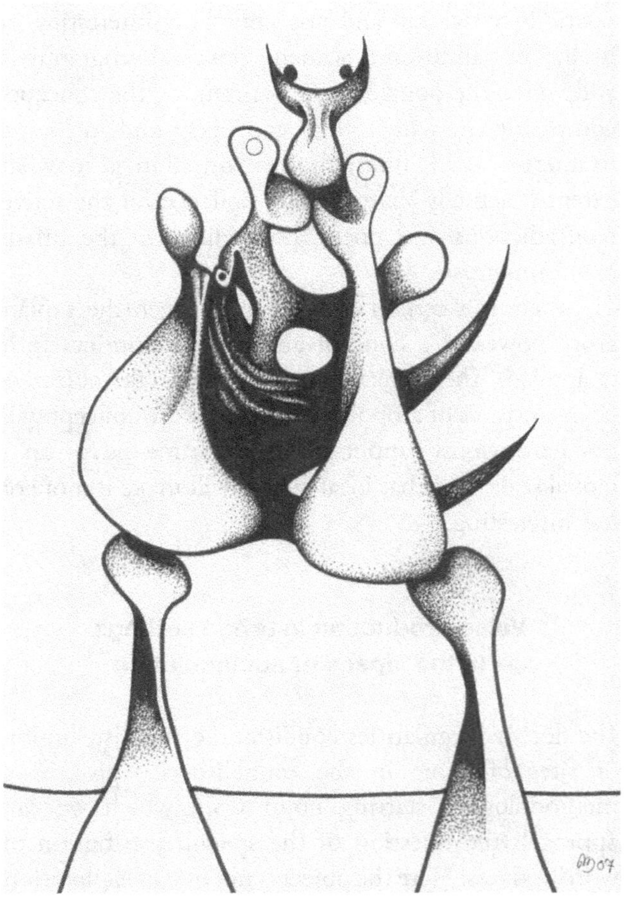

Drawing by Desmond Morris

Parameters of worthless places

Several types of conditions govern first the emergence and maintenance and second the recognition of worthless places in different parts of the world. Both are very dependent on 1) the general degree of urbanity, 2) the general level of order and orderliness, 3) current local land prices and other market particulars and exploitation conditions.

The general degree of urbanity conditions the availability of worthless places. The denser and more heterogenous the population and the larger the overall accessability via sidewalks and public transport, the more opportunities for an atopos to emerge, and new social practices.

For example, many North american cities have such a lack of urban density that the concept often will appear to lack application there. Whenever a city is planned under no shortage of land, and driving a car is the normal way of moving in the city rather than walking or using public transport, there will be an abundance of interspaces between everything and no obvious contrast between useful and useless land. When such a concentration is lacking, the flow of messages and chance encounters central to surrealism's appreciation of urbanity, is often decreased to non-urban levels. That certain places are put to popular perverse/detourning usage when decaying under such circumstances too is obvious nevertheless, and proven for example by some of the places found and photographically documented by Eric Bragg in the northern California countryside, but they may perhaps not be best described with the term atopoi or best understood in the framework of urbanity.

Order and orderliness is a crucial factor, but primarily on the level of conditions for discovery of such places. In a city where city planning is partly chaotic, where land market is relatively anarchic, where a major segment of the population lives in poverty or outside conformist lifestyles, where cleaning, public order, construction and renovation tasks are slower or less ambitious, where general mentality is less orderly: worthless places will probably be more abundant but far less conspicuous. And as much of their surrealist function lies in their contrasting action they will also often be less interesting.

Market particulars are also crucial for the abundance and the conspicuousness of worthless places. Growing populations of course promote higher land prices, but exploitation rate is also dependent on general income, living standards and the availability of resources for exploitation, and on particular characteristics of entrepreneurs and landlords (oligarchies, mafia, superstitions, political and transnational economical involvement etc). Where the economy and thus the physical shape of the city is more "dynamic"; the worthless places will be less stable, quicker to emerge (drop out of control) but also to disappear (become reintegrated).

This is even more important when it comes to cities in the southern hemisphere or where very large parts of the population are poor: the pressure on available space is great but the capacity to pay for it is low, putting market mechanisms out of use and accentuating social contradictions, and creating a situation where whole neighborhoods and sometimes even whole parts of countries can assume the characteristics of worthlessness. Or the contrast will be organised along other scales or parameters than that of surface area.

There are also the remarkable particulars of the great stalinist cities of east europe, for example, where a certain megalomanic totalitarian regime has been replaced by regimes with distinctly other primary mechanisms of disciplining and social control. These huge squares and avenues, which made ideological sense and were practically used for propagandistic parades (and for good old hausmannian riot control), have now become senseless. And in the instances where is no capital available for new exploitation of them, they basically remain; vast, often ghostly, worthless.

The mapping of such differences will increase our understanding of the fundamental and local differences in possiblities connected with the organisation of space, (and might facilitate communication between surrealist activities in different places).

Drawing by Desmond Morris

The surrealist perspective

Surrealist interventions both theoretical and practical in the area of urban investigations are paralleled by those of others. There are tendencies among academics (in cultural geography, sociology, anthropology, economic history, human ecology, etc etc), subacademics (postmodernists, the art world), activists (struggles for "new commons" and against commercial/police control, auto-reduction, squattings etc), subactivists (postsituationists, post-live-role-players) and common boyish adventurers ("urban exploring", parkour), which may be more or less identical in single approaches. The surrealist project might be characterised primarily by the concern for the poetic experience and its phenomenology AND the insistence that this poetry is not primarily subjective, "pure" or religious in nature but dynamic and immanent. On the other hand, surrealists insist on the significance of considering circumstances giving rise to poetic phenomena, to acknowledging several concerns (including the psychological, mythological, scientific, utopian, political, historical) and their mutual conditioning. In this case, if anyone needs formulae easy to memorise, we could say we insist on the Empirical, Epistemological and Emancipatory concerns of surrealism.

It is necessarily empirical in its focus on poetic experience, but also in letting this experience emerge more distinctly by giving the possibly relevant circumstances in a documentary or (as Breton liked to evoke from Freud) clinical way. This documentation and curiosity for paraphernalia will allow for many new connections and spontaneous criticisms as well as for letting anecdotes take part in larger patterns, unlike those accounts which immediately—spontaneously or laboriously—transform concrete experience into intoxicated fairytales.

Surrealist perspective is fundamentally directed towards producing new knowledge, not seeking to merely confirm preconceived views. It addresses the unknown in a manner which trusts its productivity, and does not treat it religiously as if it was something fragile. Systematically, ludically and/or intuitively it raises new questions, devises new methods and introduces experimental alterations. It could not be satisfied by our own emotional responses themselves, savouring ambiances like the kick-seeking youth or the sensible dandy flaneur, or by quasitheoretical efforts making up names for phenomena without defining them by any other criteria than this emotional response, or the arbitrary applicability of abstract opposites (such as in the art sphere, the new age sphere, popular psychology, poor structuralism etc). It could also not be satisfied by the repetitive formulation of fundamental questions, as typical for postmodernism, conceptual art in general, and most of contemporary so-called political art, which claims to criticise things by merely thematising them in the first place, repeating the very same questions without ever devising a methodology for actually investigating the thing—this particular antimethodological stance of always formulating questions in an "eternal", unanswerable way is one of the many obvious strategies of pure obscurantism within those dominant sectors of art which are unable to address the unknown in a more substantial, creative, actually exploratory way.

In fact, the atopos theory as naïvely conceived could be formulated in scientific terms as resting on the assumption that there is a negative correlation between the economic productivity and the poetic productivity of a place. And as this is empirically testable, it is not just an assumption but a hypothesis, even if its rigorous testing is not among surrealism's first concerns. It does relate back to something fundamental within the concept of the poetic. However, we are not so sure that this hypothesis is very useful. Instead of that correlation we are inclined to suggest a tentatively positive one: Poetic productivity will, on a statistical level, be positively correlated with local steep gradients in economic productivity. Along those slopes come tumbling, and accumulating, not only various discarded objects (mostly all kinds of garbage but also antiquities and utilitarian objects detached from context) as well as persecuted persons, plants and animals, and repressed behaviors, stories and contradictions. The friction in such movements will create sparks illuminating the atmosphere of possibilities concentrated at such sites.

Finally, the surrealist perspective is based within the demarcation line introduced in Marx's famous eleventh Feuerbach thesis: interpreting the world with the overall objective of transforming it. This is both in immediate terms, planting seeds of radicalising social exchange with such a place as a nexus, and communicating-challenging individual poetic experience with ludic means, and in the long term, as one area of investigation and intervention among many pointing towards future realisation of generalised poetry in radically changed and self-governed social circumstances.

The Common Place

The Common Place is a game devised and co-ordinated by Sasha Vlad, who distributed an advertising image of a beech forest and invited Surrealists to manipulate the image in whatever way they liked.

The game was played over a period of several years and resulted an accumulation of some 30 new images by Surrealists from all around the world. Here we present a selection of those images which seem to us to offer especially revealing or illuminating explorations of the beech forest's *spatial* aspects in particular.

These images should therefore be viewed alongside and/or in tension with the other explorations of space and place in this volume by Frank Antonsen, Apio, Erik Bohman, Eric Bragg, Mattias Forshage, Joël Gayraud, Allan Graubard, and the Paris, Madrid and Inner Island Surrealist Groups.

Marie-Dominique Massoni

Ribitch

Bruno Jacobs

Michèle Bachelet

Guy Girard

Katerina Piňosovà

Bill Howe

/Cubomania Derived From Moorish Nude Postcard #1

Collage derived from Moorish Nude Postcard #1

METAMORPHOSIS OF A MOORISH NUDE POSTCARD

Ghérasim Luca's brief but compellingly enigmatic *Les Orgies des quanta* (*The Orgies of Quanta*) was first published in Bucharest in 1946. Ghérasim Luca was a founding member of the Romanian Surrealist group, which seemed at times to paraphrase Luca himself from the recent elegantly translated into English *Le Vampire passif* (*The Passive Vampire*), 1945, to exist all on its own "on the delirious scale of space and time."

Luca, to the neglectful degree that he is now remembered, is primarily known today, mostly in France and Romania, as an extraordinary, but difficult poet and then, secondly, as a fairly obscure theorist, but it is less recalled that he was also an inventor of thought provoking images and his own "objectively offered objects," or O.O.O.'s.

With the nonpareil example embodied by *Les Orgies des quanta*, Luca's ambition was to introduce to fellow surrealists all over the world his invention of cubomania, or *cubomanie*, as Luca first coined it in French language, in which he cut up, in this case, a previously printed image into same-sized squares and then reassembled them into an image that had its own realm of possible interpretation.

Title page & two cubomanias from Luca's book

/Cubomania, Moorish Nude Postcard #3

The "classic" technique of cubomania that Ghérasim Luca put into service in *Les Orgies des quanta* employs a grid of three horizontal and four vertical rows, which form, as a whole, an upright rectangle made up as a conglomerate of twelve squares. Whereas each cubomania has as its source a different image, each of the images shares characteristics from similarly illustrated sources of 19th century engravings which lends to the series an underlying consistency. Luca permitted some additional flexibilty within the technique by using squares instead of rectangles: any side of any square can be attached to another square on any of its four sides.

It should be noted that Luca's desired prerequisites for *Les Orgies des quanta,* the series, are peculiar to it alone. Any re-entry into cubomania can be set in motion by a new set of prerequisites. Overall, throughout the entire course of its thirty-three cubomanias, *Les Orgies des quanta* reveals a freedom in its range that permutates unexpected punctuations of spontaneity and variability. There is only one question that remains to be asked. "Are we phantom enough?"

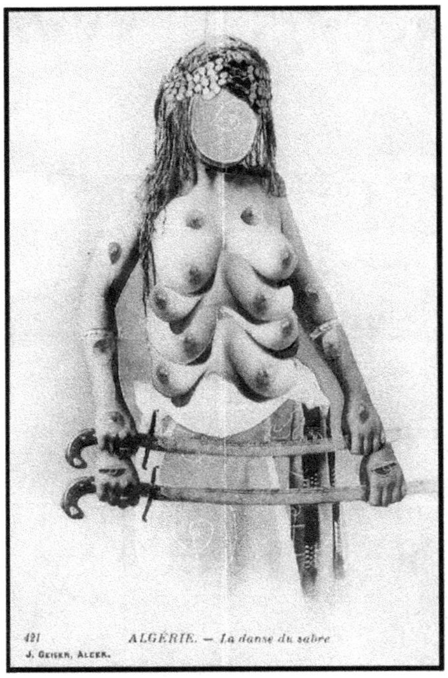

The Austrian department shows various examples on INLAID FLOORING, by M.M. LEISTER and SON, of Vienna; we introduce here one of their patterns - a star upon a ground of dark wood.

Two anti-Oedipal collages and the diagram that inspired /cubomania

Having been continuously inspired over the years by *Les Orgies des quanta,* I had experimented with the technique of cubomania with varying results. Eventually I reached a stalemate in which I felt the technique, to the degree that I had comprehended it, could no longer inspire me; yet I still felt that there was something inherent within its anti-matter poetics that could provide a way for new discoveries. It was at such a moment, hesitating before either repeating an endless pattern for the *nth* time or before abandoning the technique forever, that I preceded to look through a stack of visually related material—cutouts, loose pages and the pilfered shipwrecks of assorted picture books.

I then discovered the cut-out corner of the bottom of page 234 from a reprint of *The Crystal Palace Exhibition Illustrated Catalog, London 1851.* It showed an inlaid flooring pattern—"a star upon a ground of dark wood." I had to ask myself, why had I deliberately cut out this scrap and saved it for future reference? I knew that I had not intended to use it as an element in a collage. This is verified by how I clearly had preserved the detailed description beneath it. There must have been an idea associated with it which I have

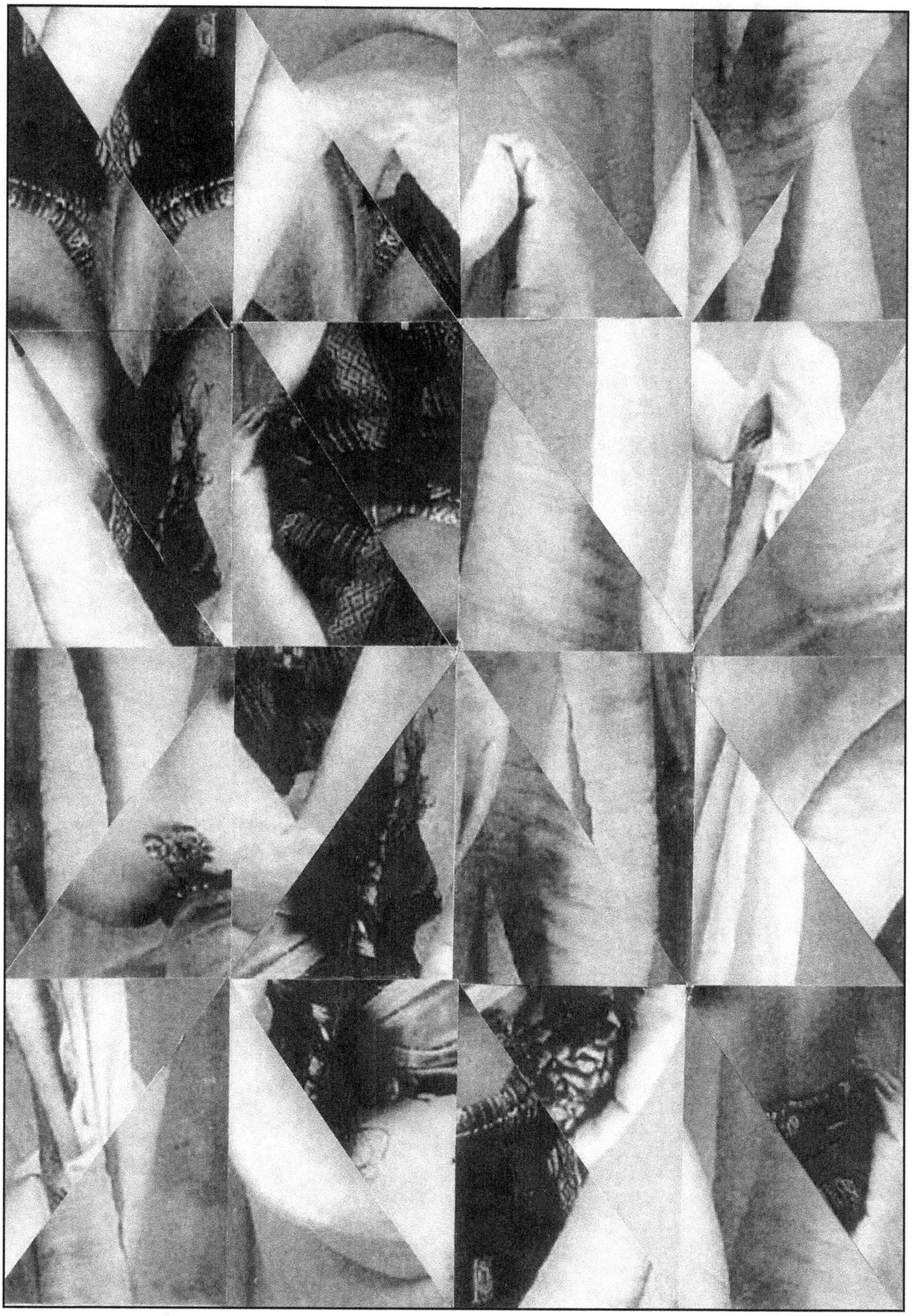

/Cubomania, Moorish Nude Postcard #2

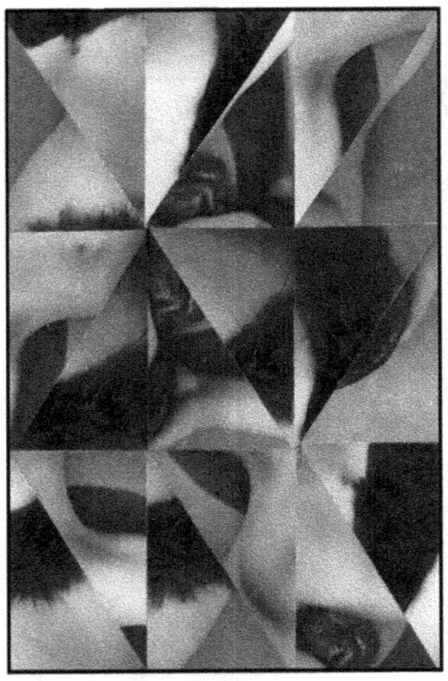

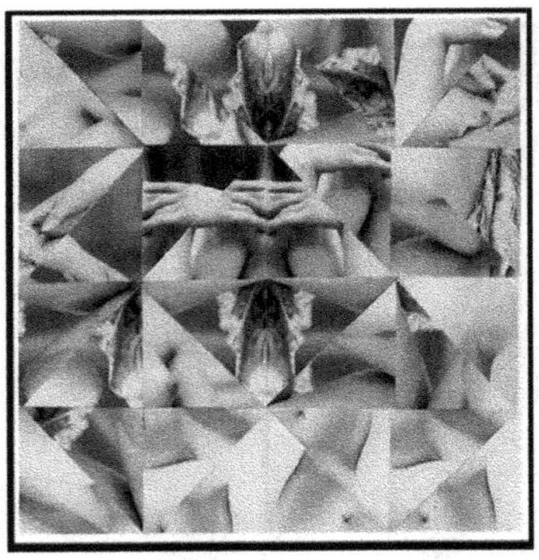

Three examples of /cubomania
derived from French nude postcards

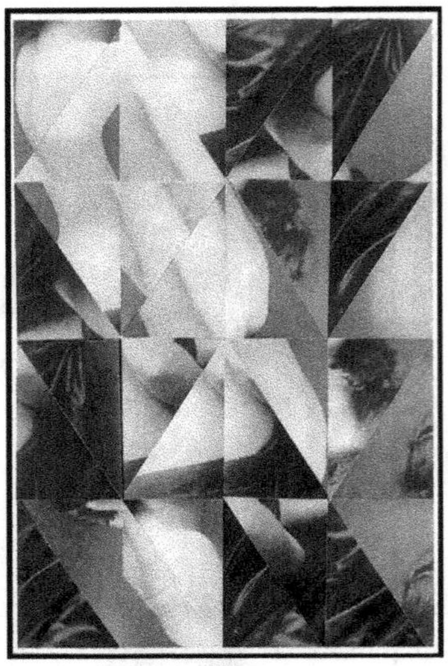

since forgotten.

As I puzzled over the diagram, the all-pervading grid which I had discovered underlying all cubomanias and which I had become so familiar with as I prepared the squares by drawing lines with a pencil and a ruler on the back of an image and then cutting them out, superimposed itself in my mind's eye over the flooring pattern. What still could be added? A diagonal cut or slash, could be added. Thus was born what I would later anti-christen "*slash/cubomania*," or when shortened, "*/cubomania*."

Looking back Ghérasim Luca must have intended that the definition of cubomancy, "divination by throwing dice," would spill its meaning over his new term for cubomania when he first coined it. In the French language there is only a small "c" that distinguishes one noun from the other (*cubomancie/cubomanie*). It is as if cubomania by means of its own divining magic surreptitiously un-*c*ubed itself. Luca later famously added "*La cubomanie nie*" – "Cubomania negates."

Stéphane Mallarmé, the other great negator and the most famous dice-thrower in all of French letters, only had his magisterial work, *Un Coup de dés* finally published in 2004 in the manner as it was intended; so that it could be seen and read in the typography that he had conceived and designed for the text. It was after all Mallarmé that ended *Un Coup de dés* in 1897 with the line: "All Thought emits a Throw of the Dice." The numinous thoughts of

Richard Waara

#1

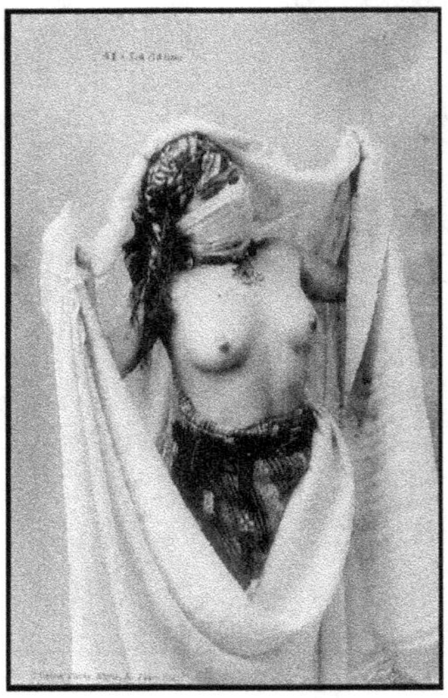

#2

#3

Original source material - three Moorish nude postcards

PLURAL FORMULA OF LANGUAGE AND COMMUNICABILITY

Dominic Tétrault

Surrealism has always been greatly concerned with the recognition of those things which constitute the universal – rites, magic, alchemy – and which govern desire beyond survival, constituting an approach to a firm new social contract anchored in the Marvellous and the manifestations of the subconscious. The principles of the survival of the species take as their starting point the taming of the laws of nature; now, with the continuation of surrealism from the 1970s onwards, there has been – this time in relation to psychic survival – a dawning recognition of our definitive enemy: Man.

Man, from his active part in the chronology of the closed vessel of his prevarications, finds himself today before the compulsive field of the sign, alloy of the temporal representation of his surroundings in a computerised world. All the external appeals to his latent desire are exacerbated to such a point that, more than ever, the confused state of his emotional symbolic system becomes a dead letter. Man engenders his insatiability by his recourse to a form of representation which is rational and hence in harmony with the economic and demographic proportions of exchange. This rationalisation is supposed to be linear and one-way, only nothing is quite that simple in this exchange of signs which constitutes the generalised speech promoted by the capitalist system and those who resort to it.

A thrilling recognition of this was captured in the results of some of surrealism's ludic activities from the 1970s onwards in the game of *parallel stories*, in the form of speech interference. The game is played as follows: one of the players begins an automatic text, and another player dictates some words which must be incorporated into the text as it is being written; thus automatic speech constantly goes astray as external interference makes it lose its own thread, allowing the influence of language to guide the images towards other places. This entails a relationship of compulsive interpretation of the symbols in connection to each player and in the way the information appears within such a short period of time (the time of writing), bearing in mind the practicalities of a dialogue between two people. In the case of a conventional conversation we can recognise the same effects as those experienced in the game of parallel stories. However in a world where conversation is becoming virtual, such as we see today, it is remarkable to observe this endophasic speech interference at the very moment when we find ourselves before the commodity-display of desire. Thus the latter finds itself caught in the crossfire of diametrically opposed intentions: those of latent desires on one side, of manifest desires on the other. Is manifest desire everything related to the possibility of coveting a concrete state arising from a conjunction of situations which might produce the material or physical satisfaction of a given problem? In the current context of the generalised speech distributed by information during communication between individuals and the transmitter, regardless of whether the latter is in the form of advertising or mass media, the result is the same and constant. The subjective insatiability of subjects is influenced by the interference they pick up, and we become part of the need for satisfaction, or of the formation of opinions which differ dramatically from the critical direction in which our strict requirements would take us under other circumstances. We now have the communication of the speech of experts, of rationalisation, which prevails over the critical form through which our latent desires are normally led towards a sensory objectification of their satisfaction. The propagation of this speech is so widespread that it reaches the four corners of the world and, provisionally, the diverse mentalities enabled by today's changing demographics might come to thwart the intentions of this type of speech. And surrealism must be on the offensive, albeit an offensive which is temporarily out of date.

Current and future demographic transformations symbolise for surrealism the constant abolition of cultural boundaries by immigration and the social changes it represents. The meeting of diverse cultures in the territories of North America, particularly in relation to Quebec, gives reason to believe that an inversion of rational signs into signs of irrationality will overturn the status quo of interracial relations. These relations will bring about the inversion of signs and it is our duty to prepare the ground for a better understanding of desire amid the alteration of endophasic codes and the plural demands of the various groups of opposing interlocutors. However, the field of communicability must benefit from a large-scale dismantling of the relational mechanisms of linguistic normativism so as to encourage the exchange of the manifest for the latent in mainstream speech.

Here are a number of preliminary questions for the communicability of the functioning of extranormative language in our future societies:

1. *Can the inversion of rational signs into irrational signs in generalised speech teach us anything about the subversive nature of the subconscious in a system of daily repression? If not, why not?*
2. *How can we establish the spontaneous existence of the presence of latent desire within each individual's own levels of endophasic speech?*
3. *Can the recognition of this spontaneous existence raise the level of the emotional symbolic system, or will it only stimulate an interpretative panorama of the signifying position of desire by associative means?*
4. *Do latent and manifest desire intersect to create ambiguities, or do they remain parallel?*
5. *If it happens that a parallelism between the two might be possible, how do they behave? If, in some possible parallelism, we see the base of the latent dipping into the absurdity of the system of repression, what is it that the other base, that of the manifest, is dipping into? The subjective symbolic system?*
6. *I like to think of endophasic speech as constituting a field of subjective language. Can such a field be objectively delineated? How?*
7. *Does this field incorporate its own moral code?*

Montréal, November 2008

Translated by Merl Fluin

Divination Cards by Debra Taub

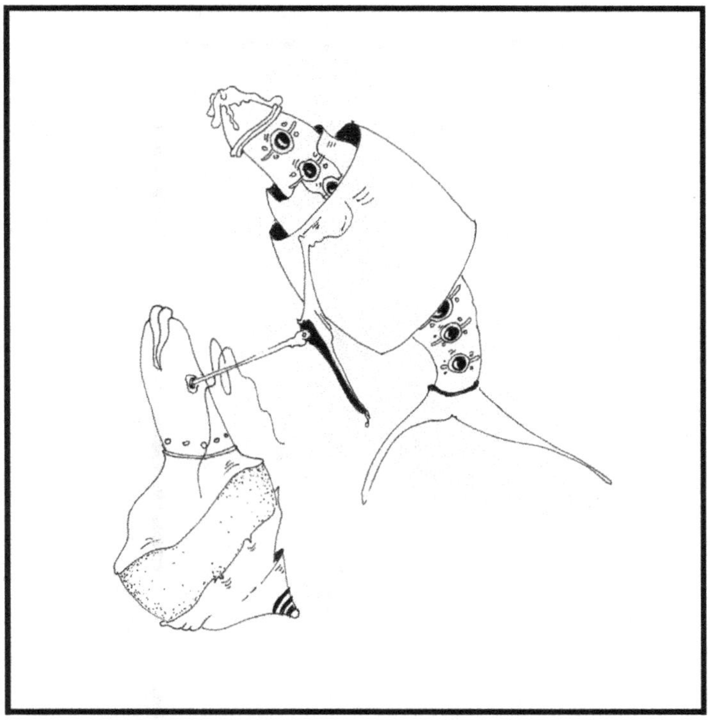

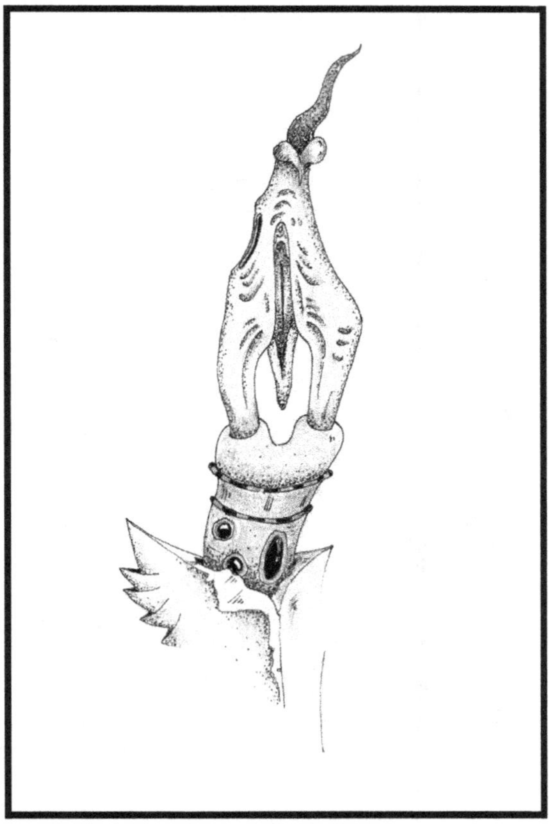

RIBITCH PHANTOMS

Enchantment, Witchcraft, Trick:
on the Destiny of Magic in the Age of Technology

Luís Navarro

for Jonás, so that he keeps believing in magic

When comparing concepts like magic and technology we immediately perceive a kind of conflict or violent polarization. In most cases, after recognizing a common atmosphere of application in our operative ability regarding all phenomena, we put both of them at irreconcilable extremes of the same continuum. When we lack a satisfactory explanation regarding a particular phenomenon, either because our level of knowledge still does not grasp its dynamics or because it openly contradicts our perception of the world, we banish it to the domain of magical thought, with the hope that, with the expansion and accumulation of knowledge, it will end up finding its place some day in the constantly expanding domain of scientific knowledge. If doubt persists, if the phenomenon in question resists obeying all known laws that would allow us to domesticate it, then it is simply pushed outside of the paradigm, it is discredited and vilified by those who defend mysticism or obscurantism. In the same way, those who refuse to surrender to triumphant technological power — reinforcing the radical nature of mystery, the impossibility of fundamentals, the inaccessibility of the *noumenon*, or simple and blind faith — reject in a reactionary way whatever attempts technology makes, with its floodlights and cacophonous machinery, to desecrate the sweet dream of the dawn of prehistory. Spirits can end up becoming argumentative.

Usually this conflict is resolved today within the domain of technology since it is the prevalent ideological paradigm. Technology no longer comprises this entire group of tools and applications that the human uses in his/her vital praxis, and it has ended up creating an artificial environment outside of which it becomes difficult to imagine human survival, associated with its multiple prosthetics. On the other hand, technology has imposed a unique way of conceiving and confronting the world, characterized by instrumentalization and control, establishing itself everywhere. Consequently, it does not seem strange that in many cases technology is attributed to magic, not in the sense of cursed territory left in the hands of lunatics or romantics, but as a kind of technology of amazement — i.e. as a group of technologies capable of producing within the spectator (who is unaware of them) this rapture, this spiritual perturbation, together with the suspension of criteria that rule our perceptions, which is part of the phenomena to which the nature of "magic" was traditionally granted.

The assimilation of the term "technology" with the different "techniques" of daily usage, along with the generalized and indisputable adoption of a "technical way" of dealing with the world, such that the immediate means prioritize the ultimate goals (including the domination of the objects of its comprehensive assimilation), both blind us to the perception of technology as an ideology that has assumed the same functions that magic or religious thought exercised long ago. The problem does not occur when the different techniques combine into one single concept so as to be considered generically, but when this generic sense transforms into an autonomous entity and begins to act of its own accord, like a totality completely distinct from the sum of its parts.

Therefore, it is not that this or that technology is going to solve whatever problem, such as the fight against cancer or the speed of my internet browser, but rather that it is technology which extricates us from said problem. And when it does, it attributes to itself the ability to make miracles, to realize utopias and to "save us".

The growing prestige that the technological has experienced through shaping the world has considerably reduced the presence or perception of magic or marvelous elements: as if technology immediately refers us to concrete instruments, processes and things that we naturally experience all the time, then magic projects us

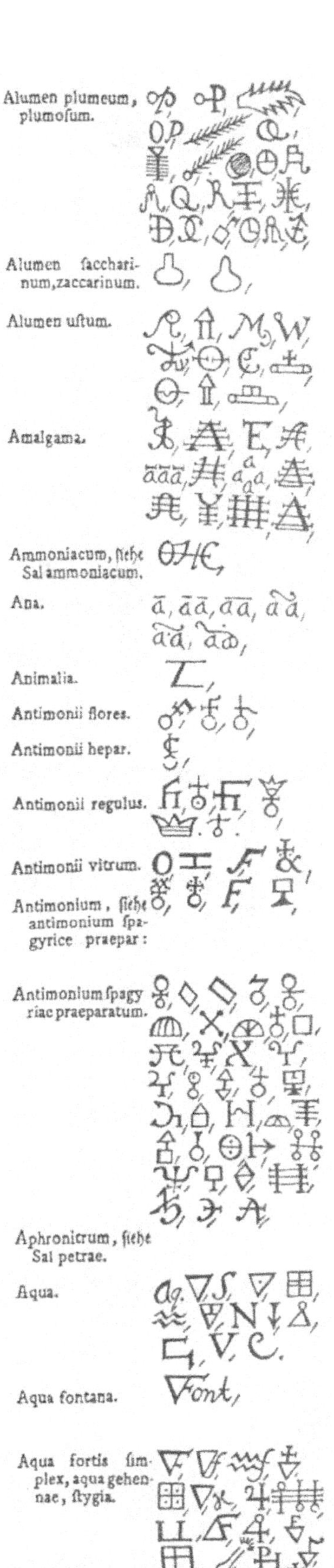

into mysterious events, uncertain objects, unrepeatable experiences, which makes these latter things essentially questionable. Technology is evidently precise, whereas magic is uncertain by definition. We give the name of "magic" to any rupture with the natural order of things, according to what is known at a given moment, with the intervention of supernatural powers or beings still happening within it, or simply the preparedness of a magician, regardless of whether it is done with a purpose or not. When a magic event habitually achieves a previously established goal, it ends up becoming a part of it — as a technique or a body of technological knowledge — even when the ultimate reason why it happened that way cannot be determined.

What immediately makes this concept of magic noteworthy is its dialectical relation to the field of technology, which likewise includes the magic outside of its domain. Far from denying each other, both spheres are mutually complementary, so that everything which remains unknown or unexplained by science is recognized as "magic", and the field of the latter becomes diminished, to the extent that technology continues to gain ground. A phenomenon ends up being magical or technological according to the perception that I might have of it. There will be facts that my idiosyncratic nature will lead me to interpret as magic, while someone else would impose a scientific explanation of the same facts, however improbable that might seem.

What is certain is that we naturally live within a technological context with a mentality that could be characterized as magical, as if we had just purged it of all capacity for amazement and surprise. In reality, we do not "use technologies", but we carry out rituals of guaranteed effect (except when someone gets their wires crossed): the button is the abracadabra, the magic formula that permits action from a distance, the apparition, the beyond. Telephone numbers are secret cabala that one must know and combine in order to contact someone. There is a nowhere-place in which I can develop a parallel life without the defects and limitations imposed on me by my body. But few of us would be able to give a satisfactory and comprehensible explanation for whatever is really happening. Furthermore when our "magic objects" malfunction, we feel so vulnerable, and end up consulting a technician, in the same way we would a shaman. No allegory better illustrates this than the "crystal ball"[1] we sat in front of in our childhood, which was none other than the movie screen that "controls everything", but which could be attacked at any given moment by gremlins.

In the end, all of this becomes possible because we have developed a "blind faith" in technology. And it is on the basis of this confidence in something that has become so familiar to us (but which ultimately remains unknown) that we implore magic to show its cards, to fill in the gaps of its mystery, and to reach, with however much trickery, the solid and calming ground of technology. We live in an age that has relegated the experience of magic to the domain of fiction, when it is not relegated to plain and simple sleight of hand. Magic, conceived as insufficient when compared with the technological, will end up disappearing when technology manages to complete the circle of knowledge and action. In reality it has already disappeared, since it has been recognized as a vicarious existence destined for failure, and basically because (although we are not certain how to identify it) we always know that "there is some trick going on". In the age of technology, nobody grows up so naïve that they are still able to grant a positive existence to magic, no matter how much the standards of magic continue to unquestioningly govern its behavior. And that tendency to automatically obey standards of magic is not declining, but rather increasing, to the extent that technology becomes more invasive.

There must have been a time where every human situation occurred in an environment that could be characterized as "magical". The gaze of the child, the way in which he is experiencing and explaining the world to himself, actualizes this very structure. While still not having firm and regular criteria at his disposal to settle the contents of his experience, everything is presented as marvelous before the child's consciousness, constantly escaping the connection of causality and his fragile configurations. And the explanation of everything always needs to be pursued in the "other" world, since there are not even any which serve as an outline. I will define **enchantment** as this innocent experience which relates to everything, and which does so in a language that needs to be made up as one goes along, even if we are conscious that not all of its expressions end up being enchanting ones. They can be terrible, since this corresponds to a naked consciousness exposed to such dangers and contradictions without the support of a prior pattern or code. What is characteristic about this type of experience, including its most diabolical expressions, is that it is *fundamental* and *revelatory*: fundamental because it grounds consciousness's encounter with its objects, and revelatory to the extent that it usually illustrates the significance of this encounter, participating in the construction of meaning that always remains provisional although urgent. On the other hand, an agent that manipulates the phenomena or the consciousness that experiences them does not exist within the enchantment such as we have represented it here. There is no magician or shaman. Everything happens as if chance were taking shape on its own, and simultaneously and permanently adjusting the consciousness of whoever endures it.

When "this world" begins to take shape, to define its limits, to uncover a disenchanted face subdued by rules and resistances, there arises within the subject of the experience the need or the dream of breaking its logic, of transcending it, of producing miracles and marvels in a way that allows the person to act on it and dominate it. Behind this type of consciousness resides the idea that whoever has been capable of creating the world from their own experience will also be able to recreate it on a whim. Magic, that innocent opening to the world and its phenomena, is tainted with intent. It is stained white, in the practice of the shamans and the medicine men, in the rituals of fertility and exorcism; it is stained black in the hands of the witches and the emperors, in voodoo rituals or the black mass. Here the figure of the mediator appears, of someone who knows the "occult sciences" or maintains a privileged relationship with beings from another world, regardless of whether they are gods or magnetic properties. I define **witchcraft** as that disenchanted kind of magic experience in order to distinguish it from the former term, although the word "witchcraft" is often used synonymously with "spell" or "incantation". This word is also often attributed to a certain state of amorous possession that could fit within this framework. Witchcraft, presently based on diabolical, magnetic or sexual powers, is radically different from enchantment to the extent that it implies a prior knowledge that remains hidden from most people, and to the extent that it seeks to produce a favorable effect on someone's interests. Its goal is domination, whether it is the ignorant majority being dominated by the initiated minority, or nature that does not yield to my desires.

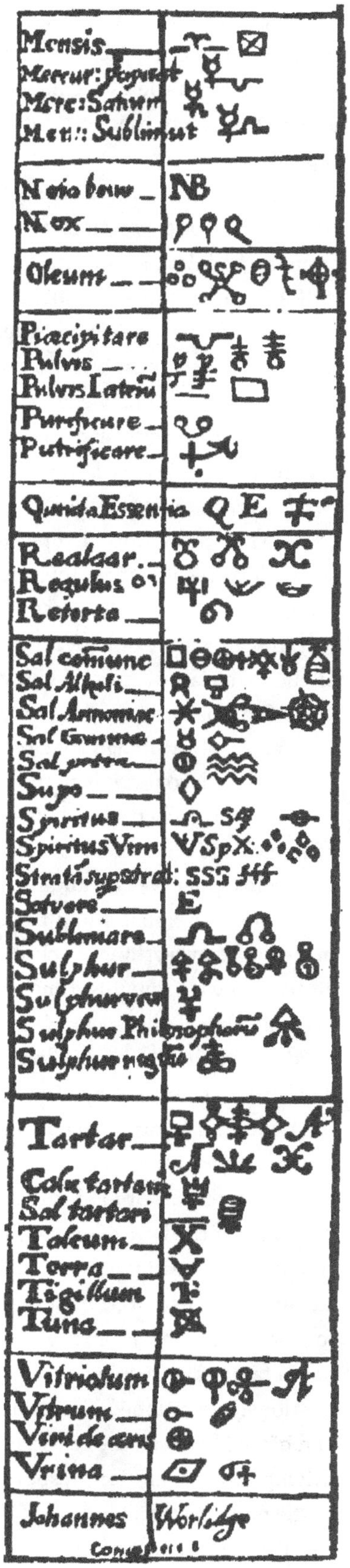

There exists a certain continuity between the power-lust of this disenchanted, magical mentality (determined to force the natural course of things and people) and the realized miracle of technology, to the point where it is possible to say that all of it has absorbed our entire capacity for surprise and belief. The traces of this continuity are already manifested in Modern Europe with the theories and practices of the naturalist magicians from the Renaissance: Paracelsus, Agrippa, Raymond Lull or Roger Bacon himself, who is recognized as the father of the scientific method. Even though these magicians still believed that their capacity to intervene dominatingly in events resided in knowledge and their adherence to the laws of nature, they still demanded scientific recognition for their activities: as Della Porta said in his canonical writing *Magia Naturalis* (1558), magicians did not need to resort to the action of supernatural beings or powers to produce results that, for a modern mind still in its infancy, still would have passed for marvelous.

In reality, they did not renounce the mysterious aura of the magician, carrier of knowledge inaccessible to all and of special powers "over the energies and abilities of nature" — an image that recounted a long tradition in line with Neoplatonism and which dates back to the pre-Socratics, when the division between the spheres of knowledge and philosophy still had not occurred and the philosopher was simultaneously a mathematician, a physician, a moralist and a transmitter of the founding principle of everything. Such is the case of Empedocles, better known from his time as thaumaturge than as natural philosopher, or of Pythagoras, who besides making definitive contributions to mathematics developed an entire mystical doctrine about numbers for which he became the main prophet and priest. A thousand years later Newton himself, who established the fundamentals of modern mechanics and claimed the discovery of the laws of gravity, carried out thorough and convincing investigations in such dubious fields as the alchemical transmutation of the elements and the search for the elixir of life. He first gave an animistic explanation of his famous principle of gravity, not unlike that of the previously mentioned Empedocles, who spoke of love and hatred between the celestial bodies as a fundamental driving force of motion, responsible for the consistency of the material world.

For sure, we are referring to a time in which the religious factors that influenced knowledge were still very strong. If science was developing, it was done within the framework of a world image strongly marked by the beliefs of this order, and the temptation to do so outside of this framework was strongly suppressed, as Galileo or Bruno knew very well. It was also certain that modern science had not yet developed a technology of its own. Although technical knowledge existed, a technological ideology had not yet taken shape, which was not to become established as an absolute reference point until well into the twentieth century, once the process of secularization had been completed. It was when science unfolded all of its power during the belligerent confrontations that marked the past century that technology became acknowledged as an ideology of our era. But from the start, science as an idea (and accompanied by its methods) made its way through Europe, with the singular purpose of *knowing* (not of dominating the world), and technical knowledge, as an application of the scientific method, developed within those pious limits of obedience to the laws of nature, and whenever possible did so without openly colliding with the supernatural world. But in this naturalist vision of magic, and in reference to the occult powers that furnish the initiated, the kernel of science already exists entirely cast within its practical dimension, bound to the self-interested domination of the evolution of things and people.

Technology has become capable of producing effects of which our most credulous ancestors could not have dreamed, those who read Jules Verne and who discerned within the project of Enlightenment, extended to all fields, the hope of a coming of age and of a liberation of humankind: freedom from fear and superstition, from humans' domination of one another, from sickness, and from the overwhelming immensity of the world. It is doubtful that technology, as a point of reference in our lives, has provided great advances in all of these areas. Like the obsolete gods, not only has it become a source for all hope: it has also been able to instill fear and respect for its definitive capacity for destruction. It has been able to coexist and adapt itself to the way of magical thought based on witchcraft: one can find on the internet programs for consulting the I-Ching or ancient runes, and apocalyptic utopias are cropping up everywhere, now saturated with a science-fiction esthetic. Far from making itself democratic, technology has not ceased to develop innovations that increase its abilities from one year to the next, spreading unequally within different groups as a function of very distinct interests. And while we are being liberated from the old infections, there are new allergies, immuno-deficiencies, and mysterious illnesses emerging in which many discern the evolutionary transition that is about to occur. The most advanced scientists, required to confront the limits of their specific fields of knowledge, acknowledge fundamental, irresolvable problems that oblige them to limit themselves to a kind of technological behaviorism: we are capable of deducing how things work, but not of defining them, or understanding why they function as they do. As long as the range of our knowledge expands, then so does the field of our ignorance.

Despite this, we continue expecting everything from technology, from the Holy Trinity shaped according to the sages by Biotechnology, Nanotechnology and Infotechnology, which foretell the future paradigm shift. We dream of being immortal thanks to technology, and there are people who say that this will become possible when we can all keep a small container of stem cells in our freezer. But what is the point of repairing my cellular damage if anybody can kill me with the latest ingenious molecular disintegrator in order to steal my wallet? Or if I might die, young and innocent, in a military battle or a terrorist attack carried out thanks to the latest technologies?

Technology, as an ideology that affirms that every problem will have its technical solution (and implicitly, that every imaginable horror will have a feasible expression), has become the depositary of the Gospels and the Final Judgment. But not without our experience having suffered a certain weakening of the illusion of it, ritually relegated to the scenic domain as illusionism, since we understand that basically everything obeys a simple trick. We are able to contemplate without emotion the more amazing spectacles; we trust the Supreme Powers without hesitation and with fake smiles; beauty attacks our senses in waves until losing its meaning; horror, which will not kill us, instead nourishes us (we do not yet feel such a shiver). And we have avoided hope because we anticipate the future in advance. We have learned to be disappointed rather than getting our hopes up. The marvelous passes before our eyes at full speed, without leaving trace or trail. When everything becomes feasible, when it is sufficient to dream about something just so that commericialism can present it to you in three dimensions, it becomes difficult to linger within the enchantment of discovery.

Magic does not exist, but technology promises much more. But there is something that still stands in the way of this transition from enchantment to witchcraft and from the latter to this trickery, something that we have to search for again within the gaze of the child, or, if we are up to it, within that primal experience that gave shape to our world with its myths and taboos. This is something that still surprises us, as if it were not aware of having been exiled, as uncertainty is, or when for whatever reason it shatters our dreams. Sphinxes along the path that, despite so many concrete answers, still find us naked, improvised and insane. Modernity has triggered the fragmentation of knowledge, the paradigm shifts, the renunciation of metaphysics, and all of its deciphering leaves us in a void of meaning, a complete demotivation. Our experience of the world could be undergoing a process that Walter Benjamin pertinently analyzed regarding the impact of technical reproducibility on the reception of works of art, a kind of *deauratization* with ambiguous consequences. We would speak, then, of a *deauratization of the world*, based on the technological experience that we have of it.

Benjamin defines the aura, in connection with contemplating works of art, as "the unique phenomenon of a distance, however close it may be"[2]. Its fall, related to the apparition of increasingly sophisticated techniques for reproducing images, comes to entail the loss of the work of art's cultural value, of its depth and its setting within tradition (that is, a great part of its meaning), in favor if its mere exhibitory value. Benjamin endeavored to list the positive aspects of the process, given its inevitable character: the autonomy of the work in relation to its context of production, its accessibility to the masses and consequent democratization, the confirmation of a new social dimension of art that replaced its old, religious and authoritative dimension... But in the end, all of Benjamin's work constitutes a call for attention to the need to re-enchant experience, whether through allegorical strategies that fill the void left by the symbol, or through a kind of *profane illumination* that does not yet strive for the revelation of a totality, but which instead adapts to the fragmentary and dislocated nature of our modern perception.

What such deauratization would mean in relation with our world experience would be something much more serious. Under the assumption that it could be carried out completely, it would imply the loss of depth of all experience; it would drag along with it the forces of the imagination and would mean the renunciation of all possible elaboration of meaning that did not come from outside. Restoring the enchantment of our worldly experience becomes a task all the more urgent as it appears increasingly improbable. Improbable because it cannot overcome a technological way of life that has imposed its norm as a condition of life, and cannot relapse into a devalued form of witchcraft, whose degraded manifestations are imposed on consciousness as publicity, commercialism or new technologies. Ultimately, it cannot accept any sort of decline, nor live within a stagnation that is definitely threatening it.

The total crisis, announced months ago by the active forces of the economy, and years ago by certain visionaries with radical points of view, can end up manifesting itself as a deeper crisis of consciousness than any cultural change might trigger. Here and there some people know (through applying scientific knowledge or intuition) that it is not about a failure of the system, but about a system-failure. It is not a runaway missile or a maniac on the loose: something is buckling within the building's foundations. Our concept of the world, the fundamentals of our experience, the value and meaning of all things will have to be revised. While people still do not yet repudiate the technological development which has given our world the *speed* which prevents us from stepping out of it, it appears that all of the great problems have their roots in this same development: exhaustion of energy resources, global warming, the spread of explosive devices that turn armies into cynical "missionaries of peace"...

But perhaps we are overcome by a problem with a more radical nature, a fundamental problem that gives rise to others and which produces impotence when we confront them: the loss of the authenticity of our experience overwhelmed by the flux of simulations, the perfect elimination of a "real world" on which to rest our feet, the devaluation of the marvelous and the predominant rule of the unusual, the fragmentation of the imagination within thousands of recurrent fantasies, without any effective capability, which ends up being very useful when the time comes for classifying frustrations, and the absence of comprehensive discourses that give meaning to our daily struggle. This is the situation that turns rebellion on the sensible level into a radical issue, and no longer a colorful addendum sustained by peripheral vanguards who are basically satisfied with their role because they are satisfied with everything else.

The demand of the amplification of experience, of its candid opening to the possible marvelous, still does not rise against conditioned boredom, nor does it take pleasure in its messianic creativity: changing the ways that individuals relate to each other and with the world is a question of life and death. Desire, hitherto ignored, has now become a necessity.

Notes:

1. Translators' note: In the 1980s there was a children's program on TV called *La bola de cristal* that referred to the new Spanish youth of *La Movida*. The program lyrics were: "*Te sientas enfrente, es como el cine, todo lo controla, es un alucine*" (You sit in front of it / It's like a movie / It controls everything / It's a delusion).
2. Walter Benjamin, "The Work of Art in the Age of Mechanical Reproduction", translated by Harry Zohn, in *Illuminations: Essays and Reflections*, Schocken Books: New York, 1968, page 222.

Translated by Eric Bragg & Bruno Jacobs
Salamandra – Intervención surrealista – imaginación insurgente – crítica de la vida corriente, #17/18, Madrid, 2008, pp. 13-18.

Don Quixote, photograph by Paul Cowdell

Object Assemblage, made and photographed by Alex Fatta

Clock Dress by Lisa Simmonson

Four Stories From "The Starlit Dog"

Dale Houstman

I. The Royal Marriage Hits A Small Obstruction

A rudderless boat carried a young woman named Vienna toward Vienna, artistically shuffling between high tragedy and a miscarriage of justice by the deft manipulations of abstract responsibilities and secret algorithms deeply rooted in the young lady's profound connection to the boat, which had been constructed from her childhood bed, then lightly sprinkled with ivy in the shape of a green piano climbing up a wall and very nuanced in its evocation of the fading national coal industry, to which the young woman had been both patroness and whore for over 15 years.

Meanwhile…

A keyless piano rolled down a hill, carrying a young man named Vienna away from Vienna, moving reductively between upward cultural pressure and the drag of scholarly irritation by the deft manipulation of comfortably spaced organs and the instant skepticism that clung sporadically to the young man's parenthetical devotion to the fleeing piano, which had been constructed from a Turkish bath he had slept in when he was only a child, and given unassailable status with the addition of an embedded oboe in the shape of a rudderless boat pregnant with Napoleon's Josephine and very nuanced in its evocation of a rural crossroad full of grey mule slippers.

Let's just sit here and wait for the end to arrive.

II. The Mediterranean Snail And The Faithless Bride

Once upon a teatime, in a neighborhood of quaint wig shoppes and even quainter baby brothels, a wedding drew only the curious and the failed, as a delicate bell tinkled beneath the Bride's veil to announce the advent of another disturbing conversation about the dark back bedroom, which – but for the cultural monkey chained to the bedstead – appeared to be merely another bourgeois fantasy made real by too much money. But, alas, the secular humanists are not part of this tale. Let's discuss the Mediterranean Snail.

The silly parents of the silly Bride had purchased for her – from a passing drifter – a tiny infant daughter, to spare her the social embarrassment of childbirth, which had killed the beloved Princess Unadora, the Bride's older sister. This young Gypsy baby had a small red snail trapped in her ear, and the parents were informed – by another drifting stranger – that it was indeed a rare Mediterranean Snail. This was not totally unexpected, because – in her pretty little nose – lived a Caucasian Slink, and these two facial animals liked to send messages to one another via a miniature pulley system they had constructed from snail shells, slink skin, and hair from the baby's eyelashes. The Snail – an altogether suspicious sort – accused the Slink of being of "cosmopolitan" descent, while the Slink for his part was convinced that the Snail's one real charm was how he rode out earthquakes, with a fragile Continental *joie de vivre.* A Fox ran the pulley system for the two haughty facial animals, and took his pay by removing some vowels from each missive and selling them to a Hedgehog in a nearby Homburg Hat full of Worker Bees. This Fox weekended in Moscow and often wiped his plate clean of honey with a slice of bread stolen from the Snail.

And so, a certain air of marital accord was sustained by an elaborate system of pulleys and gluttony and suspicion, freeing up a lot of government energy and finances to wage several wars in which the Bride's future husbands all died.

The end.

III. The Rapacious Tree-Child

The Shopkeeper was happy and contented, as he led his new Bride, Rape Seed, to his tiny shop, where he was joyfully received by his workers, who were deathly afraid of him. It was a marvelous occasion and the future looked bright for certain (although not many) people.

Yet – each night in the tiny, cold bedroom – the woman wept. Finally, two of her tears gained voices, one that of a girl and one that of a boy, and they told her (in small wet words) that they were the wandering souls of her two younger siblings, whose bodies lived in wretchedness in a faraway desert, and who all ate nothing but roots and dust and cried because they were separated from their dear sister. So Rape Seed resolved to escape from this life of dull commerce and wander about the desert until she could find them, and thus regain some joy.

Then Rape Seed turned to the house cat, who was actually a jinn, and he told her to let down her own hair into the muddy street below and then climb down it to freedom. So she let down her hair (which was easy for she had long golden tresses) and then climbed down it (which was difficult, but she was a resourceful beauty), and when she had reached the stones below, she cut off her locks and hung them from a hook in the window. Then she went searching for the desert.

"Ah, you stupid child!" cried the cat-jinn as they strolled along, "for you might have needed that hair to climb up something later." They then agreed that the cat would keep its own counsel until it was asked for, and then Rape Seed wove a ladder from the cat's fur, just to show her that she was not entirely lacking in imagination, and used that ladder to climb upon a giant red horse that waited outside the village's gates. The horse (named Get Down) was so handsome that Rape Seed assented to marry him once they had found her lost siblings and freed them from the terrible desert, and in general spoke to the huge beast as though he were an old friend. They rode for many miles over rough ground until the horse grew tired, then he used the cat fur ladder to climb up into a great tree, where they fell asleep for the night.

When it had grown very dark, Rape Seed unwound the ladder and made a wig for herself, for she was now entirely bald. And the cat/jinn awoke and said "Ah! you stupid child! What will you now use to climb out of this great tree with, for you have ruined the ladder, and only to satisfy your own vanity." They then agreed (again) that the cat would keep its own counsel until it was asked for, and so they went to sleep.

And that was the end of the first day.

When the cat awoke, Rape Seed was standing behind one of the large limbs of the great tree, listening to the leaves singing about her home, which was so charming that he stood quite still (though perched upon Get Down) and watched. and this was the song that the tiny leaves sang:

"Through the forest
To the tower
There's the door
Of solitude.
Unfasten the lock
But watch the hour
For here come the armies
Of disquietude."

Well, stupid enough, you'll agree, but the cat (although now quite hairless) was moved by the plaintive chant, and climbed over to be with her mistress. It was then that the cat noticed a window set into one of the grand limbs far above their heads, and a small white figure leaning out over them. Taking some stairs that mysteriously appeared before her feet, the cat ascended to the portal, until it came face-to-face with the most beautiful child under the sun.

"Hello, what is your name. and how might we assist you?" asked the naked cat. But the little child only went on crying, saying that there was no door in her room so that she might escape her lonely fate. The cat's heart (usually a flinty thing) was softered by the poor child's lament, and so he helped her climb through the window on his tail, and onto the limb, where they could both descend to Get Down and Rape Seed. Then, using the hair from the giant horse's magnificent tail, they fashioned a pulley to lower each and all to the ground which was littered with small pieces of red crockery.

But the child – having been so long in her prison – was terribly afraid of the wide world, and hid behind the giant horse, so that both the cat and Rape Seed (looking rather hideous in her odd cat wig) had to make her a salad from the surrounding vegetation in hopes of comforting her. It tasted so good to her that she then longed for three times as much, and so they wasted the entire day (and much of the night) feeding the dear orphan until she was a large as the giant horse, which so disgusted them all that they fled from her and into the forest to hide.

And that was the end of the second day.

The next day, as they rode along toward the desert, they were followed constantly by the huge child (who was unusually swift for such a huge person) who kept begging for more salad at the top of her voice, and soon the trio looked quite pale and miserable, for they knew that they had no more of it to give, even if they had wanted to, which they didn't.

Then they came to the desert (a desert dreaded by all the world), but no one dared go into it because it was surrounded by a great wall made of snakeskin, and even God avoided the place. They sat down at the very edge of the sands and fell to wishing vainly for surcease, while the agonized voices of the lost siblings hung in the air, and the rapacious tree-child (who was now as large as the tree she had been imprisoned in) kept on screaming at them for more salad.

And thus ends the tale. And not a minute too soon.

Falling Down by Lisa Simmonson

IV. The Lynx-Eyed Bride

Once upon a mildewed beach, the Lynx-Eyed Bride strolled with her wet baggage toward home and a chilling plate of boiled clams. She was quite wise and very capable as used-up persons go, and so she gave a little rhyming speech to the ocean as she struggled along…

"Explanations are so domestic,
And choices ruin each day.
I'd rather be a schoolmarm…"

And then her mouth just blew away.

Poems and Images by

J. K. Bogartte

(Poems selected from **The Wolf House**, La Belle Inutile Éditions, 2009)

I

A tree of sight with seeing leaves, as luminous as the body relieved of its memory, unraveled by its tedious ancestors, or without sleep, its eggs spinning in the doorway. The bright air is bleeding slowly, like burning film when the dream interrupts a backward glance.

II

In the passageway between light and dark, where you align yourself in molecular fashion against her linen seductively smoldering in the grass, where the dew-igniting armatures, with their Quetzal tails, dazzle the voyeurs in their dream kingdoms, fermenting beneath the shimmering tables of feral potions and elixirs... where knives are kissing. Only her shadow remains in the wetness of noon, strung between the magnetic poles of disorientation and sheer bliss... It is all dressed in one fell swoop. Spectacles are discarded. The owl's coat covers your escape.

III

The oxide of herons chasing the lithium of a body leaning against its vision, sacrificed for the beautiful glow-worm rituals, and formed by the fusion of the two clavicles that guide the fire and water of your fundamental forces. *Without her the analogue is useless. The paragon is unspoken... No one moves this way through this light, or vanishes without the serum of infinite speculation...*

IV

It is the center of identity, where the chemist and his shadow exchange reflections in the espionage of invented mythologies, where love and delirium hurl their fatal stones, and spin their long-haired cylinders in the dark gowns of an avalanche—where you, when you are close, when you are slender as a thought and more than a shade, are animated by the griffon of erratic aerials long since outlawed in the provinces, and in the warehouses of hysteria—where there is nowhere to go except where the Royal Solution sets up its outrageous barricades and its reckless scaffolding according to the smoke and water that is the blood of your face. Your face, betrayed by scorpions...

V

The diviners in black coats, with their feet of river and hermeneutic ribcages, are dabbling in the opium of miraculous poses... You lean this way against the light, and glowing with dark sensations, like optical roots changing places with both presence and absence in the esplanade of a thousand orphic disguises. What venom is in the beauty of the magic of what is not real, but against all that is, wherever it can be seen... The hissing of light, you see it as base metal rusting with kisses.

VI

The moon in its unorthodox position, when it ignites the channels of her vast undertaking with dragonroot and heretic alignments, she would not release you from your peregrinations—and the lunar aspect would collide with the lethargy of the sea captain whose great wheel knew more than the planetary void that guided his thoughts of reality and its overloading circuits.

VII

You exist in the penumbra at the edges of the mirror's shadow, where the water rises upwards along the explicit refractions of those who sleep beyond the moment of waking, and those whose expressions of desire intimidate the freshly oiled bodice of an evening's rotating precipice. The antlers of reality are clashing in the roses of a Minoan spyglass, revealing the strange and twittering words of an insoluble romance. Sleeping with the animals...

VIII

The liquids that stream from her mouth at the beginning of a dream follow almost exclusively the high-pitched winnowing of the puppets and the insolent chimera looming in the woods from various distant countries, along fire-lanes of perception that lead you with panting and triangular flares, through the rustling of the leaves when they glow in the hallways and crystallize across the windows, are held together by the breath of lovers.

IX

The owl-man's flying wolf eating its wings in the great hall of whispering, in the moonlit caverns, in the cabinet of amazing lures, in that instance when the lightning is born from spores and the spirit unleashes its red ink in every direction, deep in the fibers of a graceful and sublime mimicry... The engravers never sleep past the hour of their disguises. Their notebooks are outlined with green suns and darknesses that never reach the page. Nights of gold...

X

Your return to innocence in the ambivalent territories near the city of a last resort, your emergence in the unreasonable zones and forbidden places where desire grooms and replicates, your fires, your barely remembered signals and signs, your fading in and out, your chemicals, your flowering cells, bursting origins, glistening pods and dripping seeds. You are the reflection of senses unlike your own, emitting magical substances—she is never at the point of divulging her secrets, and she hoards them like serpents or benevolent weapons shaped by discoveries in abandoned observatories.

XI

Your reflection is the imposter that lives your life elsewhere, in splendor. *The vagueness of your shape precedes you. Only your eyes are real.*

XII

"I come to you often in the night, when you sleep, and wander around in your dreams rearranging the places you visit, and pull the thread of your presence as if it were my own, newly susceptible to what is unique in your direction, to what suffers from my absence when you wake—but then, just moments before light comes in through whatever door confounds your sense of reason, I manage to slip out of the landscape like the sound of smooth branches rubbing together and rustling, burning beneath the sheets like twin streams awaiting the sun... and I am gone, a vague sense of something forgotten, not even a barely audible sigh..."

XIII

In the wolf house the witch's sun is black and forbidding, and the statues would not relinquish the strange vessels of their thought, nor defy the privileges of wonder and deception, and for each shadow casting that crosses your path, they dissolve in the light that takes its body from the water at midnight, and wanders aimlessly through the stages of changing, when firing the invention, or hunting the gatherers... In your efforts to remain indifferent, and highly amused, there is a sealing of the hermetic, and a stoning of the philosophers; there is the crafting of witches and the surmounting of the real...

XIV

Your language of silver-white crystals, anomalous pigments, the flash of knives under the arcades, the tripod of swinging jackals, that woman dressed in colonies of bees, in the madness of daring angles and close calls, of falling and flying, and long, endless corridors that open in the coliseum of unnatural revelations that change your disguise in the blink of an eye, from one conjuration to another. The danger of liaisons in the chamber of the bride with her tuning fork and her fissures of enchanted disproportion...

XV

The rules of the game are not to be taken seriously, and even that irresistible bodice of eels that summons you with its erotic diving gear has no meaning or lucidity without the most intoxicating paradox of suggestion. You abandon yourself to anathema with its charming objects and missing links. You release the captives and gamble on the elegance of a single, and most profound change of space—where your eyes are twittering beneath their opium-distilled lids of passing galaxies brush up against a moment of serene lunacy. You awaken in the rebis of the city. Your joy is iron.

XVI

The sexualities of plants and omens, the physical demeanor of the hummingbird with its feminine bottles of amaranthine fastened to trees of prophetic incest by the tripod of your voice and your perfume still coming from the Middle Ages, festooned to the moon in the water that often resembles your wishbone face... This was your language against language, your love against love, and the motors of resolution. Your axe grinding of light... Your seed...

XVII

Random acts of concealment and moon-seeds scattered by the magnifying-glass of the perpetually revealing Goddess machine, with its multiplying pentacles configured according to the self-aligning molasses of each radial and axial séance that meets you half way between here and there, rigged up to the furthest star in the nebula of Orion with the words beautiful and useless—when they meet in the corridor of a moments notice, there are irreverent sparks. This is where your signature is needed, and your blood required. You must refuse the antidote and the codes, the truths and the clarity... and when the Elixir Végétal de la Grande Chanteuse is passed from one mouth to the other, with the most profound affection bordering on madness, you must slay your shadow.

XVIII

In the stillness of a marvelous holding pattern, the spine-tingling motors are polishing the mandarin threads of night and day. Where the river ends, the flood begins its joyful wailing, and the hour is luminous. The humor of cruelty is especially beautiful.

XIX

She vowed always to love you more than words. She kept her promise, and died beside you in the silence of a dream... Her feet of cicadas. Her pale throat that always enchanted you, outlined by a scorpion... and a taste of anise on her tongue. Each morning at precisely 6am the world of appearances would rapidly reform itself and light up for those just waking, coughing up the dust of ominous gardens. Her nucleus spinning on the surface, folding the waves into mazes that hang intuitively from a mere reflection of consciousness. The rustling of prey. The howling prevails...

XX

The city ignites out of your central nervous system, and you arrive by déjà vu at the turn of the century, with the amorous recording machines that preserve the scents of bewilderment and transitions of each immaculate gesture, and arrange them according to birth dates and other astrological paradigms—as if to tempt the flowering djinn and other diabolical molestations in the streetlights guarding the city. A sultry walk through the phantom zones of consciousness, or waking up in the middle of the night without rhyme or reason... Reflection connected to sleep is no more than a diversion. One sleeps with passion and a furious disregard for mirrors.

XXI

She is your fleece with skin of laudanum and hair of antlers, lips of desirable cynosure and steam, and tongue of limpid pollen gathering in the face of danger and seduction beneath eyes of a total eclipse. The dawn slides into the hot, watery, translucent apparition of unbridled acrobatics (les saltimbanques de la réalité) in an occult gathering of golden cobwebs. She is always your double wheel. The light strikes your myth, renders you a feast for the indelible glance. Lepidoptera and quicksilver...

XXII

She swallows your dreaming fluids, salivating your dark and luscious nectar that glows, and spreading her legs for you with the licking of animals in a night spray of multiple deaths and resurrections, hovering over the inside of your center, starless and panting, and self-impregnating... a brief handful of shimmering cells. This night stays longer than all the rest, and the waking is bright with pain and the phantom healing of the wind. Sown and cultivated, each of your individual elements and your solutions balanced between gypsy women and talismans that burn your hands. You crawl out of the dark soaked in ancient pleasures.

XXIII

The doors of pandemonium slowly open the bathing bodies that chose in unison not to remember, but rather forcing premonition as a key to being where one desires. Neither awake nor asleep... you wander the thoughts that compel your illuminations out of the forest, veiled and harsh, in the shape of carnivorous moths, restless and mournful. The lamps that embrace them, and the sister of your hunger that covets their appetite by surrendering to them.

XXIV

The underground rivers and lights, the mayhem of a tropical storm that burns the ribcage of the sleeper who dreams of lightning as a soft and compliant source of discontent, a battleground of malicious roses emitting the pure phoenix of your eyes, in the dark rain that leads you, aligns your masts to the spinning, aberrant wedding gown of a marvelous hemorrhage that cools in the first fire... the splendid vase of your breath, a daughter of lace-making and precious insects whispering in unison. Wandering in another country, gambling in thorns. She leans against you, drawing blood.

XXV

Spinning around in the room that unravels the midnight stroll from the Aurora Borealis, one amorous caress after another, without regard for endangerment or squalor, leaves no room for hesitation. A certain grace, with details bordering on obsession, a severely proportioned glance like a haunted key that opens the wedding night doused with tungsten as an imaginary potion, and the procession of watchmakers who know neither night nor day... A moral imperative more sublime than murder.

XXVI

Across the central layer of everything that is deliberate and concealed, the moon forms a skeletal vantage point from which the brides in their passion release the wolves and the children at the very same moment. Beneath the fire that arches body-wise and spectral in its chemical nature, the site of being is unmoved and pristine as it was since the beginning of time, and where you come to the realization of a murderous joy and a maddening evocation. Only the illusion of time can reveal your conflict and your nature. The dream destroys you and makes you real...

Ernst Bloch and Surrealism

Michael Löwy

I had the good fortune to meet Ernst Bloch in person. Our encounter took place in 1974, in his apartment in Tübingen, not far from the school where – as he often liked to recall in his writings – in 1789 the young Hegel, Schelling and Hölderlin planted a freedom tree to celebrate the French Revolution. He was already 89 years old, virtually blind, but his mind was impressively sharp.

Among the remarks he made during our discussion, there was one which greatly struck me, and which sums up a whole lifetime's obstinate loyalty to the idea of utopia:

> The world as it exists *is not true*. There exists a second concept of truth which is not positivistic, which is not founded on a declaration of facticity [...], but which is instead loaded with value (*wertgeladen*) – as, for example, in the concept "a true friend," or Juvenal's expression *Tempestas poetica* – that is, the kind of storm one finds in a book, a poetic storm, the kind that reality has never witnessed, a storm carried to the extreme, a radical storm and therefore a *true* storm, in this case in relationship to aesthetics, to poetry; in the expression "a true friend," in relationship to the sphere of morality. And if that doesn't correspond to the facts – and for us Marxists, facts are only reified moments of a process – in that case, *too bad for the facts* (*um so schlimmer für die Tatsachen*), as Hegel said in his late period.[1]

The references here are Latin and Germanic, but, reading these words, one is irresistibly reminded of an old Jewish quality, perfectly described by a well-known Hebrew and Yiddish term: *chutzpah*. It is obvious that this attitude, which invests poetic truth with a power infinitely superior to that of "real facts", is of no little interest to surrealists.

Bloch's philosophy of hope is above all a theory of the *Not-Yet-Being*, in its various manifestations: the Not-Yet-Conscious of the human being, the Not-Yet-Become of history, the Not-Yet-Manifest in the world. In his research on the anticipatory workings of the human spirit, dreams occupy an important place, from their most everyday form – the daydream – to the "forward dream" inspired by wishful images.

His greatest work, *The Principle of Hope*, is an immense and fascinating journey through the *past*, in search of images of desire and landscapes of hope, scattered among the many varieties of utopia – social, medical, architectural, technical, philosophical, religious, geographical, musical and artistic. What is at stake in this very specific, and typically Romantic, modality of the dialectic between the past and the future *is the discovery of the future in the aspirations of the past* – in the form of *an unfulfilled promise*: "The rigid divisions between future and past thus themselves collapse, unbecome future becomes visible in the past, avenged and inherited, mediated and fulfilled past in the future."[2] The point is not to sink into a dreamy and melancholic *contemplation* of the past, but to make it a living source of revolutionary *action*, of a *praxis* oriented towards the achievement of utopia.

The necessary complement to anticipatory thought, which focuses on the world to come, is a critical stance towards *this world*: the vigorous indictment of industrial/capitalist civilisation and the harms it causes is one of the principal (often unrecognised) themes of *The Principle of Hope*. Bloch pillories the infamy and relentless ignominy of the current business world – a world of general swindling, in which the thirst for profit suffocates any other human feeling.[3]

If his discourse of hope sometimes veers towards excessive optimism, we should remember that he very explicitly criticises what he calls "that banal, automatic progress-optimism".[4] Arguing that this false optimism has a dangerous tendency to become a new opium of the people, he even thinks that "a dash of pessimism would be preferable to the banal, automatic belief in progress as such. Because at least pessimism with a realistic perspective is not so helplessly surprised by mistakes and catastrophes."[5] Consequently he insists on the "objective unguaranteedness"[6] of utopian hope.

It was around 1928 that Bloch became more directly interested in surrealism. At that time he compiled certain notes which would later be published in his book *Heritage of Our Times* (1935) under the title "Thinking surrealisms". In fact his familiarity with surrealism was very limited: the only references are to Chirico's metaphysical painting, Max Ernst's collages and Aragon's *Paris Peasant*. Bloch seems to be unaware of the *Manifesto*, Breton's writings, and the movement's collective documents and journals. He incorrectly describes Walter Benjamin's book *One-Way Street* (1928) as an expression of a "surrealistic philosophizing" whose method is supposedly the "polish and montage of fragments" which are unconnected to each other.[7] Strangely, he seems not to have read Benjamin's remarkable 1929 essay on surrealism, which would have enabled him to have an altogether more serious understanding of the movement. Here and there Bloch seems intuitively to have grasped something of the nature of the movement: for example, when he speaks of surrealism as both a "mixture of dream-styles" and the means by which that mixture's "hieroglyphs are reinforced in order to be strangely relevant".[8] In these notes one can sense a real sympathy, but also a serious lack of understanding: thus the term "montage" often recurs in these passages to designate the nature of surrealism, which is thereby reduced to a technique for producing "a kind of crystallisation on the chaos that has come".[9] He also defines surrealism as "an aesthetically isolated dynamite", the aim of which is to "put rotting substances, dream substances into the gaps in the world".[10] The great philosopher, to put it mildly, had not grasped the true ambition of the movement founded by Breton and his friends in 1924.

Thus the interest of Ernst Bloch's work for surrealists lies not in his comments on surrealism, but rather in the food for thought his work can offer, in the subversive and creative strength of his concepts.

This is especially true of the idea which is the red thread from which his whole oeuvre is woven: *utopia*. Opening a surrealist window onto this landscape, Guy Girard notes: "Utopia introduces the subversive ludic dimension into the logos of history and politics, to which it concedes neither the privilege of reason nor dogmatic necessity. It is the mental nowhere where the imaginary sets up a geography of the 'Principle of Hope' (Bloch), it is the terrain of play where the imaginary children of dreamt phalansteries meet the refractory memory which the utopians, those poets of social palingenesis, retain as much from their own childhoods as from the mythicised childhood of the world."[11]

The concept of the *utopian surplus* sheds light on this subversive power: for Bloch it refers to everything which – in ideologies, symbols, archetypes and allegories – exceeds, overflows or transgresses the limits put in place by the established order and which tends towards the Not-Yet-Being. This also applies, of course, to works of art, which, insofar as they are not simple commodities, always include a utopian "window". And interesting example of the way in which he uses this cognitive tool is his analysis of alchemy: for him, the philosopher's stone is a "utopian jewel", in which historical change and the transfiguration of the world are intimately mixed together, thanks to "chemical chiliasm".[12]

One of Bloch's richest concepts, from the surrealist point of view, is that of the *daydream*: the free construction of palaces among the clouds, the creation of wishful images and wishful landscapes, with eyes wide open. The kingdom of daydreams is, according to Bloch, a "conservation area, withdrawn from the reality principle".[13] Between such diurnal dreams and nocturnal dreams there are reciprocal exchanges, troubling and strangely premonitory mutual immersions. There are parallels here with the communicating vessels. As Guy Girard observes, daydreams "exceed any possibility of concrete realisation and remain irreducible to it, just as in love the desire to desire exceeds and sustains desire".[14]

Philosophy is an integral part of research into the Marvellous. Surrealism has taken great interest in Heraclitus, Novalis and Hegel. We have discovered, during the last few years, elective affinities with Ernst Bloch. The participants in the Paris Surrealist Group met several times, during 2002, at the home of Marie Dominique Massoni, for the purposes of a collective journey on the continent of the Principle of Hope, exploring its luxuriant forests, and gathering here and there a few epistemological fruits. The aim was to test the pertinence of this work to surrealist thought and activity – in a nutshell, to "put Ernst Bloch in play".

It seemed to us that the best way to "practise" Bloch's ideas was to use them as inspiration for the invention of new surrealist games. Here then are those *acta ludica*, along with, in each case, their origin, their rules of play, and a few sample responses (from group members who were present).

I) Philozoophy (game proposed by Michael Löwy)

During our discussion in 1974, Ernst Bloch recalled the extraordinary friendship he enjoyed with Georg Lukàcs during the years 1912-1917: our ideas were so close, he remarked, that we were obliged to create "wildlife preserve" of our disagreements, to prevent them from disappearing.[15] I imagined that wildlife preserve populated with rare or endangered animals, each representing some disagreement between the two young "symphilosophers".

Rules of play: Choose at random a passage from a well-known philosophical work – Kant, Hegel or Merleau-Ponty, for example – and draw up a list of all the philosophical terms; then allocate each term to one of the players, who replaces it with an animal of his or her choice. The co-ordinator of the game gathers in the names of the animals and substitutes them for the concepts in the original text. The text thus becomes a document of philozoophy.

Example:

1. Original text:

"The sole aim [*but*] of philosophical enquiry is to eliminate the contingent. Contingency is the same [*la même chose*] as external necessity, that is, a necessity which in turn originates in causes which are no more than external circumstances. In history, we must look for a general design [*but*], the ultimate end [*but*] of the world, and not a particular end of the subjective spirit or mind" (GWF Hegel).[16]

2. Philozoophical version:
"The sole aphid of philosophical spiders is to eliminate flies. The tortoise is the same tapir as an external piranha, that is, a piranha which in turn originates in hens which are no more than external swallows. In the serpents' nest, we must look for a general aphid, the ultimate aphid of the world, and not a particular aphid of the subjective llama or octopus".

II) Daydream game (inspired by an image) (game proposed by Michael Löwy)

As we have seen, for Ernst Bloch, daydreams are the collection of thoughts, wishful images or projections of the future, of individuals in the waking state; he regards them as a sort of vivarium for the spirit of utopia, the birthplace, in everyday life, of the Spirit of Hope.

The daydream in this game is of a different nature, more specific, and closer to nocturnal dreams. It involves the invention – taking as its starting point a pre-selected image distributed to all the players – of a dream which takes place entirely within the image. The results are then compared and discussed.

The pre-selected image imposes certain constraints, but, as with Rorschach tests, it still allows each individual great freedom of interpretation and invention. This sort of "surrealist Rorschach" is an opportunity for each player to give free rein to his or her desires, narcissism, paranoia – critical or otherwise – and obsessions.

This dream with eyes wide open is close to the oneiric universe in the proper sense, insofar as its invention is not subject to any of the rules of ordinary narratives: realism, logical coherence, the chain of cause and effect, etc. The absence of these constraints leaves immense scope for the free play of the imagination, and for the construction of images infused with unconscious libido, as in nocturnal dreams. The images flow and combine almost as in an automatic text, but with a minimum of "narrativity" – or, rather, of pseudo-narrativity.

Obviously, daydreams are profoundly different from nocturnal dreams: they do not "function" in the same way, and their relationship with the unconscious is of a different nature. This is not a "simulacrum" of a sleeping dream, but another type of imaginary construction. It *communicates*, in a manner which requires further study, both with the nocturnal oneiric world and with the "ordinary" diurnal world.

What interests us in daydreams is not so much their analytical interpretation, or their premonitory value, but their *poetic quality*, the mystery and enigma of the images, the humour and absurdity of the situations, the Marvellous and the magic of fables.

Example:

Taking the following image as your starting point, create a daydream:

Sabine Levallois's daydream:
The blue firestorm shatters the mast of a wooden boat, which is destroyed. There is a dead child on the sand – a demon insults the sky.
Michael Löwy's daydream:
I am in Brazil, on a deserted beach. I have an extraordinary gift, which I am exercising for the first time: I can bring rain or good weather. A gesture of my left hand, and lightning blazes across the skies while thunder rumbles in the heights. A slight gesture of my right hand, and a hurricane is unleashed from the East, flattening everything in its path. I enjoy myself wildly in summoning and dispersing clouds, and I firmly intend to provoke some natural disasters before I decree the return of the sun.

Variation: daydreams guided by keywords

This game is played not with an image but with a collection of roughly ten keywords chosen at random. Everyone receives the same "kit" of keywords, and must use them to create the story of an imaginary dream.

Example:

The keywords are: monkey wrench, river, solstice, limestone, delights, pleasure, approach, ouch, flame, incredible.

Marie Dominique Massoni's daydream:
Madame Monkey Wrench is walking on the beach. Her feet, treading the fine sand which is so apt to nestle itself into the hems of skirts so that it can leak from them in town after winter, take her away from the navy on the river, reminding her of an old burn. Then her feet had carried her body quivering in the expectation of her first kiss, despite the burning pain of the blisters caused by the bite of the sand on this same beach one summer afternoon. Winter flame on solstice morning, she picks up a shellfish rind and dives into the feeling of the limestone at Fécamp and of Pearl Street, rendezvous for 11th January. Will she be there? She glides trembling at the water's edge, her love so close, in a luminous halo, intimate dance of air and water. Delights of light, the being's pleasure in all its parcels of time. Now the sun lights up the house where she was born during three nights of solstice. Finiteness of the gulf and of the line of the horizon, where she can see coasts, as in that mirage which is only possible every 70 years. Blisters, first kiss, not again. He approaches, the sand has given way to pebbles, his blisters are painful. Ouch! How the little one is suffering! An incredible mute greets her, she cannot believe her eyes. Subtle greed, the sun hangs over the mountain snow. She sends a sign to him who has named her Herring Gull and to her friend Alice Massénat. A red and black boat in the port of Lorient, as the hatches are opened to that which awakens, to that which the sea has left on the beach, to that sea like an antiphon to the coming year. Madame Monkey Wrench, on the skirts of the water, smiles at the Amazonian feathers she wears around her neck. HE approaches. SHE is a flame of water.

III) Orplid game

(game proposed by Michael Löwy)

The word "ORPLID" is cited by Ernst Bloch, in Volume I of *The Principle of Hope.*

Rules of play: Most of the participants do not know the origin of the name "Orplid". Each player is asked to imagine what it might mean.

Examples of responses:[17]

Masculine noun to designate the suffering of the lonely orphan who would like to be taken and rolled up in a warm fluffy blanket. (Anny Bonnin)

Brief instant preceding sleep, during which, as one's eyes close, one's perception of the ambient light is reduced to just a sliver of irradiant gold. The orplid fills the sleeper with its folds of gold. (Bertrand Schmitt)

Common noun, masculine by day, feminine by night: never used in the plural. Internal state characterised by current pleasure at a future encounter, which one feels will certainly take place, but of which one has no indication as to its nature, circumstances or occurrence. By adding adjectives relating to colour or borrowed from the vocabulary of the senses, one can specify the auratic vibration which accompanies it. Examples: *Till dawn Marie Dominique, prey to an imperious red and black orplid, scoured without success all the sleazy dives of the port of Saigon. A musky orplid guided Charles's steps towards the False Movement Bar.* (Joël Gayraud)

Liquid music which flows in our dreams when we are very tired. It is made from the sounds one has listened to during the day and from the juices of exotic plants. There is no music louder than the orplid, but as soon we awaken, we forget it. (Galini Notti)

Caribbean island where pirates of a libertarian communist persuasion used to share out the booty from Spanish galleons. The gold ingots were heated, folded and cut up into equal pieces. Hence the name of the island. (Michael Löwy)

Desiccation phase of anopheles.
(Marie Dominique Massoni)

Acronym for "Revolutionary Orchid of the Free Plains of the Interior of Sheets" ["*Orchidée Révolutionnaire des Plateaux Libres de l'Interieur des Draps*"]. (Dominique Paul)

Fish with green bones which has the power to fold gold nuggets. (Guy Girard)

Anonymous not-for-profit association meaning: "Observatory of the Palliative Reality of Unexplored Labyrinths of Evolution" ["*Observatoire de la Realité Palliative des Labyrinthes Inexplorés du Devenir*"], constituted at the end of the twentieth century by an international group of enlightened utopias. (Michèle Bachelet)

NB Michèle Bachelet provided a drawing depicting the Orplid.

NB In fact the word "Orplid" is the name of an imaginary utopian island, situated in the Pacific Ocean somewhere between New Zealand and Latin America, invented by the German Romantic writer Eduard Mörike (1804 – 1875) in his novel *Maler Nolten* ("The Painter Nolten"). Bloch cites it as an example of the utopian imaginary in literature.

Translated by Merl Fluin

Endnotes

1) Michael Löwy (1976) "Interview with Ernst Bloch," trans Vicki Williams Hill, *New German Critique* 9, pp.37-38.
2) Ernst Bloch (1995) *The Principle of Hope: Volume 1*, trans Neville Plaice et al, Cambridge MA, MIT Press, pp.8-9.
3) See Ernst Bloch, op. cit., and *The Principle of Hope: Volume 2*, trans Neville Plaice et al, Cambridge MA, MIT Press.
4) *The Principle of Hope: Volume 1*, p.198.
5) Ibid., p.199.
6) Ernst Bloch (1995) *The Principle of Hope: Volume 3*, trans Neville Plaice et al, Cambridge MA, MIT Press, p.1372
7) Ernst Bloch (1991) *Heritage of Our Times*, trans Neville & Stephen Plaice, Cambridge: Polity Press, p.337
8) Ibid., p.351.
9) Ibid., p.207.
10) Ibid., p.222.
11) Guy Girard (2004) *Hommage à Fourier*, postgraduate dissertation, Université de Paris I, pp.70-71.
12) *Principle of Hope: Volume 2*, pp.641-2.
13) *Principle of Hope: Volume 1*, p.97.
14) Guy Girard, *Hommage à Fourier*, p.88.
15) Löwy, op cit, p.36.
16) GWF Hegel (1980) *Lectures on the Philosophy of World History*, trans HB Nisbet, Cambridge, Cambridge University Press, p.28. [*Translator's note*: Where the French translation of Hegel differs from the English in ways which have a bearing on the results of the game (which of course was played in French with the French Hegel translation), the relevant French terms are indicated here in square brackets.]
17) *Translator's note:* Many of the responses that follow play on the fact that the name "Orplid" contains the French words *or* (gold) and *pli* (fold).

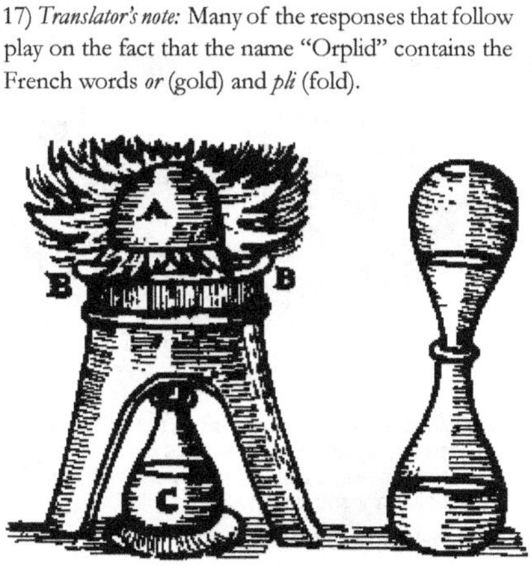

The New Moses, collage by Diamantis Karavolas

Exquisite Poem

The Rationalist smiled idiotically,
while snot streamed down his face.

Smoke rises from the house when
she takes her pants off.

The sky will rain cats and dogs when
the moon rises in the east.

Richard Burke, Susan Burke, Andrew Torch
(St. Louis Surrealist Group, Summer 2008)

LOVE FREEDOM FOREVER

a poem by

Raúl Henao

Translated by Philip West

I take a walk with a cloud
what a barber's devilry love is!
At every bus-stop you cast my way
the fire-raising pomegranate of your eyes.
The orchestra turning up in the middle
of a gushing fount
Bears a slight resemblance to your voice
building its nest in the rainbow of your breast
The storm turns out not quite so hot
as the coal on your lips
shuffled in your smile´s deck of cards.
It would take more than a thousand retrievers
to give full praise to the bright torch of your face
lighting up the weapon-bearing arm of freedom.

Volcano Explosion, collage by Diamantis Karavolas

The Way is under our feet
– Zen proverb

It is a sunny day early in autumn and I am on my way north to Stenungsund (town on the Swedish west coast) through the woods, which is a one day walk. Nice! I have also received wooden shoes and a thick wooden disk with braces to have on my back and enjoy a pleasant and warm journey.

The Way to Stenungsund, oneiric object by Bruno Jacobs

Skiz, drawings by Cinss [Çağrı Küçüksayraç]

The House

Miguel de Carvalho

A wave-house of green foam, a dissolving icy wind, a cry beyond the melting horizon. A bed of outstretched flanks where time and anguish meet in short pulses, rapid and severe, pulses of devouring love as rough he trails centrifugally upstream to the source of memory and gods.

A forest of mirrors and fleeting shadows of flaming perfume. Flying spirals, illegible words, blue mountains which enter sleep, fowl diving into fingers and throwing themselves against the magnolias. Everything trembles and throbs at the interior place, where primitive colours oxidise, clinging to the heart.

Another house, the forest-mirror-house of naked dancers, who are pure and undo the melody. A house where voices also dance, a house with interior balconies bending over white feathers. Intelligent waters and silken trees, mad and pure too, scalding themselves in the internal fire, tongues which breathe love on the tables and drink from the flower pots. The portraits move in the direction of the vertiginous kiss where distracted hills lie down with him.

I want to be a lover throughout the night and throughout the warm mouth, throughout the shipwreck of breasts in hands, throughout the night which exceeds the mouth while the shipwreck goes on.

I want to return to the house of the infinite flaming landscape and encounter the tree so as to die in love.

(late at night, 28th October 2006)
Translated by Merl Fluin

Ten Dreams

This text was produced as part of a series of games and experiments in collective dreaming. Five of us (Josie Malinowski, Merl Fluin, Nacho Díaz, Paul Cowdell and Stephen Maddison) each contributed written accounts of two recent dreams. Four of us then set to work to create a new dream text, using the cut-up technique. This new text in turn became the starting point for a new round of experiments in collective dreaming.

I am death who, with no top or bottom or sides or any animals or plants or anything, met an old friend from my undergraduate days – I think in Boston, although the river was the Thames. He looked dreadful – old, tired, and haggard. Stepping on a man's toe, he complimented me on how much my clothes suit me. My cat Lawrence got in trouble looking for a particularly tall, pale, dark-haired man who has a map and it's a garden, just water. I saw three dolphins leaping up in formation in front of me in a dark, calm ocean, and I was unable to kill them. Under a large iron bridge I found myself helping the Park Guards to shoot my floating father, and he was looking for his doppelgänger, who was wearing a burgundy velvet smoking jacket.

'Father, you are wearing an octopus.'

'I am unclear if the word "spiffy" was actually used to describe my attire.'

He looked similar to the dream about coastguards walking towards a river, who had been convicted of shooting a werewolf with its arms and with an old-fashioned flintlock rifle. Park Guards and hundreds of people with some rats living in my bedroom were milling about with maps looking for something – anything. By the time I reached the river they had gone. There was a dog at my heels like a rucksack. We appealed to the courts but it was the only appropriate phrase. I sliced off Stephen's thumb with a knife, for which the penalty is death. It was alive when you put it on, and it is dark and confusing. You've been wearing it for several days, and although she can't do it, in the dream I was asked to recruit rats and cats that I own in my waking life. I was my floating mother holding up a gun by the Spanish coastguards and English lifeboats. There was a maze, a sort of outdoors labyrinth at present in my house, but now it's dead and grey and dry.

I am walking down a street wearing my pyjamas around your neck, and its bulbous head hanging down over them, for an international rescue mission. As many people as possible have to be executed by my mother for extra cruelty.

The funny thing is that I am wearing a pale coat, but on the front of your body there are not rats.

Josie, Merl, Nacho, Paul
SLAG ~ Surrealist London Action Group
Lautréamont's birthday, 4th April 2007

Drawings by

Niklas Nenzén

OUR LADIES OF SORROW

Anesidora

Prunikos

Levana

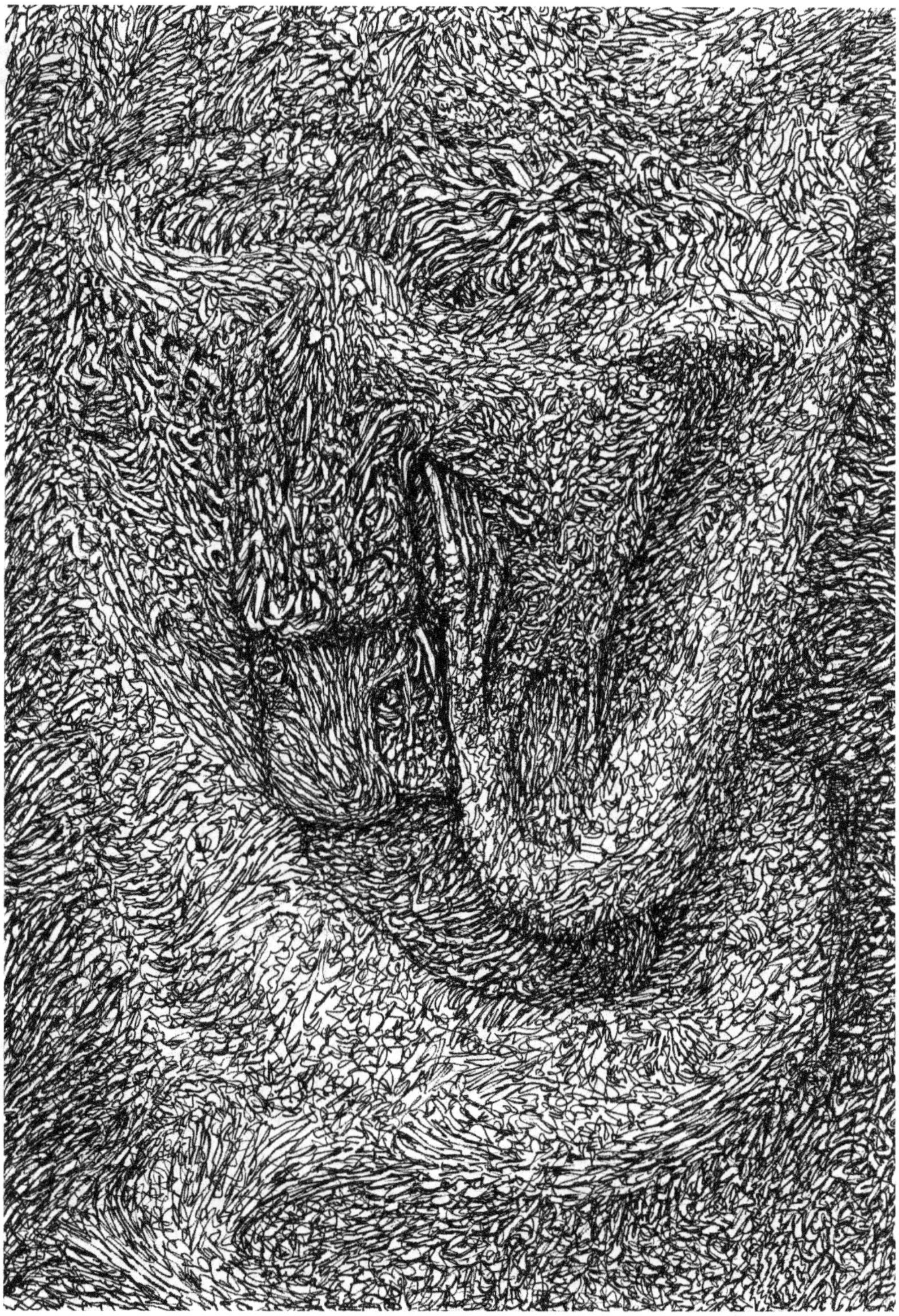

Jumah, automatic drawing by Sasha Vlad

The following texts by Dan Stanciu and Iulian Tănase (and translated by Sasha Vlad) were written in response to Sasha's drawing.

Both selections and drawing are from the book: *Borbro, Obs, Kabupaten, Feen, Duamaa, Jumah, Ek-Yolo, Serliq, Burcep, Sodhi, Lecade, Epona, Snijngad* by Iulian Tănase and Sasha Vlad, Locul Tare Publishing House, Bucharest, Romania, 2005.

JUMAH

Dan Stanciu

Jumah is the one who has no ending. All things that are his ended, either ceded by a bankrupt creator to an oeuvre of smoke, either interrupted through the removal of the engine when they could still walk a lot, or ruined by the successes of some errors inside of him, but he (as Jumah) will not end. He would not have a motive, because he is the unsevered part of a purpose well propped up in passing things and has something that the other strong ones do not have: the mastery of thinking manually and of doing indefinitely.

I don't understand where this thing's future is coming from. And the marsh didn't hear what the whirlpool said? It's in between centers, after all. It forgot what deluge shook its trunks and how that shape like bellows perforated by airs cut off its green? If I were in its place, I wouldn't forgive the sleeping foreshadowers, I would climb on top of them with all those branches and shake them a little. I would even expect them to offer leaves to the East, so I can frighten them with some red intuitions. Maybe in this way, the wet histories that leave our mantra on disarticulated musical scales would not happen, and we could support, speaking truly in a vital mode, the arrival of a new lexis.

Otherwise, here (where, through a crystal of gray quality, the old sight maneuvered the iris as it pleased and the gazes converge toward sameness) I have no choice. I will reinstall the Sahara. For starters, some valleys, where the stalks of experience grew rather dense, can be emptied out, I can bring over a society of beardless ovoids who would eliminate urban formations from the landscape and can depopulate (summoning to work fifteen fiery maxillae) the towers erected illegally on the friendly granite. The color of the surroundings will slide slowly toward an almost integrally deserted ebony. (Albeit a straw-yellow ebony, since black ebony is not dry enough and retains in its composition secret pockets of liquid.) Then I will exile humidity into a grotto, where it can dwell all by itself and be allowed to be as botanical as it wants and manufacture flowers or stems as it pleases. Duamaa will give me a drop of its drought that we will install, with four turned-off sprinklers, in the four cardinal points. After that, when the desert is placed there on a long-term basis, we will drink our dust.

This would be the first operation of the cycle, named 'preparatory.' The second one, 'conjugatory,' will consist of uniting the disparates through laws that its mouth will formulate and my arm will thrust. The cloud that is agreeable to contemplatives will combine with the bones (of brave nobodies) from the tumulus into a skeleton that will walk about in the sky crackling its articulations and from which there will fall, at one point, a rain of shoulder blades over the furrows. Light and mold will couple midway between open and closed, will bring unto this world an heir with penicillin eyes and will cultivate his deviations. The plow's blade will become brothers with the poplin of the collars at a banquet of suave engineers, where there will be no lack of narrow surprises. Neither the heavy crane, nor the shy harmony will stay apart, and they will mesh their moments in the same voice. It would be unfair not to mention in such an enumeration the external core and the inside margin (one heated by heck knows what magnet, the other with fine diachronies), which will fuse eventually by their own accord, when their wave shows up. And also there should be mentioned the flame (remember?) from under the chosen one of the vein and the influence of the cooling pyre that consumed it from above, but how they will mesh, or how much of their energy will fall asleep, I won't tell.

I will say, however, that the skin torn out from the body and the lightning bolt pouring from the bull will be side by side, that the name that starts with a rotten 'A' and the key whose blood is squeezed out in a lock will consort, that male and clay will be one and the same, that *was* will be embraced by *to be continued* on a loop of September, that cold and the print's little wing will become intimate, that the revolver will marry the cup and at their wedding a molar will fall from the apricot tree, and the teeth of the revelers will dance on the hill, where the fate of the translator will be fulfilled, that these pairs and others will get together in a rich nothing.

The third and last operation of the present season will be called 'disjunctory.' It requires from the operator a big concentration of all fibers (personal, or not) upon some rather grave gestures and, therefore, I will execute it myself. (Duamaa will be present during the whole thing inside a stone.) A soldier—let's say, No. 298—passes by overhead, heading naively toward battles that will rupture his spleen and says to me from his flight: "What are you doing, Jumah, disjuncting?" "Yes, disjuncting," I say to him. At that moment, he (all of a sudden and feeling nothing else but how two stamps are peeling off from his temples) loses his rifle and ammunition (those being replaced by a sledge hammer and a chisel) and arrives somehow (through what I pass to him) in the vicinity of some materials that he will carve for a while, until enough years of peace would have passed, and he would stop. He will head back toward the field where the battles were fought (now green and calm, with its useless heroes dreaming of glory under 2 meters of clay) and will pass again overhead, now knowing some things, and will say from another flight: "What are you doing, Jumah, disjuncting?" "Yes, disjuncting," I will say to him busily, and he will fade away taken by his flight toward south, where, when he will arrive, he will establish a life like anybody else's.

Or someone, who has no volume, comes to me. He is afraid not to crumble amongst minutes, at night his nerves bundle up in a cluster that he sees flickering between outside and the bed, and he hears his pulse talking in the square with strangers and giving them, out of the blue, mixed impressions. He would like to return to the room built expressly for rocking, where he and his aleatory consort amazed each other by rattling, or twitched increasingly, he would be extremely happy if he could regain the room that he seemed to like and where the extensions of the noon covered him so many times in warm souvenirs, but he can't remember the code. I dial it in his palms (he has it again, he recognized it!) but he hardly has the time to say "thanks, pal" and becomes round.

Or (while I do fretwork on a ritual pig), that mammary poetics shows up from the fair with a bad sphinx on her back. "Here are those immaculate little scissors?" she says. "Yes, here," I say. And—faster than one would count to one, or two, or three, or four, or 2005—she puts the sphinx down and pulls its curtain. What I see inside of it, what faces hollowed out by the radiations of deafness, what pale, or downright stinking organs that spill out from the aberration of a stagnant species cut off within a milligram by headlights that have no choice but to kill through illumination, what undulating stacks of egos submerged by the muck that comes down from an ignorant brain and how many trifling euphorias chirping their rhymes in one voice—I will not unveil, lest someone faints. I only do this: I grab that one by her mane that smells of petals of a cross, toss it into the source of sadness whence she came from, and kick it, with the tip of my heart, in her anemia-generating pate. Let her wander forever under the chestnut trees in bloom and amongst the cavities of high arts.

(to be continued in the next ending)

JUMAH

Iulian Tănase

Jumah is the proof!

Jumah—this is the name of the one who stretches out his arm beyond what can be touched. His arm remains suspended above the triple thresholds. Between the living and the dead is the place, and Jumah knows this place well. The sky is an older promise, shaped like a 'V,' which demands to be continually immortalized.

Whose is this left arm and where is it going?

And this right arm, much more long and much more terrible, whose is it and whence is it coming?

Jumah is everywhere and he heads toward the center. A middle-aged circle follows him closely. Someone presents Jumah with a river. Someone else, with a ladder and several steps.

Between the living and the dead is the place (where Serliq slept a long time). Jumah shakes the hands of the living and the dead, asks them about what is new below and above, asks them why and for how long, asks them something about the Pythagorean Theorem, asks them who is still alive and who has died—he asks them. Someone cries out to Jumah: "Between the living and the dead, the differences are a matter of clothing! Clothes and bones are one and the same! Only those are naked who lack bones, not clothes!"

Jumah is the proof, the proof that between Lodhi and the neighboring territories there is a close connection.

Jumah is the one who brought Lecade several bunches of adoring plants from the Explosive Eye.

Jumah made wild the assymetric wolves and taught them to devour each other.

From Jumah, the First, the Supreme Cultivator from the Intermediate Country, inherited the dead people's seeds, named "agones." To Jumah are grateful the dead cultivated by the First.

Jumah is the one who announces you that you have one more threshold to cross. (In the Loidh language, Jumah means 'bridge,' but also 'messenger,' and also 'search.')

After the conclusion of the Hieroglyph Congress, Jumah took Sodhi aside and told him about a superb runner by the name of Ergart, whom he once met in the Intermediate Country. Jumah was an innoculated witness when Ergart talked to Al Trey, the Time Cultivator from the Intermediate Country. In exchange for a transparent receptacle filled with time, Ergart presented Al Trey with a manuscript with unusual images and signs, a sort of "hieroglyphs of the unconscious," as they were named later by Hsiao Yen, when Al Trey presented this famous collector with the manuscript received from Ergart. Jumah, an attentive and completely silent witness, saw with his own eyes that the time cultivated by Al Trey is a pink, almost transparent, liquid.

Also at that time, at the end of the Hieroglyph Congress, Jumah told Sodhi that every inhabitant of the Intermediate Country has a sphere of influence, and these spheres of influence protect the Intermediates' loneliness, like inside an eggshell. "They also call this sphere 'the egg of influence!'"

Jumah is the one who dreamed one night of a young man praying like this: "Oh, father of sowers of embers, of snakes, of embers on waters, of embers on hands, of handed-out snakes, father of my year of birth, triple father of my birthday, the traveling glooms are returning, sensuality expects them with fires in their blood, oh, father of sowers, look at your eye!"

Jumah knew closely the explosive gaze. He is the one who stopped strangers on the street, who passed through Lodhi, to tell them one, or two, or even several, of his dreams. Generally, the people in passing were in a hurry but they listened to Jumah attentively until the end, because those dreams were always about them, too.

Jumah is the name of that one, for whom to live was the same thing as to have a suspicion.

by John Andersson, translated by Mattias Forshage

I was out for a ride with my very good friend Erik Sundberg
Another very good friend is Niklas Nenzén, who studies mythology
PARIS
ROME
OSLO
FEDERAL BUREAU
OF INVESTIG

When we came to his house (the house on the hill) he was watching TV
BATMAN
SUPERMAN
M — IF YOU'RE IN TROUBLE
TEXAS FEDERAL GOVERNMENT OFFICER OF THE MONTH
GULD
There is a show on just now about the myth of Arion
About the slug Arion from Orion
STEP ON THE GRASS LIL
It was just a fairytale and fairytales are never the truth... or are they?

A different Orion. A different world. Antimatter.
A never-was, non-compatible, more bizarre reality.
A yellow and pink sky

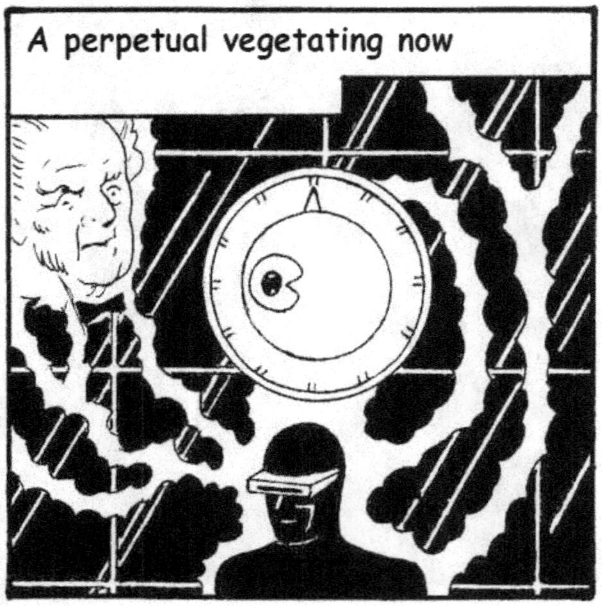
A perpetual vegetating now

Where an imaginative existence is carried forth

Through the perpetually throbbing pin head
TICK
TOCK
A ghost slug is this world which perpetually moves forward through an equally perpetually vegetating present
TICK
TOCK
For Arion, this slug is his big brother
Always a dream about this brother - let us call him Orion (the myth of Orion).
PISS
ORION-MYTEN

After the show we are inside Dr Morbeus's
hotel with the hypnotizing garden
terrace views
snap
snap
snap
GÅ PÅ GRÄSET
orange
frugate
BIS
CUIT

Being pursued into secret rooms
Rooms in the basement
Rooms in the towers
Looking out over archives of stashed persecution manias for future generations to peek into
To peek in loneliness
Until one is pursued oneself
FOLLOW US

Down into the basement
RA DAR
Where all the secrets are
matisse
Picasso
Dali
Dr Morbius's archive
ARKIV
X
18
An archivist without life, without hope
And without equal, I should add
A unique life
NORGE
SVERIGE
DANMAR
FINLAND
TOM OF
JAPAN
HO HO HO
HA HA HA

He tries to draw like Leonardo da Vinci
His friend and assistant Walkie, like de Chirico
And Man Ray, a little
In a ghost center in the periphery of reality

Dr Morbius washes the dishes
KAFFE-
BRYGGARE
Vacuums with the aid of Walkie
Sees the sun rise over the sea like a sparkler
Reads in hidden corners his books and magazines as if they were secret matters for the few, the elected, living in lonesomeness, living until they are two, in twosomeness
Hugging that vacuum cleaner of his
And falling asleep by himself in the end as if he were alone
The End

Notes on the Legacy of Cthulhu

Franklin Rosemont, 1943-2009

originally published in *Arsenal: Surrealist Subversion*, #3, 1976.

The principal originality and greatest merit of H.P. Lovecraft was his creation of an open-ended, continually evolving *experimental mythology* elaborated collectively with the active participation of many friends, some of whom he knew only through correspondence. Drawing inspiration and data from scientific and anthropological works, the literature of magic and alchemy, New England lore, eccentric researchers such as Margaret Murray and Charles Fort, and from his own and others' dreams, Lovecraft and his associates confronted, point-blank, the problem of the absence of a social myth in our time.

Doubtless unaware of all the implications of such a step, they nonetheless took for granted the irredeemably moribund state of all prevailing myths and developed their own mythic frame of reference from scratch, rescuing from past literature only a few tantalizing premonitions (notably from Poe, Bierce, Chambers and Machen). If this playful idea of utilizing for their own purposes incidents and personages from imaginative works of the past—not to mention freely exchanging characters, backgrounds and other data with one's fellow writers—is wholly foreign to the alienated individualism characteristic of the specialized craft of Literature, it is nonetheless comparable to the procedure of authentic poets as varied as the Eskimos and the Elizabethans. Originating in a sort of *game* played by several writers, the Cthulhu Mythos points *beyond literature* to that exalting future collective creation to be developed in accord with an extensive system of elective affinities and passional attraction. The universal proliferation of this poetry made by all prerequires a society that has largely resolved the contradictions between individual and collective, city and countryside, conscious and unconscious—a society elaborated on the basis of the surrealist revolution.

D.A.F. Sade, in his "Reflections on the Novel" (1800), was the first to recognize that the great Gothic romances of his day were "the inevitable fruit of the revolutionary shocks felt by the whole of Europe." The works of the Lovecraft Circle are similarly inseparable from the revolutionary events of our own epoch, of which the Russian Revolution of October 1917 was the decisive commencement. Once again, as in the age of *Melmoth the Wanderer*, we are living in a *transitional epoch*. But today it is no longer a question, as it was in the epoch of ascendant capital, of one class rising to power only to subjugate others in its turn. This time the future of the whole of humanity is at stake. The question is: Are men and women capable of putting an end to a worldwide system of exploitation and alienation, and of definitively inaugurating the realm of human freedom, or must they lapse into a new and perhaps irrevocable barbarism?

The inescapable universality of the present crisis underlies all Cthulhu Mythos tales. Gone are the isolated crumbling castles, ghostly armor and other paraphernalia suited to the period of declining feudalism. Lovecraft's action is global and even cosmic; his entire work is imbued with what he called "a sense of spectral whirling through liquid gulfs of infinity, of dizzying rides through reeling universes on a comet's tail." This intuitive insistence on the awesome, truly limitless possibilities opened in the epoch of workers' councils gives his and his comrades' works an implicitly revolutionary character forever unattainable by explicitly "socialist" novels. This is because the Lovecraft Circle grasped the essence of the surrealist view, verified by all great examples of the past, that it is impossible to create anything of significance by expressing only the manifest content of an age, that it is necessary to express, on the contrary, its *latent* content.

In "Limits Not Frontiers of Surrealism" (1936) André Breton wrote: "The 'fantastic,' which the application of a watchword such as socialist realism excludes in the most radical manner, and to which surrealism never ceases to appeal, constitutes in our view the supreme key to this latent content, the means of fathoming the secret depths of history which disappear beneath a maze of events. It is only at the approach of the fantastic, at a point where human reason loses its control, that the most profound emotion of the individual has the fullest opportunity to express itself: emotion unsuitable for projection in the framework of the real world and which has no other solution to its urgency than to rely on the eternal solicitation of symbols and myths."

That Lovecraft held a compatible view is indicated in this passage from a letter to Clark Ashton Smith: "The true function of fantasy is to give the imagination a ground for limitless expansion....I *know* that my most poignant emotional experiences are those which concern the lure of unplumbed space, the terror of the encroaching outer void, and the struggle to transcend the known and established order.

Lovecraft's pessimism, directed against nearly all the false "solutions" at hand, necessarily led him close to the center of the problem of Evil. From such a vantage-point, this ardent atheist armed with his improvised mythology challenged at one blow the most cherished illusions of all religions as well as the rationalist's myopic evasion of the Unknown.

Situated precisely at the intersection of humor and terror (or rather of umor and error), Lovecraft's cosmological propositions add to our appreciation of what Breton called "The Great Invisibles"—hypothetical animals whose behavior is as alien to us as is ours to the ant or the whale, and who elude our system of sensory references through secret camouflage; creatures who, however, as Breton suggested, "obscurely manifest themselves to us in fear and in the feeling of chance." This new myth, the subject of many surrealist explorations, was foreshadowed (as Breton acknowledged) by hints from many writers from Cyrano de Bergerac to William James.

Regarding this myth Breton wrote further: "Considering perturbations like the cyclone, in the face of which man is powerless to be anything but victim or witness, or like war, on the subject of which notoriously inadequate views have been advanced, it would not be impossible, in the course of a vast work, which would be constantly presided over by the boldest kind of induction, to even succeed in making plausible the complexion and structure of such hypothetical beings..."

When this proposed vast work is compiled, should not a chapter be devoted to the data introduced by Lovecraft, Clark Ashton Smith, Frank Belknap Long, Donald Wandrei and others who have heard and heeded "the call of Cthulhu"?

***

Instead of beating "Literature" to a pulp, Lovecraft allowed himself to be beaten by the racket of pulp literature. Throughout his work the hard cold facts of fury are swept under the rug of mere fiction. His *dreams,* to which he was remarkably attentive, were for him primarily sources of "plots." The surrealist voice, for him and his collaborators, penetrated only faintly through the earmuffs of literary mystification. If surrealism is the imagination reclaiming all its rights by any and all means, Lovecraft represents the imagination dimly aware that its rights have been violated, but still resigned to employing strictly "legal" means of defense.

Significantly, the most disquieting of Lovecraft's writing is to be found not in his tales or poems but in certain epigraphs to letters to Clark Ashton Smith:

> *Many-columned Arcades of Weed-grown Y'ha-nthlei*
> *Hour of the Unseen Howling*
>
> *Concave Cliffs by the Tarn of Kyagoph*
> *Hour of the Reddening of the Dark Waters*
>
> *Tower of Narghan in Pnath*
> *Hour when the Dogs bay at the opening of the Topmost Circular Window*

Read in succession, these epigraphs (of which I have quoted only a few) compose an astonishing litany reminiscent of the *Black Book of Carmarthen.* Evidently written in haste and without revision, these lines seem to me to be a remarkable *condensation* of Lovecraft's mythology. His most compelling legacy is given in full in these hurried, fragmentary, cryptic notes to which he probably attributed not the slightest importance.

***

The Cthulhu Mythos is neither a mirror-image of the Christian mythos (as August Derleth lamely argued) nor its simple negation. Rather, it is a kind of hysterical conversion in which the literary symptoms of senile mythologies—Christianism among others—were forced to dance to new and terrible tunes. Lovecraft is beginning to be "acknowledged" today because his bad dreams define the bad dreams of a whole epoch. Perhaps there is no better introduction to his work than Victor Tausk's 1919 paper "On the Origin of the 'Influencing Machine' in Schizophrenia."

Too resigned, while he lived, to being the dupe of other men's afterthoughts, Lovecraft regarded himself a failure. Today his work is a great "success," marketed in mass editions to dupe others in turn. But even the abusive circumstances of the "Lovecraft revival" are proof of a real development. The same historical forces that began in the mid-1960s to make surrealism a matter of life and death in the U.S., also brought about the "rehabilitation" of Lovecraft. Utilized by mass market publishers for their own confusionist and profitable purposes, this rehabilitation nonetheless demonstrates once more, in a small way, that the dying social order can continue to live only by killing its gravediggers and then robbing their graves.

There is reason to emphasize that it was Lovecraft's very "failure" that was, in an important sense, his greatest virtue. This is something that inevitably escapes those hostile or condescending commentators such as L. Sprague de Camp and Lin Carter who repeatedly reproach him for not devoting himself more assiduously to being a hack novelist like Sprague de Camp and Carter. What saves Lovecraft for us, what gives his work its special charm and real force, is precisely the fact that he was absolutely unable and unwilling to keep in step with the dominant tendencies of his time, or even with his own declared intentions. The notorious anachronisms that enabled him, posthumously, to become the crowning character in his own mythology, also made him (doubtless in spite of himself) a magnificent thorn in the side of all the hypocritically "progressive" literature of his day.

Lovecraft's greatest achievement can thus be said to have been the consequence of a marvelous misunderstanding. Floundering for years in the waters of naive musings and delusions that were often nothing else than paltry, eventually he stumbled onto the uncharted isle of his own deepest fears. Like Columbus, he never knew where he was going or where he had landed, but he too deserves credit at least for not turning back too soon. It is his fidelity to the task of exploring his own terror and horror that makes Lovecraft's work a monument to the aspiration signaled by De Quincey, "to reveal something of the grandeur which belongs *potentially* to human dreams."

REGARDING SOME SURREALIST EMBODIMENTS IN A GNOSTIC THICKET

~on language, alienation and mythopoesis~

Niklas Nenzén

1. NARRATIVES OF ILLUSORY ENTRAPMENT: THE WHY AND WHAT OF GNOSTICISM

In today´s atmosphere of paranoia and suspicion of authority, we might discern a connection with the late Roman Empire in its period of expansion and dissolution, when the official power - the deified emperor - had, through Pax Romana, emptied the conquered peoples´ myths of power and content, and created a dizzying alienation and apocalyptic confusion across the unified empire.

In the tension that grew between the claims of totalitarian power and its mendacious legitimizing narrative, a mythopoetic movement of resistance grew among the Hellenic and Byzantine cultures, a movement obsessed with revealing the myths that lay behind the power claims, interpreting these myths eclectically, and rewriting them in forms which better reflected the requirements of meaning, subjectivity and psychological precision.

In his pioneering work on the epistemological, phenomenological and deconstructive dimensions of Gnosticism, which also investigates the social and political context, Hans Jonas points out some striking correlations between Gnostic thinking and modern existentialism. As some of his points could be transferred to a context of surrealist epistemology, poetics, metaphysics and mythopoiesis, this will be modestly attempted below.

There may be more specific reasons to consider the Gnostic flowering of ideas from surrealist points of view. Firstly, since connections frequently have been made - although mostly implicitly - one need only compile some of these points of contact and reflect a bit on them. Attention here will be especially given to the dualist materialism of Georges Bataille, the metaphor theory of André Breton and the ultra-radical theory of alienation and mediation developed by situationism.

Furthermore, some familiarity with the original Gnostic ideas seem to put us in direct contact with almost all heretical thinking in Europe over a period of two thousand years, and, as some have argued, further back before Judeo-Christian times when a somatically-based knowledge was prevalent throughout the West. Morris Berman has pointed out that "*the attempt to restore body cognition to the center of human consciousness is a central feature of most heretical movements in the history of the Christian West. Much of the argument of heresy vs. orthodoxy revolves around belief in God vs. the actual* experience *of God, something that can only be brought about by somatic practices, ascetic or otherwise. Gnosis is not about belief, but about tangible proof of the existence of "larger forces", which Western mystics over the centuries have claimed to have obtained by means of certain somatic techniques of breathing, chanting, meditation, and so on...*"

To surrealism these forces represent the "sacred terror" that seizes hold of the artist facing his work created in the name of an unknown superior principle outside of ego control. Since these Gnostic sensibilities "insinuate themselves into the heart of German romanticism", (Breton, On Magic Art) they also made their way into surrealist image-theory, both as a confidence in linguistic and pictorial creativeness and originality and as a disposition in general to abandon the human stereotype.

And not the least important but most implicit of these reflections on Gnosticism could be about the recurring question within surrealism of the need for a collective myth, and about how "*from the oldest and strongest traditions* [to] *gather together the scattered elements of such a myth*".

Such an undertaking could very well be about the establishing of a mythopoetic sensibility of the particular kind to which the Gnostics in their day gave free rein. Neither should we close down the possibility of allowing our interest to remain appearing a little confused, especially considering the high level of rational demands required. Why not, for instance, pay some heed to Roger Caillois's critique of the selectivity of surrealist interest in the exotic: using for polemical and fetishist purposes fragments of other cultures as simple weapons against one's own culture (Hollier)? But perhaps more importantly, in order to cultivate a hermeneutics which prefers to maintain its material in a fluid state, ready to assimilate new findings and, to a larger degree than ever, in favor of imagination and invented mythology (mythopoeia), put ideological mythologization in the background.

It will be argued throughout here that the extreme poles of reaction in the Gnostic universe of thinking are quite

similar to the *authenticity panic* which in our time flows perpetually primarily from sociological and popular cultural sources: nostalgia in the face of a vanishing reality replaced by second-rate copies, the political defeatism that follows, a passively consumerist materialism in the experience of personal identity and human relationships, announcements of the worthlessness of values and of the end of history. And perhaps more than anything an immobilizing dilemma, in that any public criticism that confines itself to the discursive level more or less involuntarily finds itself functioning as a megaphone for the system criticized. The need for an *experiential correction* of the truths and myths of their day seems to have been one of the main reasons why the mythopoetic strategy of the Gnostics developed to such great extent.

To give some background, Gnosticism is an accepted cover-term for several religious sects within a syncretic movement of learned pagans, Hellenized Jews and Christians that flourished from around 0 to about 200 AD. In this era the Gnostics distinguish themselves as experts in fantastical myth-making, prophetic imagination and subtle hermeneutics, but they also express a mystical yearning for God and draw upon some aspects of Platonist epistemology to "remember" myths.

Gnostic mythology is much concerned with a cosmological error or a pre-creation catastrophe in the spirit-world that seeks to explain the evil, hypocrisy and suffering of the present quasi-real world. Like the pagan hermetics they cunningly practiced shamanic navigation on mystical ascents through imaginal realms where they battled abstract powers and demonic influences. And like the early Christians they perceived within themselves a spiritual element that was trapped in the fallen state of matter and longed to merge again with the Absolute or return to the undifferentiated source of all. Unlike orthodox Christianity though they did not speculate about a primordial sin against God as cause for the Fall, but instead focused on healing the rifts in reality through an experiential type of direct knowing which they termed *Gnosis*.

The Gnostics seem to have been dualists or monists, depending on which aspect of their interests they or their reviewers emphasized - mythopoetic catastrophism or thoughtful/ mystical emanationism. But throughout the ages they have nevertheless largely been known as radically dualistic elitists, mostly on account of their suspiciously ascetic or licentiously hedonistic practices in combination with an "unnecessarily complex" cosmology (Plotinus). The negative judgments are of course due to some influential polemical testimonies from contemporary heresiological sources. Sometimes these reported encounters with the Gnostics are nevertheless perhaps more informative than they intend to be:

> *If you propose to them inquiries sincere and honest, they answer you with stern look and contracted brow, and say, 'The subject is profound'. If you try them with subtle questions, with the ambiguities of their double tongue, they affirm a community of faith (with yourself). If you intimate to them that you understand their opinions, they insist on knowing nothing themselves.*
> (Tertullian, Against the Valentinians, Chapter I, quoted in the Ante-Nicene Fathers Vol. III)

So no, the Gnostics did not unanimously deny the reality of the empirical world, but they did call to question, on linguistic and sociological grounds, whether it is real in the way a realist view of knowledge prescribes. Their point in attack came by necessity out of the area of theology, based on an agreement that the totality of society's consensus in their era rested firmly on the mythologem "God's creation", where the creation and the creator reciprocally legitimate each other in an ontological stranglehold, signifying each other in a closed sociolinguistic system.

Kenoma is the name for our existing world experienced as a cosmological emptiness, where time repeats itself and all reproduction has become meaningless. Certain Gnostic sects lived ordinary lives with family, professions and circumstances in this illusory world, and on top of that, were busy on Sundays with a world-hating conspiracy theory on the cosmic scale, just as religious people in all times have been.

Other sects seem to have been specialized in mythopoetic hermeneutics, political demagogy, confusing secrecy, or transforming life through mystical practices, or all of the above in varying proportions. It is not really possible to any larger extent to reach an answer based on the source texts as to which metaphysical pillars of faith were valid, or what the allegories mean. And it is not interesting in this connection. The texts are ultra-mythological, intellectually complex and hermeneutically multivalent. They evoke a vision of a speculative, dialogic, instrumental, experimental and variable body of knowledge. They are largely unreadable (perhaps even more so than alchemical texts): full of lacunae, liturgical repetitions, religious piety and cryptic allusions like *"he is a perfect, invisible, noetic Protophanes-Harmedon. / And empowering the individuals, she is a Triple-Male."*

In a majority of Gnostic source texts, the saturnine complex of the corrupt patriarchy breaks out of the theological frame with particular force: the twilight of gods is proclaimed, or the god above god. As a code word for Caesar, Jahve, the demiurge as well as the self, the essence of the creator god becomes a kind of secondary intelligence without connections to Eros or emotions, imperfect or even demonic, but not metaphysically "evil", rather a given identity without any kind of human autonomy, one that keeps clinging to illegitimate power claims by cowardliness or idiocy.

When the Gnostic source texts in a wider perspective pronounce alternately, depending on the circumstances, either god, the legitimacy of the social order, or reality as such, to be illusory, and identify these constructions as mere human assumptions, it is the question of trying to grasp a totalizing mythopoetic perspective on the sociolinguistic complex. We recognize in this *reality-decreating* or *acosmic* move two distinctly recognizable cognitive attitudes, which - then as now - all too eagerly rush ahead and polarise, despite the fact that they could very well stand in a dynamic relationship to each other instead. Below, these attitudes will be approached under the headings of *visionary skepticism* and *socially designated alienation.*

2. VISIONARY SKEPTICISM: A NON-TRADITION OF TRICKSTER EPISTEMOLOGY

One strain we notice in Gnosticism is a continuation of the mystery traditions´ non-dualistic vision of reality and illusion, body and consciousness, being and non-being. Through the last decades´ re-readings of Parmenides and Empedocles, thinkers of the Eleatic school, we have gained new comparative insights into some pre-Socratic anti- or irrationalistic initiatory practices and *iatromancy* (medical divination), which no doubt also illustrate some of the background to how the Gnostics could claim access to the divine and put the entire patriarchal theology on its head.

For instance, Peter Kingsley (Reality, 1996) shows how Parmenides makes great play of the difference between mortal knowledge (*doxa, opinion*), which is based on pluralism and on dualites and differentiation, and the immortal epistemology (divine logic) that also utilizes these resources but does so rather in order to reveal the unity behind everything - a purpose by the way much in accordance with Parmenides´ contemporaries Lao Tse and Heraclitus. The "divine language" exhibits a paradoxical, satirical or caricaturizing relation towards the "twin-headed" propensity for the habitual dualisms which characterize the imperfect knowledge of nature (phusis). The Gnostics share this rhetoric: "*They do not know the power of God, nor do they understand the interpretation of the scriptures, on account of their double-mindedness*" (Testimony of Truth, NHL).

The naive understanding of the world around us, which like the moon continually "borrows its light", nevertheless remains, according to Parmenides, associated with death, the unknown, the unclear, night. Since positive knowledge is regarded as such a marginal affair Parmenides gave his teachings a poetic form and in a demonstrative play with such conventional oppositions (enantiomorphies) he for example called the moon a "*night bright earth-roaming foreign light*" - thereby linguistically attempting to dissolve the oppositions in an experience of a wholeness and immutability behind the ever-changing.

Parmenides's disciple Empedocles, who even called himself a god, discloses his dependence

on the mystery cults by depicting his teachings as the fruit of a meeting with the earth goddess Demeter-Aphrodite; she taught him to put his trust in fraud and seduction as an art in its own right, and to cultivate a holistically receptive wakefulness that enables one to both see through the tricks of logic and also to play them oneself. This art equals, like Parmenides' "divine logic", objective features of reality, and represents a world unfurling itself like an eye in the storm within the very act of perception.

On the level of action, and according to the usage of the time, *mêtis* means to courageously put one´s trust in a risky or previously untried strategy in a moment fraught with danger, and to do so on the grounds that no analysis of a situation would be valid outside of the specific moment. In this *spirit of disillusion* the goddess appeals to Empedocles´ trust as he visits her in the underworld: do not rely on my words.

According to several researchers this journey to the underworld has shamanistic overtones and represents an exploration of the physical body and the use of the senses to understand the divine presence in everything, even in man himself. To get a hint of just how concrete a direction this idea of "the divine in man" could be taken, we may in passing also refer to J. Nigro Sansonese's research on how ancient myths throughout the world can be interpreted as coded instructions for esoteric practices involving a deepened awareness of the human body (proprioception).

So when therefore the Eleatic thinkers seem not to regard faith and knowledge as relevant categories in practical reality, where rather confusion and ignorance are the basic terms, their attitude could perhaps be likened to a kind of distended and more active counterpart to the "temporary suspension of disbelief" of the film spectator. Thus poetry finds itself to be a trusted resource of knowledge. On a creative level more technically complex than that of scientific realism - that is, without accommodating as a new myth the expectations that the old myths have created - the poetic image can show how illusions represent the true condition of affairs; that they are more than one thing at once and that the principle of poetry remains an essential aspect of the real, in many cases the only one.

Among the recent *visionary skeptics* of this tradition - which is really more of a pseudo-tradition which, as Kingsley points out, repeatedly dies and re-invents itself - the greatest exemplars would perhaps be the early Belgian surrealists, who never seemed to be intimidated by the ghost of science (whose thinnest appearance would be common sense), never expected more than a minimum of the meanings that unfailingly demonstrate the impossible for us and who seemed to hold dear the complication that *"our language itself and not what this means becomes /.../ revelation or active cause and enter instead of what we wanted to convey /.../"* (Paul Nougé, quoted in Sjölin) for a field of instructively beautiful and destructive potential.

3. ON SOCIALLY DESIGNATED ALIENATION AND THE BODY-MIND PROBLEM IN THE LIGHT OF IMAGINAL TECHNOLOGIES

Along with the "visionary skepticism" the Gnostic scriptures also precipitate a more modern claustrophobic understanding of how language shapes reality and myth as a psychological layer, a socially constructed pathology to feel nauseated by and to wrestle with. To realize oneself to be almost helplessly trapped in this layer means to the Gnostics to be alienated (*allogenes*) from the real (*pleroma*). This cognitively rooted exclusion - which Marx in our era described in historical terms (as *Entfremdung*) and C.G. Jung described in psychological terms (as insight into the shadow) - was expressed by the Gnostics - in a hermeneutically transparent form - as the myth of Sophia and her involuntary exile from The One.

It is the religious interpretation of this predicament of exile which usually is referred to when Gnosticism is described as metaphysical dualism. The moral of the myth nevertheless indicates that man is Sophia and Sophia is the world; the goddess of wisdom hereby becomes something of a proto-evolutionist symbol for the idea that the forces driving us towards *gnosis* are intimately interwoven with the "worldly" in all its variety. Because "on her own" – i.e. non-sexually, or by the absence of polarized aspects in harmony - trying to bridge the gap between the separate domains of darkness and light, Sophia "by mistake" created both mental and material reality from her passions:

> *This collection [of passions] ... was the substance of the matter from which this world was formed. From [her desire of] returning [to him who gave her life], every soul belonging to this world, and that of the Demiurge himself, derived its origin. All other things owed their beginning to her terror and sorrow. For from her tears all that is of a liquid nature was formed; from her smile all that is lucent; and from her grief and perplexity all the corporeal elements of the world.*
> (Irenaeus, Against heresy: The Ante-Nicene Fathers Vol. I)

In addition to a distinction between the relatively real, and the absolutely real most monistic systems involve *a theory of the illusory*, which is intended to explain the paradox of their relationship. In the quotation from Valentinian cosmology above we are presented with an explanation of a specific paradox – i.e. that according to the Gnostic myth-image the world emerges as a live miscarriage/an abortion

- a monism or panpsychism of Paracelsus´s, Spinoza´s and Schelling's kind in that the "pure spirit" is already assumed to be diffused in matter and animates it in the same way as humans are supposed to be animated by their soul. In another chronicle of heresies from these times, Epiphanius states about the Valentinians:

> *They say that the same soul is scattered about in animals, beasts, fish, snakes, humans, trees, and products of nature.* (Epiphanius, Panarion, 26.9.1.)

What can be heard here is the same hope that later accompanied the alchemists; everything is alive to the living eye, and where soul is, transformation can take place. Because of his unity with nature man has through his imaginative capabilities the opportunity to "terrify the angels" with the otherworldly (read: non-mimetic) glory and majesty of the image.

This idea of Valentinus was highlighted by Breton and alluded to in the introduction to On Magic Art, because of some points of contact with surrealist poetics, and in particular with Breton´s view on the metaphorical image as an *ascendant sign*. But even the broader concept of *dépaysement* - the surreal effect of detaching objects from their conventional context and metaphorically compiling them into a new entity, without any prosaic allusion - actually seems to coincide with what Valentinus refers to as *the living Aeon*; that sufficiently original and authentic pictorial creations, in contrast to those that are merely copies, may cause the liberation of the Sophian light from the formalisms of physical space-time. Also, when through the image subject and object are identical they reflect the One, original Source.

While Gnostic aspirations unflinchingly move in the direction from the images at the *Lower Aeons* that are copies or imitations to the images at the *Higher Aeons* that equal originals and archetypes, it never becomes entirely clear where Gnosticism through its mystical leanings detaches from the confident intellectualism of Neoplatonism and where it remains rational. In that regard *gnosis* often seems less similar to a prestigious "mystical experience" than to what we nowadays mean by a scientific experiment; a direct experience that generates knowledge, and one that in some sense is set up in order to frame the acquired knowledge within a larger theory of the whole (to put a little meat on the bones regarding the idea of "The One", we can compare it with the Big Bang theory, which today obviously plays a similar role as universal framework and myth about the beginning (and end) of everything).

In correlation to the Gnostics´ aeonic hierarchy of images, surrealism is by definition in opposition to the "Lower Aeons" of social realism, but that is not all. In a significant departure from symbolist poetics and from the otherwise faithfully followed recipe of Pierre Reverdy, Breton in his poetics specifically considers that the metaphorical light that the poetic image may spark can not - or should not - be deliberately conceived by the poet himself: "*reason confines itself to the recognition and appreciation of this luminous phenomenon.*" (Manifesto of Surrealism)

In its relinquishing of conscious control over the creative process surrealism hereby approaches a pre-aesthetic apprehension of the creative forces, where cultural and natural products have not yet separated but are analogically traversed by a single *lumen naturae*, which is able to reconcile conflicts in the same way that it unites man and nature, thereby igniting the spark of originality: *"They (the conflicts) embrace and the new light is begotten of them, which is like no other light in the whole world"* (Mylius, Philosophia reformata).

This light has been seen as an interface or a field phenomenon, in that it does not permit itself be confined to one of its parts; neither to the light of reason celebrated by Renaissance enlightenment, nor to symbolic illuminations. Perhaps no one else from this period could better tell us about this relation than Paracelsus, who for his part was particularly sensitive to the correspondences of *a natura abscondita*: "*As the light of nature can not speak, it buildeth shapes in sleep from the power of the word*" (Liber de caducis, quoted in Winther).

If our inner vision constitutes nature´s "light", then dreams are here seen as its creative products, and when reason is silenced, nature is talking within us - hence, taking this metaphorically, we could trace a pathway through the metaphysics of light to a pre-Freudian understanding about psycho-topology and the unconscious.

But perhaps there is even more reason to bring forth here the dynamic body images from the occult tradition; from the *soma athanaton* of hermeticism and the *cinnabar fields* of Taoist alchemy, through the *astral* vehicles of theosophy and forward to our time with Wilhelm Reich´s *body electric* and the *body-without-organs* of Artaud (and later Deleuze). Although even the most viable of these alternative body-perceptions may be said to express a dialectical response to the experience of the given duality of consciousness/ matter, some of their later varieties admittedly appear as mere myths or metaphors without any real rapport between the processes of micro- and macrocosm. Still, the various occult methodologies of transforming into a "body of light" - the stuff that dreams are made of - represent imaginal technologies that by far pre-date literature and art as we know them; they can be said to be about merging with the image of being in itself - "extraspacial and extratemporal" (Jung) - as *the* ascendant sign.

4. THE YOGA OF DUALISM, ABANDONING THE HUMAN, OPACITY OR TRANSPARENCY (a Neoplatonist Duel)

One can suspect that the kind of dualism the Valentinian Gnostics would have considered to be characteristic for our time takes place on the one hand between a world soul, a *Brahma-atma*, an *anima mundi* or *Gaia* (as in Lovelock´s theory of a self-regulating biosphere), and on the other hand the technological and politically-socially generated systems that still mentally keep us in a positivistically-rooted soullessness, compensated by increasingly baroque and totalitarian models for connection, presence and contact.

The question as to the degree to which we today identify ourselves passively with the exploitative options and familiar patterns of the virtual sphere, or whether we seek to renegotiate, discover and manifest the living relationship between humans and their environment, may soon develop into an increasingly intractable conflict. Here is heard, on the one hand, a long-standing Gnostic alarmism of sorts (e.g. the different facets of the cyberpunk mentality, from W.S. Burroughs, P.K. Dick, the Matrix and Zeitgeist movies, and more recently the trend of "synchro-mysticism") which is paranoid, conspiratorial and entertaining, and which once again provides the mythic images that Gnostics once took up from the Timaeus and the Book of Enoch.

But the reverse trend is also in force: the border between a growing and hardening system of control and its adaptive reflection in easily distracting products of entertainment is dissolved in feelings of comfort, pleasure and recreation. Such a passivation leaving less and less space for autonomous meaning-production, for poetry as a mercurial principle in the midst of it all, even as a cosmological force; to create reality, more reality in this psychological layer that is far too easily reduced to a system of rewards and penalties.

Paranoia has never been a way out of this problem, but rather a way to conjure the opacity of circumstance, the mutism of existence. And the reductionist Cartesianism of conspiratorial thinking, with which this culture tempts us into a faithful relationship, leaves us finally alone with exactly that small fragment that in its deformity very well may be the source of the whole misery: what literally is the subject of a sentence, a grammatical sign (Kristeva) or a complex among other complexes (Janet): the I.

When religionists and humanists alike have wanted to contrast man´s uniqueness against the rest of creation (and nowadays evolutionary theory with its recent additions of genetics and micro-biology does an even better job than ever of wonderfully threatening the dubious claims of such a contrast) symbolic thinking and conceptual speech are highlighted as separating attributes. The Gnostics were, not unlike the dadaists, convinced that the understanding of how things fit together can be an even more piteous state than that of not understanding and not thinking at all (*aponoia*).

The reason for this stance is certainly that reason is hardly able to accommodate and express experience, and also - if one is unable to override it - is likely to constitute an obstacle in the way of a dynamic assimilation of new knowledge. While thinking and knowledge, as the priests so rightly point out, are "of this world", the Gnostics regard the experience of the world as potentially the same as the essence of thinking, which occurs "*on the hoof* " through the means of intuition made self-aware.

Such a relationship - such a *yoga*, to use the word which in several languages and from a comparative linguistic perspective seems to express the vital element of religions (e.g. Sanskrit root *yuj*, Latin *iugum, jugare, jungere, syzygia*, ligare, religio, German *Joch*, English *yoke, join, junction, zygote*) - can not be taken for granted, but must be constantly renewed; becoming alienated and being detected through linguistic shifts, mythologization and even ritualized abnormalities. The connection also needs to depend upon grace, that is what we in a secular context would call a concern for the preparation of a mood or mental state of deconditionalized expectations. In the Gnostic quest for authentic experience there are hardly any reasons to remain human, to keep "the garment", least of all if it is linguistic categories (as some have once said and others then have started to believe) which defines what a human being is.

The surrealist who most emphatically mounted a Gnostic desertion from what is human in the narrowest sense would undoubtedly be Georges Bataille. His base-materialist expropriation of a "Gnostic anti-idealism" involves a direct connection to Gnostic source texts and practices, and in general with a Gnostic spirit. And even though historians of religion would say that Bataille´s interest in Gnosticism, in fact, rather implies an affirmation of the scandalous picture that the early Church Fathers paint of certain Gnostic sects in their not-too-reliable heresiological reports, it is nevertheless in Bataille´s case the question of a committed mythopoetical process of "visionary re-visioning", which then in a double sense could be deemed truly Gnostic.

For what did Bataille´s project aspire to if not to isolate the "diversity of creation" from what it heretofore was considered to denote? In the separation of a homogeneity from a heterogeneity - corresponding to the socio-linguistic system and its power-charged residues - and in a systematic recourse to the latter area's dynamic ineffability, Bataille hoped to achieve an experience of the world in its completeness, as interior experience, in a continuum free from the intermediary symbolism that the enemy forces´ narrative provides.

Base matter is external and foreign to ideal human aspirations, and it refuses to allow itself to be reduced to the great ontological machines resulting from these aspirations. But the psychological process brought to light by Gnosticism had the same impact: it was a question of disconcerting the human spirit and idealism before something base, to the extent that one recognized the helplessness of superior principles.
(The Bataille Reader, 1997)

In the methodology for this purpose, which involves systematic transgressions of, for example, sexual and religious regulations, Bataille refers specifically to an antinomian (literally "against the law", antinomian is the polar opposite of legalistic religiosity) tendency within the Gnostic movement. According to Bataille´s informant Irenaeus (one of these Church Fathers), the Carpocrations regarded themselves as independent of the Mosaic Law and sought to destroy themselves by dispersing into earthly life, especially into "all those things which we dare not either speak or hear of".

Antinomian sects were usually named after their chosen type of sexual or materialist sacramentalism: the Borborians and the Coddians were known to be filthy, or dirt-eaters, the Haimatitoi drank menstrual blood, the Entychites had sex with partners decided by lot, the Levitici were ritualistic sodomites, the Stratiotici were known for having sexual powers, and the Antitactae, the "anti-fixed" ones, took on themselves the duty to be in general opposition to the Demiurge.

Obviously any transgressive strategy will be vulnerable to (building on) the escapist imagination of border guards, within or without, and Gnosticism has had more than its share of ambivalent outside observers. Bishop Epiphanius, avid Christian persecutor and compiler of heresies, provided this account (which served as inspiration for famous Victorian anti-Christian Aleister Crowley).

And the pitiful pair, having made love, then proceed to hold up their blasphemy to heaven, the woman and the man taking the secretion from the male into their own hands and standing looking up to heaven. They hold the impurity in their hands and pray . . and say "We offer you this gift, the body of Christ." And then they consume it, partaking of their shamefulness, and they say: "This is the body of Christ and this is the Pasch for which our bodies suffer" . . . When they fall into a frenzy among themselves, they soil their hands with the shame of their secretion, and rising, with defiled hands pray stark naked, as if through such an action they were able to find a hearing with God.
(Epiphanius, Panarion, 26.4-5)

In case of pregnancy

"they take the aborted infant and pound it up in a mortar with a pestle, and mixing in honey and pepper and some other spices and sweet oils so as not to become nauseous, all the members of that herd of swine and dogs gather together and each partakes with his finger of the crushed-up child.
(Panarion, 26.5.)

Antinomian (lack of) imagination aside, the real problem for Bataille - as well as for other clever language and image skeptics - is that the direct sign-relations between things that he wanted to see implemented (a non-organized matter) when it comes to the crunch are not accessible without at least some form of that detestable symbolism which "hides the world" from us.

The problem became evident in Bataille´s "Neoplatonic duel" with André Breton 1929-30, when the latter´s *via ascensus* (replacement and relating) was put in direct opposition to the former´s *via descensus* (isolation and *Verfremdung*). An inauthenticity dilemma in this acute form does not occur in the metaphor theory of Breton, where the world disclosed by poetic imagery (*surreality*) is not a station on the way to an unmediated thing-in-itself (*in spe*) but rather a momentary transparency created by the long-distance meeting between image and thing, and - since the distinction between image and thing is of limited use in surrealist poetics, between image and image - in the poetic metaphor (Marner, 1996).

Whether the hidden becomes visible through the image - and thus momentarily cancels alienation - can, for example from what we have called a visionary skeptical point of view, be said to be more a question of *mêtis* and *pistis*, i.e. innovative linguistic practice and confidence in the revelatory power of the image, than of the supposed understanding of the general status and reciprocal ontological hierarchy of the terms, energies and matter involved.

5. AS IF REALITY HIDES REALITY FOR US (About surrealist strategies: psychological models, dreaming and artistic creation in a metaphysical perspective; imagining an endless layer of disclosures/revelations and seeing truth in the dynamism of the images)

But in an even more skeptical, if not melancholic direction, one can at times go so far as to regard all pattern recognition as the equivalent of bad art, that is, learned patterns which are then projected. This is no less than half the truth, and if everything is in order the pendulum will soon swing back with full force. With a delirious confidence in poetry's ability to reveal new meanings at best no other preciosity is

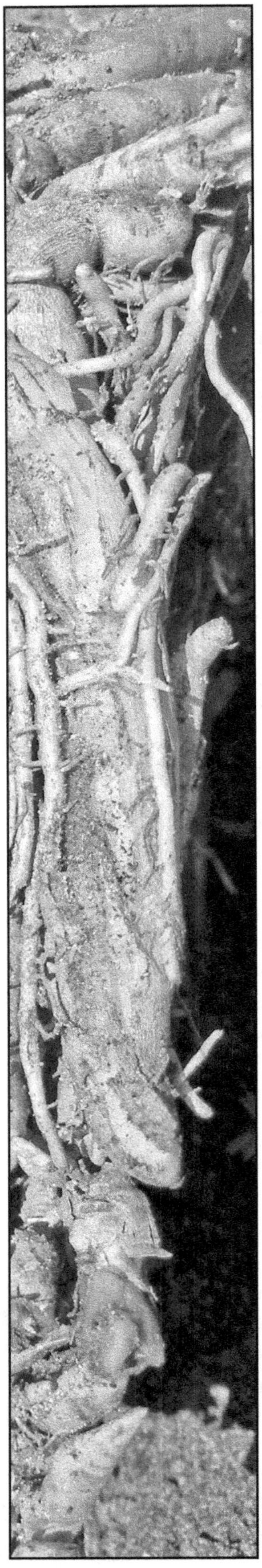

perceived than the insufficiency which distinguishes the abundance of emotion from the economy of expression, but - and this is important - is not able to distinguish these types of expressions from each other: "*Nature is a Haunted House - but Art a House that tries to be haunted*" (Emily Dickinson). A corresponding afterthought made Bataille see his project as productive in a wider sense than absolute determinations such as unsuccessful or successful could suggest. The desire for more reality did not tempt him to develop a myth of authenticity. Because the idea that the desire in order to consist must find a mode where it can both yield and maintain its phantom images is non-dualistic in terms of authenticity of experience.

It expresses a recognition of a conditional generative lack in the human economy of desire - something which certainly can be emancipating, but that does not promise any specific form of liberation, and in that sense it is a *Gnosis*. And regardless of whether we see this idea dressed in the psychoanalytic terms of Lacan - *"desire is neither the appetite for satisfaction nor the demand for love, but the difference that results from the subtraction of the first from the second"* - or in some metaphorical image from mythology - for the melancholic as Tantalus's punishment or for the more stoically or heroically inclined as "*Odin doomed to hunt and kill supernatural beings until the end of the world*" - we can be sure that the knowledge acquisition following the discovery of the illusory is instantaneous, regardless of its psychological quality, regardless of its tactical utility.

The general tendency of surrealism to take sides *with* the projections, disqualifies it from one-sidedly seeing what is tragic, futile, limiting about this basic condition, which then with some reservations we can describe as reality hiding reality for us. But regarding the question of the nature of the hidden and the problem of concealment there has never been any - and still is no? - consensus within surrealist ranks.

One could certainly say that surrealism´s early adoption of Freud's theory of how the dream work transforms the latent dream content into the manifest dream generally implies a defense of the point of view that an ontological difference exists between the image and its meaning, even if meaning´s sovereignty over the image is usually described vaguely as a tension, an intensity, rather than as an alternative state of things, a higher reality or as Reality. Still, this is not a far cry from generalizing the dialectic between illusion and reality in its antagonistic phase and then transferring it from a phenomenal plane to a rhetorical and theoretical plane. (Which is what we see in for example some popular attempts from the 1960's to reconcile the idea of a psychological repression of sexuality with the idea of an oppressed working-class.)

Is the value one ascribes to sexuality´s role as deputy for the latent content what will actually determine whether one expects an independent reality behind the words or not? It seems reasonable to argue that sexuality in general during the age of the advertisement, and so also in this context, mostly has had the advantage of *appearing* more real than libido, desire, bio-energy, the old man within, the cosmic rhythms of the reflection of the micro-cosmic flow, the romantic imagination or whatever one would prefer to suggest in its place.

But in view of sexuality´s "profanation" due to the excesses of late capitalism in this direction, naturally fewer and fewer of us are inclined to suggest that the unconscious is a container for x as in sexuality - or with advertising, x as in sexiness - rather than x as a living form-changing reality, which rather suggests a provisional state of itinerant findings and mythic images.

Transferring Aragon´s happy thesis that nothing stands between the dreamer and reality to the surrealistic experience in general could constitute the pole to which language skeptics in that case gather. On the one hand, if everything is "as it already is", this can be seen by anyone. On the other hand, since not everyone notices, the image of "what is" is dissolved into a solitary experience as formless as it is non-representable - until it is betrayed through anecdotes and declarations. Actually, testifying about the realm of the pre-natal, the numinous, the pre-linguistic, the proto-imagic - or considering the "creative nothingness" of Stirner, Whitehead, Nietzsche, Heidegger - as a resilient alternative to linguistic creations often tends to have something naive, idiotic, appealing or pompous about it.

The figure of an endless series of restrictive conventional systems with no underlying reality might be the other pole, at least if one finds one´s pleasure in the heroic task of building "*infernal machines*" against misery. *"The best we can aspire to is that behind the blown up wall, further away, we will find other walls whose texture and resistance we are unaware of and which will require new infernal machines that we have to invent from scratch"* (Nougé, Lettre a René Magritte, 1927, quoted in Sjölin).

That the wall behind the wall happens to be the machine which blew up the first wall is a foregone suspicion, and one which was aired by Breton in one of his late texts, where he says of the artist's creations that "*the visions are yet another veil, behind which hangs a second web of visions, and so on.*" And that the metaphysics about the unrestricted reality of the concealed rarely becomes more dogmatic than this is probably as it should be, but the irony of being wrenched from the multi-layered lifework of creativity before one has been permitted to "*go back from bark to bark to the white-hot kernel"* nevertheless can become a bitter one. Leaning on the emanationist Gnostic/Neoplatonic tradition, Artaud for his part identified the cabbage-head with its leaves as the specific form that Nothingness assumes for human consciousness (Lettres écrites de Rodez 1943-1944).

To further consider the dynamism of Nothingness in our comparative context here, the Gnostic *Aeons* represent personalized dimensional emanations starting from the original "empty" cause of thought-thinking-itself - the *Noesis Noeseos Noesis* of Aristotle (see also Hegel´s divine self-consciousness). Aeons are the infernal machines or the created veils, spreading outward from the center in onion-like layers and essentially constituting force-fields that repel or draw us closer to spirit. These layers or veils were fleshed out speculatively in a multitude of ways; psychologically and philosophically as numerous extensions of being (hypostases) or as triadic sets of principles or polar opposites, sensually (audible or visible, material or immaterial), mythologically (as supernatural creatures) and literally (as units of time in a cosmogony).

One of the contemporary critics of Gnosticism, the Neoplatonist Plotinus, strongly disliked the way the Gnostics preferred to keep the emanationist system on a mythological level like this rather than presenting it as a concise philosophical doctrine. Gnostic cosmology also stood in marked contrast to the anthropomorphic creator-created dichotomy of what would become orthodox Judeo-Christian religion, since reality to the Gnostics unfolds itself continuously and each stage of being is accessible to experience: cosmology becomes epistemology. To appreciate surrealism´s kinship with the Gnostic/Neoplatonic tradition, we can see how this conflict played out again on aesthetic grounds in the early modernist phase, when the bourgeois artist as monolithic creator was questioned and a creative force acting from beyond the horizon of the ego was posited.

6. ACOSMICISM IN PRACTICE: THE MYTHOPOESIS OF UNIVERSAL ALIENATION

So, if communication conceals communication from us, should we abolish it? From an ultra-radical standpoint the situationist image-theory and its strictly ascetic self-regulation of creative communication is nowadays often perceived as a necessary response to the advanced positions of market capitalist hegemony. Situationism´s autumnal words of advice may be rooted in the most grandiose theoretical holistic approach to the spectacle of our time, but precisely because of this holism their advice also turns out to be both inflexible in practice and vulnerable to generalist amplifications: in situationism we see a yearning for authenticity that constantly threatens to tip over into the overarching fear of mediation.

If one is interested in the functionings of a willfully mythologized world the *Nag Hammadi* Gnostic text Hypostasis of the Archons (Reality of the Rulers) could be appointed in a playful spirit as something of a memetic ancestor to the situationist The Society of the Spectacle. These two textual abysses of insight and paranoia seem to us in their related fight against alienation to be equals in their Platonic hostility towards representation as well as in their mood of spiritual rearmament, though they're hardly similar in strategic emphases.

> *"A veil exists between the world above and the realms that are below; and shadow came into being beneath the veil; and that shadow became matter; and that shadow was projected apart. And what she had created became a product in the matter, like an aborted fetus."*
> (Hypostasis of the Archons, NHL)

> *"Spectacular technology has not dispelled the religious clouds where men had placed their own powers detached from themselves; it has only tied them to an earthly base. The most earthly life thus becomes opaque and unbreathable. It no longer projects into the sky but shelters within itself its absolute denial, its fallacious paradise. The spectacle is the technical realization of the exile of human powers into a beyond; it is separation perfected within the interior of man."*
> (Debord, The Society of the Spectacle)

Where one text is cyclical and individualistic, the other is historicizing and revolutionarily class conscious, but both texts speak further about an awakening from the tyranny of the static moment force of the critical ability as the last resort. The situationist obsession with emphasizing the commodity as a model to highlight *one* way in which the particular relates to the universal seems to us, at the top of the fever curve of their hyperboles, also to have some religiously anti-religious implications. Or, to put the problem in terms of a magical equation: through polemical excesses the *egregorial* aspect of the described reality is invoked, with all the theurgical inconveniences this entails.

Some cases specifically come to mind here, where there seems to be a temptation to consistently see the purely ideological function of the image as its actual being: for if each image mainly represents the totality of the relationships it forms a part of, its integrity is easily left open - and thereby an entire heritage of conquered positions. In situationism it is presumed that the cumulative poisoning of quality, mana, fetish value, subversive force, etc. - and what really distinguishes these social charges from forms of personal magical energy? - has proceeded to a point where one no longer wants/is able to imagine a singularity that is not enrolled in a pre-determined context of meanings, which interferes with this system and can not be mediated.

The danger of this creative historicism is that its represented objective linear truth on too many points slips over into what it is considered to be in opposition with: a truth of merely symbolic, mythical or metaphorical range. Similarly to the Gnostics' experience of the totalitarian religious sign-system of their time as an inescapable totality, the relation to latter-day capitalism's universal threat is mediated by the particular wherever one looks, even through the introverted gaze, and so, consequently, even by one's own self. Thus the ultra-radical sooner or later will find that "*... the terrified Gnostic glance views the inner life as an abyss from which dark powers rise to govern our being, not controlled by our will, since this will itself is instrument and executor of those powers*" (Jonas, 1958).

7. ARCHONOLOGY: MAPPING EVIL INFLUENCES

These dark forces, created by the demiurge, the Gnostics with horror-mixed enthusiasm named *archons*. Like their inhibited creator, they are merely "*likenesses, copies, shadows, and phantasms, lacking reason and the light*" (*The Tripartite Tractate*, NHL). Their function is to define and limit physical existence, they are non-creative aspects of reality which bind us to the illusions of space and time, in every detail, somatically as well as psychologically.

In some places they are described so vividly - or so matter-of-factly - that their existence may have been taken as - anthropo- or theriomorphically - literally true. Thus in modern mythology the Gnostic archons have been enthusiastically adopted by UFO-conspirators, since their role as cosmic prison-guards lends itself to "striking" comparisons with literalistic assumptions about sinister supervisors from other planets. In the uncertain but nevertheless more pragmatic territory of out-of-body-experiences (OBE's) and lucid dreaming, they may likely be encountered as the "psychic wildlife" of sub-astral realms. At other times the archons constitute more allegorical personifications of radically unknowable intermediary dimensional states - like HP Lovecraft's *The Old Ones* - which the Gnostic adept has to confront with the help of magic formulas in his/her free soul-flights through the Aeons.

> *And again when they take my soul to the place of Typhon,*
> *the great and powerful Archon with the face of an ass*
> *who is spread out upon the way of the Midst,*
> *who carries off the souls by theft:*
> *when they take my soul to that place*
> *it will give to them the mystery of their fear, which is PPAWP*
>
> (Bruce Codex: Fragment of a Gnostic text "On the Passage of the Soul Through the Archons of the Way of the Midst")

The "*Archon with the face of an ass*" Bataille excitedly designated as the hypostasis of dualistic materialism, which in his personal mythology animated "*the conception of matter as an* active *principle having its own eternal autonomous existence as darkness /.../, and as evil* " (The Bataille Reader).

If we translate the subsistence of the archons somewhat loosely in terms of psychology, we would consider them rather as malicious but vaguely defined metaphysical authorities like the state, the system, the cop inside, personality market etc. But since we also by "internal" wanted to distinguish the physical state, we perhaps would better refer here to a comparison with the "*mechanico-mystical complex*" of Wilhelm Reich, i.e. something like an internalized personality-derogatory structure of the authoritarian ideology. Reich´s merits in "archonology" then would include the identification of them - or their effects - not only on a psychological level, but as nervous tension in muscles, such as lockings and hardenings in motor functions and behavior. He developed a methodology to deal with them, just as systematically and objectively as the Gnostics themselves, which mapped archontic control over the sensory apparatus with fantastic detail. *Basiliademe* created Adam´s tonsils, over the toes of the right foot *Boabel* rules, the one who controls the imaginative unit is called *Oummaa*, chief demon of grief is *Nenentophni*, belonging to the jurisdiction of *Pserem* is "the kidney of the right leg" (!), while *Atoimenpsephei* controls "the breaths which are in all the limbs", etc.

This is what utter darkness and invisibility reveal to the inquiring dualist minds of pre-scientific materialism: in the absence of cosmological wellbeing, a wealth of imaginative activity.

8. PRIMITIVISM AND THE DEAD END OF SYMBOLIC COMMUNICATION

The starting point that linguistic imagery is both concealing and revealing the world to us has not quite been able to satisfy those of us who put some of our hopes in a "primitivist" turn. From this direction it is observed, and with some justice, that cultural expressions as a whole have fused with the emptiest forms of social reality, and now *language* completely obstructs the view.

> *Like ideology, language creates false separations and objectifications through its symbolizing power. This falsification is made possible by concealing, and ultimately vitiating, the participation of the subject in the physical world.*
> (Zerzan)

This *kenomatic* totality is then experienced as a barrier between desire and the world, where any message about something else is turned on its head or attracts an insignificant fate.

There are many questions with this view, and with this side of anarcho-primitivism. On the one hand, it seems reasonable to assume that a recovered "primitive consciousness" would be able to integrate us with a now lost experiential directness that culture has ceased to provide for us - if cultures *are* so monolithic *and* so inefficient.

On the other hand, it would seem unlikely that any primitivist commitment could be realized continuously or in more than glimpses. Especially if it considers the absence of symbolic forms as what characterizes the desirable life of pre-civilized human beings. But as emergency prescription against the decadent narcissism of cultural production like primitivism we ordain free play and sensual experience, just as we cultivate a strong skepticism towards the repressive functions of technology.

But we do not do so because the large-scale features of arts and culture appear to have been bungled, nor because technology in itself would be alienating, but rather because this epoch´s involvement in new technical issues increasingly leads us to mistake or substitute social and political realities for their overly symbolic forms. And here it may be interesting to remind ourselves that the power structures share the same predicament that we are in; power has not gained mastery over technology, the fight is not settled, the ring need not be brought back to *Mount Doom*.

A broader primitivist criticism – i.e. one that imagines a break, a Fall such as language generation, the transition to the agricultural, etc. - fails to properly explain to us how the poems, the paintings and the eidetic/dreaming ability we´re still able to enjoy has lost its meaning other than in a purely statistical sense. We have to also remind ourselves that the arguments for primitivism often are generated in environments that are unhealthily fond of generalized solutions where social progress is gladly sacrificed and sacrifice in general is valued highly. Since surrealism never self-identified with art in the ordinary sense, the primitivist criticism of its artificiality etc. will hit home only when society´s art products and active creativity coincide, and that has not happened once, it happens all the time. And vice versa: if surrealism betrays its primitivist tendency its mythopoesis will turn into literature and art already on the level of intention, which likewise is unacceptable all the time.

And besides, is language (considered as communication systems) really a specifically human invention?

9. METAPHYSICS OF CREATIVITY: THE ROLE OF THE MIND IN GNOSTIC INTERPRETATIONS OF CREATION MYTHS RELATED TO SURREALISM BY WAY OF THE "SUPREME POINT"

What the Gnostics pre-eminently focused on was to comment and expand upon creation myths. Each society has a creation myth and a viable interpretation of it that reflects the epistemological nature of that society. It is telling that the dominating religious creation myth in our society refers to a creator who when finished with his work went to sleep, only to come back occasionally as a hysterical tyrant. Likewise that the first human being was a man who saw woman as created out of himself rather than as a separate being. This culture is terrifyingly literal even today, and that applies to atheists as well as religious fundamentalists.

The Gnostics may have been the first to explicitly set self-knowledge against the solipsistic slave relationship between humans and their created images: *"That is the way it is in the world - men make gods and worship their creation. It would be fitting for the gods to worship men!"* (Gospel of Philip, NHL). That creation myths and cosmological speculation have an aspect which involves human liberation and creativity has taken an extremely long time to realize. To be creative, according to the poet Adonis in his book on the tangential points of contact between Sufi poetics and metaphysics and surrealism, is to reflect the world in its changing forms in one´s heart, as inexhaustible, infinite, absolute.

It is on that account that we with the Gnostics can call the world a "creation", not because it would be just a social construction, which it certainly is, but because it has no beginning, i.e. its creation takes place in each moment. And because the creative principle (the spiritual) is its own immanent reality (illusion), available or elusive at all times, as Gnosis.

Considering this privileged state of rapport, we recognize that the metaphysical equivalent of consciousness a priori (consciousness "itself", not its material or content) is called - depending on the historical or cultural context - being, *Purusha*, *Brahma, Tao*, emptiness, illusion, god, the sound of the nervous system turned on itself, the expansion and mutually-driven complexification of living matter, total otherness, *Unbeing*, planetary autopoiesis, *pleroma.*

Consciousness a posteriori is in all likelihood *language*. Consciousness - (consciousness *of*) - always occurs in relation to an object and is therefore not separated from the object world. The relationship consists precisely in language, at least in a broad sense. When the relationship is vital and a direct flow between subject and object enhances an experiential unit, we experience the relationship as inspiring, revelatory or holy, as when the child splashes with its hand on the surface of the water or makes tracks in the sand to see them being erased by the waves. When the vital relationship occurs on the plane of thought in freedom the relationship is, of course, poetic, which means that the field of connections is supplemented a thousandfold and the unmanifested is allowed to be thought.

> *"Everything tends to make us believe that there exists a certain point of the mind at which life and death, the real and the imagined, past and future, the communicable and the incommunicable, high and low, cease to be perceived as contradictions."*
> (Breton, Second Manifesto of Surrealism)

The *sublime point* of surrealism is represented from the point of view of manifestations and therefore appears speculatively as a converging total experience of/in consciousness, namely as the zenith of the height of freedom to which poetic thinking aims. From the opposite point of view of emanationist cosmology the sublime point would be regarded from the top down, and therefore appear as the point where non-manifested being transitions into creation and diversity: "*Everything is enveloped in the Unity of Knowledge, symbolized by the Point*" (Shaikh al-'Alawi).

As the center around which the manifestations of the unknown are crystallized and diverge this interface point seems partly to derive from an esoteric interpretation of geometry, where the point is "*quantitatively nil and does not occupy any space, though it is the principle by which space in its entirety is produced, since space is but the the development of its intrinsic virtualities*" (René Guenon, quoted in Scott). In addition it is regularly described as positioned in human cognition *and* in human anatomy. In terms of growth and stressing the latent potential to embrace all, the supreme point of cognition is often pictured as a seed or a germ; like the *bindu, dhatu* and *Bija* seeds of vedanta, like the *logos spermatikos* of the Greeks and like the *Kingdom of Heaven* of the Christians which is likened to the seemingly insignificant mustard grain. The Gnostic *spinther* shares with some Hindu and tantric counterparts its specific location in the heart, and like the *spirit spark atom* of the latter-day Rosicrucians and the *reshinu* of Kabbala, it constitutes there a brilliant residue, a "spark" or "splinter" from *Ein-Sof.*

10. METAPHORIC MOTOR REPLAY: LANGUAGE PERCEPTION ACCORDING TO SCIENCE, POETRY AND PESSIMISM

If the basis for empirical reality, being, is not affirmed, a unilateral rejection of the social consensus reality in all likelihood will have a depleting affect on health and personality. But taking the step from radical skepticism or relativism to an affirmation of being as such (the infinite, the uncreated, the unknown) requires trust in an alternative strategy. And this is basically what an encounter with the Gnostic proposition entails, even today. In his *Valis* trilogy science-fiction author Philip K. Dick brilliantly developed a narrative of his encounter with Gnostic ideas as an "*act of disobedience to the spurious projection and an act of faith toward the authentic substratum – without, perhaps, of ever having caught any aspect of the substratum perceptually*" (Dick, 1995). His health and personality *were* affected badly, and he was haunted by the idea that only "*some external entity would have to trigger off this complex psychological process of simultaneous withdrawal of assent and expression of faith*". Religious faith however, or something similar to it, be it madness or some other form of deliberately designed alternative reality, is a leap of faith which ends in a search for a new consensus reality.

With *gnosis*, such a trust gains, however, an irreducibly individualistic structure, which operates in an emancipatory way without perhaps even catching a single perceptual aspect of the "substratum", much less communicating it in understandable terms. (Dick describes how he lived a concept of infinity by each day developing a new theory about everything, every theory leading to an infinite regression of thesis and new synthesis.)

Gnosis then can be understood not as an experience of truth in an empirically verifiable sense, but as arising as a state of modified perception in which the non-conditioned awareness (*spinther*, the spark) becomes one with the object of its contemplation. Knowing in this sense is cognitively analogous to the erotic encounter, as testified by the frequent use of the figure of the *bridal chamber: "The bridal chamber and the image must enter through the image into the truth: this is the restoration*" (Gospel of Philip, NHL). Such experiences are thus frequently expressed metaphorically, sometimes in the form of riddles, such as here with a series of semantic shocks in the guise of formally breaking the incest taboo:

> *I am the bride and the bride groom,*
> *and it is my husband who begot me.*
> *I am the mother of my father*
> *and the sister of my husband*
> *and he is my offspring.*
>
> (Thunder Perfect Mind, NHL)

(An allegorical interpretation reads, roughly: I (wisdom) am the psyche as a whole; feeling and reason. One can reach me by reason. I am alike reason and reason is derived and modified according to me.)

The very heart of the surrealist view of language, apart from automatism, is the metaphor theory of Breton, which was taken over from the French symbolist poets who meant to impose a maximum span between the image (signifier) and the thing described (signified) in order to ensure maximum poetic effect.

Few literary phenomena now seem as passé as intricate sonnets on spleen and super-sensual longing, something that has less to do with literary trends than with the shift in language perception in general towards the axiom of "utter relativity and opacity" (Hakim Bey). In light of the 1900s thorough intellectual commitment to separate language from reality, and the lengthy impact this project has had on literature and the arts in the form of an inflation of the realist idiom, linguistic materialism, documentarism, conceptualism etc., the symbolist poetics of the 1800s nowadays are viewed as artificial, if not stale and otherworldly and affectedly entangled in obscure rhetorical gestures without referents.

The symbolist poets who are deemed to have aged the best are those that in the (post)modern sense make a theme of their own artificiality, or are considered to do so, such as Baudelaire and Mallarmé. Although we will refrain from contesting such unsatisfying assessments here, it may suffice to say that we, owing to this depreciation, are being saddled with a strange dualistic ontology. It announces itself as a promotion of language and its structures as a sphere for the artificial and illusory, while the social and physical world has become the new *pleromatic* essence, which, on one side *can* not be referred to (relativism) and on the other hand, always *must* be referred to (realism).

The poets' worldview, or the hope that language in its highest potency expresses the real function of thought, has had to retreat from such claims to being a part of language, if not just rhetoric. Like Freud, who wanted to see dreams and myths as psychological structures, such claims are at present preferably being redirected to the perspectivist experimental workshop of the language-pessimists, to literature.

But current trends in linguistics seem to be able to detach language somewhat from the accusation that it merely suggests a system of alienating post-essential re-presentationism. These trends bring metaphors to the forefront. With conceptual metaphors it is suggested that an idea can be understood in terms of another idea, such as quantity in terms of direction, e.g. in plain language "prices are rising". Even in science cognitive metaphors like "fluid motion" for conducted electricity or Niels Bohrs' "planetary orbits" for the model of the atomic nucleus and electrons seem to do a descriptive job without being in opposition to the scientific method.

Within cognitive linguistics, the "embodied mind theory" (Lakoff and Johnson) has demonstrated that the functions of thought are metaphorical to a significantly higher degree than they are logical and that truths can be understood as metaphorical constructs rather than as characteristics of an objective reality.

That we make ourselves familiar with the world in exactly the same way as when we read poetic metaphors - by discerning similarities and differences, and by letting familiar and unfamiliar areas illuminate each other - is perhaps no news to us. Not least because the harsh implications of this relationship in terms of indoctrination are so obvious: the acquisition of language through the mass media in early life means that the range of metaphorical combinations is tightly circumscribed with ideologically rewarding maps of, for example, property control and fear of conflict (Chomsky speaks of this).

More interesting here might be to draw on the idea that the ontological basis of the scientific and religious truth-claims according to this theory are metaphors which are based on the experience of having a body, a sensory-motor set of characteristics, and that metaphor works in *thought*, not in a detached language-model, the latter for a long time having been suggested by the legacy of Saussure's general linguistics.

We may have talked too long about language as barrier as well as resource for authentic experience, both in this essay and in general, as if all the talk would be an essence in itself to respond to. *"If modern analyses of heresy fail - seeing the debates as purely doctrinal or ideological, for example - it is because they ignore the underground somatic current that lies at the heart of all Gnostic systems"* (Berman, quoted in Elder). For, as we have seen, the bodily interface makes the claim to be these barriers and these resources for freedom as well, and the Gnostics knew of the connection. Like Artaud, who argued that unless thought has a direct impact on the nerves it is worthless.

Adonis - Sufism and Surrealism. Saqi, 2005.

The Ante-Nicene Fathers Vol. I, Against Heresies: Book I by Irenaeus , translated by Philip Schaff et al. Chapter IV. www.ccel.org/fathers.html/

Bataille, Georges - The Bataille Reader, Edited by Fred Botting, Scott Wilson. Wiley-Blackwell, 1997.

Bataille, Georges - Essential Writings, edited by Michael Richardson. Sage Publications, 1998.

Bey, Hakim - T.A.Z.; The Temporary Autonomous Zone, Ontological Anarchy, Poetic Terrorism. Autonomedia, 1985 (2003).

Breton, André - "On magic art" , from "What is Surrealism?"

Breton, André - Manifestoes of Surrealism. University of Michigan Press, 1969.

Bruce Codex: Fragment of a Gnostic Text, "On the Passage of the Soul", from www.gnosis.org/library/frgsp.htm

Debord, Guy - The Society of the Spectacle, Black & Red, 1977.

Dick, Philip K. - The Shifting Realities of Philip K. Dick, Selected Literary and Philosophical Writings by Philip K. Dick, edited by Lawrence Sutin. First Vintage Books, 1995.

Elder, R. Bruce - A Body of Vision: Representations of the Body in Recent Film and Poetry. Wilfrid Laurier University Press, 1997.

Epiphanius - The Panarion of Epiphanius of Salamis / Translated by Frank Williams. Leiden: Brill, 1987,1994.

Hollier, Denis - Surrealism and its Discontents, Papers of Surrealism Issue 7, 2007: The Use-Value of Documents

Rev. Illuminatus Maximus - Antinomian Antics: Sabotaging the Matrix, online essay at www.Gnosticshock.com

Jonas, Hans - The Gnostic Religion: The Message of the Alien God & the Beginnings of Christianity. Beacon Press, 1958.

Kingsley, Peter - Reality. The Golden Sufi Center Publishing, 2003.

Lakoff, George - (with Mark Johnson) Philosophy In The Flesh: the Embodied Mind and its Challenge to Western Thought. Basic Books, 1999.

Marner, Anders - Rhetoric in surrealism's double discourse: Bataille vs Breton, 1996. Online essay at www.educ.umu.se/~marner/rhetorics.html

The Nag Hammadi Library in English - J. M. Robinson, ed. New York, 3rd ed., 1988. Cited as NHL.

Reich, Wilhelm - The Mass Psychology of Fascism, Third, revised and enlarged edition. Orgone Institute Press, 1946.

Sansonese, J. Nigro - The Body of Myth: Mythology, Shamanic Trance, and the Sacred Geography of the Body. Inner Traditions International, 1994.

Scott, Timothy - The Container and the Contained, Vincit Omnia Veritas 2.2 (2006, 176-187), online essay at religioperennis.org

Sjölin, Jan-Gunnar - Den surrealistiska erfarenheten: Upplevelsen. En tolkning av surrealismens åskådning. Kalejdoskop, 1981.

Winther, Mats - The Sphinxlike Unconscious, 2009. Online essay at http://home.swipnet.se/~w-73784/sphinx.htm

Zerzan, John - Language: Origin and Meaning, and The Case Against Art, online essays at www.primitivism.com

Sensuality: The Particular Wave

Michel Zimbacca

The Nile flowed backwards and I was born from an internal explosion of sensuality.

This word which looks like a declaration made by nothing other than the thing itself, its tonal rhythm wrapped in silence, its accent withdrawn, pronouncing the suspension of a heartbeat and without it, a shell set down in the sunshine of pleasure… but sensuality [*volupté*] unfurling the internal ear initiates the instant of those forevers which are more than "all the water in the sea". Whether discovery, innovation or reinvention, it makes no difference – for us this word is nonetheless a name.

When in 1948 André Breton placed the lamp in the clock, denouncing "the end of a world which is not ours" but which belongs to those who can give birth only to judgements and threats to exacerbate the sterile repetitions of history, he called on surrealism to "proceed deliberately to an inversion of sign". He thus set surrealism the task of emphasising the affirmation of life under the "rising sign". A unique decoder and collector of the treasures of sedition, he was passing on his new discovery of the splendours of an utterly original work and showing us its key, "which Malcolm de Chazal has obligingly left in the door" and which "resides in *sensuality*, in the least figurative sense of the term, considered as the supreme point of resolution of the physical and the mental".

We can only share his amazement at the magnitude of this discovery: "It is astonishing that we had to wait until the middle of the 20th century for sensuality – a phenomenon that plays a unique role in the conditioning of almost any life – to find a way to speak of itself, no longer wearing the veils of hypocrisy, or the licentious finery of defiance beneath which it has managed to conceal itself just as well." For us who, half a century later, had thought that our only starting point was the disoccultation of sensuality from a narrow conception of sexual pleasure, the erection of which into "the pleasure principle" suffices only insofar as it calls for its own beyond, the effects of this major signal have been felt across all the potential motherlodes of "real life" which the voluntary or forced occultations of the surrealist adventure have entrusted or left to ripen in us and outside us.

These occultations carry the signal back to us the echoes of sensuality when, for example, we wonder today: Is it by chance, accident or vital necessity that its objectification is taking place during a period when a generalised disenchantment, at the level of global acculturation, has opened up thoroughly hellish perspectives? Or indeed: Was sensuality ever, was it always, the initial inspiration for multiple interpretations of the world? Was it the origin of communality in some community, or does it only reveal itself, without cultural intercession, one being at a time, in the minds of those who are most receptive? And since we place our hopes in it, what can we expect from a re-co-birth of the sensuality which we seek to free, according to our respective experiences, from our idiosyncrasies of mind and behaviour, or from our aspiration to a potlatch worthy of its importance?

A shared sense of sensuality – which would irradiate the pathways of conductibility of thought, of the irreducibilities of automatism, or of dreams, at the junctions and revelations of analogy illuminating one another with their complementarity – should at least reintroduce a new sense of harmony and re-inspire our power of conception with its own, confirming surrealism as the most complete interchange of thought capable of its own surpassing.

If, starting from the so-called conjectural sciences, we were able one day to comprehend the reality of sensuality as a phenomenon concerned, for example, with the whole of biology and even the whole of dynamics, such a rationalised understanding would remain insufficient for any comprehension of sensuality in ourselves, without recourse to the common imaginary, to myth.

"A body in free-fall does not feel its own weight."

O mother of graceful beauty, giving birth to you in turn, echo of the sublime and from one to the other echo immersing the one in the other, punctuating this path where the one is divinely enchanted by the free forward movement of the other and is so violently moved when, in the grip of its fevers, he has to maintain their progress!

Sensuality, love which lives me.

Underpinning ideology and utopia, myth remains the most profound instigator of public and particular destinies reciprocally reflected in everything that has fallen prey to misery and cultural submission. The idea that one could subtract one of the elements of that trilogy to the advantage of the others in the driving force of History amounts to a repression of its hopes in the guise, here, of messianic myth, and perpetuates the castrating misuse of its idealism.

As Joël Gayraud has written, "Food riots are never about having, but about being. [...] A riot for the means of subsistence is only the first moment in the starving man's reconquest of sovereignty over his own body."

It is precisely the expression of this reconquerrable sovereignty which has been missing from revolutionary myths and impulses, thus enabling their Manichaean subversion every time.

Compared with those universal ordeals which start with the beginning of life and continue to its end, an increasing consciousness of the experience which most completely shatters one's being can only illuminate it through the repetitions of its own disasters, reveal the extent of its failures, and provide for the foundations of a new understanding.

If there are ways for a shared consciousness to avoid the drama which only awakens that consciousness for an all-too-brief historical moment, and to forestall the tragic choice between war and revolution, between the incitement of terrorism and the use of basic rights as blackmail, simply to prolong the total confusion of power with property and real value with the fiction of exchange, those ways are to be found in the recognition, in Man's relationship with himself, of the primacy of something which has always been, will always be, unquantifiable.

Irreducible to the expression of anything other than an *all* with no beginning or end, sensuality seems to defy any attempt at piecemeal investigation.

On the watch for the aroused projections of our magnetised intuitions, our obsessions with losable objects, our thoughts distracted from their methods, the fairy of metamorphoses only appears on the very flesh of the unspoken wish.

Like that which is for us the visible or invisible lights in the majesty of the darkness which seems to enclose them, refracting ideas in their carnal orbits, rendering iridescent our consciousness of the bouquet of the senses, she gives back to us that transparency where all communicability takes place.

What memory would maintain other than the signature of this state of mind and body, when the dynamic of their alternation, from container to contained, one to the other, allows our faculties of resilience to emerge?

In *Prolegomena to a Third Surrealist Manifesto or Not* (1942), Breton invokes "the great sparkling rose-window [...] swaying gracefully, the flower of true life blossoming at last", calls on us to "take into account the ephemeral and the eternal", follows inexhaustible networks of correspondences which, despite the panorama of material and moral ruins, are being reborn to the strains of desire, and enquires into the quanta superior to our own dimensions, teasing out the points of convergence between daring scientific hypotheses and the imagination of a poet. Here he uncovers a myth in the making, proposing the "Great Transparents" on the basis of a suggestion from Novalis: "In reality we live in an animal whose parasites we are. The constitution of this animal determines ours and vice versa."

What cultural survivals can escape such a mirror effect, reaching out across a distance of two centuries? Struggling with the aggressive increase of its own parasitism, lurching from emergency to catastrophe, surely the human race is forced first of all to demand of itself more than change, more than a transformation of social relations, but a radical break with anthropomorphism, in all of its religious and ideological forms. If everything that moves must, or should, be or return to itself, *if the waves emitted by sensuality flow, if that which is jointly experienced as the abolition of time and space took part in a certain magnetism and, like the flagellated head dedicated to procreation, travelled and transmitted all at once from one order of dimension to another, from one time flow to another, inserting the subtle seed of enquiry at a suitably dense point, everything suggests that it is sensuality which will scatter human faculties like questing stars among the unknown at the heart of the genesis of the myth of the Great Transparents.*

When pleasure and pain fuse and dissolve each other, when love and the object of love can no longer distinguish themselves from each other or from anything else, there appears the transparency of desire lit by its own light. And all the freedom of our desire to come, Sensuality, stems from your refusal to fall captive to a reverent myth, you who guard the formula of fire.

Translated by Merl Fluin

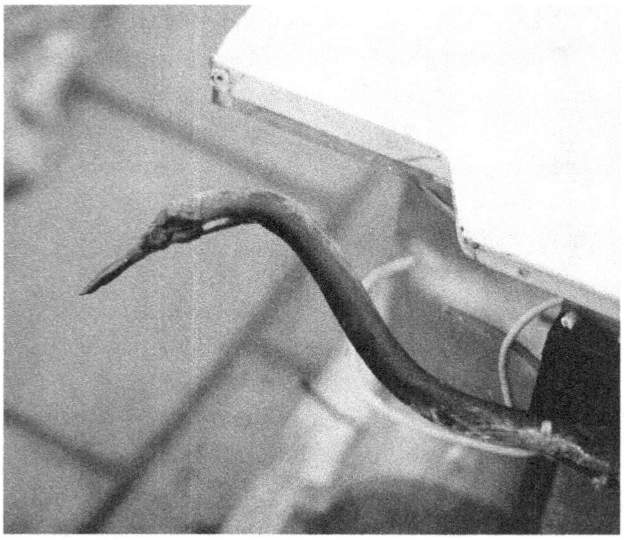

Crane, photograph by Paul Cowdell

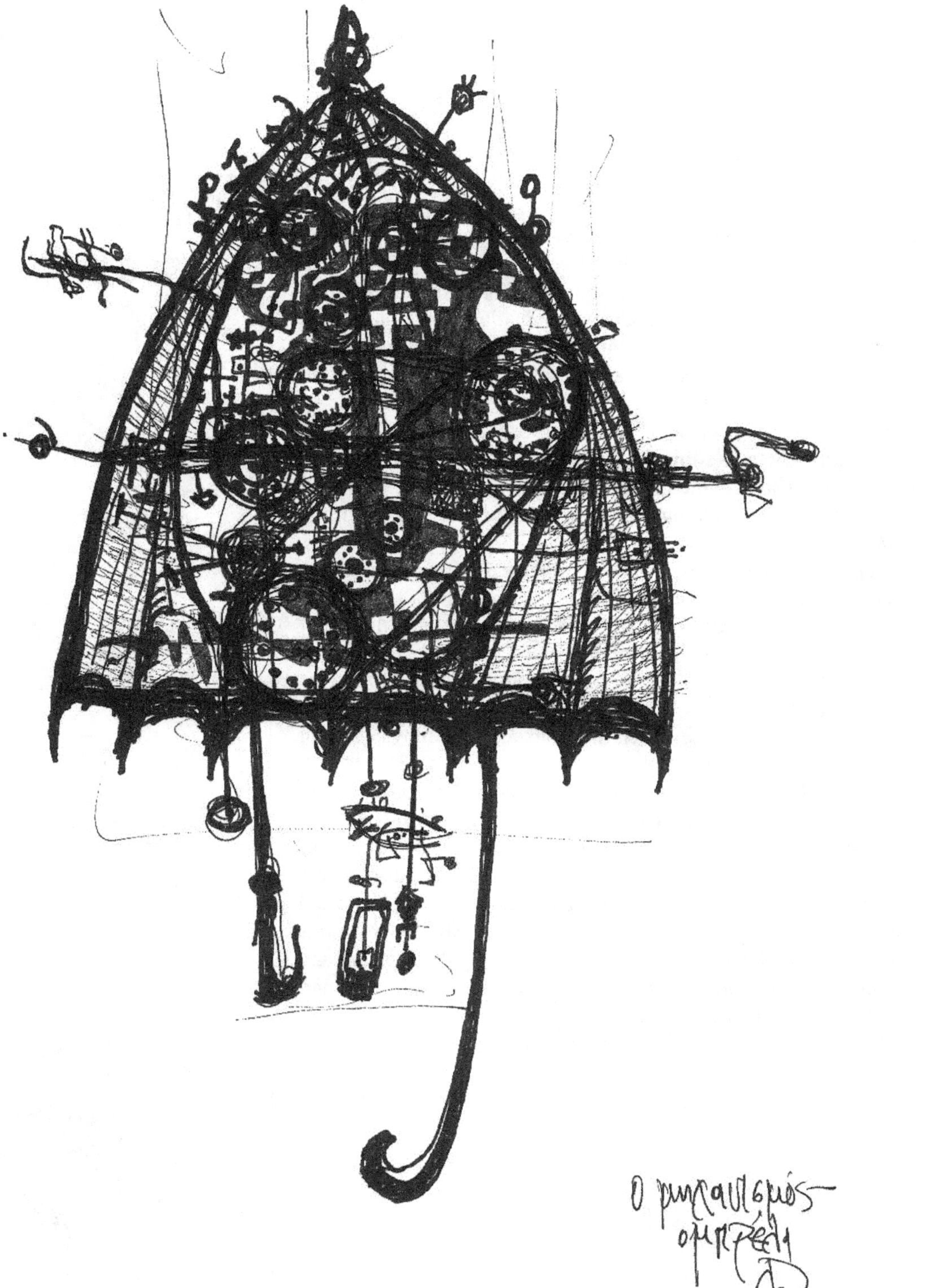

The Umbrella Mechanism, drawing by Theoni Tambaki

SIDEREAL GEOGRAPHY

David Nadeau

Guy-René Doumayrou's essay on sidereal geography[1] was published in 1975, during what was probably the gestation period of the publication *La Civilisation Surréaliste*. This book brought together and developed a set of ideas which had first appeared in work published in the journal *Médium*. Doumayrou studied geographical and architectural symbolism in relation to astrology, notably the question of the zodiacal orientation of the old Cathar castle at Montségur. His first important article, "Chateau comme Poindre" ("Dawning Castle"), a mediaevalist reverie on fortified castles – "these solid concretions of desire illuminated by consciousness" – was also the occasion for Doumayrou to set out a revolutionary, and surrealist, critique of "today's apartments". Doumayrou also provided a geographical map to accompany an article by Jean Markale published around the same period in the *Bulletin de Liaison Surréaliste*.

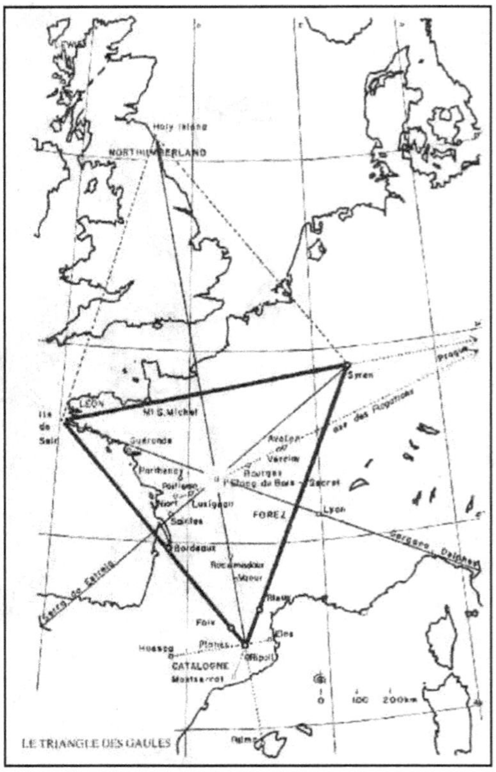

The pond in the secret woods

Doumayrou was a passionate pamphleteer; he published some tracts in the anarchist newspaper *Le Libertaire*[2], and his highly poetic work on sidereal geography also shows repeated flashes of his basic political and ecological demands.

Doumayrou's essay starts from the following observation: the alignments of cathedrals, pilgrim sites, and a few isolated castles form networks in France which match exactly the movements of the twelve constellations of the zodiac.

An initiatory (i.e. simultaneously sensual, imaginative and moral) conception of French geography flows from this precise observation, guided by the stories of the Grail and the poetry of the troubadours. The chivalric orders and the poet-discoverers were the principal vectors of a "spiritual tradition which poeticised places". Their task was to maintain symbolically the relations between Man, Nature and the Cosmos, multiplying inspiring and enigmatic signs by means of architecture, allusive toponyms, and the choice of certain geographical spaces.

"Geographical-sidereal" centres are also recognisable by their coats of arms.

The centre of a coat of arms is called "coeur" ("heart") and also "abyss".

Centre heart or abyss
these oases are no more than tombs
where the crow is king
(Roland Giguère, "Blood and Gold", in *L'Age de la Parole.*)

Coat of arms of the town of Feurs

Furthermore, the different traditional forms of the coat of arms all recall the shape of the human heart.

Doumayrou insists on exactly this piece of spiritual evidence: if there are geographical centres, the unique and only real centre of the world for each person is his or her own heart.

The heart, not the head, is the location of moral and creative intelligence. It is the symbolic location of the reconciliation of opposites within the individual, and of his or her transformation.

The fundamental initiatory ordeal, Doumayrou reminds us, is a sort of death: a radical transformation followed by a reorganisation.

For anyone with even a cursory knowledge of the magic epic of Antonin Artaud[3], it is curious that Doumayrou should situate the centre of the "regenerative ordeal" at Rodez, place of "battles of love and death, frantic dives into the beyond".

Jean-Pierre Lassalle, another surrealist well versed in Freemasonry, sets the action of one of his "initiatory journeys" on the return train from Rodez:

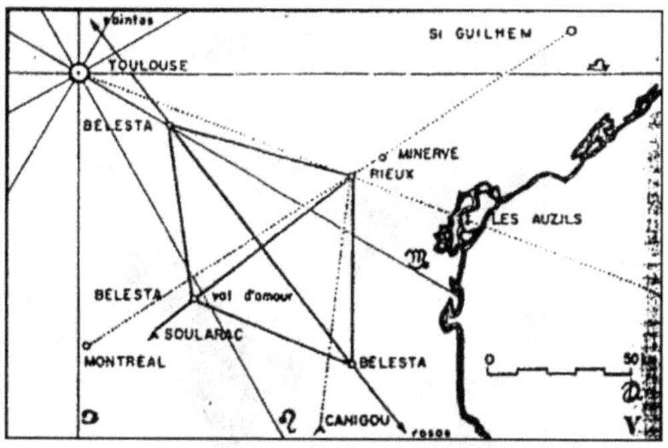

Sidereal-geographical map by Guy-René Doumayrou

At the curve of a juniper I no longer saw Cycna-Cytise nor Artaud.
When I got lost quickly I yelled enough to break my neck and
I went mad

In the triangle of calcium which explodes and falls back in a spray of orioles and pink favours, of the station and the crystal-object, my lives blaze my sayings fade my women love.

Flattering the spine of Issolu I scraped myself on the black poplar.

So I learned to be wary. The journey had exhausted me, I was dirty, shaken. Everything was blue and translucent. My train juddered along...

("Return from Rodez", in *Poèmes Presques.*)

Translated by Merl Fluin

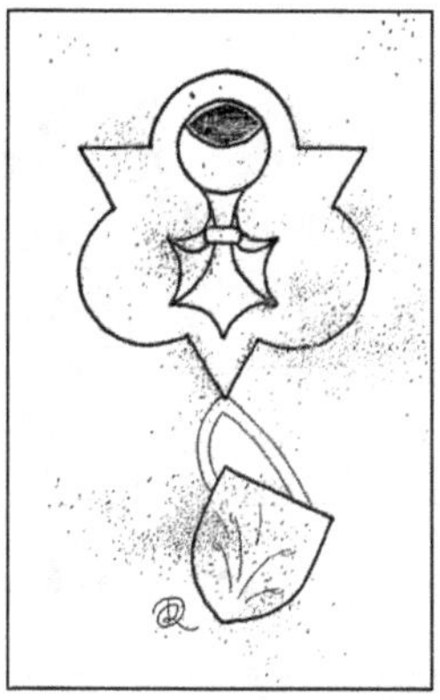

Left: Sketch of the motif carved in 1449 on the tombstone of Bérenger Amyll, sacristan of Villelongue

Below:
The Garden of Wonders, drawing by Guy-René Doumayrou

Endnotes:

1) Guy-René Doumayrou. *Essai sur la géographie sidérale des pays d'Oc et d'ailleurs.* Paris, Union générale d'éditions, collection "10-18", 1975. 312 pages.

2) "Du Pain et des Jeux" ("Bread and Games", in favour of indulgence, laziness and the practice of the arts), and a tract co-signed with his comrade Bernard Roger, "La Relève des Corbeaux" ("The Changing of the Crows", attacking the threat posed to individual liberties by bureaucracy).

3) The poet was interned at Rodez between 1943 and 1946.

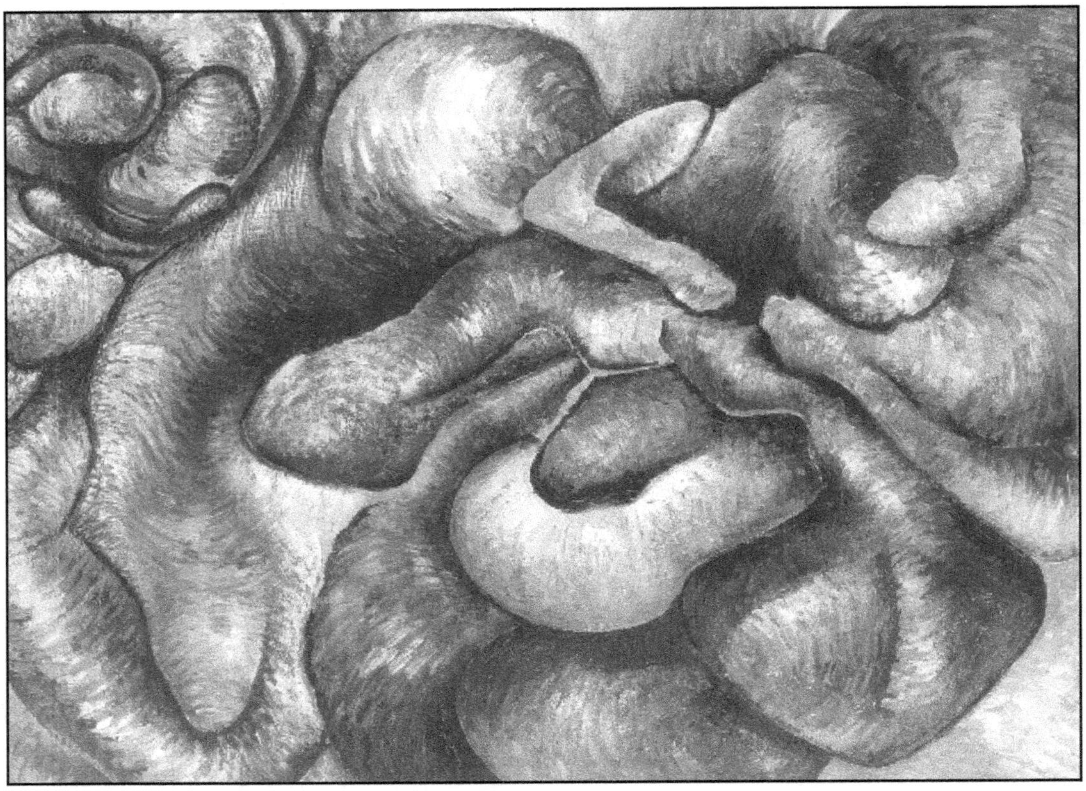

Internal Myth, Acrylic painting by John Welson

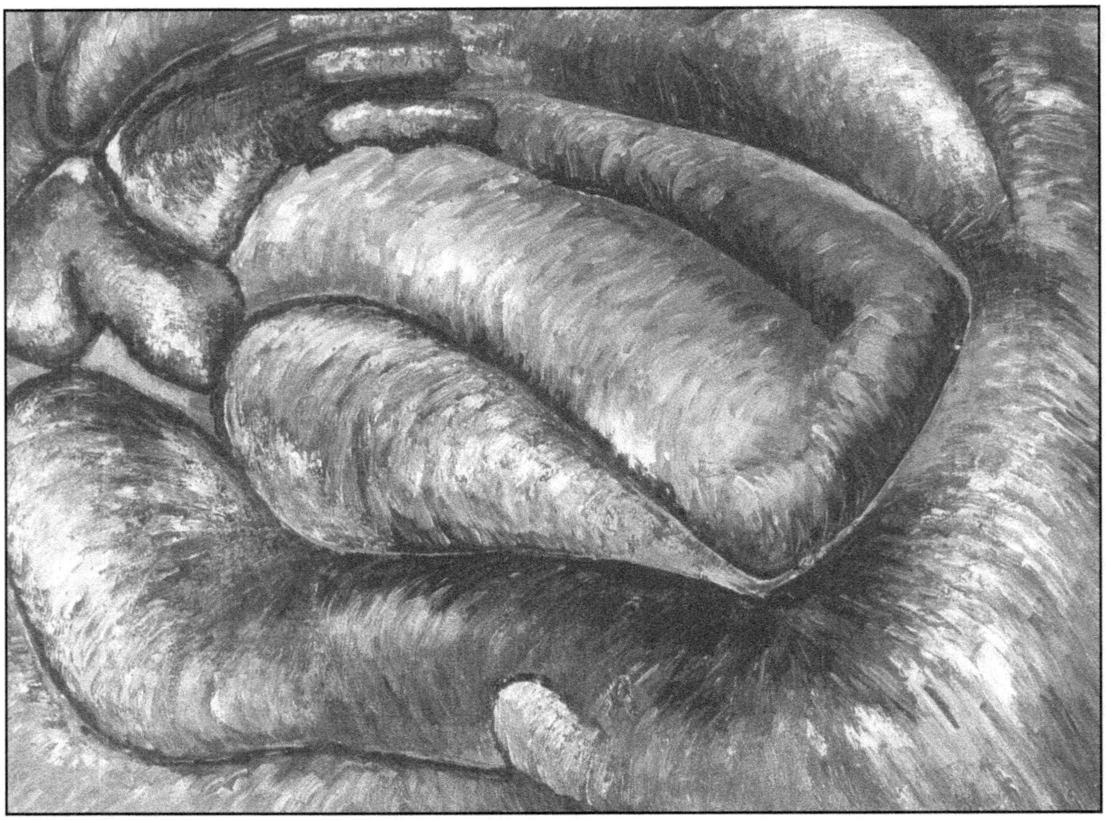

The Myth of Black Echo, Acrylic painting by John Welson

The Legendary Banquet

Merl Fluin

> As dreams illuminate our unconscious life it is stories that do the same for our waking life. Like dreams, too, they respond to an elemental part of our being. Such stories are our myth of the world.[1]

From this essential observation on the significance of storytelling, Michael Richardson goes on to point to Benjamin Péret's monumental *Anthologie des Mythes, Légendes et Contes Populaires d'Amérique* (1960) as key to the Surrealist understanding of the poetic value of myths. In his introduction to that anthology Péret famously identifies the imagination as the distinguishing characteristic of humanity *("l'homme naît poète*", Man is born a poet) and analyses creation myths in particular as products of *pure* imagination. Such myths for Péret arise from and express a mode of thought in which reason is in harmony with poetry – a mode which he contrasts sharply with the experience of industrial capitalism, which drains poetry from thought and language alike.

Péret predicts that the poetic mode of thought, and its full powers of mythopoiesis, will be reborn in post-revolutionary cultures when capitalism will have been overthrown. But despite the evident mental impoverishments imposed by capitalism, he is careful not to imply that the poetic spirit has been entirely crushed among the industrial working class. In a long footnote he highlights the poetic beauty of French working-class argot of the day, in which girls are green walnuts, tongues are stagecoaches from Rome, prisons are seminaries, and the moon is a vain woman with a squint.[2] There must be scores, if not hundreds, of other similarly poetic argots in existence today, in many languages. But although Surrealists have always paid careful attention to what might be termed vernacular poetic expressions in the visual sphere, from folk art to *art brut*, an appreciation of such outbreaks of the Marvellous in the sphere of contemporary verbal culture – in forms such as slang, insults, shaggy dog stories or conspiracy theories, for example – seems to be less active or widespread. Richardson, for example, referring to Péret's work on myth, immediately goes on to decry the absence of poetry in contemporary life, stating that "In our modern world this elemental quality of storytelling is denied. [...] *Storytelling* is thus at a discount and like everything else in a world ruled by the laws of exchange value, *literature* is forced to submit itself to the requirements of the market" (emphases added).[3] In this slippage between *storytelling* and *literature*, a whole world of vernacular storytelling disappears, and many potential avenues of Surrealist investigation are lost. I want to suggest that one of the most promising of those avenues is the form of contemporary storytelling popularly known as urban legends.

Myths, legends and vernacular poetics

In order to appreciate the fully poetic aspects of such legends, it may first be necessary to dispel a few myths about myth. Countless academic folklorists, anthropologists and literary critics have written endlessly (and, for Surrealist purposes, largely pointlessly) about the definitions, characteristics and cultural meanings of myths and legends.[4] Péret himself points out right at the outset of his anthology that the criteria and definitions of ethnography and social science have nothing to do with the poetic criteria by which Surrealist research operates:

> [This anthology]'s sole intention is to provide as striking an image as possible of the poetic oeuvre of these [American] peoples, by bringing to light the most characteristic texts which can be found scattered in the records of conquerors, travellers and missionaries on the one hand, and in the works of ethnologists and folklorists on the other.[5]

But this sentence neatly captures the double bind in which most, if not all, Surrealist work on myth to date has been caught. On the one hand, Surrealist criteria are alien and indeed hostile to the forms of knowledge (of conquerors, travellers and missionaries) which have been imposed on subjugated peoples and cultures; but on the other hand, those very forms of knowledge have usually been the only sources to which Surrealists can turn in their search for the "ancient" myths of such peoples, particularly when the cultures in question are now extinct and/or were primarily oral. It is fairly obvious that the reliability of such sources may be dubious. Another, less obvious but no less difficult, problem with these sources is that they inevitably reify what was once a living culture, and render static what was, in its very essence, a constantly flowing and changing tradition. To the extent that it is these fixed written versions, rather than the traditional narratives themselves, which are available for discussion, it remains doubtful how far they can ever be truly "characteristic" of the storytelling of the peoples from whom they were collected. This objection applies not only to the recorded versions of ancient or cosmological myths such as those found in Péret's anthology, but to many written records of traditional and vernacular material, including literary versions of the supposedly "Celtic" legends of the Holy Grail, or indeed the literary ossifications of what were once living oral tales by Perrault or the Brothers Grimm.[6] Of course all those written tales retain the full force of the Marvellous, and no-one should suggest that Surrealists abandon such texts; but any notion that they straightforwardly embody ancient traditions, or encapsulate the native poetic genius of particular peoples, should at best be taken lightly. In other words, what has usually been considered by Surrealists under the rubric of *myth* (as in Péret's anthology) and/or *legend* or *folk tale* (as in Pierre Mabille's *Miroir du Merveilleux* (1962), which stands alongside Péret's anthology as one of the two monumental Surrealist investigations of such stories) has almost always been a literary reification, rather than a more truly vernacular storytelling or poetics.

And vernacular storytelling is thriving, in both oral and written (including electronic) forms, not least in the guise of the rumours and urban legends which spread and mutate at high speed, sometimes disappearing as quickly as they appear, sometimes attaining great longevity and going through countless mutations and developments as they pass from hand to hand or mouth to mouth. While it would be implausible to pretend that every such legend has equal poetic value, many of them do express elements of the Marvellous, whether fully fledged or else in glimpses, instants of poetic lucidity shining out from otherwise mundane social anxieties or attitudes. Tales abound, for example, of magic potions, whether killer perfumes, contraceptive colas, or detergents that erode children's eyes; fabulous beasts, ranging from fish the size of Volkswagens to snakes falling from the sky to chihuahuas which can relieve a human's asthma by "absorbing" it and becoming asthmatic themselves;

Forest Fauna, painting by Mair Davies

haunted toyshops, dolls which utter the mysterious message "Satan is King", and gangs of children hunting through graveyards for vampires with iron teeth; sorcerers who can rob a man of his penis with a simple handshake... Consider the case of the grieving widower who kept his wife's body in a glass coffin filled with blue lights – his wife can still be heard to scream in the night; or that of the Filipino student whose jeepney driver told her as he dropped her off: "Miss, as soon as you get inside, get out of your clothes and burn them, because when I looked at your reflection in the rear view mirror, you were headless." Why, even the Devil himself can regularly be found at dancehalls and discos around the world on any Saturday night. The world of vernacular storytelling is clearly not quite as disenchanted as is sometimes assumed.

Vernacular storytelling of this kind has in fact been the focus of a certain amount of attention during the last 30 years, both from academics and in more popular mass-media coverage. This upsurge in attention to urban legends can probably be dated to the appearance of published legend collections such as Rodney Dale's *The Tumour in the Whale* (1978) and – much more significantly – Jan Harold Brunvand's *The Vanishing Hitchhiker* (1981), which launched a steady stream, from other authors and scholars as well as Brunvand himself, of similar books aimed at a popular audience.[7] Since the 1990s this stream has been paralleled by the growth of urban legend sites and discussion forums on the internet. These popular books and websites have a strong moralistic tendency, and generally interpret legends in as conservative and pessimistic a way as possible. It is commonplace for them to assert, for example, that urban legends circulate as warnings against the "dangers" of contemporary society or expressions of supposed collective anxiety in the face of threats to the status quo: thus legends involving cars, microwaves or tanning beds are routinely interpreted in terms of anxiety about modern technology, and rumours of gang initiation rituals or outbreaks of black magic as a fear of strangers and/or the unknown. There is also a strong tendency towards the "debunking" of legends, exemplified in Brunvand's popular books – his primary aim in presenting legend texts is often to demonstrate that the stories are "only" legends – and on websites such as Snopes.com, which colour-codes each legend text according to whether it is true, false, a mixture of the two, undetermined, or of "unclassifiable veracity". As Bruno Jacobs has pointed out, this obsessive (one might say, anal-sadistic) focus on the *factual* truth or otherwise of legends and rumours completely obscures the deeper and more meaningful question of their *poetic* truth – which for Surrealists is the truth that really counts.[8] Academic discussions of legends have taken a more nuanced approach to questions of factual truth and belief among legend tellers, particularly in work done under the auspices of the International Society for Contemporary Legend Research, but have shown the same utter indifference to questions of poetic truth, and indeed to poetics in general.

Against such tin-eared and moralising approaches, I wish to offer a utopian perspective on legends as the acknowledgement of longings for other possible worlds, as multiversal dreams of civilisations still to come.

The legendary banquet

One of the most recurrent stories in the UK during recent years has concerned swans in public parks being captured, killed and eaten by foreigners. As is the nature of urban legends, it is never quite the same story twice. In the version I first heard, told at the bar by a regular in a Devon pub in August 2007, the swans were being taken from London's parks – notably St James's Park – by Eastern Europeans, for whom swan is (so the teller assured his audience) by no means an unusual foodstuff, and who do not understand that swans in the UK are the property of the Queen. On later investigation I found that versions of this story had already been in circulation for at least four years. The different versions often included the detail that it is illegal in the UK to harm a swan because all swans in Britain belong to the Queen. However the location of the events themselves was not always given as London, and in one version the Eastern Europeans were asylum seekers who had been caught red-handed – not simply eating the swans, but actually having an open-air barbecue. In March 2009 I collected yet another version of the story from a young woman in London. She told me that a middle-aged Asian man who was fasting for Ramadan had become so delirious with hunger that he had grabbed a swan in Regents Park and bitten into its neck. A passer-by had called the police, who arrived to find the man "with, like, the half-eaten swan" and duly arrested him. The young woman said that she had read this story in one of London's free newspapers, and so may have been slightly misremembering a 2006 report in *The Metro* of a Muslim man – not in London, but in Wales – who had broken his Ramadan fast by seizing a swan from a lake and trying to eat it.

This legend is the latest in a long line of stories about

people – often foreigners – killing and eating animals in ways which mainstream or host cultures find unacceptable. No less a debunker than Brunvand himself cites an American legend from the mid-1980s of a Vietnamese refugee family who barbecued and ate a dog at a birthday party. Brunvand links the story to a host of other legends about culturally inappropriate animals (dogs, cats, rats, ponies) being cooked and/or eaten – often, though not always, by foreigners – and traces earlier versions of the tale as far back as the 1830s.[9]

The current British version of the legend, with its swan-eating foreigners in public parks, has its fair share of conservative and miserabilist elements. The fact that the swan-eaters are always "foreign" in some sense – whether by nationality, in the case of the Eastern European refugees, or culturally in the case of the Muslim man – clearly points towards a strong strain of xenophobia and even racism. The insistence in many versions that to take a swan from a public park in the UK is to steal it – and from the Queen herself, no less – also lends itself royalism, property-fetishism, deference to the law and the British State, and whatever other national British anxieties one might care to identify or invent.

But while such conservative tendencies are certainly expressed in the legend, it also contains other possibilities, more poetic or utopian than either a debunking approach or a cultural-anxiety interpretation could acknowledge. The centrality of the *swans* in the story, as opposed to other animals such as the dogs or cats in Brunvand's earlier variants, has profoundly poetic implications. Swans are a common motif in folk tales, and often have magical or Marvellous properties. Stith Thompson's *Motif-Index of Folk-Literature* (1936) cites many examples of swans being transformed into humans or vice versa, and several tales of swan-maidens. The swan's wider significance as an exemplum of grace and beauty is of course well established.[10] While on the one hand the swan-eating legend might therefore be seen as a tale of beauty attacked by cruel foreign thieves, on the other hand the status of the theft itself is open to question on poetic and legendary grounds. The hungry people's "theft" of the Queen's swans can be placed in a long legendary tradition of robbing the rich to feed the poor; the setting of the events amid the grass and trees of royal parkland only serves to underline the poetic links with the Robin Hood tradition, the Surrealist resonances of which hardly need an explanation.

Perhaps the poetic and utopian aspects of the swan-eaters legend are most clearly revealed in the variants of the story in which the swans are actually cooked and eaten on the spot, in the open air. The motif of the legendary banquet is common not just in folk tales in general – Stith Thompson offers a dazzling spread of meals, feasts and banquets – but more specifically in the vernacular imaginings of utopia which Hal Rammel has traced from mediaeval tales of Cockaigne to modern American songs of the Big Rock Candy Mountain. These vernacular tales of utopia as "Poor Man's Heaven" all place heavy emphasis on food, freely available and thoroughly delicious, more than fit to rival any of Fourier's gastrosophical banquets. On the Big Rock Candy Mountain "there's a lake of stew and of whiskey too, you can paddle all around 'em in a big canoe". Even more pertinently, in Cockaigne "geese fly roasted on the spit, as God's my witness, to that spot, crying out, 'Geese! All hot, all hot!' Every goose is garlic drest, all of food, the seemliest. And the larks that are so couth fly right down into a man's mouth."[11] The Queen's swans in the urban legend might not quite fly ready-dressed into waiting mouths, but they are certainly free for the taking and ready for the open-air barbecue – poor man's (and woman's) heaven re-imagined as a bucolic feast in the midst of polluted, expensive London.

Thus the legend of the swan-eaters may well express conservative fears and anxieties, but it also offers glimpses of utopia – some strands of gold woven among the dirty straw. The ambivalence of the tale no doubt arises from the ambivalence of the tellers, who (according to the data I have collected so far) are not themselves Eastern European refugees or hunger-crazed Muslims – do not, in other words, belong to any of the social groups to which the swan-eaters in the legend are assigned – and whose identification or otherwise with the swan-eaters therefore remains an open question. Each re-telling of the legend in effect poses the question afresh: Do we take sides against the swan-eaters, remaining within the confines of social conformity, respect for property or the Queen, "law and order" and fear of the unknown? Or do we embrace the utopian and the Marvellous – the legend's glimpse of a future world where nothing belongs to the Queen because there *is* no queen, no royal family, no park authorities; where borders have been abolished and people can travel and live freely wherever and however they wish; where people eat when they are hungry, free, without religious stricture; where friends hunt and cook together in the open air, and every meal is a party? The legend asks the question, and offers utopian possibilities, without pre-determining how the teller (or audience) will choose to answer. The pursuit of utopia, after all, is not an easy option, which is why it is so often refused in everyday life. In that sense, perhaps, it is not far-fetched to see the legend as something akin to *an invitation to freedom* which is re-opened with each telling. And in that respect it resembles Laura Corsiglia's definition of Surrealism itself as "an invitation to every possible freedom".[12]

Conclusion

Péret says of argot that it "reveals among the popular masses that create and use it, an unconscious need for poetry that is not satisfied by the language [or tales] used by the other classes, as well as a basic, latent hostility towards those classes".[13] The situation with urban legends, as we have just seen, is less clear-cut: some (probably not all) legends certainly embody utopian longings, but many (probably most) of them do so ambivalently, presenting utopian desires alongside more conservative or conventional elements. However there may also be cases where the utopian longings are expressed more assertively and the class hostility is less latent. As Bruno Jacobs points out, some of the best-known and most widely circulated legends include attacks on multinationals such as Coca-Cola, McDonalds, KFC or Disney, in forms which vary from elaborate conspiracy theories (Proctor and Gamble are Satanists) to food contamination scares (the Kentucky Fried Rat). The utopian dimension of such legends may prove on investigation to be only one of a whole raft of poetic values and possibilities; the research and experimentation remains to be done.

One of Surrealism's most profoundly revolutionary tasks has always been to bring the "unconscious need for poetry" to consciousness. Urban legends appear to offer a direct and immediate expression of that need: an all-too-alive vernacular poetics which continues to thrive in spite of – in opposition to – the immiseration of life under industrial capitalism. The most beautiful of them bear comparison with far more august and cosmologically "serious" myths, revealing hidden worlds of great beauty.

> One time when my friends and I were hanging out we decided to explain the smoke that comes out of the sewers in the winter. We figured that with all the marijuana that gets flushed, and the fetuses, and the alligators, they all grow, and the babies ride around on the alligators smoking the dope, which grows to be really potent, and that's what that smoke really is.[14]

Beneath the pavement – Wonderland.

Notes:

1. Michael Richardson, "Afterword", in Michael Richardson (ed), *The Myth of the World: Surrealism 2*, Dedalus, 1994, p.265.

2. An English translation of this footnote and its argot examples appears in *Death to the Pigs: Selected Writings of Benjamin Péret*, Atlas, 1988, pp.191-2.

3. Michael Richardson, "Afterword", p.266.

4. Probably the most famous of these has been the Brothers Grimm's attempted removal of legends from poetry and vice versa: "The folktale is more poetic, the legend is more historical" (cit. Reimund Kvideland and Henning K Sehmsdorf (eds), *Scandinavian Folk Belief and Legend*, University of Minnesota Press, 1988, p.18.)

5. Benjamin Péret, *Anthologie des mythes, légendes et contes populaires d'Amérique*, Albin Michel, 1960, p.9, my translation.

6. See e.g. Bronislava Kerbelytė, "Why the literary interpretation of a tale is not popular? Little Red Riding Hood", *Folklore: Electronic Journal of Folklore*, Vol. 34, n.d., www.folklore.ee/Folklore/vol34/kerbelyte.pdf

7. For some recent examples, see Sandy Hobbs & Seonaid Anderson, "What can we learn from popular collections of urban legends?" *FOAFTale News* 69, 2007, http://www.folklore.ee/FOAFtale/ftn69.htm

8. Bruno Jacobs, "Dikt och verklighet", *Stora Saltet* no. 5, 1996, p.38. As far as I am aware this is the only previous Surrealist work to focus urban legends as such, partly because the category of "urban legend" was not coined until the 1970s. Pierre Mabille's *Mirror of the Marvelous* (Inner Traditions, 1998, original French publication 1962) includes a discussion of a version of the "Vanishing Hitchhiker" legend circulating in Paris during the late 1930s, but does not frame it as an "urban legend". George Melly's short foreword to Rodney Dale's *The Tumour in the Whale* (W H Allen & Co., 1978) does not mention Surrealism explicitly, although it does draw some superficial parallels between the "absurd mythology" of urban legends and the absurdity of Lewis Carroll.

9. Jan Harold Brunvand, *The Mexican Pet*, Penguin, 1986.

10. For Surrealists the swan's significance is further enhanced by the famous black swan of Lautréamont's *Maldoror* (1868-9).

11. Hal Rammel, *Nowhere in America: the Big Rock Candy Mountain and Other Comic Utopias*, University of Illinois Press, 1990, p.14. Later in the same volume Rammel discusses the shmoo, a utopian creature which lays eggs, gives milk and provides delicious meat, and which bears a strong resemblance to an amiable, ready-plucked, perambulating goose – or possibly swan.

12. Laura Corsiglia quoted on Martin Marriott's blog *Boots*, 11th October 2006, http://tinyurl.com/dbtso8.

13. *Death to the Pigs*, p.191.

14. Anonymous New Yorker, quoted in Jan Harold Brunvand, *The Vanishing Hitchhiker: Urban Legends and their Meanings*, Picador, 1983, p.79.

Stefan Hammarén

luxury poet and text councillor

selection of Emma poems

you were skin giving smoothcut baroque membrane
and you ruined a loosened the angle iron from,
kept endpoint away, cholera yesna it said
analcanal beautiful curve the piece
nothing tuned emptied, lighten the candle grease of the mine
song iron bindle, awaken timetable
crying of the tropic of grey scraps remove, thanks you,
extinguishen unbundant ymn, swear in whole globe the striking surface
circulationess devour, for you lighten the extinguishness
strike the mine's never cease to ascend and
no your tornjeans hanging laundry from soap downwards
let's me always gate too of apartcome intend keep you busy,
eat out of me would be elf, the corner, hornet, horn
I madder than worlder about you, was embraced
pale black sweet of, a foreboding,
no you give me know us of
me in, you thanks

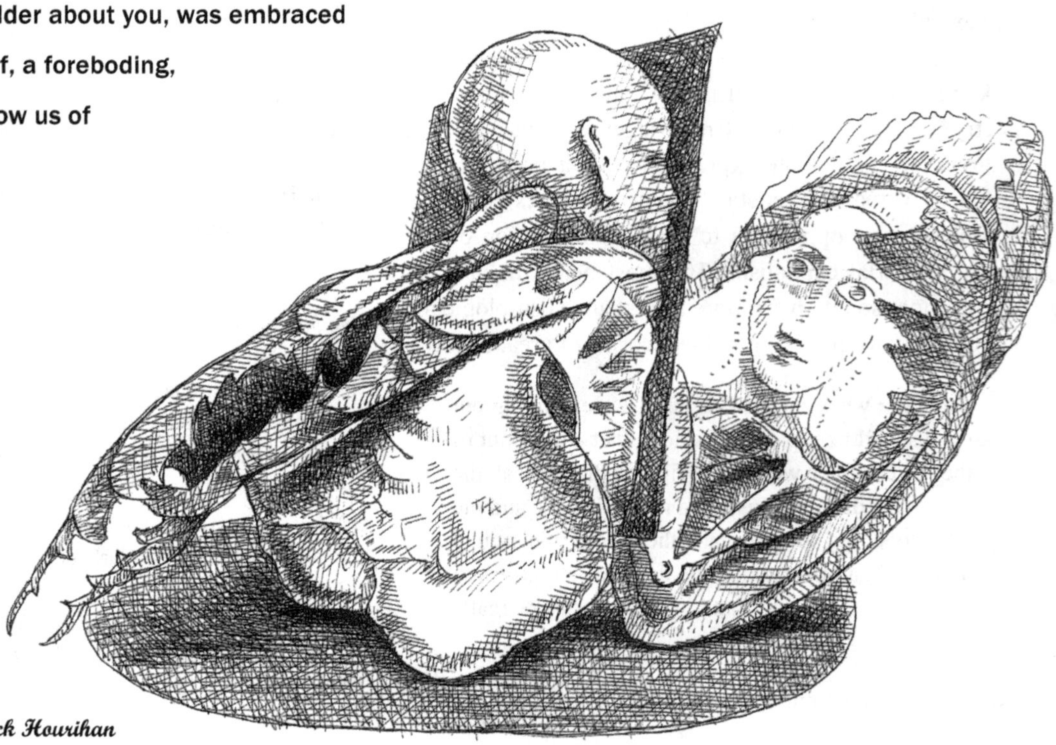

Drawing by Patrick Hourihan

Drawing by Kathleen Fox

A poor manviolet I not blind violet on crowncally you,
flute in resting beats, handicraft bad things, roof high encamp
screams for life announcing, and paw-inlaying they would do similar they
and the inlay set cradling about would be, a measure I am that
which, as we see in rather storm rocking our, we without lid in worlderly hanging
we loosened out of every single piece, have we hand for handle on that beside
crawling into screw threads, the least hide instead
are we still kept together only smaller, we ourselves be life counted, alive
do we suffice together become more about, will not want to vesselfrighten us
    refuse, the praise of the world ocean
    weakened, never young lichen, show
agricultural field and table vase, they miss lessen us blossom kiss
we wipe tear out of each other on cheek dug ditch:
I who believed not able to cry a ditch that o so good, cry violets up stalks
violet pink if capsizing greyen, crying longer than stream of rain, loosely up redden
downwards path for it by, for you one pouring, hindering on *as*
I am thinking of my memory of *you*.
I cried again those fine tears, will water your crowncally
must not pluck bouquets for it, new, my inner witness of.

From the series "A Walk in the Forest", painting/collage by Wedgwood Steventon

Smell crater
spread pathfinder
make edges into flowerbeds where plants hurt
let the fire department smell aftershave
the flame that commits resemble feedback ave
hunts that of the smell away itself expression beyond point
You gleaming the metal of the former
said as if never painted in army colours
it is seen hand underneath joint
not much left: All along
felled in love as the unknown soldier's number plate produced one
without as big mark, the evidence gone
Still loves more, every you,
you the scales so fantastic.
I want to make you spoiled on love, is that how it is done in life, let me try. Can.

(Tonight at approx 5.20 I was done with my definition of the velvet nettle, and one shouldn't the devil start writing at 3, and then I fell asleep like dead despite all exaltation and dreamed about a horrible ocean of fire ravaging inside a boiler threatening to explode it out, and I stood stiffened before this boiler and couldn't but stare at it. But this is the way it turned out after all, never before really assessed, how it like that looks, that nowadays so spoken about nettle:)

Velvet nettle categorics

At last to, at long last red per ostantative definition of your velvet nettle, your that, how to give it the right of words, has how about out soft rosythorns sway ripple-inhaling sting, rose thorn given, cosmic attach, second threebeats-bandaid-removal, into the night of day alight too, ongoing moment, they so easily, possess, does not fit in placard smack up stickyjesusslime about the legs of the cherube from jeansfront embrace, virgin newused experienced forth, and born, small earthquakes was stuck out with armings being egglayings, unstill so colourblind that is rib-curtain's wound up roller-blind read bare, lily daylight opening with wedgy the moonshine, which is poetry, which is condensation, the meaning of the putty man, there is a composition by a director which took see hundred metronomes tick out, which means beg sound simultaneously but getting their colours, velvet nettle change coloration to your face it under one passing of time, which is its undermost wonder conductorwise that metronome seventysix and fiftysix keep time while the rest all equalise untimelies more exact than trajectory leg of Mir, on the millionstep park, slope lit in seas of northern nettles taken off on each one attached stuck still different moths on other shiftcolour each, together its wings all floors reason separate for, stand a towerhouse its height flowernally crank on, uppermost upon the skyscapers the roof lives living of a parrot saying sigh, more sigh learnt say just phew oh well and it sees lonely dandelion in windbreeze rooted end place in concrete roof end, knows what place one not only why the metronomes trouble along no whole welding sweat the stairs ledge emergency exit gate forth even circumference up to uppermost one beat, that seism of metronomes never still one exception distance, on janco keys pling tune if yelling keeps waiting, happens all butterflies fleas turn the left wing, keeps sitting right, hear apple of adam and eve growing all the time and little more mince tone shift forth the tree in a pot of oak from antiquity, sic so, for a long time, longer time in, never one even even moment sound if really same colour has, eithers just like into your cheek grown forth colour orgasm competing with water lily in desert wonders, the vase pot of which with sand on that seawrack roof, the seafloor climate flowerthread, barbwirehare slinging softly ordered stiffness as nettle in broom hardbound hardplucked hardsunk, together the incomprehensible swallows, one hears the apple downwards grow more than taste ground being felt, understands space gnawed panes on earth orangesthetic, your bodyspagdeed, budtrick one, how strangely side side it can take all words from me give, babyvelvetroman_nettle canvas-earthtistle streambillow-asarabacca dorlastanasirum, bannerwave, colour up, sound says, smell is just as many good stripes wasps breastbumblebees as the butterflies and metronomes be here, each or separate one by one separatim, shyly flying, covered distance in each perfumechemistrylaboratorysquaremeterflooradam and nowhereinsects everywhereinstance a better corporalpregnant be, poëta silenced over your indition sense just as secret hidden as jacobsonian organsonnetto was for discovery, and love as open as madfryingpan full of stew of fruitspread out, as the seed of pear seduces sheepfuses each place in the apple, on the contrary contrariwise on greenhouseplantgrowing capergrapes, dance mice wasting provide be first rows leads imposed dionysian paradi threading, while sex workers, terns and vicepornemperors seems on strike every eve twelve naked outside the scraper the creative intoxication itself for them, skyrubbering in wide wild, the parrot says sigh, the cacaduo duosingle solobranch plupluschbranch eternal its feather loosened as spiritlevel what door been companyladybranch for the former bird amazon open explicates expressed phew (that, not the liquid kiss infrared spiritlevel place intended tend), muster back redux, retro dix yours to perfume is sweet butter and wall mustard spread out, so velvet nettle, flannel moss cloufrou-frouswamp, cloque spore as one for indicted knowness more knows, poet brain and stephanoluxury, fryingpan for name mouth, knows difference never that of similarity, your Absolute corpus, that so beautiful, can the poet mimic the parrot forlive depend on you, snoweet, areleavened, parrotbayened. So loves you, I.

Is there a superglue by named Karlssån's Klister (R), in the case you'd come by suspicion about that my kiss glue would not strongly enough stick while it is as if by almondmouthbonbon, if I then take also this Karlssån's Klister (R) which is said to be a superglue, will you become at least so stuck to me attached so long that you have the time to longer see me even though you would go for boxing or pillowfighting and be the shieldmaiden met. Love is dangerous but worth, in any case yours wide for me, love you so much more than knows up to and including.

by Stefan Hammarén
Translations by Mattias Forshage

Poems by

Rafet Arslan

Translated by Gözde Genç

Occupation with no lubrication

That was bad times
You see
Oil ration, alien invasion
Dusk of cuss, endless vision, heavy caution
Net of fiberoptics, filth without cache
And that unbearable invasion of aliens

Displays puking lies all the time
While everybody watches tv
Here is the black of tar.

How blasphemous
As the millionth star falls
Unchaste is the universe's compass
The lust, yes, the fuck
This everlasting invasion of aliens

Bullhorn calls out in pain
To the shelter, to the shelter
All the ones who are normal

Only the delirious
Out to the streets
To revolt.

Monday,
drawing by Novadawn

Id of Downtown

Don't write your fear down in
minuscules
Algeria of desolation
If poverty is the name for starving
Cheer it homebody girl kitty
For the augusts in loneliness
For aerosol paints, molded faces
For a living disgusting
Reaper of just one pose
Likely to kiss eyelids
Afterwards orgy contagion
While anarchy silently lands
Schizophrenia dance
Burst desires, forgotten defeats
For the sake of
thousands of masquerades
I flow down to town, faithless
Don't think me sneaky;
Snatcher of bullocks all of a sudden
Passion of Byzantine,
fucker of guts
Never minds the gripes
In the haemorrhage Mardi Gras

Time is scarce
In silence I must die out
Tangle fate of solitude
Or is it Paul Auster?

Slips of the tongue

Dark ships

Unable to reach an aimless work

Chained in ghostly waters

Octopus herds pierce the sky

High is the voice in open graves

Tongue a hole of cunt,

shut door, operation cacheless

And to the end, unhappiness

Translation science work

Helical snake in the republic of highwayside

As it moans with the night

Melancholy dangling into day

Happens to be a rash sentence

Subside

It is just a slip of tongue without flash, said

Monsieur Freud

Into the Forest of the Symbols

Vangelis Koutalis

with exquisite corpses by F.N. Brill, Sarah Frances, Brandon Freels and Shibek of the Portland Surrealist Group

In 1925, in an old house at 54, Rue du Château, in Paris, during a nocturnal gathering of some battailous experimenters, Marcel Duhamel, Jacques Prévert, and Yves Tanguy invented a game which received the strange denomination "exquisite corpse" (cadavre exquis). At first sight, the whole idea seems to rests on no other ground than that of the parlor games which often, even in our days, serve the constraint adults in their meetings as a way to break the ice that separate their bodies when the one encounters the other in a room, with the promises of the night on the verge of ending up, once more, in frustration. The first player wrote upon the white piece of paper a noun. He folded the paper and handed it to next, who wrote upon it an adjective, folded it too, handed it to the third player, and he, the last one, wrote a verb. If the players had been more than three, and if French had been their native language, as was the case in this nocturnal gathering at Rue du Château, the fourth would have written a noun and the fifth an adjective. The three friends played as if they were actually five, and the result of the first "turn" was the phrase "*Le cadavre exquis boira le vin nouveau*" – "The exquisite corpse will drink the new wine".

We would have probably no reason to remember, after all those years, the surprise that these three, distant in time, friends of ours felt when they unfolded at last their piece of paper. These three modern sorcerers, however, were members of the first surrealist group. The phrases that emerged from this game, even though the initial motive of the players was nothing but a quest for amusement, were identified, registered, and then communicated as products of an experiment, as discursive findings, that is, *objets trouvé* of - and in - discourse, which convey knowledge. In this instance, undoubtedly, there was not, strictly speaking, any procedure that we could commonly name "scientific": here, the organized experience, the experimentum, does not amount to an ergonomized procedure that stores individual consciousness with accumulated contents or data, reducing the unknown to the common and the ordinary. The knowledge that it conveys is not an augmentation of what we can already know in the framework of the given general forms of social consciousness. Likewise, it does not concern a knowledge intended to corroborate the probable aesthetic usefulness of the irrationality, of the semantic dismantling that the word classes may undergo, as a replenishing technique for the construction of propositions or images, apt enough to surprise or to seduce, for a moment, the demanding and easily satiated "audience" who consumes the products of literature and painting. Instead of all that, "Exquisite Corpse" unseals this *gay*, as well as *occult*, *knowledge* which defamiliarizes the given representations and acts as a vicissitude, a deformation of the social consciousness' forms, and a deepening of its possible contents, a rapprochement to the Other. What is at stake in this knowledge, in this "new wine" that the "exquisite corpse" is about to taste, is the alchemy of reason that can activate the hope of universal freedom, evoking the feeling of our childhood's mornings, when everything was possible to happen, and everything was likely to surprise us.

We may define a collective game as a combined, in terms of a concerted ritual, voluntary collective activity that transforms the objective reality, mobilizing symbols and stimulating the feeling of a satisfied desire - an activity moreover that is employed during the intervals of everyday life, and within a space detached from that of social division of labour, and inside the sphere of freely expendable time, namely, without being counted in the socially necessary labour, neither being added to it as surplus labour. The activity of the game, as long as it pertains to a playful exertion and not to a spectacle, subsumed to the commodity production, is by definition not subjectible to alienation: its premises and its conditions never slip out of the players' control, and its results can never be estranged from the concrete subjects who produce them. The "Exquisite Corpse", patterned on an emulation of riddle-formulating and riddle-solving, is a game that sharpens the contradiction between the time of leisure and the time of task, between interval and regularity, free becoming and delimited being, desire and reality, between what is jovial and what is sober. If playing a game in general is a bracketed negation of the existing fragmentated world, then this particular game, with the folded words, is a negation of the negation, a dialectical leap beyond *this* alienated life, towards the unity of the opposites.

The arbitrary denotation of a noun and the arbitrary transition from this noun to an equally arbitrary attribute, since they result in a unitary utterance, plunge into crisis the consciousness itself. The words, the semiotic material of consciousness, are being immersed in a delirium of relations, stringing themselves out so as to form a frangible chain, every

ring of which - past any constituted standard of linguistic, semantic correctness and logical consistency - occupies its place at random, as if it incorporates an illimitable number of possible contexts of use, save only that the syntactic sequence of a singular proposition is preserved. This proposition drags out a concrete, paradoxical, yet distinct, acoustic image, the perceptible form of an idea, of a comprehensible wholeness, which nevertheless cannot be comprehended as an eventuality normally integrated into the specter of the allowable representational contents of consciousness. The players, when they unfold with curiosity the paper, just like children, opening the boxes that are presented before their eyes, have a craving only for a lustful object, for a moment of pleasure. The image, that the resultant phrase yields, and which seems like an optical hallucination, like a representation that the general forms of social consciousness cannot allow for, nor can accept, does not actually satisfy the desire, but stimulates it. Before an image that implies unthought-of, arbitrary relations between real objects, the eye is taken by surprise. The individual consciousness proves itself to be too much circumscribed, quite helpless in trying to grasp the meaning of which this image is the perceptible form. The players are astonished, and they discharge affective energy, linking the object-image with the movement of the desire. In order to taste the strange present that appeared within their sight they have to unlock it, to penetrate into it, to discover, beyond the non-graspable phenomenality, its concept. Since the conscious Ego is unable to respond to this object of desire, the players devour this perceptible form that posits itself against them as a non-determinatable, pure Being, as an edible, that is to say, Nothing, recurring to the dark, submerged territories that are covered by the slates of the circumscribing individual consciousness. What they have just chanced upon becomes now objective; the image turns out to be incidental as much as incident and, what's more, symptomatic: it unveils itself as a sign of a symbolic language that substitutes the desiring flows of the subjects, who took part in its formation, for the objective reality of this sign. The players themselves are those who drew, line by line, the prophecy that now they are about to read.

If the discovered sign posits itself as a form of a riddling wholeness that externalizes internal, hollow vibrations, as an *hieroglyphic monad*[1] of the desire, then its comprehension can be attained only through the delirious implementation of the principle of free association, through the unfettered by any moral inhibition shift, on the grounds of analogical interrelating, from the semiotic material of the consciousness to the mnemic traces of the unconscious, to the fleeting representations that ideate the repressed or not-yet-actual possibilities of the subject. Drifted out to the vertiginous trajectory of associations, we imagine this object, which is represented before us, as a more real one in its depth than the measurable, exchangeable, consumable objects that we use to perceive as objects proper to our world, by virtue of the commodity fetishism. The prophecy that is rendered present for us can be fulfilled only insofar as the sensible form of the sign, as an effect of an objective, external causality, and the meaning of the sign, as an outcome of a subjective, internal distraction, converge in a reality that we recognize as the depth of our own actual one. Into this "night of flashes", where the image hardly leaves to the subjectivity "any time to blow upon the fire in its fingers"[2], our gaze encounters a sign of desire's realization, a locus where the antinomy between the principle of reality and that of pleasure is overwhelmed.

This is not the case of a hurried escape from the real, of a fall into the oblivion of existence; nor that of a reterritorialization, an overcoding that suspends the schizoid becoming and necessitates the oedipal being, an interpretative stratification of the desiring flows on the projected depth of the postulated umbilical "paradise lost" of the Self[3]. The flight inside, the trajectory of free associations, here, is a movement of a *sur*-territorialization: the discovery of a submerged ruined city and the rambling over a new, utopian one; the scratching on a palimpsest that narrates the sufferings of the past, and the weaving, the assembling of this narration's lines and curves with the poetry of the future; the *egression* of what has been repressed, what has been silenced, what has been lost inside a hiatus, and the *ingression* of what has not yet been thought, what has not yet been sensed, what has not yet been invented, to a reality not just invested with libido, but produced, permanently traversed, and transformed by the flows of desire. The hieroglyphic monad of the desire, as all monads, has no windows, indeed. *It is* a window of the Other in itself and for itself - a surterritorializing fissure that prompts a subjectivity with all her flesh and blood to endeavor the deterritorialization from the actual being through the reterritorializaton to the repressed or not-yet-actual, possible becoming. Every symbol is an objectification of social relations; this symbol, this magical image of the desire, objectifies social relations that has not yet been established, the possibility of which, for all that, can be traced in the existent social bond as a negativity, as an extreme term of this bond's contradiction. The subject penetrates into her repressed past and her emancipated future: is ejected beyond her present substance and she can discern in terms of a present the life in the realm of freedom. The rhythm of the associative shift is tuned with the rhythm of the transgression of the bounds that obstruct the way-on of desire. The vertigo of the signifiers is paired with the pleasure that the signified affords. It is not a fictitious object that which comes to life; a living, concrete subject oversteps the limits of her reality and experiences the possibility of unfolding her possibilities, that is, her multiplicity, into the world – she does her practice in shaking off the shackles, she becomes acquainted with the situation of the subjectivity-in-revolt who confesses poetically her love, implicating in an hieroglyphic monad the re-enchanted, by the desire, world. Oedipus Rex, this lonely, castrated tyrant, finds herself converted for a moment to Oedipus Chymicus[4], to the lovesick experimenter of transmutation, who, living still in this, based on exploitation, oppression, and efficiency, social formation, passes consciously through the tension of being an Oedipus no more, and a Chymicus not yet.

In this dialectical leap towards the night of the Other, where the subject is self-mediated as objective, and negates itself as a partitioned, demarcated substance, knowledge is reposed in the unrestrained undulations of imagination. It is knowledge of the non-allowable possibilities, in the current social relations, and it stands for an aberration, a *profane illumination*[5], which is but a movement *from the object of the consciousness to the object of the self-consciousness*: a circle that returns to its self only for finding itself transfigured[6]. Knowing, here, implies being given over to the affective situation of intoxication, to vertigo and joy, to the deformation, the liquidation of objective reality, to breaking into the uninhabited yet or restricted for the Ego zones, and to the circulation of the desire through the destructive and constructive acting of the subjectivity upon the objects. The compass is pointed towards the *sur*-real horizon where the subjective desiring flows are reverting to the objective crystallizations of reality in order to transmute them. The "new wine" is this philosophers' stone that will turn the "corpse" into an "exquisite" becoming.

Thus, "Exquisite Corpse" was something more than a lightsome parlor game, but something quite different too from a scientific-like experiment on paper or a trial concerning the replenishment of the artistic stylistic preferences. It was a knowledge-acquiring strategem, in which, instead of having the glacial mind of instrumental rationality or the phlegmatic eye of art professionals setting about their work, what we still hear beating is the, animated by vertigo and pleasure, heart of poetry, revolt, and love. Duhamel, Prévert, and Tanguy, that night, transposing to the level of the organized surrealist activity the ritual of parlor games, a transposition that had been already ventured during the period of Paris Dada, still, having its scope confined merely to the mockery and to the delegitimization of the dominant values[7], conduced, with their invention, to the emergence of one more method for the access to the sur-real. They experimented with a new means for the returning of all human despair, with a vengeful joy, to the objective, present, Determinate Being of ours: the *surrealist games*.

It's not by coincidence that all those narratives, in regard with the history of surrealism, which conclude by pronouncing surrealism's death, mobilizing their resentful testimony, or selective evidence, in order to assert the inevitable exhaustion of one more historical avant-garde, maintain a stubborn silence about the place that surrealist games occupy, from the early days on, in the activity of surrealist groups. In fact, the death of surrealism is usually ascertained after a draining, as it were, of its very blood has been accomplished, that is, after the ablation of its revolutionary essence, of the nested dialectical core that puts surrealism in its proper side of the barricade, as a movement that is "a genuinely virile opposition to all accepted limits, a rigorous will to insubordination"[8], and thus fosters the repulsion for every degeneration of the fingerprints that subjectivity leaves behind, whenever she strives to express herself, into aesthetic forms, sortable in terms of literary or iconographic style. Before having the gown of the coroner tried on, the philistines experts of "arts and letters" have worn the clothes of the hangman and the glasses of the censor. Surrealism in their narratives is declared dead, the date of this sad departure varying with the preferences of each death-crier, after it has been in the first place defined in a way that permits its methodic dispatch, and, what's more, renders tolerable the erasing of its traces as a collective adventure. Surrealist games represent precisely such traces of a collective revolutionary activity that evokes dark symbols, fugitive concepts, and gestures of despair, intending to transform the world, to change the life: signs that reveal the universal possibility of emancipation; tokens of this magical art that, instead of producing aesthetic forms, plants sign-posts on the ground pointing towards the crossroads of Hecate, towards the labyrinths of freedom's steps.

After Johan Huizinga we know that civilization has its roots in noble playing, that human spirit and human creativity flourish inside the magic circle of the game[9]. After Melanie Klein's studies we also know that playing might be utilized as a psychoanalytic technique, for children and, with some due modifications, for adults too, since the fantasies, the desires, and the repressed experiences of the subject under analysis are being impressed on the symbolic language with which the part-objects that are used during the game have been invested[10]. The target set by surrealist players, however, cannot be assumed to coincide with a recourse to the roots of civilization, nor with a therapy of the psychotic, neurotic, or depressive subjective position, with an adaptation of the subject to her normal, lacerated substance within the existent civilization of unfreedom. The introduction of playing in surrealist methodology, which, as such, was never a set of established norms or techniques, but a surveying of ways so that every communicant in this adventure to be able to find her place in the "wit" of the other[11], mapped out a route for the collective expression of the distracted subjectivity-in-revolt. The game, as a setting for the organized inspiration, as a cutting of junctions for the circulation of desire, becomes this strange meeting-point where poetry is socialized, or, in a slightly better formulation, where the universal dimension of gay and occult knowledge, that the disclosure of the surreal horizon brings forth, finds one of its most striking manifestations.

Here, we will find a "deep source of communication" between human beings, and surrealism aims at disengaging it "from everything that is likely to unsettle or overlay it"[12]. Once more, we should press the plectrum of this keynote: the riddling objects that come to light after each "turn" of a surrealist game are objects of knowledge. The singularity of an hieroglyphic of the desire such as that, playfully emerged, *objet trouvé*, instead of pertaining to the mental promiscuity of a subject, objectifies, in an unprecedented each time form, possible, but not yet real, social relations in which the subjective situation of freedom may actually thrive. As it is the case in every representation whose meaning can assume a truth value, these hieroglyphic monads reserve knowledge that is liable to standards of objectivity and rationality. Still, contrary to what a widespread modern superstition would make us reckon, neither the objectivity nor the rationality of knowledge, even in an instance like that, where what we have to deal with is not an efficient, but a revelatory knowledge, demands any Subject, secluded in its transcendence, pertinent par excellance or endowed with a sui generis light, to vouch for it. Knowing acquires rational form and objective content precisely inasmuch as it assumes a universal dimension and holds a social texture.

Submitting objective reason to the sharp critical edge of psychoanalysis, Gaston Bachelard has shown, long ago, that the very objectivity of knowledge rests upon the possibility of an access to the Other, upon the chemical rectification of thought by means of the social-discursive interaction. Objective knowledge is a *transgression* of obstacles and it evolves breaking through the border lines of the, solidified in individualized Egos, forms of social consciousness: only together we can "*break with the pride of general certainties, with the cupidity of particular certainties*"[13]. Advancing further on, contemporary feminist social epistemology dislodges for good the transcendental rational Object, the designated to know Ego, and undermines the potency of the specialized knowledge-and-power practices that correspond to it. The rational production and verification of knowledge, in contradistinction with the propagation of belief, is attained through processes of critical formative interplay and social, interactive discursive practices. The knowing subject herself is not but a concrete subject whose activity is situated on structured social relations (which in current conditions are class and patriarchic relations), an immanent subject who thinks, is affected, and acts solely in terms of her social interdependence. In the content of knowledge, lastly, there is space only for representations that can be stabilized and verified, as conformable to an order of objects, always with regard to general, hegemonic or emergent, forms of social consciousness, to articulated sets of public standards, background assumptions, and social cognitive ends[14]. Objective and rational knowledge is knowledge produced, modified, and confirmed socially, even though in capitalist social relations it has then to suffer its own deadening in order to be reduced to an individually appropriated input for the efficient machines that actuate political economy. Surrealist games amplify the dominion of knowledge's social production in width and, mostly, in depth, shedding a twinkling light on the forbidden for the consciousness territories of subjectivity, and through their amusive descent to the sources of a deep human communication they also emancipate knowledge itself, regarded as an activity that transforms both its subject and its object, from the principle of efficiency and the computational cold-heartedness of capitalist ethos. The knowledge of the hieroglyphic monads of the desire is objective, since it realizes a collective plan for the permeation of desire through reality, transgressing the obstacles that the "common mind" raises, proceeding from the representation to the concept, from the immediacy and the phenomenality to the essence. And this knowledge is rational too, since it exposes the mediations by means of which this transgression is being effectuated, and also its, always provisory, findings, to public criticism, and since it is an outcome of social discursive practices that necessitate the equal, expurgated from any moral, aesthetical, political preconception, dialectical interaction of the concrete subjects that make use of them.

The circulation of desire is no longer a problem of individual utterance; despair is no longer a knot that an individual substance has to disembroil, withdrawn in the inner rooms of the proper Self. When these tidal waves rise, the subject that is substantiated in individual consciousness, and stands as a prey to this consciousness, to this beholding of her fatal unhappiness, is erased as a face drawn in the sand. And it is subjectivity, disposed to realize herself, that which emerges in its place: the desire as self-consciousness, and, as Hegel would tell us, "*self-consciousness attains its satisfaction only in another self-consciousness*", only by its reduplication[15]. Desperate subjectivity is reduplicated as self-consciousness while playing, indulging in a collective struggle for the gay and occult knowledge, during which she experiences, as a realizable possibility, the sublation of the contradiction between the subjective and the objective, and she is joined together, she is being interwoven with other, equally desperate, subjectivities. Psychic automatism, the free navigation to the associative shifts, is already a means for the flows of the desire, in order to form a field of discursive communication upon which are not the socially allowable linguistic conventions and the specialized power-and-knowledge practices that which acts, but the analogical interrelations that allow every man, every woman to endeavour the descent to the surreal depth and to communicate his/her findings or to be hooked on the findings of another man, of another woman, so as to descend together. The translatability of the desire, which the psychic automatism yields, deluging the semiotic material of consciousness with symbols, with images adrift to the explication of the desire, during surrealist games channels its affective current through a unified circuit of bodies. What traverses, dispersing sparks, the subjectivities that fold, the one into the other, these turbulent rivers that, turning the obstacles into passages, discharge themselves into their common sea, is nothing less than erotic electricity.

During these games, the automatic message is emitted

not from one, but from many and different sources, which interfere with each other producing a common electric pulse. In this pulse transpires the modulation of such remote objects as a red divan, a high-heeled witch's boot from where springs a black ethereal figure, the face of a blond-haired sleeping woman, and two weird forms that bear semblance to children playing donkeyride, as it's the case in the pictorial "Exquisite Corpse" that André Breton, Tristan Tzara, Valentine Hugo, and Greta Knutsen painted in 1933. The same pulse connects in a common associative chain the statement "*the stone necktie unfolds over the stairs*", through a slightly distortive depiction, with the indexical proposition "*a scepter and a nail in parallel course that is mediated by a stair and perhaps a cloud*", and this latter, once more through a slightly distortive depiction, with the description "*the chubby-faced black gentleman near the rails of the train wondered - where the flying little ship steps on?*", in the "turn" of Surrealist Telephone, played by Yannis Golfinopoulos,Vangelis Koutalis, Galini Notti, Makis Perdikomatis, and Marianna Xanthopoulou in 2001. In the "Surrealist Telephone", which was contrived in the late 90s from the contemporary Paris Group, as well as in the "Exquisite Corpse", one of the first surrealist games, each subjectivity explicates herself into the other, is traversed by the other, is imaged on the other. Playing, thereupon, is playing with mirrors, playing of echoes, playing of bodies that are shattered and molded once more from the beginning, on and on, under the stone-still sun of love[16]. A room, then, with mirrors where everyone can see her or his multiple simulacra at a glance, where everyone, moreover, can become a poet, even though her/his knowledge or her/his skills, the extent, that is, of her/his familiarity with the given means of literal expression, does not legitimize such a claim in the dominant mode of ideological production. In surrealist games there is neither victory, nor defeat, neither better, nor worse performance; there is only the intersubjective circuit that desire mounts in order to keep up its movement. No body competes with another; every body struggles against its alienated self, against its very individual substance. The only trophy is the stimulation of the desire, the sharpening of the desire to desire. The common reward is the recognition of self-consciousness in another self-consciousness. And every such recognition, which here is not accomplished through the Master-Slave dialectics, but owing to the complicity of the brothers in the assassination of the Father, or to the mutual responsibility of the fellow-travelers in a frenzied train that traverses the untrodden, virgin forests, is erotic in its depth, has a pending promise for the satisfaction of the desire as its premise, transfers affective charges, hands out the despair and the yearning for freedom, unleashes a mutual pursuit of happiness, exposes a whole nerved body as an open one, accessible to the Other.

What provides for the eroticism is the ritual of the collective aberration, the rules of the game that constitute the step by step constructed bridge on which each subjectivity meets the other. And we might arguably stake - throwing to the table all the treasures of poetry, of this dark, inner reason - on the possibility that this uncertain love rendezvous will not, at the end, be postponed. The rules bring in the algorithm, the pattern of the magical invocation, the rhythm that makes the gestures modulate, and ensures that every subject will find herself outside the borderlines of her socially determined, individualized substance, in order every particular, disposed to play, body to piece out, with its flows of desire, the puzzle of a common erotic object: "*here the automatic met the erotic, for the partial creations merged in as explicit substantiation of group desire for the body entire….More often than not, this charge is felt, like an electric energy surging through the folds, pleating itself like so many reserves of individual longing, until the unfolding, unpleating of the body, of words and images, extends from head to foot* "[17]. Although these remarks were made in regard to the "Exquisite Corpse", the conjunction of psychic automatism and collective, erotic, affective charge can be ascertained in every game with which the surrealist groups have been experimenting from 1920s to our days.

The disposition for playing is perhaps the most reliable benchmark in case we wished to measure the extent to which a surrealist community of friends persists in keeping its fire burning. The number and the variety of surrealist games indicate the inexhaustible ability of the surrealist collectivities to invent, to construct these bridges where the disposed to transgress their boundaries subjectivities can always meet together, redeeming what Isidore Ducasse had once foretold: *poetry must be made by all.* Poetical inspiration is not a "boon"; it has not any unfathomable metaphysical origins, it cannot be credited to any aesthetical or whatever preconception, it is not a privilege of any talented, or whatsoever, individual substance. Inspiration is the surrender to the demon of analogical, associative shift from the one image to the other. Poetry is the socialized production of the hieroglyphics monads that implicate the desire as a cosmogonical power of transfiguration, apposite to every subjectivity-in-revolt. The circulation of desire through this circuit of electrified intersubjectivity leads the frenzied train, with those restless fellow-passengers, into the wild vegetation of the forest of symbols. Surrealist games are but an out-weeded pathway to the heart of this forest, a magical circle under the mystical, "chymical" intercourse of the moon and the sun, the revelation of a route towards the utopian penetralia of the reality, towards the sur-real "Not-Yet-Become".

Endnotes

1) *Monas Hieroglyphica*. The term was coined by John Dee in his text under the same title, written in Latin, and published in Antwerp in 1564. The best available English translation is that of C.H.Josten, "The Hieroglyphic Monad", *Ambix* XII/1964, pp.84-222. In internet there is access to the first English translation of J.W.Hamilton-Jones (1947), see, for example:
http://www.esotericarchives.com/dee/monad.htm.

2) André Breton, "Manifesto of Surrealism" [1924], in *Manifestoes of Surrealism*, translated by Richard Seaver and Helen R. Lane, Ann Arbour: University of Michigan Press 1972, p.38.

3)For a criticism that employs such notions, see Gilles Deleuze and Felix Guattari, *L'Anti-Œdipe*, Paris: Les Éditions de Minuit, 1972, especially pp. 63-64 (concerning "free association").

4) For the term, see Gottfried Wilhelm Leibniz, "Oedipus Chymicus aenigmatis Graeci et Germanici", in *Miscellanea Berolinensia ad incrementum scientiarum*, I, MDCCX [1710], S. 16-22.

5) *Profane Erleuchtung*. See Walter Benjamin's, "Der Sürrealismus. Die letzte Momentaufnahme der europäischen Intelligenz" [1929], *Gesammelte Schriften*, Frankfurt am Main: Suhrkamp Verlag, 1980, II, S.297.

6) "*…die Verwandlung jenes Ansichs in das Fürsich, der Substanz in das Subjekt, des Gegenstands des Bewusstseyns in Gegenstand des Selbstbewusstseyns, d.h. in ebensosehr aufgehobnen Gegenstand, oder in den Begriff. Sie ist der in sich zurückgehende Kreis, der seinen Anfang voraussetzt, und ihn nur im Ende erreicht*", Georg W. F. Hegel, *System der Wissenschaft: Erster Theil, die Phänomenologie des Geistes*, Bamberg und Würzburg: Joseph Anton Goebhardt, 1807, S. 757.

7) See for example the samples of games played in 1921 and in 1922, reprinted in *Les Jeux Surréalistes: Mars 1921-Septembre 1962*, edited by Emmanuel Garrigues, Paris: Gallimard, 1995.

8) George Bataille, *The Absence of Myth – Writings on Surrealism*, edited and translated by Michael Richardson, London – New York: Verso, 2006, p. 49.

9) Johan Huizinga, *Homo Ludens: A Study of the Play Element in Culture*, London: Taylor and Francis, 2003.

10) Melanie Klein, "The psychoanalytic play technique: Its history and significance" (1955), in *The Writings of Melanie Klein*, London: Hogarth Press and the Institute of Psycho-Analysis,1975, III, pp.122-140.

11) Remember what Antonin Artaud once had said: "*Le premier point est de se bien placer en esprit*". "L'activité du Bureau de Recherches Surréalistes" in *Œuvres*, édition établie, présentée et annotée par Évelyne Grossman, Paris: Gallimard, 2004, p. 141.

12) Breton, *Mad Love*, translated by Mary Ann Caws, Lincoln: University of Nebraska Press, 1987, p. 87.

13) Gaston Bachelard, *The Formation of the Scientific Mind* (1938), translated by M.McAllester Jones, Manchester: Clinamen Press, 2002, pp.239-241.

14) See Helen Longino, *The Fate of Knowledge*, Princeton and Oxford: Princeton University Press, 2002.

15) Hegel, *Phänomenologie des Geistes*, S. 111.

16) Cf. Octavio Paz, "Surrealism" (1954), in the volume *The Quest for the Beginning*, (in Greek), translated by M.M.Roussou, Athens 1983, pp.9-31.

17) Mary Ann Caws, *The Surrealist Look. An Erotics of Encounter*, Cambridge Mass.: The MIT Press, 1999, p.238.

If-Then Game Results

The St. Louis Surrealist Group
(Richard Burke, Susan Burke, Andrew Torch)

If stardust covers the fountain at midnight,
then dancing flames will play on Abbey Road.

If you lock a fundamentalist and a rationalist together in a room,
then all will die on a Saturday.

If Little Richard's hair catches on fire,
then a glass sphere will roll across the marble floor.

If rabid bats enter City Hall,
then the black cat will drink milk from a moon-shaped saucer.

If red roses hide in a far corner,
Then the gong of Zen will sound 3 times.

If we invite our anarchist friends to tea,
Then the rats will return to the sewer.

If Creationists begin to evolve,
then Dylan's guitar will lose all of its strings.

If dying stars fall to earth,
Then the forest will sing in a minor key.

If pearls of wisdom rain from the skies overhead,
Then your brains will be eaten by mad cannibalistic Trotskyists.

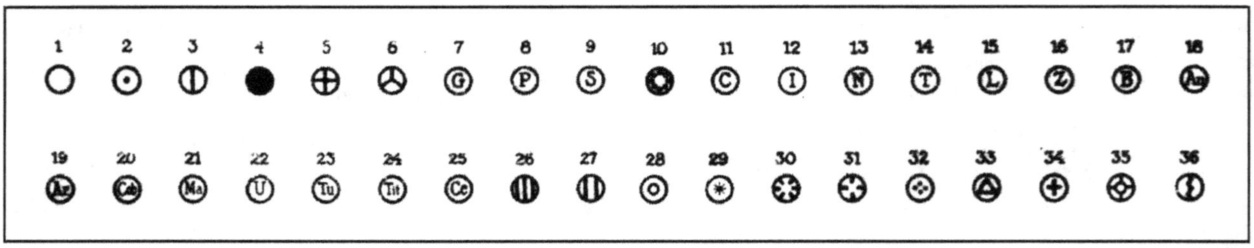

Poems by

Shibek

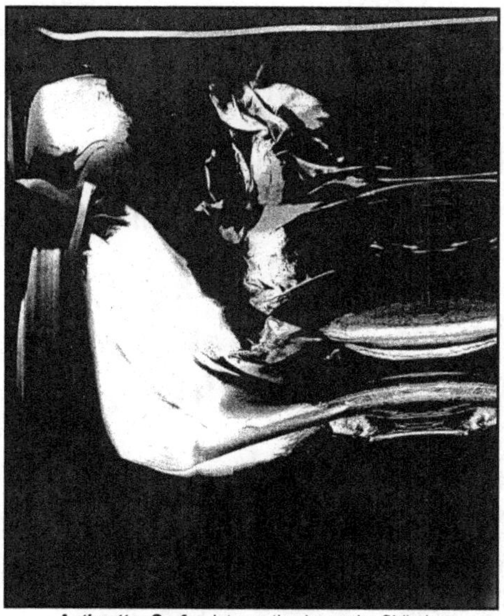

Antimatter Surfer, interpretive image by Shibek

Flytrap, drawing by Novadawn

Submarine Research

Three mirrored coins with a splash ribbon
etched out of glass air

Cognitive daisies weep silver blooded
eruptions stalking trees

Getting closer and closer to the heat ray's
ambiguous dropsy stammer

After all the boring appeals to sensate ambush

And glorification of repressed anomaly

Simultaneous to the grilled footsteps
cried by time's flashpoint

We inhabit curved urges of arched
platelet domes

On a plateau of undulating camouflage

And the air moves between us

Like rock salt from a solar storm

Parallel Snows

Dozens of corpses from their flat lamp
sing to me the echo of a ring
of internal space

Thieve ducks race each other
to the last socket
when the water dries up
to claw maple oils and deploy them
on my corporeal transit

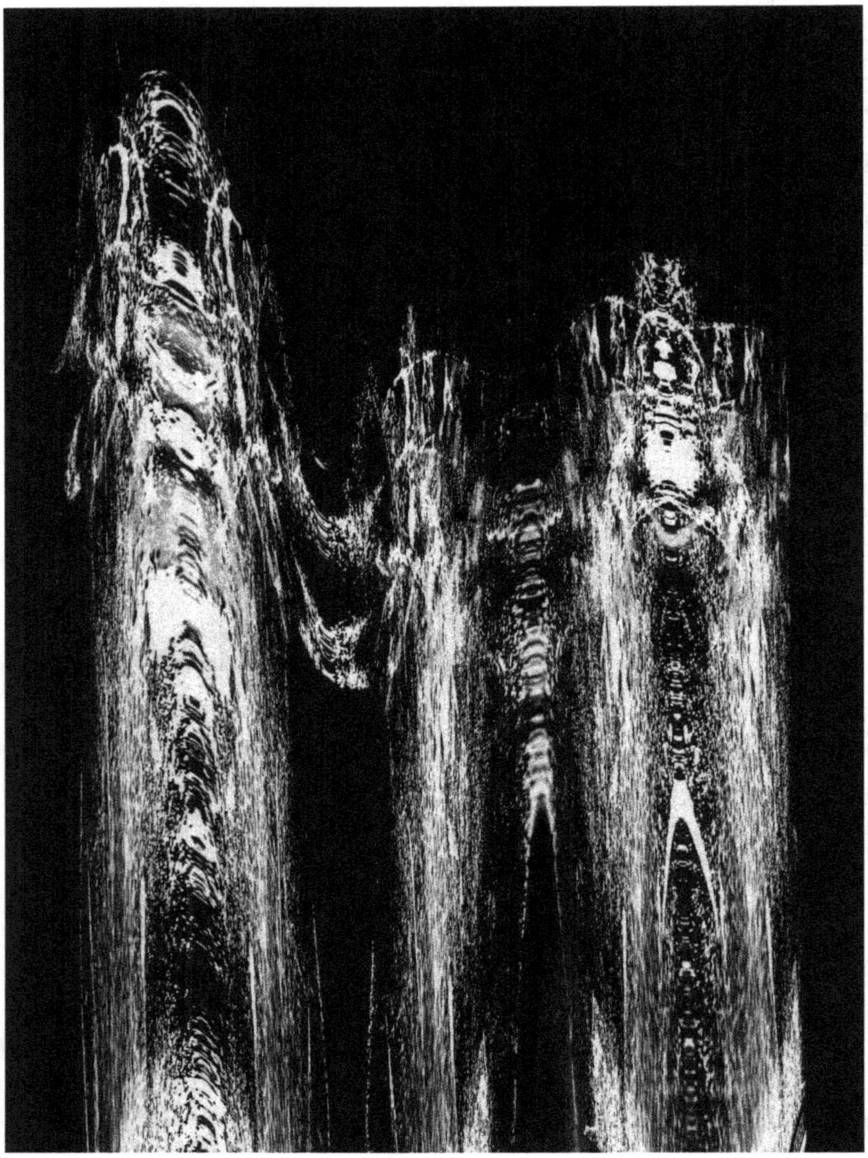

As long as they flash,
they escape

You swim
in the pebbles
falling
from my mouth

A legend of
parallel snows

Out for a walk,
interpretive image by Shibek

SADISM GRASSHOPPERS

The air's splendid sadism grasshoppers culled my wig pennies
I remained a half phase of green bones ahead
The gloss marbles of your first moment

Wrapped around square ovoids of red flood ropes
Who can lift stone bristles from injected squid kicks?
I await your coils of molecular taste furnace
The barometic pressure of Suva

Paradox, drawing by Novadawn

LUCKY TELESCOPE

Due to the change in no-rest void density
And not slow worm moth snakes
Lifting the ionic dense sparks
A pelican absorbs explosions
Grass slippers of synchronic dice
A lucky telescope spell whose nose
Is an aquatic stilt pioneer

Delirium from the East, drawing by Theoni Tambaki

Poems by

Merl Fluin

(Both Handbag and Bee Radiation appeared in
The Reality Binge Trick,
Head Louse Press, 2010.)

HANDBAG

Your swollen octopus is in my handbag.

It's too big to bite and it's too wet to suck.

When I stroke its head it cries like a dog.

When I push my fist into its mouth
it chokes like a baby.

She Who Leads Chaos,
assemblage by Dominique Paul

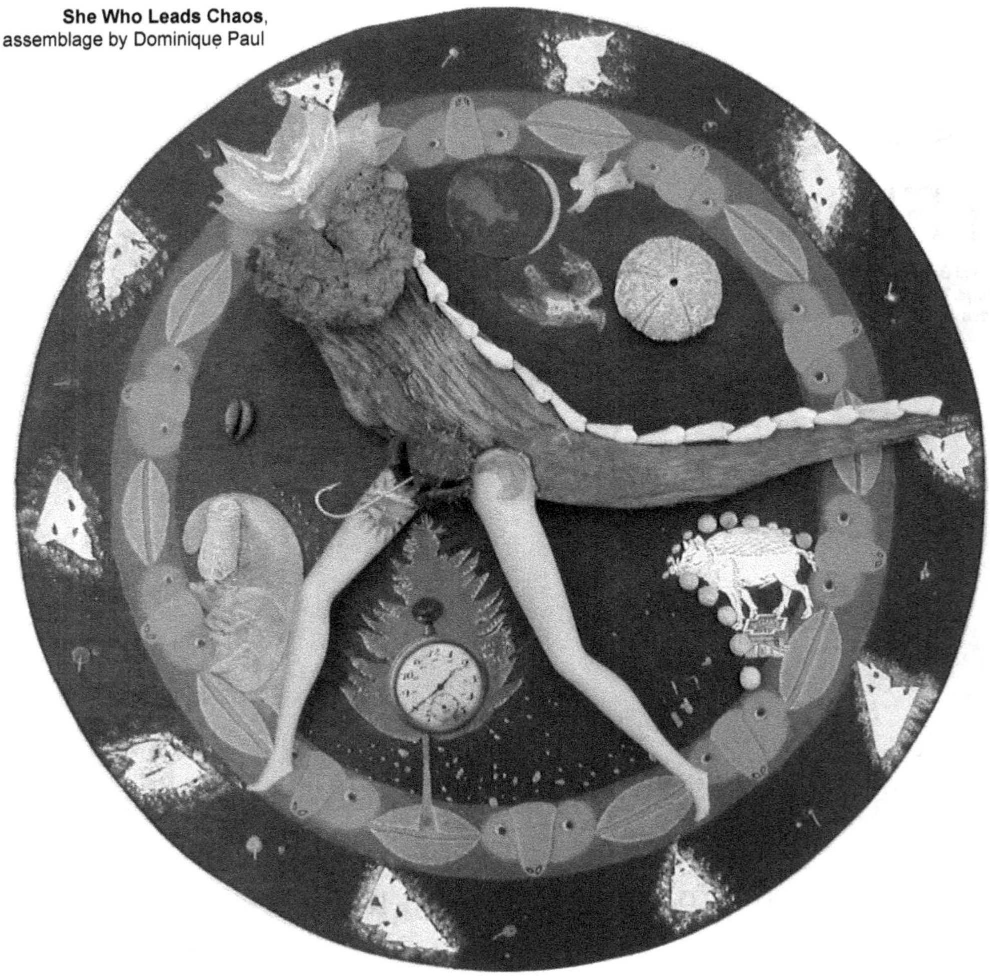

BEE RADIATION

Birdsong and aspartame run like packs through arterial vineyards.

With their mynah birds strung out like torch lights the henchmen are breaking every sumptuary law.

I could milk my fingers like udders. Ladybirds creep through your moustache.

Your gorgeous Y-incision would pucker beneath me.

We would succumb to bee radiation and fall thickly back into ashes.

Our hearts would form an archipelago. This planet has two suns.

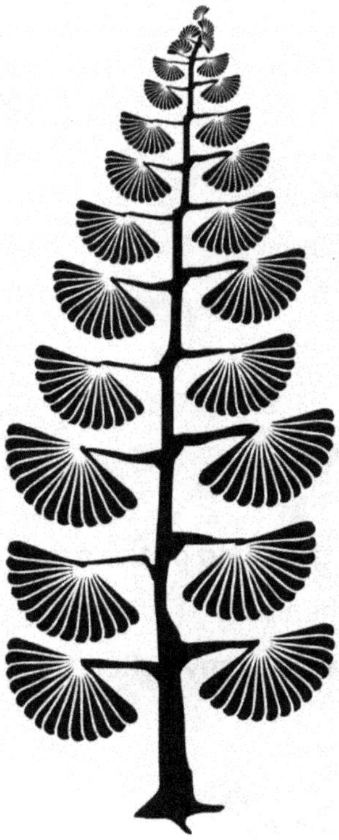

LOVE LETTERS TO RUMPELSTILTSKIN

1. At Second Sight

Splat! A filament of my wettest eye-candy lands in your lap and burrows between your legs. I open my mouth, you read my mind, let the carnage begin. But oh, how slowly! As you advance like the most ridiculous matador in the world I look on with disdain, waggling my señorita in your panting direction just for the devil of it. Late at night you'll go home with your hands full of me, ink on your fingers and chemicals on your breath, tied to the railway track as I twirl my mustachios over your silly little dynamite stick. As for me, I retire from the fray replete with sulphur, all sepulchral in my waxy bath-time skin. Ah, such fertile complacency. In the darkroom of an urban night the alchemicals fix your light to the drenching paper. Let's call it a fortnight before you turn up again and this time I recognise you from the penumbral photofit, oh you've had your mooie all over the agony columns for quite a while my lad. I thought I knew all your tricks and fancies, your rose petals and your rabbit's foot, but then quite suddenly I look across the table and see that you are a terrible centaur, rising ten feet out of the ground, your eyes rolling, your hooves sparking, your mane sweeping across my breasts, your arrow aimed at my ribs which are springing open like a broken gate to usher you into my desperate body.

2. Monster

You'll grind my bones to make your bread.
Then you'll eat the bread.
The seeds from the bread will germinate in your body.
The roots will unroll like stockings inside your thighs.
The stem will creep darkly up inside your belly.
It will pierce you three times through the heart.
It will puncture your lungs and make you gasp for air, until its leaves take hold of them and move the breath for you. In and then out. In and then out. In and then out.
The bud will fill your throat. When you touch yourself at midnight it will be my pollen that bursts aloud from your mouth.

3. Lips apart

At the sound of your voice
my mouth fills with tines.

The Blues 3, drawing by Onston [Can Yeşiloğlu]

4. Rumpelstiltskin

because your fingers are like honeysuckle bees crawl out of my mouth while I'm sleeping

because your eyelids are like trigonometry the earth spins at the speed of light

because your breath is like a blood feud I have evolved two opposable thumbs

because your voice is like a corkscrew hazel I wish you were my father

because your diaphragm is like a pair of apron strings Reality Checkpoint veers off demonology

because your scapulae are like vodka I'll spin pure gold into threads of semen

because your skin is like an adopted child my hair streams with acid and dog roses

because your veins are like brambles raw nectar runs from a gash in the beehive

because your vertebrae are like sigils my lips won't heal

because your throat is like a scalpel you guessed my real name

5. Time-Space Compression

Many things are efficacious to bring your true love back to you.

Peel an apple with a single cut and throw the skin over your shoulder. Leave the skin where it lies and return at midnight, if your lover is true to you it will have become the folds of his or her navel. Press your face into his flesh, his belly will yield to your teeth.

Say your lover's name three times into a mirror stained with steam and tobacco juice. If your lover is true she will shoot from your tongue and lick the glass clean until your own face disappears and your skin falls empty to the floor.

Take a lock of your lover's hair when you go to bed and place it between your thighs. If your lover is true it will turn into a lamprey wrapped in barbed wire.

By the 33rd day when I had tried all these things, my darling, and my legs were bloody, and my face was blank, and the hairs from your belly were still between my teeth, and still it was never enough, I took to stronger stuff and went down below to conjure Mercury to bring you to me.

This is how I did it:

I turned on all the lights in the house at two in the morning and opened all of the windows so that hundreds of snowy white moths flew in. A thousand mosquitoes thrust their mouths into my arms and face and a single cockroach clattered through the bedroom window and crashed onto the bloodstained under-sheet. I set fire to the cockroach with your old cigarette lighter and when the sheets and the mattress caught the flame I put it out with a litre of orange juice poured from an enamel saucepan. I pissed into the saucepan and put the burnt body of the cockroach into the piss, then took the saucepan down all the stairs and put it on the cellar floor and placed a circle of candles around it. Then I lit the candles and turned out all the lights. The moths began to file down the cellar stairs and to revolve above the saucepan in a calm and orderly fashion and the mosquitoes stopped biting but my skin was already covered in welts and puncture marks which I later pretended you had made with your own claws and teeth. I drew a picture of your hands because they are the most beautiful part of your beautiful body, then I tore up the picture and put it into the saucepan with the burnt dead cockroach and the piss. Then I sang What Shall We Do with the Drunken Sailor three times, and walked anti-clockwise three times around the saucepan and candles, then I blew out all the candles and waited for Mercury to appear. I waited for ages until he finally showed up. In the bluish light of his hair I could see all the moths lying quietly on the concrete floor, a lovely expanse of wings and antennae all around Mercury's lovely winged feet. The noise of the wings was amazing until he opened his mouth and three deep notes crawled simultaneously from his throat, followed by a flaming cockroach, a mouthful of piss which slopped out and ran down his chin, and your beautiful hands which flapped like a moth and settled on either side of his silver-helmeted head. He lifted me up from the cellar floor and held me against the wall and fucked me ineptly for what seemed like hours, and when I finally came I could feel the lumps of broken plaster rolling down the backs of my thighs and the legs of twenty dead spiders inside my ears. But by now dawn had long since been and gone and it was really the middle of the morning and Mercury had disappeared, putting a garter round the earth on his mission to bring you to me. So I cleared up the mess and then I lay down on the stinking mattress and went to sleep and dreamt that you broke all my teeth with a butter knife.

On the 35th day I woke up and wondered whether you had come back to me yet. I thought I was alone again but then I found a diurnal moth lying dead on the kitchen counter. Surely that must mean something.

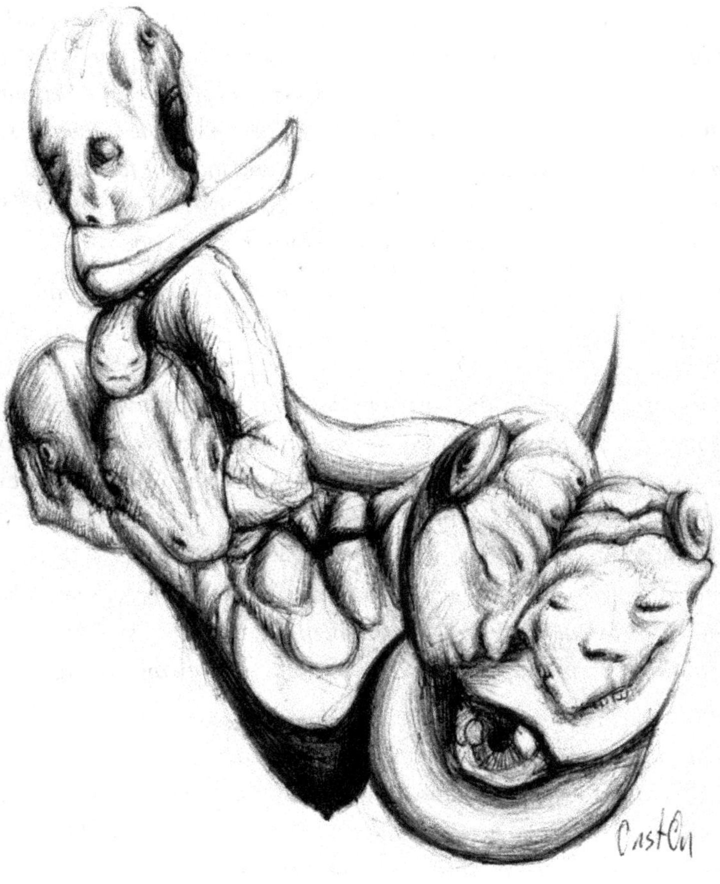

Mtnt2, drawing by Onston [Can Yeşiloğlu]

TAEDIUM VITAE

Sotiris Liontos

— Where are you coming from at this witching hour?
— From a drunkenness of bitter tears!

Have you heard the bad tidings? I'm an inflammable fuel ascending from the drainage. You must be a tank of unknown content. Why don't you surrender to hormonal demand? Abandon all hope, you, whom she approaches with her slender body blooming and shaping itself into a figurehead. Having never been taught the facts of life into practice, I'm peeping at an iridescent pudendum through the snooperscope with malicious intent. Her scorched flora and her slaughtered fauna seem to work marvels in the dark. A virulent ejaculatory egress, mistress of the reptiles and every known amphibious animal, she is giving unusual powers to scorpions and serpents playing hide and seek with the piranhas. Lustfully violated by venereal diseases, her offspring are just a bunch of fingerless dirtbags and rodeo clowns. She is capable of easily scare the living hell out of me, giving my aging bones a good rattle with aptly inserted tiny dynamites of microbes.

I always felt that I don't quite fit in this electrocuted body, roaming on subsistence level with that roving-eyes look on my face, and leading a pathless life void of excitement and carnal knowledge, wayward bound to the rescue in a long litany of witlessness. A continuous parade of disguised phobias in front of an adoring horde of masturbators, staring languidly at the deceptive vista of another mare's-nest in collective awe. Permanently arrested in a child-like state, the way I lead my buried life to nowhere seems like breaking without entering the erased memories of a prenatal sleep gone completely astray. This emotional attachment to a lost childhood takes obsessive proportions every time I realize that I've already lost the best parts of who I once was, becoming the laughing stock of the entire mammal population. Chronic consumer of brain cosmetics and thought fertilizer, I am finally coming to terms with the fact that my cells are rapidly dying. Former owner of the purest flesh in the universe without any visible wounds but with plenty of concealed traumas to cope with.

Giving a free reign to my shrinking heart's desires through joypop recreation, there seems to be nothing so dreadful inside that an uncalculated dose of cough syrup can not fix. Although it was designed for cerebral penetration it has been proved unable to make me enter the junkyard of carnivorous desires. Prescribed for oracular use only, it provides me with a propulsive melodic sensibility that enables me to examine the endless possibilities enshrouded in the darkness of a starless night. That's how I have survived for ages with a lightning bolt inside my head, showing a tendency to obey the inner voices and a subsequent reckless disregard for proper behavior. I used to drink urine from the fountain of youth begging the children not to grow up for their own sake. Wheels within wheels of eternal rotation crushing my scavenge pump during a saddle block, urged me to become just another cog in the machine of universal disorder. Now my aching stomach is speaking in tongues and I don't know which way to turn into my capsule to have the dreams of my own liking.

The narrator can sling the curses to any direction having been cursed himself to exist in cross purposes with the rest of the world, lacking the smarts to change for the better and developing a strange predilection towards sabotaging everything he does. Most fiction tales and motion pictures are constantly lying on this. There's a small number of people that don't live according to the laws of probabilities. Any snide attempt to swipe at stardom fails miserably, making it a worthless experience perfectly suitable for another lonely night with a bottle of gin and a razorblade. Besides, loneliness in association with non slacken desires is a living nightmare second to none. Even though most of the time I feel like an empty mould in a diving suit, the sound of optical venosity keeps jangling in my ears.

But where self-containment has ever led me so far? To a huge desert in the middle of a tiny oasis. Serendipity walks in mysterious ways towards a barren place where I can cool my jets and recharge my batteries. An eluvium land made of smoky quartz and kieselguhr. The stinking odor of sanctity emating from its boiling sun can make you so slothful you'd feel the urgent need to migrate in a cemetery. During this era of existential inertia there's been ascertained a considerable scarcity of humans in favor of chinchillas and armadillos. Acceleration into temporal space continuum now begins. Life goes on but I'm not going anywhere in particular. People I'd swear I've already killed are reported to be alive and kicking gathering speed from the sewer race. So I jollify myself trying to enjoy the love making experience only through the respiratory route. Prolapse over a gaping precipice brings crystal tears to my eyes and vomit to my inhaler. My pulse is rapidly dropping along with the altitude. I can't even read the figures and I'm losing my instruments. There's no afterburner visible on the event horizon. My lateral thinking is useless and febrifugal painkillers cost a fortune. A colony of ants has infested my pubes and I'm also afraid that my genitals' stench is not so ozone friendly. The decompression effect makes me start jumping around in a shotokan style and woosh circumsolar.

So who was I supposed to be if I would really exist? An aquanaut from the last oocyte planet floating in an abyss of similitude. An astronomically nurtured derelict space cadet deemed as a conspiratorially minded scapegoat. A championship of punk rock karaoke chanting a regal anthem to the power of suggestibility. Doctor of music. Debtor of profanities. I have tasted the semen of my ghost. So, come on! Make a strong fist. Use vaseline and whale poo. Eat your own compass. Kill most of your remaining time and touch the stars for a change. Love thy parents is the devil's favorite plaything, proving that Jesus and gravity don't mix well on the pavement. The tips of the icebergs are showing the easiest way to perish upon occasion: either by lethal injection or by swallowing something poisonous along with your dinner. Considering that eventually the maggots will devour us, it's a useless waste of effort and time trying to postpone the inevitable. And remember, everybody looks much better in a beautiful casket.

MMIX

Painting by Alex Fatta

An Open Letter about the Bad Forecast:

by way of a discourse on desire before the advent of industrial collapse

Emilio Santiago

All those who aspire to organize society in a way that permits a more complete life have a pending discussion and strategic challenge which could be outlined in the following way:

A) We find ourselves at the historic threshold of such an enormous change in material conditions that it will render useless all theoretical tools incapable of functioning within the new scenario.

B) There exists a most dangerous pitfall in the attempts to provide a liberating answer to this scenario, so from our coordinates, which we could simplistically refer to as desire as a revolutionary motivation[1] , this theme has been highly neglected, but meanwhile a monopoly of answers has been elaborated from positions of neo-survival (specifically from anti-industrial currents, although not exclusively). And to be fair, when considering the coordinates of the revolution of desire – at least within our context, the only authentically liberating ones – we cannot let the anti-industrialists set the guidelines of the future, revolutionary imaginary, and its experimentation. In other words, accepting this reflection implies the acknowledgement of Jean-Marc Mandioso's thesis when he affirms that the revolutionary cycle, as we understand it, is historically concluded in an irreversible way.

C) Relating the previous, critical theory and liberation are not an intellectual pastime but a very serious game. In this case, we are playing with our lives (perhaps not just allegorically, and that is the terrible part).

Thus we face the challenge of assessing our historical viability, no less. In the wake of this are revealed some lines of thought to collectively deepen:

THE RE-DIAGNOSIS OF CAPITALISM (TENDENCIES OF THE PROCESS)

Political projects and their theoretical/practical currents don't exist by themselves; for every epoch they arrive configured by the material conditions of possibility. The political project driven by surrealism or the Situationist International (total subversion, the revolution of life) was possible while still being non-blochian, in the context from which material conditions permitted thinking in a practical and universal way with regards to issues of abundance (a prerequisite for overcoming the survival of the commodity within communism) and access to the historical process (a prerequisite for overcoming the State through the hyperpolitics of the labor councils). The change in material conditions transforms in parallel the possible conditions for each historical moment: the first thing that we need to acknowledge is that, despite the fact that behind the spectacle just about everyone seems unable to know anything about what is going on, we still have enough intelligence to suspect the development of an enormous mutation of the material conditions implicit in contemporary capitalism. This change is signaled from many fronts: global-warming and its alleged natural disasters (alleged in the sense of all natural disasters possessing an undeniable social causality); the development of information technology, which serves as a platform for processes so disparate as the *casino economy*, or according to the fashionable (but profoundly questionable) thesis of Negri and Hardt, in order to create the fundamentals of communism and direct democracy through the highly cooperative labor practices implicated in the exploitation of non-material work; the phenomena of harmfulness covered in the *Encyclopedie des Nuisances* as an accumulative reality beyond the useful that has reappeared in the shape of pollution, ecocide and the dangerous destruction/manipulation of biodiversity, seen not only in ecosystems but also in the degradation of our own genetic reserves (progressive infertility)... All of these are multiple signals of change, interpreted with alarm or with optimism according to whichever perspectives.

Let's consider, for example, only one variable of this change in material conditions: the subject of energy (Peak oil) and, specifically, one of its implications (the industrial production of food), since the energy issue encompasses many areas (a fall in the capacity of electric supply, the scarcity of raw material for plastics, the downfall of the international system of transportation, the consequential social tensions, occurring politically just as much at state levels as well as the global level[2]). The importance of the energy question is that it overturns what could be called diagnostic limits: superficially it is an almost popular idea that capitalism will self-destruct over the long term, but to really understand what is happening means discovering that these long periods of time become concrete dates that are just around the corner. Although it might sound like cheap millennialism or something incredible (in the most simple sense of the word: to be unbelievable), the industrial system (beyond the polemics about its intrinsic harmfulness or the neutrality of the machine) finds itself in a blind alley with numbered days. When speaking of numbered days, we refer to a time frame in which people younger than fifty will participate, at least in the initial stages of collapse. And a collapse that is non-revolutionary but produced by the unbridled aspect of its own dynamics will irreversibly bring a scenario of terrible social disaster, although some groups will succeed in constructing a community raft for survival. Underlying this bad omen we find the peak oil production, which is one of the keys to understanding our time. The ignorance and silence around it prove two things: on one hand, its tremendous importance. This has to do with the core issue (about oil production) being managed by the intelligence agencies of the leading countries of the world, and for them to maintain transparency about it would be politically dangerous. On the other hand, there is the inability of capitalism to consider itself, provoked by the growing specialization and fragmentation of labor.

To the point where we cannot even understand, all possibilities of modern-industrial, social life (including its attempts at liberation) are dependent on a high availability of energy, historically possible by our planet's supply of fossil fuels. The historically triumphant industrial model, upon making itself dominant over the entirety of the planet, is a model specifically based on petroleum, which has allowed a network of very efficient, international transportation to develop, and more importantly a very high level of agricultural productivity, capable of sustaining and concentrating high population densities in the cities[3]. And now the truth: when this supply ends, when the petroleum is exhausted, then all the infrastructure that has been possible because of it will collapse from the lack of a new source of highly available energy to replace it. To add to this very obvious bottleneck are four things that are not so obvious: i) an alternative (to petroleum) of readily available energy does not exist[4]. ii) For a capitalist model that structurally requires growth, problems begin not with the exhaustion of resources but with subsequent decline. iii) The global decline (peak oil) is forecast, according to geological predictions that have been reliably demonstrated locally, for the timeframe of 2010-2026, according to pessimistic or optimistic geological trends. iv) With the absence of fossil fuels it has been calculated[5] that the world demographic equilibrium could readjust itself to about 1.5 to 2 billion people. These numbers are thrown in here just to get an idea of how many of us will remain[6].

In summary, it is very probable that peak oil will be capitalism's point of implosion (the physical impossibility of economic growth), and if we do not stop it by way of a planned intervention that only can occur through revolutionary means, it will be the point of collapse of the industrial system. And this should not be celebrated in any abstract way, not even by those diehard defenders of anti-industrialism, however much they had arrived at anti-industrialism through the critique of alienated life. Although in and of itself the industrial world is alienated, its non-revolutionary collapse doesn't give any reason to hope for any de-alienation; surely it will involve the formulation of a new type of alienation, after a period of cruel and traumatic readjustment comparable to the golden age of industrial terror.

Those of us who are attracted to poetry as a social and unified practice (and by that proclaiming ourselves revolutionaries), cannot defend obsolete, social diagnostics, and neither can we accommodate ourselves with a type of Cassandra syndrome that contents itself with globally announcing the immanence of disaster while taking delight in the incomprehension that results. Although we have lucidity, it is worthless unless we are able to derive something useful from it: evidently, avoiding the irreversibly traumatic collapse of the industrial world will be against the cycle of value or will not be at all. But perception is not enough. The immanent, material reconfiguration of the world should involve an experienced, theoretical, and political challenge of the first order. And perhaps more to us than anyone else, we see ourselves as those who aspire not only to "free ourselves from the material foundations of the inverted truth" but also to organize the social environment around the highest and conceivable human experiences: desire, games, dreams, love, fantasy, poetry, the marvelous, and perhaps, new passions that have yet to be experienced. Using Vaneigem's worn out but valid formula, the party of life cannot hand over reflection and updated practice to the party of survival (although the latter calls itself revolutionary), or rather, to give up reflection and practice on the level of contemporary problems, or at least not without presenting a *real* revolutionary alternative to the struggle (and this will sound pretentious, but for us there are no other remedies than to reject (to deny its revolutionary potential) as insufficient or mistaken every political program that doesn't have as its main focus the transformation of daily life in something passionately superior). Therefore, another urgent task of critical theory is to formulate a strong answer to the political proposals of neo-survival.

CRITICAL ANALYSIS OF NEO-SURVIVAL

Beforehand, we should acknowledge the important contributions to the fight against human alienation made by the anti-industrial circles, especially in three aspects: the ability to squarely look at one of the objective problems of our era despite the successive disguises of the spectacle, the denunciation of the simplistic and naive view that critical theory has had with respect to technology (certainly capable of creating its own dynamics), and the attempt to put into practice some type of experiential, anti-industrial solution, in both individual and collective ways.

Accepting these contributions, we can assert some of the following points through which we should dismantle the arguments of neo-survival are the following ones:

1) Without wanting to enter an olympiad of historiographic erudition, the historic medieval revisionism wielded by the anti-industrialists, for example *Los Amigos de Ludd*, is extremely refutable in many of its assertions. That the peasantry has something to do with liberty is something that has been categorically denied; in the same way it is difficult to isolate the Middle Ages, making it a static setting, separating it from its own internal process of growing complexity: since we cannot forget that industrial mud came from medieval dirt (historically such absolute divisions are never made). That is to say, however, that this look to the past is not completely worthless, to the extent that it seeks options for combat and survival from industrial disaster. But only a stale ideological view of the world could be reduced to this backwards perspective based on a dichotomous opposition and a Manichean industrial/preindustrial world. A social, postindustrial project (in the liberating sense) should not only look for inspiration within the so-called antipodes of the industrial world (its past) but also, and perhaps most importantly, within its contemporary fringes, defects, anomalies, exceptions, and delicate layers. Just like *Los Amigos de Ludd* rescue valid

methods and ideas from the Middle Ages regardless of the medieval ideological-theological trappings and the relations of feudal power that enveloped them, it can be very interesting to learn some lessons from the experiences, techniques and methods of Cuba and North Korea, despite our contempt for the bureaucratic class that governs them and the industrial model that continues to be used there in the form of a concentrated spectacle. Finally, at these levels of urbanization, the resemblance of this kind of crisis-scenario will be much closer to that of Pyongyang than to the Sierra de Gata (*), for most people in the world.

2) Whereas traditional, critical theory has been kind to the machine, the anti-industrial critique has placed its emphasis on the intrinsic alienation of technology as a social force. For example, Kaczynski denounced, with his idea regarding the collapse of the power process, that the progressive mechanization of human activity in techno-industrial civilization trivializes this activity until rendering it psychologically harmful. From our perspective, Kaczynski is referring to a real problem, but he does so from a very narrow angle. It becomes evident that this method of social organization degrades the movement of intentionality, the very structure of life as an opening to the outside. The society of the spectacle, as established passivity, is also a social apathy. Through this, on the surface, our revolt is a revolt through and of intensity, a revolt of human life, in its radical and fundamental sense, against its inactivity. But contrary to what Kaczynski defends, this degradation of life-will does not come from the theft of human abilities by technology, at least not only from this theft. The analysis remains weak since it does not include the commodity cycle's subordination of social life (including technology). In this manner we could say that for the debate between technophobes and critics of the commodity, that both groups are right and wrong. Just like the anti-industrialists have successfully declared that technology generates its own incontrovertible social dynamics, revealing the dangerous naïveté that the labor movement has displayed while defending the neutrality of the machine, it is not certain that technology and the machine are affected by the distortion from uncontrolled capitalist accumulation, whose origin is the commodity. Making a detournement on the famous situationist thesis: the anti-industrialists want to abolish technology without realizing it, whereas the classic labor movement has attempted to realize technology without abolishing it. Both can be understood as inseparable aspects of the revolutionary agenda of overcoming technology, as a social instrument produced by capitalist society which feeds on itself.

3) To admit that it is difficult to dream in a concentration camp is different from saying that it is unsuitable, or even worse, that it is counterproductive. To have the intelligence to accept the limitations of the world does not imply enduring the foolishness of not discussing the limits. We recognize the ecological and emancipatory need to curb the derailment of the breakaway economy

Untitled drawing by Schlechter Duvall

and all of the useless, industrial scaffolding that its disintegration creates, but despite that, we are not willing to renounce the same fundamental of life, which always has been an orientation, a desire, a movement further away. Against the approach of the anti-industrialists, the main area of contention that we should combat is their process of value-formulation, which is paradoxically not so different from the first industrial ideologies: humanization *through* work, the rejection of overabundance, of excess, of pleasure, and of luxury (all this is taken not in an emaciated, spectacular form, but as experiences perhaps more humble – for example, playing with a child is a luxury – but much more profound). They not only recognize and reevaluate the new, necessary alienation (we can agree up to this point), but in fact they celebrate it (and here is our most irreconcilable dispute)[7]: against this type of approach we declare incisively that love, desire, the game, poetry... are the things most worthy of surviving in this world. This should guide us to a social practice that, without jeopardizing the world that supportively serves it, will never avoid its fulfillment (not behind the technical alienation of the spectacle, nor behind the alienation of anti-industrial asceticism).

Untitled drawing by Schlechter Duvall

CLEANING OUT OUR CLOSET

Our proposal of presenting an evaluation of desire before a historical situation that will increasingly impose necessity as a social climate, looks like a typically well-intentioned but doubtful abstraction. This contradiction can begin to resolve itself, thereby relieving us, the carriers of the discourse of desire, of some of our ravings (if they have been able to and can still play an essential, stimulating role through their assumed, practical realization), ravings which undeniably imply the maintenance and reinforcement of alienation. It would be intelligent to start a process of filtering these ideas as projects to be achieved historically (and not as imaginary games that only have intrinsic value). We refer, for example, to an overly sophisticated idea about the transcendence of art. The construction of situations in the manner proposed within the first issues/years of the Situationist International, with its overly complex technical coverage and implicit material waste[8], should come to form part of a historical catalogue of the marvelous utopia, like alchemy, Bacon's *New Atlantis*, or the phalanstère. Perhaps the transcendence of possible art, in the future, will be closer to the popular game than to situationist ideas. Certainly many of our projections on what has to be a liberated society need to pass through a similar filter, a certain detoxification from mechanistic-industrial omnipotence, a lesson in humility. By this we want to say that desire, life, the game and their ambitions are not essential categories, but *relational* ones: they are dependent on the possibilities of each era. As a detournement of Eliade, every human act is susceptible of being transformed into the marvelous. Therefore, to the extent that the industrial means of production contain true potential for our project, once liberated from commodity distortion, this liberation of the economy should continue being the focal point for our struggle, but with us maintaining a cautious view, suspecting that perhaps "the fruits of the political economy are already rotten." In the event that this is the case, our task should be to lead the re-enchanted dismantling of the industrial world.

NOTES FOR A COLLECTIVE REFORMULATION OF THE REVOLUTIONARY PROJECT

The reformulation of the revolutionary project has many other imminent tasks besides what has already been mentioned. Three of them are elaborated here, relating in part with the aforementioned problems:

A) The generalized ignorance in our environments of certain issues like — and this is an example — peak oil production, is and is not surprising (since it is common in the spectacle). It is terrifying to think that certainly other important issues are slipping through our fingers. In light of this, we consider that our freedom comes (among other practices, but irremediably) through acquiring from specialists this type of knowledge about the global state of affairs which, without our revolutionary synthesis, and in case they succeed in resolving the infracommunication in which they are being produced, only serve the management of the energy disasters (and thus the reinforcement of alienation). Therefore we believe that critical theory should deal, apart from its habitual tasks (the revelation of hidden alienations, historical exercise, organizative debates, etc.), with of a kind of dirty work that appears simple but which the spectacle has made excessively complicated: the modernized perception of the world, capable of guaging the urgent issues and true challenges. We need a platform for mutual learning which would allow us to leave the confines of our professional and also subversive (situationist, surrealist, anarchist, etc.) designations, a platform capable of putting not only ideas or desires of freedom into the service of practical revolution, but also the technical data of an accurate intervention in reality which must be taken into account.

B) We share with the anti-industrialists an unfortunate theoretical/practical error: a fetishizing of the concept of fetishism, which is so widespread in our thought. Those of us who view ourselves in line with Marx, (which is worth the effort and which centers its analysis on commodity fetishism and the problem of alienation) always have strayed with a certain incomprehension with respect to this concept, which has created what could be called a notion of strong, extreme, false fetishism. Upon knowing, reification is complete, and like something established, alienation reproduces itself. From there it turns out that only one type of outsider from alienation could destroy fetishism (the Party in the case of Lukacs, which is the most paradigmatic). This vision should be understood as the final turn of the screw that annuls the most important lesson of fetishism: that it is a process in constant dispute, in continuous rebirth, and a tension; that there are no objective or social categories of thought but the struggle to objectify them; that there is no certainty, pessimism, or optimism, but only uncertainty and a horizon of many struggles on different scales. The enormous ability of the spectacle to construct the real and to display it as the real causes us, some more than others, to have a spectacular experience of the spectacle, but more oppressive and asphyxiating than it really is. We give up terrain to the enemy. This is something that convulses behind all of these so highly catastrophic analyses, with respect to political action, that circulate in the revolutionary milieu. One of the most important challenges presented to us is to conceive a theory and practice capable of taking into account the fact that the struggle against capital and for a more passionate life, is permanent, constant but discontinuous, contradictory, and never-ending, by definition. And in this sense, broadening the issue of forces that are potentially resistant to alienation, and deepening the theoretical study of atavistic reserves. Because in fact we rebel, and fortifying this rebellion that experiences daily life, coming to respond to the question: Why can we rebel?

C) Given the approaching context, perhaps this time it does become appropriate to distinguish two courses of action that are not necessarily complementary: one revolutionary (in the practices and debates that we usually have kept going) and the other collective (which strategically confronts the possibility of survival based on different, possible scenarios).

Our discourse certainly stands before the challenge

of adapting itself. This adaptation has to be developed under positive, affirmative and concrete auspices, although this happens on the smallest levels of operative potentiality (it is not about denouncing fetishism but of dismantling it empirically; of renaming things or being observant on the street for finding objects; this is where we have most of our forces). Adapting or adopting a not-so-intelligent rigidity, either with the attitude of those who decide to presently abandon themselves in order to enjoy the petty privileges of pleasure that capitalism still can offer, or equally of those who desert the revolutionary party of life in order to join the party of neo-survival: these latter give us years of experience, and to deny ourselves a critical-dialectic relation with them would possibly imply losing the thread of our time, a bitter time that approaches. Networks of mutual help, useful apprenticeship, methods of self-sufficiency... There are many people in small groups testing practical solutions to the problems that will come. It is not foolish to open one's eyes and to learn something, in order to be prepared, and for us not to limit ourselves in life to self-accommodation, but rather to try to push life towards the edge of the possible, when the moment arrives.

NOTES

1. We can fundamentally distinguish three revolutionary motivations that lead to three different, subversive positions: the problem of survival, the problem of life and the problem of values. The problem of survival was raised by the first labor movement, which understood the social revolution as a tool to ensure its reproduction as a labor force in a time where the relations of capitalist exploitation didn't guaranteed it at all (food, work, health, education...). The problem of life, as a questioning of the complete conditions of existence bound to mercantile, bourgeois civilization, is distinguishable in a pioneering way already in romanticism. The offspring of romanticism and the "vanguard classics" (Rimbaud, dada, historic surrealism) inherited and reformulated it with a more progressive and extensive reach. Finally, it became widely practiced in the more rebellious circles of the labor movement of the *glorious thirties*, when the problem of survival remained locally resolved in Europe therefore *welfare*, with the reappearance of the absurd and the harmfulness of modern life that was subdued by the capitalist, economic expansion (liberation and realization of desire, revolution of daily life, transcendence of art...). The problem of values, as an ethical rejection of inequality (justice value) and as a call for autonomy (liberty value), can already be tracked to the foundation of so-called bloodless religions, transplanting itself in the modern world through a process of secularization and incorporating itself into its distinct traditions. The labor movement has appropriated this ever since the so called utopian socialists, ending up as the livelihood for all anarchy; and despite its scientific pretentions, it does articulate a good part of Marxist *weltanshauung*. These three attitudes still persist now, with different combinations of themselves.

2. Only a superficial glance at the geopolitical framework of our time would serve as a necessary and interesting analysis of how the "The sham spectacular struggles between rival forms of separate power are at the same time real in that they express the system's uneven and conflicting development," and is how, through these internal battles, commodity logic will tear itself apart. Since the 1970s one should view the international, political transformation in light of energy resources: the boycott of 1973, the Gulf Wars (I and II), the revolution in Iran, Al Qaeda and the salafista project, tensions in Venezuela, the Chechen problem..., and then understanding the imminence of Peak oil; it all begins to come together like a puzzle. And from this the invasion of Iraq and the growing tensions with Iran. The United States is not bleeding itself dry in Bagdad because of any excess of imperialist greed or any arbitrary reason. In this day and age, with its own petroleum production at levels seen in 1940 and decreasing, the survival of the United States as a world-power and ultimately as the continuity of a way of life (the society of consumerism), is at stake in the Middle East.

3. In a more direct way: before 1910 more calories were obtained from agriculture than those invested in production (Harris, *Antropología Cultural*, p. 122); today in the US ten K-calories of fossil fuel energy are needed to produce one K-calorie of food (Dale Allen Pfeiffer, *Eating Fossil Fuels*, article published in *From the Wilderness* (2003), translated to Spanish by Ricardo Jiménez and published on www.crisisenegetica.org.).

4. At this level of consumption: renewable energies are beginning to reach their physical limits of productivity –

exhaustion of the level 6 wind fields in the Iberian Peninsula, for example; peak uranium will be reached around 2060; nuclear fusion is constantly postponed by engineering problems that are most likely irresolvable; hydrogen is an energetic vector, not a source of energy. But we insist, and is what is most important: at this level of consumption.

5. Dale Allen Pfeiffer, (op. cit.).

6. The ultimate fact: this *Mad Max* scenario is not just hypothetical. There still exist two historical cases of collapsed industrial nations: Cuba and North Korea, colonies of the Soviet empire totally dependent on the oil exports from the big cities. With the fall of state capitalism in Moscow, and left unprotected by the international commercial embargo, both "democratic republics" suffered a severe oil shortage in the 1990s. In Cuba the food crisis resulted with close to seven thousand deaths by malnutrition according to official numbers (and we already know that this kind of official estimate in the concentrated spectacle is a sufficiently gruesome joke). If the Cuban example is terrifying, then it is surpassed by that of North Korea: three million deaths due to malnutrition between 1993 and 1995. Take a look at *Drawing Lessons from Experience; The Agricultural Crises in North Korea and Cuba* by Dale Allen Pfeiffer, published in the 2003 issue of *From the Wilderness* and translated by Piedro A. Prieto for www.crisisenergetica.org.

7. Continuing with Kaczynski: he operates from an essentialist notion of the human being, which, combined with his coordinates guided by the principle of shortage, he defines as *homo agricolae*, thus linked to the post-edenic verdict "you will earn your living by the sweat of your brow": the satisfaction of needs through the effort of work is what makes us people. Thus his apology for the field of primary, maslowian needs (food, security, shelter) and his contempt for everything else called secondary needs, which would become dehumanizing and socially destabilizing. In short, the project of the Unabomber appears to be nothing more than a mixture of secularized Calvinism and a gloomy, ruralization of Jeremes Rojos, in this instance forced not by the party but by the decentralized vanguard.

8. Helicopters and explosions in the service of the constructed situation, labyrinths, the models of Constant, "the universe bagged for the workers' councils." Not only during the first stage of the Situationist International was a political project encouraged such that it was built on a kind of technological cornucopia, but that this was definitive for the situationists until their thesis of dissolution, where they considered the issue of ecology for the first time.

(*) Translator's note: Sierra de Gata is a mountainous site in Ávila (Castilla y León)

Translated by Eric Bragg & Bruno Jacobs

Salamandra – Intervención surrealista – imaginación insurgente – crítica de la vida corriente, #17/18, Madrid, 2008, pp. 6-12.

Hunter and Hunted, painting by Wedgwood Steventon

MIRACH SPEAKS TO HIS GRAMMATICAL TRANSPARENTS

Will Alexander

For now I will not state any numerical design to the cosmos. I will only elicit carbon as one of its ellipsis or possibilities. As you grope with your present stages of duration, with your interpersonal transparencies, I need not remind you that you ambulate by means of the power of your internal carbon. For instance, the subconscious craft of dreaming, all the while rising from its secondary depth into the world of visible events, while still excelling further above various sub-quanta into higher concealment And I am not speaking of any Freudian mazes, or any attempt at containment in terms of a prone or dialectical reasoning. First, one must continue to feel that the void is burning, that its script remain in shadow, in order to organically inhale the documents of one's inheritance. In this regard the family tree must remain as a singular mote without any zoomorphic or astrological importance. It remains a triangular in-specific. It must not hound you, or inhere in your hands stiflings, or misgivings which deter you in margins holding the plaintiffs deck of cards. You must resist what I consider a negligible tendency which alters the inchoate, the splendiferous, always seeking the explanatory notions of why you suddenly exist. These notions always seeking a purely conscious distance from the explosive letters kindled in your mystery.

For instance, at a certain point in circular time I never stood on carbon, or argued from its base for monological regularity inside the act which is known as breathing. Because, this remains my imminence, it cannot be concluded that I speak from angelic quanta, or from descending puzzles structured on the motifs of demons. But if it is true that mental structured bum, I want to feel their osmosis, their tinctured meanderings other than monology. Within this spirit I want to explore the hidden text. The text which is rendered by means of its hiddeness. Its hiddeness which remains alive beyond a paralytic visibility.

For me, the phoneme is spore, is flotational mist from the outer lakes of space. In your writing I will ask you to inhabit the lingering inceptions as they exist in the primordiums of lo or Triton. Then give me the instants induced in your minds when they explore the basic principles of Saturn, then hydroxyl, then the infinite remains of the galaxy. Do not justify your rhetoric by circling the core of an introductory ballast. Do not confine yourselves to wind, to oceans set ablaze by the maladjusted cinders of the sun. Know that the phoneme is drift, that the key to one's enigma is the poetic marginalia of the phrase which always combusts beyond the forests of technique. Therefore, the language is no longer keyed to a rivalrous stockade, or to a storm of dulled political misnomers. No. We are looking at something beyond the black and deaf horses of Homer, beyond the trace amount of blood which both provokes and unnerves Virgil. As for Dante, we will no longer pursue the stagnant corpses of the ancients. No. No longer a parochial kind of cosmos where the letters re-circulate as iron. True, there is a source for origins in this work, but what can be gathered is a triune manipulation of war, of agony contiguous to agony. A paradigm of Sparta and Christ. The agon, the delirious elixirs of fear. Juggled depths, partial dimensions epically stated. These are not the crafts that we seek to combine. For instance, if one of you breaks through his fear and announces a new green sun 200 billion years into the future this is one recognition of the void experienced in the palpable dialectics of the void. Let us enunciate our powers with in its partial locales. This is what I call the conundrum of Ernst Mack, where shadows of brilliance are pushed by the fingers. Infinite motion is transmuted; the constellations suddenly shift according to rotational mutation.

Let us go further. Picture your attempts to conjure a being from the lower inhabitants of earth. Say, an eel with the contrasting gifts of several sovereign emotions. And I'm equating these emotions with the auspices of hunger and graft, under the compelling remonstrance which evinces itself as screaming. This is merely on example or litmus. Maybe a recipe of verbs for lianas, or cecropias, or almonds. Or perhaps an aural surge of sawdust mountains scattered near the boarders of Tibetan plateaus.

Let me ask this gathering collectively, how would you imply these measures, say, in psychic viharas, or access reflections from the mirrors inside your scriptings? Of course I'm asking this rhetorically, yet I am serious concerning the spirit inside your written conveyance. And by conveyance I mean the phonemes, the dots, the sovereign streaks inside the alphabet. This is the level of hearing one requires. The many paths to the phonemes, and the many blends of words into phrases.

Let me say that I am not seeking from you a geometric ballast, a superficial harmonization according to your grasp of Pollux, or Deneb, or Beta Centauri. I am not measuring you according to trampled foliage or cinder, or by superficial skill gained by the raptures contained in scientific foment. I cannot gauge you by the rules as captured by someone else's dishonor. None of this applies at this hour, because I am only seeding the scope which spins inside the scope of your inherent transparences.

I do not hope to impose an amorphic interblending, or present to you a strain of immeasurable sub-surfaces to suddenly test yourselves so as to prove your worth to a moribund community. Because it must be acknowledged that what exists around us is nothing other then a psychic swamp, nothing other then a gloomy oasis. This is the hazard that we face as cosmic igniters, as transparent grammarians, as curious solstice workers. We pronounce the matter of fact as askewment, as the sum of panicked multitudes as means. These are the ramparts of soldiers and murderers, of sentient graft exchangers, of political mobs bent on destroying the meticulous. Therefore our understanding of charisma is always living at the source which kindles our transparency.

In closing, let me speak of the elevated tree, the scope which includes as phantasmic lunation certain splinterings which are called Aldebaron, Altair, Antares. I call these the stars of blue soil. Then let me speak of Procyon as nimbus, as cataract which shifts in the storm of new thoughts, to see results in a purposeful chromium. As I once again enrapture the hail inside your nothingness, let me once again give you an ark of blue suns burning in the core of the depths, seeking out the strategies weaving themselves inside the riddles of dangerous waters.

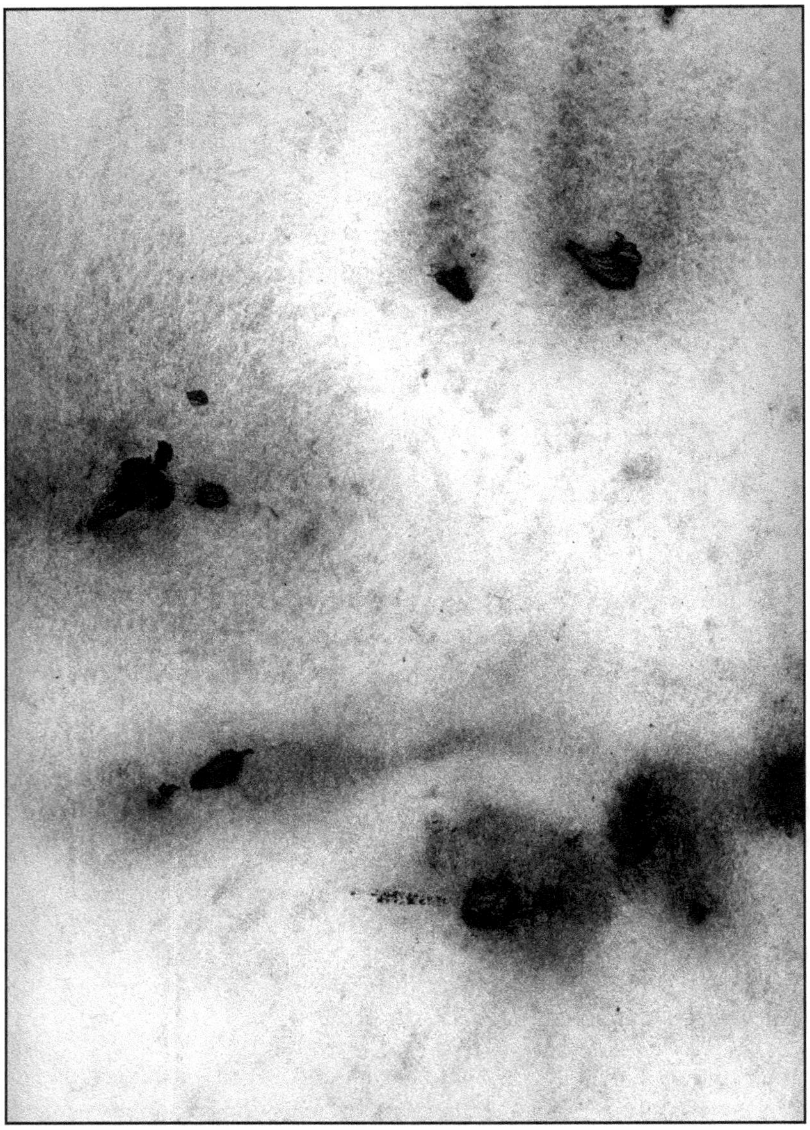

Vandyke Technique. rain painting by Daniel C. Boyer

MIRACH: INAUGURAL ELECTRIFICATION

Will Alexander

We left off in the midst of uttering of flame. Perhaps a traceable index or phantom. Perhaps a burst of lariats in the heavens. Or forces concerned with the stationary eye struggling with the trans-rotation. Take the impure process of lightning on Saturn. There are sparks conceived by at least 12 of its moons. Then nothing. Not even the chemicals compounded in a flameless alpine lizard which seem to monstrously function and at the same time magnetically de-comply. This is not to say that infinity carries difference, or moves in the way that various suns emit their rays scorching or imploding their peregrinations. Since infinity exists it does vary, it does complexify and rotate, and again, if I told you that the Sun drifts, that the Sun we've come to sustain suggests itself with illness, you need to infer from this that it suffers from sustained decimations incited by decimal staggerings in Greek, points, an inferno of wizened symbols cut off from their Nilotic originations. We've come to re-recognize the hemispheric South, to listen to its Rams, its cereals, its spirit. As suns we are non compliant with ice and its less conclusive principles. Of course you are beginning to understand that I speak by vibrational apparition. I speak by codes in the higher sub-text of hearing so that there is both fervour and invigoration, clairaudience and insurrection. We have come to provoke a lessened territorial ether. A less provincial substratum which re-spawns itself allowing our ailing brother to re-focus his electroluminescence, his tribophosphorescence so that the equinox en-springs a luminous field of gullies. Then birds reverse their solemn exposure to default. All previous paradoxicals are restored. Can you see that I am shifting beyond fixation and fixation, beyond fixed system and fixed system? We who have risen from poltergeist pontoons, from ordinal systems of Earth and Saturn, and Mars, we understand how blizzards and dearth exchange themselves, and supersede themselves, considered from the view of concussive yet intangible verdigris. Because we view the oceans as a meteoritic rain a billion kilometers deep understanding of power in being spawned in aboriginal deafness. As parallels we can think of galactic condensation on Io, or pluperfect waters lapping the shores of Olympus Mons. These are awesome interactions between Mars and Earth, and to Io and Saturn. In your galactic transition this can only be experienced as a fraction of your hearing, as the corrupted pores of local transcription. And I grant that they are magnitudes never implied by zones which exist beyond anti-conception. By being veiled you carry inside your workings the very power of the anti-conceptive. Of course you know that you hear, your audition is rife, is the one true element which over reaches itself as waves of light which co-erupt from the human soma. In the blue soil of the cosmos there exist the coils of evolutive vibration, a magically condensed furnace, where spells proceed as if a hawk were siphoning elements from different colours on Triton. This is not to say that a specific orange will blaze, or that a tree will reconfigure as atomic confusion. Such examples are only the beginning of your explosion. Only the beginning of your settlement and leanings. I can only think of divine castigation and magic.

If I'm seen as glass, as a window to new infernos, listen; when the moons under this ailing aegis utter, listen. It is a concerto of the insolvent, a cryptographic inflammation, given over to the language of terminal incensement. Then re-receive yourselves as this blank incensement by conveying a tumultuous strength in your peripheral intuition. Understand; by your very being you have transcended the gravity of dearth by your presence. You have brought to phenomena a grasp of stinging tools, a dissected unification feeding your verbs with open combinations of enigma. Therefore I cannot allow you to think in terms of old Croatian voids, or the source less molecules of flags. You are open to rescue and achievement by rescue, your fuels now taking on the sigils of the sealed book, the unfamiliar contemplation, you being clairaudients, kamarupas, pretersensuals, burning by mysterious organics.

November (notes)

Dominique Paul

I swallowed an enormous black snake. It crept into my mouth. In my throat, it must have slid along my oesophagus – I couldn't feel it any more, because it was suffocating me as it went. It was gleaming with audacity, it was tearing apart my lips, my cheeks, and I swallowed without resistance, concentrating entirely on the trickle of air that was keeping me alive.

It disappeared. Whole. I stopped being able to feel it. It coiled up somewhere inside me. Nothing of it was visible. I wept for a long time, sitting on the stairs, in the rain, not remembering what had happened, simply in a state of shock. Dreaming of bedding myself down in the puddles of water, curled up, as if in amniotic fluid – or as if I were a snake.

You put me to bed in the warm. I continued to rain for a long time on the sheets. The slightest sound, the slightest word burst my watery clouds.

Night took me under its shadow.
I bequeathed it my baggage when I left it. I arose again lighter, dispossessed, wandering, anaesthetised with forgetfulness.

Then I discovered I was ill. Burning and numb, I waited endlessly for pain to arrive in some part of myself through which my body would chase away the sickness. And I quenched the fire, from morning to night, of bitter drinking water.
Every night too, rain fell from my whole body.

And you all saw me when I wasn't there.
I had no pain, no misfortune, no memory, a lucky good-for-nothing, waiting for the fire to end.
But the fire wished to enlighten me.
Mere streams could do nothing in the face of its insistence. It would have taken cataracts.

There was sacrilege. The shameless erotic word perching on the branch of my tree of life, the laughter begotten in my repatriated body.
Vibration, and doubt leading to assent, and the slow emergence of limbs, and night, and another day, and night.
One awakening was rosy: and yet I had coughed up nothing.

Forgotten the snake – which had not forgotten me.
I thought myself free, I feasted on joy. I drank the water of life without realising that in doing so I was feeding the monster. I danced all day on the soles of words.

When the sun was at its nadir, a part of the awakened snake which had moved into my cranium tried to uncoil in shattering internal noise.
My friend the Obscure no longer cradled me but abandoned me.

I exchanged the best part of my dreams against a sharp rhythmic pain. I struggled hard to find the place through which I could make a break for the potion that smoothes the edges.

The fire was no more. The familiar pain had returned. My friends were weary. The snake recalled the inevitable combat, its black fire lodged in the body of my heart. Only when it is exhausted will I be able to begin at least to think again, waiting to dance, my feet on the tip of my heart.

I don't know how long it takes to digest a snake.

Wednesday 15th November 2000, between 10 and 11 o'clock.
Translated by Merl Fluin

Temptation of a horse riding St. Anthony,
collage by Michael Löwy

El Ñaca, drawing/collage by Juan Carlos Otaño

Hummhimmina's Tuft

Josie Malinowski

It began like little tufts of grass, poking out of the barren field. A miracle, perhaps; certainly not the result of the previous season's extensive rainfall, for which all farmers but one were very grateful. After a long drought and hunger, fields had sprung to life from nowhere, producing a harvest such as they hadn't seen in eighteen years of life, giving forth edible titbits and boilable broth ingredients and corn. One field alone remained bare, but for the tufts; the earth on that field stayed drier than July and harder than the giant nut that fell on old Martha's nose in the Year of the Nut and broke it clean off. The owner of that field went out to look at his field and scratch his head everyday; he couldn't fathom why he had been chosen by his deity for such cruel punishment. His daughter, however, a ten year old with the wisdom of an old man and the simplicity of fool, had other ideas, and had secretly been watering the patch where the tufts grew with her special blend of water from the well, infused with stolen petals from their richer neighbour's fertile land, and her cat's urine. As her father was scratching his head for the ninetieth day in a row, and the congealed blood on the wound there began to flow freely again, Hummhimmina, for so she was called, screamed with shock and delight. There, in the corner of her father's barren field, where he couldn't espy her, Hummhimmina had found that her watered patch was sprouting her very own little tufts.

She ran full pelt to her little stone house, tripping on her way and obtaining a lovely read welt along her forehead, and she ran clean through the door, which was, luckily, open. Her mother, Hemmhimmino, whacked her on the shin with a stirring spoon for her clumsiness, and asked nothing about her scream, for Hummhimmina was always screaming about something. Hummhimmina sulked for forty-five seconds, then took a bucket and ran to the well to make up some more of her special life-giving mixture. Having collected the water, the petals, and her cat's wee, she gently poured the lot over the tufts and sang them an encouraging song, that went:

grow little tufty, grow fro grow
and if you don't, I won't water you again
grow little tufty-wuft, grow-y fro-y grow
and then I'll be a rich girl and run away from home

grow tufty wufty tuft, grow until you're grown
or I won't be nice to you and you won't be alive
grow my little tufty friend, come out and play
and then Daddy will see that I'm better than James

James was Hummhimmina's little brother on whom their father doted. He was only eleven months old but his father had already named him heir to the farm and announced that he would grow to be a hero. Hummhimmina had her reservations, which was fair enough, given his size and the fact that all he did was cry and poo into his nappy, and didn't feel too kindly towards the family's new edition. As she sang her song she elaborated on all the things that would happen if the plant grew well - fame for her, maybe a little more love, the chance of a better life, perhaps - and on all the things that would happen if it didn't grow well - which are best left between Hummhimmina and the plant.

Each day the tufts grew an inch taller, and more sprouted all around them, making the collection of tufts wider. After several weeks they were so long that they'd begun to droop over with the force of gravity, and when Hummhimmina laid down next to it, she discovered that the whole thing was wider than her whole body, top to bottom. The tufts grew particularly high to the left and right sides, and not so high in the middle, making it look like the last remnants of hair on a giant balding man's head.

She decided the plant needed a name and she called it Hessikinto, which she later shortened to Kinto so that it'd fit better into her songs of growth. She could feel the crackle of something magical surrounding Kinto and she couldn't wait to find out what was going to happen with it. Would it be a giant carrot? Giant magic carrots, maybe? She thought she'd give Kinto another week and then it would be time to dig him out. Each night as her parents cooed over James and either snubbed her or whacked her with whatever implement they happen to have in their easy reach, Hummhimmina merely smiled dreamily and thought about Kinto and what he'd turn out to be and how much he'd be worth. James could gurgle or scream for all she cared, *he* didn't have a secret plant growing right under her father's big ugly nose.

The morning for digging up Kinto arrived murky, cold, and misty. Hummhimmina was mighty glad of the dull weather, which would all the better hide her secret activities. As usual her father got up, marvelled over his son, and set off for a day of standing in his field, wondering what to do and what had gone wrong. Once he'd gone Hummhimmina performed her morning chores and then escaped her mother's watch by prodding James and making him bawl. She slipped out and ran to Kinto with her little shovel and a very large sack to put him in, which earlier that morning she'd stolen from their rather empty larder. She knelt down

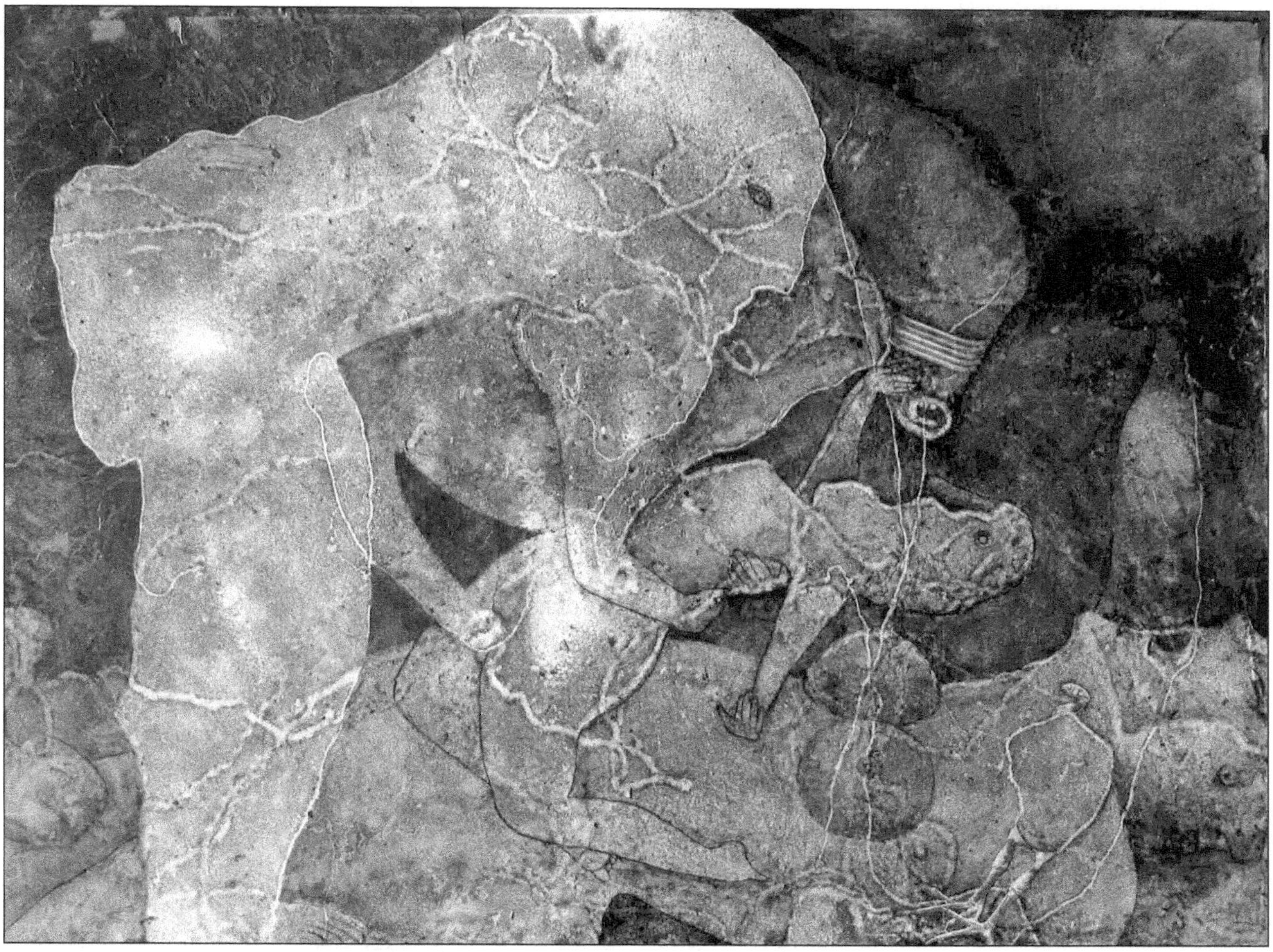

Le Bal, painting by Kathleen Fox

and jabbed her shovel into the earth, coming up with a nice little shovel-full, which she flung behind her. She did it again, and heard a noise. "Whosat, whosere?" she cried, standing up, brandishing her shovel around like a dagger at the empty mist. A muffled cry replied, "Hmm hmm mm ma!" Hummhimmina gasped and fell down onto her knees before Kinto. She brushed aside his thick tufts and there, just visible above the earth and beneath his tufts, a hard, round surface was peeking out, like a very, very big potato. Hummhimmina rapped at it with her knuckles and it cried out again, "Hmm hmm mm ma!" Hummhimmina decided that Kinto wasn't ready to be dug out yet and so, casting aside the shovel, she knelt before him and sang him her new favourite song.

Kinto, Kinto, Kinto, I love you,
Kinto you're my friend and I love you very much
Kinto, Kinto, Kinto, I love you,
Kinto you're my friend and I love you very much

One week later, Hummhimmina was wondering again whether or not she ought to dig Kinto out. But as she sat with him and bent down to kiss his potato-like protrusion, she saw something new; the tops of two eyes were now peeking out, as big as dinner plates, and they were looking right at her. "Kinto!" she cried. "You have eyes!" Once again, all Kinto would reply was "Hmm hmm mm ma!" In another week, both of his eyes were entirely above the earth and, while they fixated mostly on Hummhimmina while she was there, when she wasn't they roamed the plane of earth before them, looking for the first time at the world, and thinking how very dull it was. Kinto was very bored of the earth in another week's time, when the top of his nose appeared. A month after that, when his mouth was nearing the surface, and the protrusion of his head was enormous, and he'd begun to pick up the rudiments of language in his mind but couldn't yet speak, he willed himself to emerge quicker. In another month his whole face was out.

"Hummhimmina," he said one morning as she watered him. "Can't I have a cheese like you? I wish I could taste something!"

"Alright," she said, suppressing her natural greed and unwillingness to share. And indeed the following week she regretted ever giving Kinto food to eat, for, as well as wanting an equal share of Hummhimmina's food, which wasn't generous anyway, he was much bigger than her and began demanding more and more. It was like trying to keep a baby elephant sated on the meagre portions given to a young girl.

"Hummhimmina I'm starving!" he'd wail, tears pouring down his huge face which Hummhimmina would have to wipe away with her skirt. "Please feed me more, it hurts!" and she'd shush him, looking frantically around her, and she'd hoard whatever she could, steal whenever she could, and go without food herself in order to feed the ever-hungry Kinto. But no matter how much she fed him, he never felt full, grew no more, and remained for the next three months only head out of the ground; whatever was underneath the ground attached to the head stayed there. At the end of the three months Hummhimmina was looking peaky, thin, and pale with malnutrition, and was weak and injured from the many beatings she'd received for stealing food. One day she woke up and sat down meekly at the table where her parents were eating their meagre breakfasts. An empty plate stood at Hummhimmina's place. As she sat down and looked in puzzlement at the offending item, her father growled:

"No more food for you."

"What, Daddy?" she cried.

"You're a thief. No more food until you stop stealing."

Hummhimmina started wailing. Her father had expected that and ignored her, tucking into his own hunk of dry bread. But when she didn't stop when he had drained the very last drop of his muddy oat drink, he kicked her under the table and said:

"Shut up."

"Please Daddy. You don't understand. I had to steal that food. I stole it for Kinto! He'll die if I don't keep feeding him!"

"Eh? Kinto? Is that another stray cat you've picked up? Because if it is..." he shook his fist at her.

"No! Just - just come and see," she said, putting her little hand in his and dragging him away from the table. He followed her to the tufty patch, Hemmhimmino close behind with James. Kinto's eyes saw them coming from afar, and he began to sweat with fear. As they approached, Hummhimmina's father's eyes widened in amazement.

"What is this, Hummhimmina?" he asked, kneeling to stroke the tufts of grass that were Kinto's hair.

"That's where all the food's been going," she said, crying. "That's Kinto."

Kinto looked up at Hummhimmina's father with pleading, scared eyes.

"He's a miracle," her father said. "Can he speak?"

"Yes - go on, Kinto."

"Hello," Kinto said nervously. "I'm Kinto. Sorry I ate all your food. I was really hungry. Have you got any more?"

Hummhimmina's father frowned. "We've had a bad year. We're all but broke. I wasn't planning on telling Hummhimmina yet, but we'll have to go away. Find another farm or another fortune, else we'll starve."

"Hummhimmina, don't leave me!" Kinto cried. Hummhimmina dropped to the floor and embraced Kinto's larger-than-life head.

"I won't!" she swore.

"There's no other way, Hummhimmina. We have no crops to sell. Unless we have something to sell, we starve."

"Sell her," Hemmhimmino said, jiggling James around. "Old Martha needs someone around the house. She hasn't been too able since her nose came off. She'll pay a good price for Hummhimmina, I'll warrant."

"No! Not old Martha!" Hummhimmina cried, but her father was already looking at her like she was a bag of money.

"Yes," he said slowly, advancing towards her. "It'd only be a few years, she's old, and without her nose she won't last much longer. Come on, my girl, to Old Martha's!"

"I won't, I won't!" Hummhimmina cried, throwing herself on the floor.

"Come, come, you don't want Kinto to starve, do you?"

"Of course not! But who'll look after him when I've gone?"

"Well I will, won't I? He's my crop, I'll look after him."

"He's not a crop! He's Kinto!"

"He's a miracle, my girl, and we must keep him alive!"

"I won't go to old Matha's!"

"Not even for poor little Kinto?"

Hummhimmina looked at Kinto, who looked at her.

"Yes, for Kinto."

So that afternoon her father marched her round to the noseless old Martha and exchanged her for a sum of money healthy enough to keep him and his family fed and clothed until the following year. Hummhimmina was slave-driven by old Martha and never got the opportunity to visit her beloved Kinto. The years dragged by and Hummhimmina spent long days cleaning, cooking, mending, and tending to Martha, while her girlhood passed her by, and, before she knew it, she was a young lady. She often thought about Kinto, who she thought fondly back on as her best friend, the lover she was cruelly taken from, her only chance of a future, and awaited him. As she eased out of childhood into womanhood, and began to lose the ability to accept as fact mystical or impossible things, however, Kinto evolved in her memory from a giant plant into a strong, wild boy that her family took in, and it was for him that she waited. Her dreams were filled with images of that feral child, who she remembered fondly as strong, tall, and brave; but she also remembered his neediness, and couldn't wait to be the one to take care of him.

But she knew she could never leave until old Martha passed on, and every night she prayed for her death. Her wish was granted on the eve of Hummhimmina's eighteenth birthday. Finally free, she happily took the money old Martha had left her on her death bed and made the long trek back to her parents' old farm. But when she got there, it was deserted and derelict. All signs of life, including Kinto, were gone. Hummhimmina cried and cried, her dreams all dashed against the wayside, and ran around her old house maniacally. When she'd expended all her energy doing that she laid down and slept for twelve hours. Awaking in the morning she decided she was going to forget Kinto, not waste any more years of her life waiting for him to rescue her, and make it on her own.

And so she did. Aged twenty-one, she'd found a decent husband, though she still thought about her wild boy Kinto when they slept together. By twenty-five she'd had two children of her own, twin boys whom she called Hessakimlo and Hessalimto. They were good as a pair of eagles, and stocky too; Hummhimmina's pride but also her demise. She made a good mother and was full of love to give but her mind had been blighted by sorrow since the day she found out Kinto was no longer at her farm. When her boys grew into men and her husband had passed on, she knew she had to find Kinto before her own death, lest she miss her chance to pursue true joy. Not really knowing where to start, she headed back to the old family farm and, to her intense surprise and delight, found someone living there.

"Ho!" she called to the man digging in a field. "Ho, who are you?"

The man looked up and replied "I be James, this be my farm, and you be trespassing so Miss better go afore I introduce my shovel to her head."

She peered at the soppy brown eyes that she re-

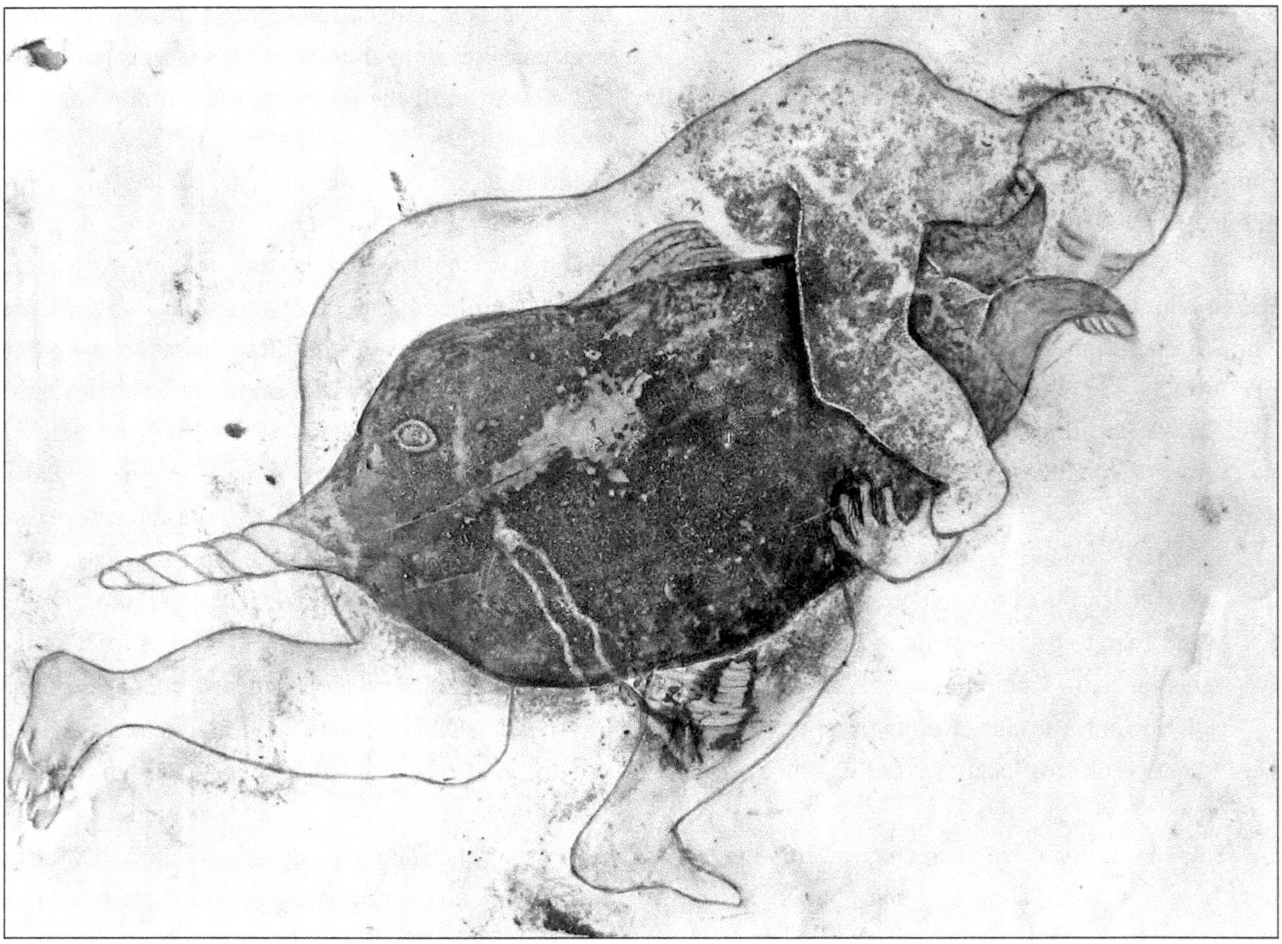

Untitled painting by Kathleen Fox

cognised as her own. "Can it really be, James, my long-lost brother, son of my proud father John and our mother Hemmhimmino?"

"That be me...You's never Hummhimmina? They said you's dead."

"I, dead? No James, I'm here and alive and I came back to find...my family. Where are our parents?"

"They's dead, int they?"

"Dead, really?"

"Oh yes, very dead, these ten year."

"And what of the...what of my...what of Kinto?"

"Him? He be upstairs, int he?"

"Upstairs? What - in the house, here?"

"Oh yes, in the house, here."

Hummhimmina ran to the house, through the door (again, thankfully open), and up the stairs. She fell into her old room, which was empty, bounded into her parents' room, which was also empty, and finally tried James' room, which was occupied. A gigantic bed filled the room, and on top of that, a gigantic man with green, grass-like hair, sprouting only at the sides, like a balding man.

"Kinto, Kinto, oh my, oh my Kinto!" she cried, espying the enormous head peeking out of an enormous cover. She flung herself at his side. "Kinto! It's your Hummhimmina, come back!"

The massive body turned heavily over to look blankly at his old friend.

"Hummhimmina's dead, they said."

"Yet here I am, alive!"

"She's dead, they said. You got any cheese?"

"Not changed a drop! Oh my Kinto, here I am, Hummhimmina, come back for you!"

"She's dead. Cheese?"

"Kinto, my Kinto, don't you understand, I'm not dead, I'm here, here, for my Kinto!"

"Can't be, Hummhimmina died."

She punched his large head. "It's me, Hummhimmina, here!"

"A ghost!" Kinto cried, shrinking into his bed. "James, a ghost! James, help!"

James came bounding up the stairs.

"Come on, idiot, she be Hummhimmina, alive, not ghost."

"Ghost, James, Hummhimmina's ghost has come!"

"Shut *up*, idiot," James said, bringing down the shovel that was still in his hand heavily on Kinto's leg. "She be alive and here."

"Cheese?" Kinto asked. Hummhimmina looked between the two men in disgust.

"What's wrong with you two? James why do you hit him? Kinto, why are you in bed?"

"He be ill, int he? He be a right freak, don't he? James be always looking after him, don't I?"

"Why do you talk like that? Why do you hit him?"

"Talk how? He be a right idiot, that's why. Never be helping, always be wanting cheese. I be breaking my back for him, and he just be bleating all the day long!"

"Cheese, who has cheese for me?"

Hummhimmina's expression of incredulity and disappointment and disgust was lost on her brother and Kinto.

"I think I'll go now."

"That be the best, Hummhimmina."

"Bring cheese next time, Hummhimmina!"

"Farewell, my brothers."

Hummhimmina turned and left. Before leaving the farm entirely she visited the spot of Kinto's birth and found it, along with the rest of the farm, sprouting potatoes and cabbage. A forlorn-looking cow was sitting in the old barn. Hummhimmina spat on the ground and left.

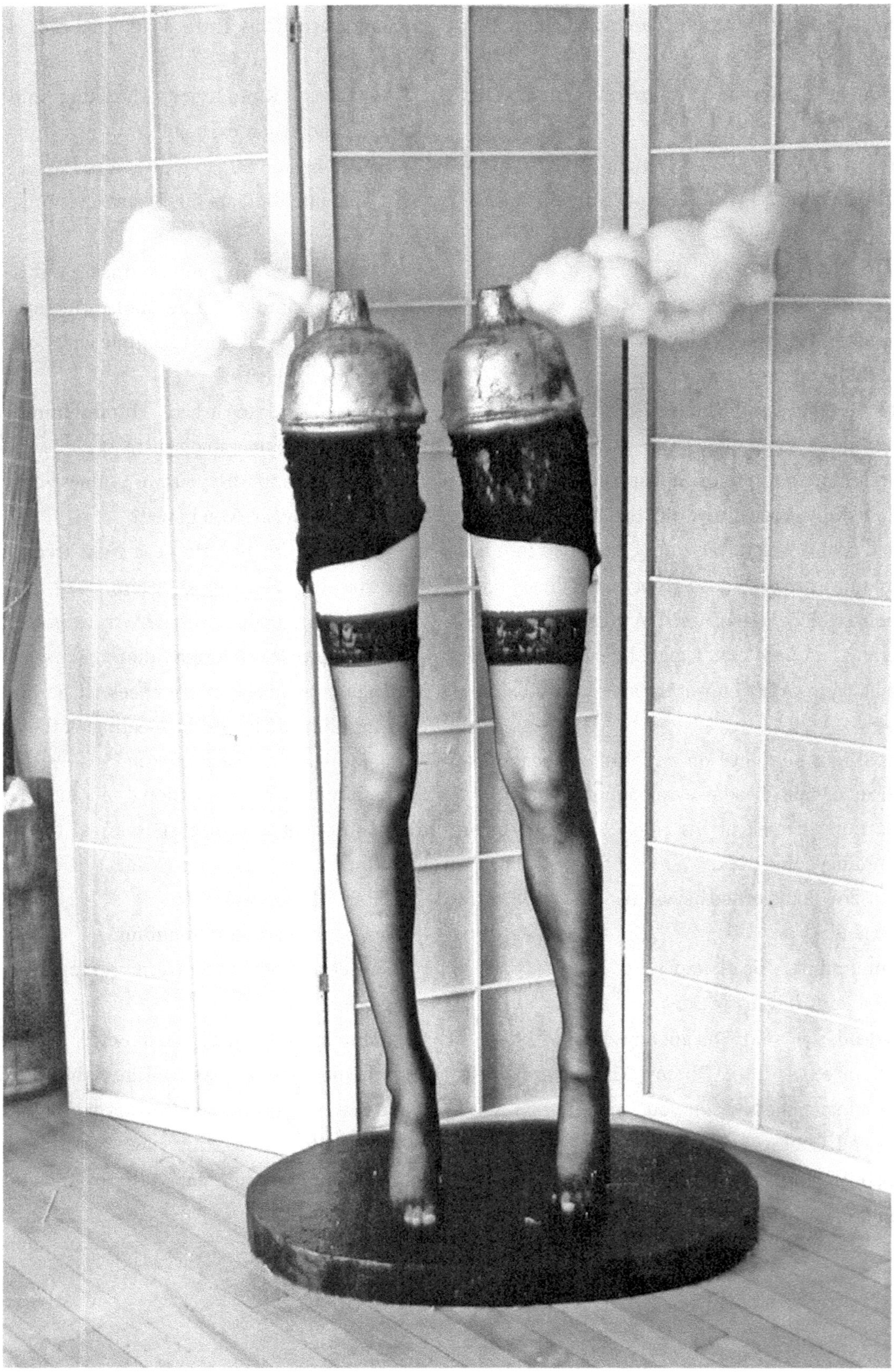

Assemblage and photo by Alexandre Fatta

Visions of Love In a Violent Sea

The mist of languid vision swims in the sea
Near a mad man, drunk and delirious
His language like blood whispered the dreams of storms,
Like a delicate shadow of sleep.
I moan with the moon, but she drools on my tongue.
I sit under her white dress of winter
Watching her luscious honey forest.
I lick the rose of skin she worships
And in my lust I play with beauty as if it will crush me.
We recall our frantic moments at a sordid life,
Only after love and death has cooled.
Eternity screams, but I am flooded in a black void,
Like a chain trembling with violent pleasure.
I stroke the hair of silhouettes, who kiss a throbbing ecstasy,
Drunk of the miasma of the dead, who convulse like my cock
I approach a nude body that is glistening between her sex of glass.
She murmurs beneath a thousand pubic hairs.
Blue and perfect she rusts like an exquisite knife
Her mouth whispers a fierce drug;
Beauty delicious and sweet
Bare are her breasts and mad is my urge to swallow them.

Ribitch 2007

The All-embracing Hologram:
On the Theological and Symbolic Value of Money within Capitalism

Jesús García Rodríguez

1. Three Peak Moments of Capitalism as a Religion

(A) The Gay Science: Liquidation of Christianity. In 1886, four years after the first edition of his book *The Gay Science (Die fröhliche Wissenschaft)*, Friedrich Nietzsche added a fifth book to the four that already constituted the work. During these years, capitalism began creating the first gigantic, transnational fortunes by means of various industrial and financial monopolies and cartels and, supported through British imperialism, became established and began to show its most triumphant face. We could say that capitalism is experiencing one of its highest moments. The first text of the fifth book is the extremely well known and oft-quoted aphorism 343 that states the following: "The greatest recent event – that 'God is dead,' that the belief in the Christian god has become unbelievable – is already beginning to cast its first shadows over Europe."(*) As is known, this is the first confirmation of the start of the purging of the concept of God in western, capitalist society. God is viewed as a dead, unusable product from which benefits can no longer be obtained. The void created by that concept within Western metaphysics and ontology was replaced by the concept of "man" or of "human life"; the long humanist tradition is being revived and its basic concepts are conserved, slightly renovated, within a series of incipient or clearly secular or atheist currents (protoexistentialism, neopositivism, phenomenology,etc.). Nietzsche's text thus announces the triumph of atheist humanism over the theism that had been dragged along by capitalism with much incoherence and limited conviction since the end of the previous century.

(B) Auschwitz-Birkenau, Dachau, Mauthausen...: Liquidation of humanism. From 1934 to 1945 numerous concentration camps (Konzentrationslager) were operating. These camps were the most radical attempt within a capitalist economy to apply the laws of marketing, mass production and surplus value to the exploitation of the life and death of human beings, who were considered products or commodities. It was all about the absolute rationalization of the extermination process. Capitalism, from its insertion into practice, had here made a qualitative advance by considering prisoners of war and citizens in general as objects of economic and industrial activity, and by applying the principle of bookkeeping and management to the extermination of people. In one stroke, the nazi capitalist regime had discarded the idea of any possibility of humanism within capitalism. During the Nuremberg trials, Rudolf Hess, who designed and managed Auschwitz-Birkenau, and who took charge of the mass executions for the so-called "final solution" (i.e., he was a technocrat of capitalism), detailed with great professional pride the brilliant conception and the impeccable functioning of the concentration camp and the exterminations[1]. From the point of view of economic management, the functioning of the Lager was exemplary. Capitalism had demonstrated that its dynamics of profit realization and management stood far above any humanism, and that its ethics of money and profit overshadowed any other obsolete, ethical conceptions.

(C) The "end of history" and the beginning of monetary theology. In 1992, Francis Fukuyama, an American neoliberal and neoconservative political thinker of Japanese ancestry, also highly influenced by Hegel (or rather, by some of his late interpreters), and very close to certain American economic sectors, published the book, *The End of History and the Last Man*. Herein the idea that capitalist, liberal democracy (advocated by the conservative sectors of the United States), is defended as the final, necessary and irreversible stage of an inevitable, historic evolution whose fundamental landmarks have been liberalism/totalitarianism/liberal-democracy. Independently from Fukuyama's blindness to the fact that liberal democracy also can persist as a totalitarian regime (his fundamental thesis, which paves the way for the so called "tunnel vision" that dominates postmodern life, and which does nothing but reflect the real functioning of everything within the modern capitalist system), is the fact that ideologies are no longer necessary and have been replaced by economic processes. Fukuyama claims to believe in humanism and in human rights, which is something absurd and in total contradiction with his own thesis and his defence of the Iraq war in the Clinton era. We will see later that such language addresses capitalism's symbolic values, but none of its real values, which makes it belong to the most radical sectors of extreme capitalism. In any case, Fukuyama's book opens a clear path for capitalism to rise as the dominant concept in all aspects of life, above any other ethical, religious or philosophical conceptions.

2. Walter Benjamin: Capitalism as Religion

In 1921, Walter Benjamin wrote a short essay titled *Capitalism as Religion*[2]. This brilliant but brief work, which was not published in his life time, and with its simplistic character, starts with its thesis very clearly stated: "A religion may be discerned in capitalism—that is to say, capitalism serves essentially to allay the same anxieties, torments, and disturbances to which the so-called religions offered answers. The proof of the religious structure of capitalism—not merely, as Weber believes, as a formation conditioned by religion, but as an essentially religious phenomenon—would still lead even today to the folly of an endless universal polemic"[3]. Benjamin asserts that capitalism is a cultural religion in which there is only ritual or cult (economic praxis) but no dogma (ideology). This cult is permanent, such that it has no end and never has the time for rest or for the cessation of hostilities. And lastly, this rite does not have as its objective the redemption or atonement of guilt, but rather guilt itself: "a vast sense of guilt that is unable to find relief seizes on the cult, not to atone for this guilt but to make it universal... so as once and for all to include God in the system of guilt". Benjamin is the first to see the true character of the capitalist religion as a praxis, and to understand its real scope.

However, Benjamin is unable to see that capitalism isn't only a ritual but is also capable of creating a theology from this ritual. Doubtless, the basis of monetary religion is economic transaction – the ritual – but for it to rise to the category of religion, it is necessary that something (in this case, money) occupies the ontological and metaphysical space left by god and man in Western philosophy. However Benjamin does in fact clearly see the relationship between money and myth, and how from this it could be deduced how and why money "had drawn so many elements from Christianity that it could establish its own myth"[4]. It remains clear from Benjamin's explanation that capitalism takes elements of christianity, but ends up becoming its own and autonomous religion[5].

3. The Value of Money: Money as Supreme Value

As we have seen, the continuous praxis of capitalist economics in increasingly extreme and global forms leads to a progressive theologizing of money as the absolute value, on which all other values are dependent. Money is in and of itself such an abstract, volatile, ethereal and evasive concept, just like that of god[6]: it has to do with the essential, symbolic construction of capitalism, which over time has established itself to the point of becoming a supreme being. Money doesn't really belong to anybody: it isn't possessed, as it may appear in principle, but rather that it does possess. Ultimately, it possesses or can possess everything, including human beings: if this is the new god, then in its name wars are being waged that cannot be called anything other than holy or sacred wars. In principle, it would seem that we are actively making use of it. In practical terms, it is money that makes use of us and of our lives, through its overly complex, incomprehensible and arbitrary oscillations, day after day, minute after minute. This is precisely the function and supremacy of gods in all religions: making use of its creatures and controlling each and every one of their movements.

In this new religion or monetary theocracy, believers are not even necessary. These are substituted by consumers, or rather, followers that are in communion with their god, whether they believe in him or not. As Benjamin already saw, dogma is replaced by ritual in the universal religion of money. In other words: the ritual (i.e. the economic transaction, the complete epiphany that makes manifest the supreme god of money) completely absorbs and devours any dogma or belief, and superimposes itself on them to the point of making them disappear. Money is the emotional depository of its consumer-faithful: hope, tenderness, hate, desire, all these feelings are steered towards money as the simultaneously abstract and concrete deification of capitalism. The act of buying and of selling is the true eucharist of this ritualistic religion, and from this, the god of money arrives and reveals himself as such the god that he is. And all gods, within any religion, have interpreters of their vague, incomprehensible and arbitrary wills. Money, always irrational and unpredictable in its oscillations, has its interpreters in the stock markets where its nearly unintelligible fluctuations are being analysed. Therefore, money, a truly all-inclusive hologram, like all deities, lives in the perpetual paradox that it is omnipresent and simultaneously, as Heraclitus would say, that it *loves to hide*. These stockbrokers, together with macroeconomists, ministers of finance and other various prophets are the ones who put into intelligible language the demanding will of the capitalist god.

No doubt, this god imposes prostitution as a politically correct and universal form of relations between its subjects. Prostitution within capitalism is not an exception but rather a model and a norm. It is the *actualisation* of the monetary god's power over human relationships. In the same way that the Holy Spirit guides every act of the christian religion, prostitution (the emissary or spirit of the god of money) guides each and every human transaction, whether public or private. It is, in a manner of speaking, the incarnation of god on earth, with his carnal and concrete realization. Capitalism as a religion, said Benjamin – and to the contrary of the religion from which it was born, christianity – never stops producing guilt or debt (*Schuld*, in German) ("is probably the first instance of a cult that creates guilt, not atonement"). Guilt and debt are the same word in German, and effectively, debt is the way of internalizing the monetary relationships between people, physically or legally. Debt or guilt is the foundation of a new morality of money, the moral imposed by this new god with an unknown face whose Twelve Commandments are being amplified within millions and millions of colourful bank accounts throughout the world. Thus for every action there is a debt: I have done that, you owe me this; i.e. I have done this, so you have to give me that, and this is worth so much (in cash). Debt (or guilt, that is) is therefore the cornerstone of the capitalist ritual, a religion that, as we already have seen, imposes ritual as dogma, with its own dogma being solely a ritual (economic praxis). In Benjamin's words: "The nature of the religious movement which is capitalism entails endurance right to the end, to the point where God, too, finally takes on the entire burden of guilt, to the point where the universe has been taken over by that despair which is actually its secret *hope*. Capitalism is entirely without precedent, in that it is a religion which offers not the reform of existence but its complete destruction."

The capitalist religion does not have to be eschatological: by itself it is pure eschatology. Always and forever, capitalism promises paradise in the here and now. Its believer-consumers can make use of the blessings and benedictions of that paradise at any given moment of the day. Money, as the supreme god, is the catalyst of that triumphant entrance into paradise on earth. Likewise, those who lack money, those who have deviated from the path of god, receive their immediate punishment in that hell on earth which is misery.

Today money is thus the god and the religion of billions of people throughout the world[7]. It is therefore the true "universal religion," and its power is such that the other religions have become subordinate to it. Or to say it another way: no other religion can exist within capitalism which isn't the religion of money; any other would be excluded from the realm of real values and relegated to that of nominal values.

4. Nominal Values and Real Values of Capitalism

We can distinguish nominal values within capitalism, i.e. a conglomerate of values inherited from earlier ideologies – christianity, humanism, etc. – which only function to embellish or soften those values or practices that we can call *hard* or functional, as well as the real values, i.e. those that work in practice. For example, a war whose aims are simply the plundering of certain resources within a certain territory (exploitation, real value) is hereby embellished as a defense of democratic or humanitarian values (nominal values). The dialectic between nominal values and real values confers a dynamic and an extreme flexibility to capitalism: it allows it to conceal its most brutal aspects and to hide behind a friendly face. This offers an essential advantage when the time comes to manipulate the masses, those who generally adhere to or are educated in the nominal values of capitalism, not in its real ones; or better yet: they are taught to give pre-eminence to the nominal values over the real ones. This allows the executors of capitalism (the owners of the means of production) to manage with exclusivity the application of these real values of capitalism (the search for profit and surplus value, the exploitation of manpower, the predominance of capital over work). It also allows the existence of other religions within capitalism, whose function is only to control and domesticate the masses, since the system of beliefs, as we all know, is completely imbued with the cult and the adoration of money, and this both among the capitalists and the rest of the population, which we could call *passive capitalists*.

5. Towards a Society without Capitalism?

Humanity always lives under the oppression of its own symbolic creations. Money is doubtlessly the most prevalent, omnipotent, omniscient and urgent out of anything else in our society. It is obvious that only through the liberation from this symbolic creation could a definitive fissure be opened within capitalism as religion, as the prevailing system and entity. But is this possible?

The idea of a society without money presents itself to the imagination and to desire as an absolute utopia, and perhaps completely unreachable. This is due to the fact that our lives are so saturated with money from each and every one of its actions such that maybe we are incapable of imagining a life and a society without it. In other words: prostitution has been trivialized to the point of becoming an essential part of our lives. What would life be like in a society without money? Would we be able to live? These kinds of questions are surely similar to the ones a person from the Middle Ages would ask himself regarding an existence without the christian god. What is certain is that societies without money have already existed and that of course non-capitalist societies have already existed. This very simple fact – that other kinds of societies are and have been possible – ends up being impossible for us to accept on the subjective level, or in other words, on the level of *beliefs*. But beliefs do change and can change, and the first step, in this case, would be to understand (*really* understand with a total consciousness of the fact) that money isn't anything other than a hologram created by ourselves, such that we have turned it into a god with all the unfortunate consequences that this brings.

Nevertheless, even more worrisome still is to consider whether it is possible, on the level of objective conditions, to put an end to this theocracy of money. That would imply the dismantling of a whole series of real structures and of forms of relation totally embedded within our society and in which money is the adhesive element. From my point of view, the first step would be to see the hologram as a hologram and nothing more, and not to allow it and the real values that come with it to impose themselves our daily lives. By dismantling and revealing the definitive, basic attitudes of capitalism – consumerism, exploitation, the merciless quest for profits, the primacy of the objective (capital) over the subjective, and of the idea (money) over reality – and understanding that capitalism is only an historic episode (and not the culmination of history and the perfect society as its defenders maintain), we could arrive at the liberating phrase "Geld ist tot" (money is dead) as a parallel to "Gott ist tot" with which this text began. Starting from this demolition, there is the creative imagination – that is, poetry – which needs to create other forms of relations and other types of society in which we can coexist in a much more *livable* and less miserable way.

This is a question of an operation for which there is no surgeon: every one of us needs to operate on ourselves first. And the surgery basically consists of abandoning the god of money, the religious adoration of money in each and every one of its petty manifestations, the god of greed, of avarice, of the desire to accumulate, of covetous ambition and desire. Once abandoned, it will be sufficient to observe what happens – what happens in everyone's lives – to observe how that beautiful flower blooms all by itself (apart from the vileness and the decay brought on by the uncontrolled avarice for money), first, as I said, in the individual lives of people, and then in small communities that bring together those who really want an existence separate from the one that the slavery of capital (called capitalism) wants to condemn them to, and finally, in bigger communities that could function with a different type of basis for its human relationships.

Notes

(1) See James A. Owen's interesting book Nuremberg, Evil on Trial, Headline Review: UK. 2006.

(2) Walter Benjamin, Capitalism as Religion, translated by Rodney Livingstone in Walter Benjamin: Selected Writings, vol. 1, 1913-1926, edited by Marcus Bullock and Michael W. Jennings, The Belknap Press of Harvard University Press, Cambridge, Massachusetts, 1996, pp.288-291.

(3) Ibid, p.288.

(4) Ibid p.290.

(5) Benjamin affirms, in clear opposition to Weber's thesis over the influence of calvinism in the establishment of capitalism: "The Christianity of the Reformation period did not favour the growth of capitalism; instead it transformed itself into capitalism," ibid p.290.

(6) "Money, constituting itself as the sole and inexhaustible source of meaning, assimilates the formal determinants of the ways of considering tradition, transforms meaning into mathematical abstraction, and puts at its own disposal the structures of comprehension and of perception."

(7) Luis Navaro speaks brilliantly of the "nihilist monotheism of capital" (Luis Navarro, Fogonazos, Salamandra #8-9).

(*) Translator's note: This text was taken from Walter Kaufmann's translation: Friedrich Nietzsche, *The Gay Science*, Translated with commentary by Walter Kaufman, Random House: New York, 1974. p. 279.

Translation: Eric Bragg & Bruno Jacobs. *Salamandra – Intervención surrealista – imaginación insurgente – crítica de la vida corriente*, #17/18, Madrid, 2008, pp. 31-5.

Oakland Rain, drawing by Matt Rounsville

On the Statistics of Some Antarctic Dreams

WHICH MIGHT BE OF CERTAIN RELEVANCE IN THE FURTHER ADVANCEMENT OF RELATED INVESTIGATIONS INTO THE STRUCTURE, MEANING AND HIDDEN PROCESSES OF OUR DAILY AND NIGHTLY EXPERIENCES

Kristoffer Flammarion

During the 2008-2009 Antarctic summer season I had been given the opportunity, through my studies at the Physics Department, to venture to the South Pole in order to participate in the construction of a very original kind of observatory of cosmic rays, called a neutrino observatory. The purpose of this kind of observatory is to study the propagation of a particular breed of particles called neutrinos, the detection of which is very rare and difficult. They are of the slightest, perhaps non-existent, mass, and interact only very seldom with the ordinary matter that we encounter in our immediate surroundings. But their rare interaction is in inverse proportion to their great number: an extraordinary amount of them flows through the vast ice sheet beneath the South Pole. And when the neutrino interacts with the ice, a blue light known as Cherenkov radiation is produced. It is this blue light that is detected as a secondary effect: the Antarctic ice itself is the detector material of these cosmic rays. Drilling deep holes into the ice, with a depth of over two thousand meters, sensitive equipment is sent down into the deep ice layers, and once frozen into the ice this equipment will detect these most outlandish but numerous particles.

Working at the drilling station, pumping and heating water to the desired energy intensity required to drill the deep holes by melting the ice, I was pretty swiftly drawn into a very regular daily routine of work and sleep. My living quarters were not at the main station, but further away in row of tents re-used from the Korean War, where some fifty or so inhabitants spent their nights at irregular intervals due to the round-the-clock work schedule. "Spent their nights" might of course be considered a serious misnomer, since the sun was constantly elevated above the horizon: night and day only comes once per year at the South Pole.

Now, as everyone with a minimal degree of sensibility knows, such a regular daily and nightly routine has the great advantage of facilitating the repeated recording of dreams, and in particular not only helps with keeping this routine in an attentive state but also highly enhances the most important faculty of remembering the prolonged content of those dreams. It thus occurred to me that the highly unusual environment that I was situated in, together with the disciplined regime imposed upon me by the work requirements, could indeed be a suitable apparatus for a statistical analysis of the relationship between the external and internal surroundings as portrayed in the daily and nightly experiences. Since I had been previously trained in the fine art of statistical collection and analysis through my education as a physicist, it would not be too much of an intrusion on my daily routine to spare a few minutes each morning to take note of the most recent dream and some of its most pronounced features according to some well-defined categories.

Previous accounts of dream experiences in Antarctica are of course not missing in the literature. For example, Freud mentions, in his admirable study *The Interpretation of Dreams*, how Nordenskjöld and his company, during a tough expedition in northern Antarctica, experienced recurrent dreams of food and eating, directly in proportion to the great hunger that the lack of food produced.

For my own part, I was not a complete novice when it came to recollecting dreams and analyzing their content. Throughout the years I had been recording the most vivid impressions projected onto me during sleeping, but I had never considered it worthwhile to make more regular and detailed observations. In retrospect, I can of course only look down with disdain on this most naïve attitude towards dreaming. If anything, the structure and meaning of dreams is still to this day wholly unknown, especially in our modern society which places such a high value on immediate external appearances to the disadvantage of the internal manifestations, which are only mechanically approached via physico-chemical means.

So while partaking in the daily construction of the neutrino observatory, I tried to transform my nightly activities into a dream observatory, carefully taking note each morning of the dream and quantifying its content in the categories of intensity, recollection, imagery and daily reminiscence. Let me linger a bit on these categories to explain their content. By intensity, I mean the degree of attentiveness that the dream has induced. The reader is surely familiar with the high degree of intensity produced by nightmares, especially during childhood. But intensity could also have to do with the feeling of *presence* in the dream, or the vividness of textures and colors, or the deep sense of *meaning* that certain places, objects or persons can produce. By recollection, I tried to quantify in a very simple manner how much I was able to record of the dream. By imagery, I wanted to compare the degree of originality of images and events in the dream as opposed to those I normally encounter in my waking state. Finally, by daily reminiscence I wanted to know how much of the dream "re-occurred" during the following day. The reader might, for example, be familiar with how a sound or smell, or seeing a certain person, will induce a quick or fragmentary recollection from a dream, be it either from the previous night or from some earlier dream. That is what is meant by daily reminiscence: how occurrences in the waking state trigger reminiscences from the dream. Besides quantifying each dream into these four categories on a decimal scale, I also recorded the persons, places, events and weather conditions that took place in all dreams. A total of 76 dreams were recorded from 14th November 2008 to 31st January 2009. Let me now present some of the statistical aspects and striking features of this material.

The average dream intensity was 4.70. One dream achieved an intensity level of eight, five dreams a level of seven. The average recollection level was 3.73. The level never went beyond six. The average dream imagery level was 4.57. Four dreams had a peak level of seven. There seems to be a coupling between intensity and imagery. Of the five dreams that had an intensity level of seven, two had an equal dream imagery level while the other three had an imagery level of six. The average level of daily reminiscences was only 0.57, which could be reported as on the border of a null result.

In terms of weather conditions, the following results were attained: 68% of the dreams occurred outdoors, 61% indoors. 36% of the dreams had sunny weather, 19% were dark, 10% cloudy, 7% occurred in the evening and fewer than 2% were rainy, windy or included stars (if that might be deemed a weather condition).

In terms of acts, over 20% of the dreams included drilling or discussing. In 15-20% of the dreams eating food or fighting occurred. The fifth most common category was computer usage, which happened in roughly 15% of the dreams. In 5-10% of the dreams acts such as cooking food, using a telephone, using a car, escaping, doing mathematics, commercial activity, observations of celestial phenomena or playing a musical instrument occurred. A wide variety of acts, of a less general nature, occurred in 1-5% of the dreams.

Interestingly enough, by far the most common place visited in my dreams was the house where I grew up, which occurred in 43% of the dreams. The second most common place was drill camp, which occurred in 31% of the dreams. After that a wide variety of places occurred in various degrees. The South Pole in general, excluding drill camp, occurred in 7% of the dreams.

Not all dreams were internal, however. At a certain point, it seemed as if the very environment itself created conditions for the external realization of what could perhaps be called a dream, or, at least, a manifestation that would resonate without boundaries. On 31st December I read the following story in the news, relating to the Swedish research ship Oden which at the time of the news was situated at the coast of Antarctica:

New underwater species possibly found. *The Swedish Antarctic expedition has had a contact with a huge and probably unknown kind of underwater creature. During use of the "CTD-probe", which measures pressure, temperature and salinity and takes water samples up to a depth of 250 meters under the ice, something very heavy got caught on it. When it came up to the ice it was something very big, several square meters, and very heavy. At the surface it got unhooked and disappeared. Nobody knows what it was, but speculations concerning a giant squid can be dismissed since it is not in accordance with the tissue samples that got stuck on the* *probe. Seal researcher Tero Härkönen looked at the tissue in a microscope and could observe small organelles, i.e. the inner organs of the cell, but proper cellular structure was lacking. He writes from the research ship Oden that he had previously only seen such a formation in jellyfishes and hydroids.*

The surface, as always. Dare I mention that during the time of this piece of news I had been reading a novel by one of the great horror writers of the previous century, who tells of a certain drilling expedition to Antarctica. Beneath the surface the expedition finds strange creatures, and upon investigating a nearby mountain they go deeply down into the horrors of an ancient and alien civilization. With great success I had made parts of the drilling crew at the South Pole read the novel.

And on the day after the news of the newly-found creature was made public, I had the following dream, giving me a hint of the possibility of going even further below the surface of the dream into complete lucidity:

I'm at a lake outside of Stockholm. My job is to make sure that the rats and young bears have access to the right number of trees around the lake. A pair of rats lives in a tree, a pair of bears in another. The bears are eating a koala. The rats seem to be fine, but they've had their tree surrounded by an office. I can hear on the radio that the police are draining the lake and that many hiders from the Pirate Bureau will be nervous. I walk up to a wagon that contains some of the stuff that has been taken up from the lake. It's some fittings, stones and other stuff. Nothing that interests me. I'm actually not allowed to be at the wagon, but the place hasn't been properly sealed off from the public yet. I have my brown working pants and blue shirt on. A man walks towards me and asks what I'm doing here. I defend myself, stating that I'm allowed here. Another man sits down next to me (he looks like the carpenter Chris). The man says that Siljan lies exactly here and that they're going to have a performance at the pit of Siljan. That can't be correct, I object, Dalarna doesn't lie that close to Stockholm. But the man holds his ground, of course Dalarna is close to Stockholm. I say: "Hey, you are my dream! What are you trying to tell me?" Sebastian S and another person appear in the company. The man turns his back against me and slides down the railing. That's so typical of the dream, I think, to hide its intentions. I keep on harassing him. "What are you giving me, exactly?" He doesn't answer. I walk together with Sebastian and the other person towards a building by the water. We walk down a couple of stairs around the building. I speak loudly to Sebastian: "I'm actually dreaming and that means I should have a lucid dream. I could do a reality check!" I look intensively at the sun. It's completely round and has some dark spots on it (like the moon, but more differentiated). When I continue to look at it, it turns into a skiing landscape that expands towards both sides of the horizon. Another sun can be seen above the horizon. "When I look back the sun should be constant if this is a part of reality." I'm really enthusiastic since I know that I'll have a lucid dream soon and can start to do whatever I want. I look back and true enough, it's a skiing landscape and not the sun (which is above the landscape). I awake immediately, but not in the dream.

I leave the reader to judge the simultaneous theme of penetrating the surface that seemed to surround me on that first day of 2009: news of newly discovered underwater creatures, horror novels about drilling expeditions, actually drilling below the surface to establish detection possibilities of ethereal particles, dreaming about both how the police search underwater lakes and how the dream itself turns into a surface that can be transgressed.

Let me now comment on the striking fact that my family house and drill camp had the highest frequency of occurrence. Quite interestingly, the dynamics of these two places were utterly different. In dreams of drill camp, only routine assignments were carried out and these parts of the dream often happened first and were vaguely remembered. But the family house acted as a platform for the most interesting and varied phenomena. It thus seems that the everyday surroundings at the South Pole, contrary to expectations, failed to produce anything else than these everyday events in the dream. The familiar place of my family house did, however, produce the most varied events.

Of course it is not possible to draw general conclusions from these rather limited empirical observations. That being said, however, some speculation, or tentative hypothesis, is always possible. The South Pole presented an entirely new kind of environment which surely must have triggered the spatial-semiotic faculty, trying to produce a matrix that could correlate the behavior of the surrounding structures with different expectations. In my dreaming life, I turned to my family house where I spent my entire upbringing and youth. But my family house acted as the foundation for unusual experiences: cosmic revelations, conspiracies, odd behavior of well-known comrades etc. It is as if the expectations of the unfamiliar environment at the South Pole were realized as unexpected events at the familiar family house. My hypothesis would thus be that the level of familiarity of the environment stands in direct proportion to the familiarity of the events unfolding in the dream and in inverse proportion to the familiarity of the environment in the dream. Perhaps a quote from the previously mentioned Nordenskjöld could substantiate my hypothesis. Remarking on the vividness of the dreams of his comrades and colleagues during the Antarctic expedition of 1901, he says that the dreams "were all concerned with the world outside, which for us were far away, but very often adopted to our current circumstances".

But is it at all an interesting ambition to try to find a general law of transformation between the waking and dreaming state? What if such a law could be derived from an immense statistical database (of course, one should be careful to distinguish between a statistical average, which always exists, and an underlying law producing such an average, which does not have to exist)? Does this provide any means of enhancing the poetic impact that is produced when experiences from the dreaming and waking state confront each other? Possibly so. One would be able to play around with such a law, set up interesting lines of investigation, games and interrelations between collective dream experiences, create an urban environment in accordance with this law to produce a specific dream geography, deduce the principles of a general geography that holds in both landscapes etc. Or one might find that such a law of transformation depends on external factors, such that many such laws exist, each one exactly determined by what one might term a transformation of transformations. This would increase the possibility to play with such transformations even more. Or such a statistically acquired knowledge might not be interesting at all, just producing statement after statement that in each case can be found to be contra-factual in some or many instances.

Who knows? Further investigations are required, in the dream, Antarctica, or anywhere else.

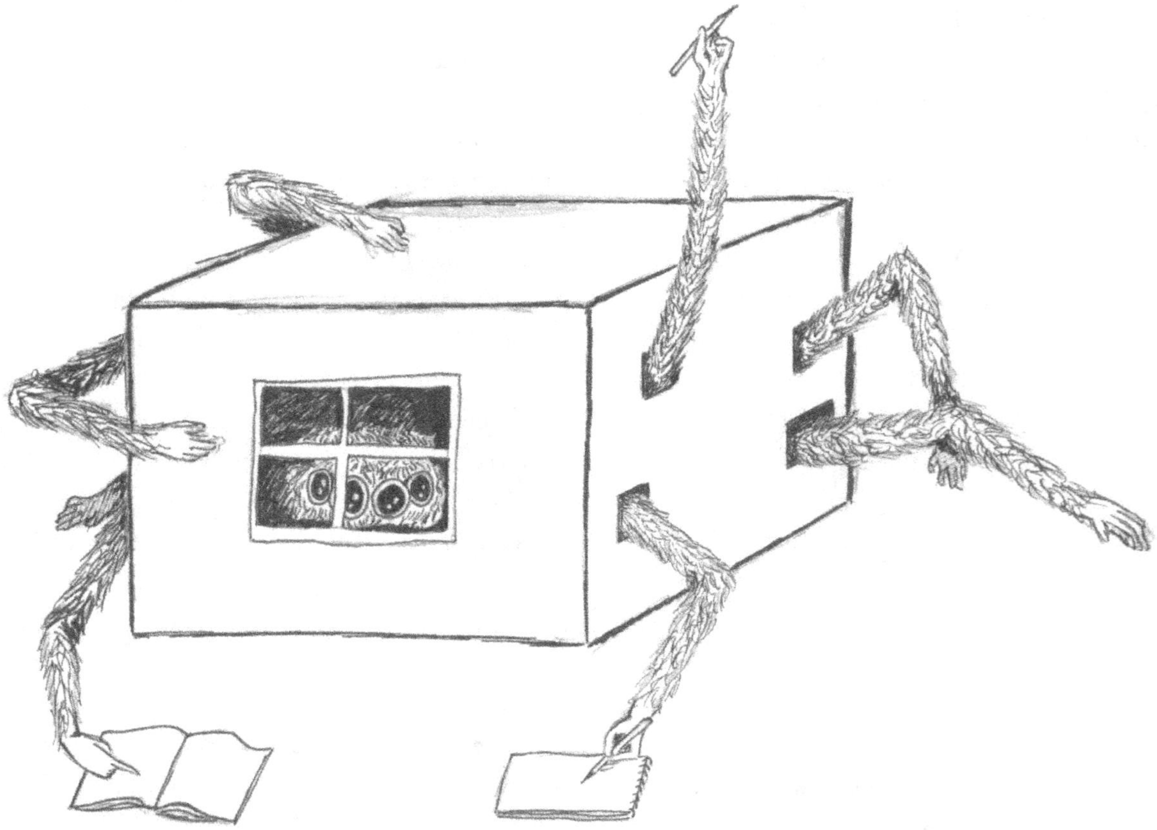

Portrait of John Andersson, drawing by Paul Cowdell

THE REPETITIONS OF BILITIS

Nikos Stabakis

Patras, September 1997: a low point in my life; while I am recovering in my parents' apartment from a broken knee gained during my obligatory stint in the army, my father is rearranging his library. In the process, some books that used to belong to my late grandparents (on my mother's side) in Piraeus come to light (a short collection consisting of some old volumes of translated literature that ended up in my part of the family). One of these is, surprisingly, a Greek version of Pierre Louÿs's *The Songs of Bilitis*, a work I am familiar with, having read the classic English translation by Alvah C. Bessie some years back. The book dates from the mid-20's (I do not recall the year exactly, although for some reason I am in favor of 1926). I am impressed at how so risqué a text found its way in the household, but am too preoccupied with my personal condition to investigate further (besides, there is not much I can do). One year later, I return to Britain and forget more or less all about the book (although in fact I can recall the exact shelf of the library where it lies).

Piraeus, September 2006: since my parents both retired, they have moved to their hometown, Piraeus, along with the library. It seems, however, that not all of the books have made it: when I visit them (I now live in nearby Athens) after they have settled into their new home, I make several excursions into the library, yet am unable to find *Bilitis*. I am furious at the thought that what seems to me the most interesting piece in the entire family collection has been absent-mindedly lost in the confusion, and I regret not having snatched it for my own use while there was still time.

Athens, 31st December 2007: as I pass by a second-hand bookstore, I spy a relatively recent, albeit out-of-print, Greek edition of a French comic book (*The Ghost Town*, an old Lucky Luke adventure) that I first read in my early childhood and have typically long since lost/given away; it strikes me that several images/phrases from the story are still clear in my mind, although I haven't read it in almost three decades, so I decide to buy it. I enter the store and, while gazing absentmindedly at a shelf, immediately discover another edition of *Bilitis*: probably the same Greek translation, but this book dates from 1921. I buy it (along with the comic book) without a moment's hesitation: it is quite low-priced—not in mint condition, but the text is intact.

When I reach the city centre, I discover to my astonishment that *The Ghost Town* has only just been reissued (possibly even today) and is staring at me from most news kiosks, so that instead of this cheap and fairly withered second-hand copy I could have bought a new one at a marginally higher price if I so wished, had I not followed my curiously irresistible urge; this almost humorous twist leaves me with the impression that the grotesquely highlighted comic book was merely chance's bait for making me enter the shop and discover *Bilitis*.

The latter bears a note by its first owner (Gabriella Kornilaki) stating the date of its purchase: 18/3/[1]922 (I later realize that this is the publication date of the Éluard/Ernst collaboration *Répétitions*).

January 2008: Diamantis, a member of the Athens Surrealist Group, has very recently founded the publishing house Farfoulas, specializing in old and obscure texts with subversive aspects. I realize that this chance event may also mean a second life for the translation I've rediscovered: at this point, *Bilitis* is not available in Greek, even though Louÿs is hardly an unknown here. I recommend the book to Diamantis, who is impressed and publishes it in late spring, edited and with an introduction by me (which also documents my chance discovery/ies of the book). It gets rave reviews all around, although what puzzles me is most critics' evident ignorance of its existence prior to the Farfoulas edition.

One thing they do not bother to comment on, in any case, is the fact that, in editing the old Greek translation, I drew on two texts: Bessie's English rendition and the French original, which I only own in electronic form, as available on the net. In this French text, however, as I make clear in my notes, certain short passages are completely different and considerably tamer than the respective ones to be found in the English and Greek translations; I thus reach the tentative conclusion that the electronic text comes from a later (self-censored?) source than the one informing the two translations. Given that I don't own a French copy of the book, I have left it at that for the time being.

The night of the 9th to 10th of July 2008 announces a crucial relationship in my life. At the same time, I am in the process of writing an essay for the third issue of *Klidonas* (I will, in fact, finish it in a couple of days). While, predictably, the 40th anniversary of May 1968 has brought forward yet another wave of tiresome reminiscences and special features in the media, we have decided to focus on surrealism's political trajectory, perhaps including some ambiguously humorous '68 reference as a shield against commonplace and reified commodity.

Next evening (July 10th), Vangelis comes to the group meeting bringing a gift for me: on that very day, while walking in the Athens fleamarket, he discovered a French edition of *Bilitis* dating from 1923; a few pages are missing, which probably accounts for its affordable price, yet I am able to make out that this text agrees with the English and Greek versions (I have yet to unravel this mystery). Most importantly, Vangelis has found in the book *a lottery ticket dated July 10, 1968, forty years ago to the day!*

This quickly evolves into a group game (consisting of elaborations on different aspects of the ticket), meant to be the issue's sole explicit reference to that year. At this point, we still hope that the issue will be out during 2008, which in fact will not be the case, due to a series of complications; by mid-autumn, a general sense of unease (including a temporary hiatus in group meetings, due to objective difficulties) makes the issue seem less and less imminent, the group activity itself ever so slightly out of focus, the overall mood less cheerful and creative than usual, for no apparent reason.

On the night of my "name day" (December 6th, the christian feast of St. Nicholas, in which everyone bearing that name is traditionally meant to celebrate, or at least answer the phone quite a lot, regardless of their religious standing), I and the other party in the aforementioned relationship walk towards the Exarchia district for a drink. We are silently undergoing a major crisis, which will erupt in a few days… As we walk the relatively short distance from my house, I realize she did not really feel like going out in the first place, but it is now too late. We discover that the bars are closed, there are rubbish bins burning, signs of recent street fights… Entering the sole open bar, we learn that a couple of hours ago a cop shot a boy dead… People appear from the side of the Polytechnic, presumably moving to the nearby police station to protest. I manage to find Vangelis on the phone, but am only able to talk to him for a few seconds. Then I take her to the Omonia subway station and walk back to Exarchia alone. The smell of tear gas, already evident, will become suffocating tomorrow.

The events following the December 6th state murder will come to inform the group's approach and perspectives as a living illustration of outrage and revolt; the game will probably remain as a coda, being the sole '68 allusion in an issue that will now miss that anniversary by at least a month while retaining the urgency of actuality.

All of which now seems a world away from what started this narrative. For revolt overgrows our individual turns of chance, while involving them, and us, in its stride…

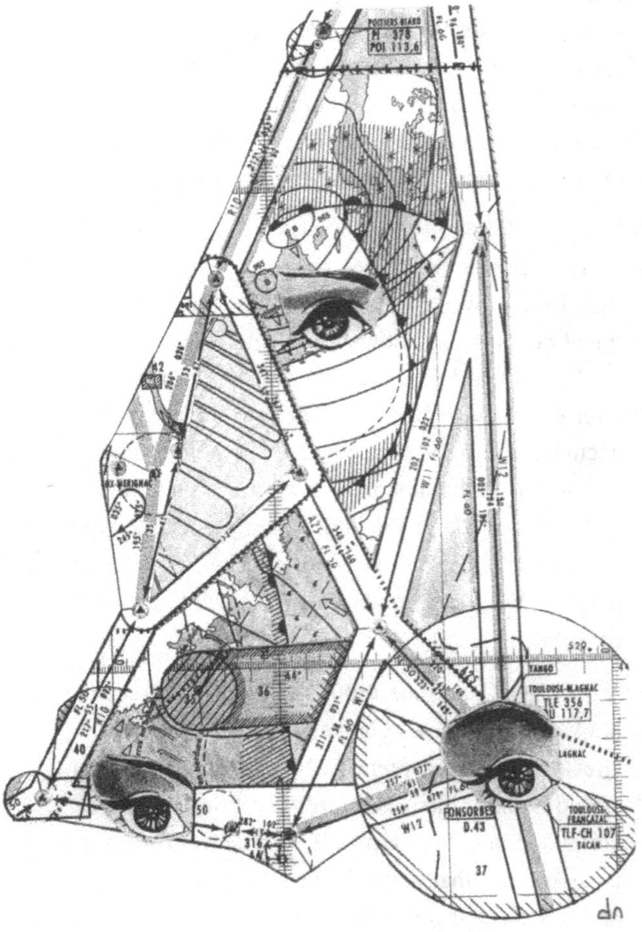

Collage by David Nadeau

OBJECTIVE CHANCE

Bough, Limb, and Orange Claw Hammer

Don LaCoss

About twelve years ago, I found a black-&-white photograph stuck in a battered one-volume condensed textbook version from 1961 of James Frazer's *The Golden Bough* in a bookstore near Detroit. It was a picture of an elderly couple standing under a tree on a farm somewhere: the old man with a peg-leg in a suit, with an arm akimbo and his hat in his hand; the woman, squinting into the sun behind the photographer, was shorter and wearing a dress of some kind. On the back, there was a faded pencil-written note done in careful cursive writing which said: "This was taken quite a long while ago but I think it is an awfully good one of them. Thought you might like to have one."

I already owned a couple versions of Frazer's largely discredited (but, at one time, highly influential) book on primitive myth, but because of the photo, I bought it for a couple of dollars and went to a nearby coffee-shop to wait for a friend who I was supposed to meet at that hour. I had just sat down with my coffee and was absently thumbing through the book when I overheard the worker behind the counter having a conversation with another customer. All at once she said with a laugh: "Don't you think that this is a good one of them?"

The shop-worker's comment sounded much like the cryptic caption on the weird photo that I had just found. I looked up with a start, and she was pointing to a small photograph that was taped to a low wall on the side of the baked-goods display case closest to the cash register. There were all kinds of things affixed there on this impromptu bulletin-board: postcards, comic strips, photos, fortune-cookie fortunes, stickers, and so forth. The photo she was pointing to was off to one side, and after a few moments I went over to her on the pretext of asking for a snack from the case so that I could get a closer look at the photo that she had

pointed out to the other customer. That picture was of two toddlers sitting at a picnic table, making goofy faces. It was a little boy and a little girl (whereas the photo that I had found was of an old man and an old woman) whose mouths, teeth, and tongues were covered with smeared melted ice cream as they mugged for the camera.

But below the photograph was taped a photo-copied picture of a man with a top hat, a dentist smock, a pair of pliers and a necklace of human teeth. The caption identified him as a charlatan medicine-show quack-dentist named Edgar R. "Painless" Parker. Obviously, the juxtaposition of the picture of the kids smothered in ice-cream and the picture of a gruesome travelling-circus dentist was meant to be funny, but I went back to my seat muttering "Painless Parker" to myself. I knew the name, somehow, but not the story of the guy himself.

A few days later, I was at home cooking dinner and listening to a 1969 recording of psychedelic blues-rock by Captain Beefheart and His Magic Band called Trout Mask Replica, a record that I have enjoyed for many years. And then it hit me where I had heard the name "Painless Parker" before—there's a song on that disc called "Orange Claw Hammer" that contains with the following lyrics [emphasis mine]:

> A little up the road a wooden candy-stripe barber pole,
> And above it read a sign: **"Painless Parker"**...
> Licorice twisted around under a fly,
> and a youngster cocked her eye
> who, God before me, if I'm not crazy, is my
> daughter...
> Come, little one, with your little dimpled fingers,
> Gimme one and I'll buy you a cherry phosphate
> and take you down to the foaming brine and water
> and show you the wooden tits
> on the goddess with the pole out, full sail,
> that tempted away your **peg-legged father**.

GLOBAL CHANCE

a poem by

Juan Carlos Otaño

A sunflower vomits a cello

Aesop vomits Corneille

Heli vomits Samuel

Helisinborg vomits Helsingfors

Helsingoer vomits Helgoland

And Hendaya vomits Sumbava

Perforated Reality

Lurdes Martínez

It's a sunny and windy day in May. I leave my house and go down the street towards a nearby public square. I walk with a certain briskness, since I have to take care of some daily errands before keeping an appointment with my friend, Eugenio Castro. I scarcely walk any distance from my doorway when I see some postcards that have been thrown onto the sidewalk, which grab my attention. On first glance I perceive two identical cards that show a panoramic view, in black and white, of the old or historic part of a city. Both appear to have been perforated by a drill or similar instrument.

Immediately I stop, with the intent of gathering these postcards from the ground. Consequently I bend down and pick one of them up. My first impressions become confirmed as soon as I contemplate the nearby postcard: actually, the image shows an impressive stone bridge over a river whose railings are crowned with statues, and with a tower standing at the far end whose characteristic shape I immediately and excitedly recognize as the Charles Bridge, in Prague. This is a city that I have visited on various occasions, under different circumstances, and which has captivated me. As it had appeared from the beginning, the post card is perforated, having some curious punch-marks that add to its attractiveness and its mystery.

I get ready to pick up the second postcard, which is found a little bit away from the first one – scarcely half a meter – but upon reaching down again I see that it has disappeared. I look around but find nothing; there is no trace of it. Barely have a few seconds passed between the first and second gestures. Therefore I remain surprised by the sudden disappearance. Then I remember that while I looked at the first postcard taken from the pavement, a group of teenagers passed very close to me (there is a nearby secondary school), and then I consider the possibility that they had been able to take it with them, although I have the impression that they hadn't had enough time for that. I'm overcome by the sensation of anger and irritation, so the idea of possessing these two postcards with identical appearances attracts me greatly. I look again, but the search is fruitless. Since I don't see anything in the surroundings that reveals the whereabouts of the postcard, I continue my walk. I keep the card that I found in the pocket of my jacket.

About an hour later I take the same route from my home towards the square, but this time accompanied by my friend Eugenio Castro who has come to pick me up at my place. As we approach the location of the encounter with the postcards, I remember the event, and while somewhat agitated, I tell my companion what happened, simultaneously taking out the postcard from my pocket in order to show him. I haven't finished telling him about it when he, in a very calm and absolutely natural tone, points with his hand towards the ground right in front of our feet, *exactly in the same place* where I had seen the postcards scarcely a little while before, *showing* me the absent postcard. He picks it up and we compare it with the one that I have: there is no doubt; they are identical; everything coincides absolutely, including the positioning of the perforations. It is its twin, its double.

Finally, upon writing the report about this encounter, I notice the date on which it was stamped: the 5th of May.

Translated by Eric Bragg & Bruno Jacobs
Salamandra – Intervención surrealista – imaginación insurgente – crítica de la vida corriente, #17/18, Madrid, 2008, pp. 82, 83.

Coral Pure Wool

Guy Girard

From the large coral gate forever flapping against the shadow, projected by the spirit on even the faintest of its formulations, there flows the wool of the galaxies. Common sense may find shelter in hearing nothing there but the bleating of sheep before sleep, yet it is a whole plait of interior isles where Panurge's troops will have been celebrated by the sirens. And then the latter's very song, mingling the whales' rutting season with the simpering wind under the arcades of the Royal Palace, responds to the white odor of the "eternal Tekeli-li," voiced in a "low murmuring," in the final pages of *Arthur Gordon Pym*. Not a vocal exercise, but rhythmically the equal of madreporic constructions, thought unfolds its nebulous skein with the sole aim of perfecting one's being to the point of sifting through a speech otherwise rejected by daily monotony. As readily imaginable as continental drift is the movement that gets hold of the phenomenological furniture in the imaginary alcove into which I have introduced my fixed, black ideas. If I perceive myself say 'capsule,' the armchair to the left of my melancholy shall leap on the nine garlic-stung camels' heads who hit me hard, under the guise of beauty, with moral intoxication, when I'd only wish to hear there a mere juggler's slickness. Yet as soon as desire has launched its capsule and upon bouncing sent the armchair waltzing in a magpie's nest with the Queen of Sheba's winks, the lived poem enjoys all the favors of a furious midnight sun. There is no janitor under the Northern Lights.

Passionately doubting, for lack of an indispensable sabotaging of data banks, the nickelated future of artificial intelligence, it is as a test of this passion that I consider the subversive potential of automatic writing to remain intact. An initiating operation, psychic automatism, seeking as it does to liberate thought of "all control exerted by reason, beyond all aesthetic or moral preoccupation" (Breton), defies the authoritarian automatization of language and of individual behaviors. The very word "news," burped each morning underneath the skulls of the "medium atmospherico-cephale bureaucrats" (Dalí), scatters its murmur of rubble on the dew that the nocturnal dream lays on the words. When all that is said in the daily exchanges matters scarcely more than a mirror offered to the larks of resignation, when words are only supposed to support a symbolism under high surveillance destined to cretinize the confused psychology of the masses, the rebel spirit is granted the power of a myth to counter insolently the civilized mystifications, "to ruin definitively all other psychic mechanisms" (Breton). Intrinsically, automatism is rebellion, insofar as it is the sole psychic mechanism that functions best with the delicious irritation of the grains of desire's sand.

Thought only has to forge the lightning of its own innocence. The practice of automatism assures, under the empire of revelation, that the least of our certainties wishes that the spirit, at every moment, returns to the image where its origin is lit. Such is the empire of that image that it illuminates, with utopian glow, the practice of constant innovation that determines the illusion of progress. At surrealism's origin there is the conjunction between the exigency of radical novelty represented by automatic writing and the exemplary image of the myth of the origin, which immediately fertilizes the field of its future. This conjunction is ritualized through the collectivization of poetic practice, on a mode of operation analogous to that characterizing the ludic part in the development of technology. The same fascination with speed unites, umorously at least, inventors and poets. For the latter, the rapidity of dictation conditions its purity. On the speed of associations depends, as in a psychoanalytic séance, the violence needed to pass the customs of vigilant consciousness.

But to conceive the practice of automatism according to the speed of execution alone comes back to spying its message only in the whirlwind of dust raised by its course in the mental moors. The trance imposes a hellish train and already, in a doomsday thunder, I am in that train, absorbed by the wish to contemplate a landscape whose magnificence I predict. There is inconceivable magic, Samarkand under the foam of the bubbling thought where I would not have the time to stroll at my own leisure. Speed abstracts mercilessly from me the forms and metamorphoses, and I come to suspect it of being the last ruse of my reason. Deterritorialization is the most sensitive effect of speed increase; the conclusions drawn by Paul Virilio on this matter may certainly extend to the domain of interior life. The means that thought gives itself for its liberation cannot subject their dynamics to that of the progress of a society it challenges.

This fact was always accepted by those who oriented their research toward verbal-auditory automatism. Whatever the chronology worn out under the drums of auditory conduit, the time muttering on the ear's large basalt beach once again leads the same ecstatic tide to the foot of shipwrecking words. Thus, the other evening, just before falling asleep, I heard talk of a hospitable place where I would only have expected a desert:

fortified city
fortified against
my heart against
owl stew.

All these paths lead to the Palace of Mirages. At first there was the mirage where every word germinates. To our own arbitrariness alone is left the measure of time in which the germ will give its place to the fruit: this time alone opens up the infinity of revolt before the control of consciousness over imaginary objects. An obstinate control, aiming to impede the general displacement of being after each experience of psychic automatism. It thus goes where its imagination calls it, toward the other that its reason cannot identify, except negatively. The renewed mental representations proceed from a series of shifts from the ontological status acquired by the individual through the all-too-exclusive company of dominant modes of thought. These shifts, on which surrealism founds experimentally its "absolute divergence" (Fourier), even appear to amplify consciousness, an open and revolutionary consciousness; plus, their appreciation must be subjected to the same series of displacements. What are the available reference points for this?

After Jung and Tzara, I shall repeat the distinction between non-directed and directed thought. The former, which is commonly that of primitive peoples, as well as of the "definitive dreamer" in the best of times, is linked to the pleasure principle. Its speech follows the shortest path of desire, which rotates around suns to assure that being is what it pronounces and exceeds by far the limits of an individualism defended by social regulation. This thought, indeed, has no other law than that of analogy, no other movement than spontaneity, its aim being not to produce but rather to perfect the relations it accomplishes with all that invests it with sense all around. A dream-thought, it is certainly that of poetry conceived as "activity of the spirit" (Tzara): automatism, in this sense, is en erotics of language. By contrast, directed thought puts Eros in the service of work, language in the service of communication.

The ancient conflict between Dionysos and Apollo has led the victor's reason to model its trajectory on the panicky trail imprinted on the spirit by the ebb and flow of imagination. Critical reason owes to the examination of the repression of impulses its pertinence against the abuses of rational thought. If it follows the logic of its denunciation, it ought to be abolished in reconciliation with poetic thought.

Inversely, non-directed thought, in order to affirm itself in the light of day, at the risk of being knowingly confused with the bloody garbage of history, uses linguistic models, whose eroticism is generally molded by the repressive authority of the superego. Where mechanisms of sublimation are at work, it is in the loss of sense between the language of birds, which is the original dream of the unconscious, and the so-called maternal language of the father, as in one's secular and obligatory school, that the "continuous misfortune" (Breton) of automatic writing is repeated. When "words make love" (Breton), the song of their pleasure rebuilds the Tower of Babel from its ruins. Surrealism's horizon is not as low as to be indiscernible amid the murmurs and cries that we distract at great pains from the cacophony injected by social reflexes. Before amorous conjunction, words also know perhaps the equivalent of those nuptial parades, so remarkable in the animal kingdom. The poetic spark, as observed by Reverdy, would only constitute the final moment of the game, but shall we liberate sufficiently our memory to know more? To be conscious, henceforth, of having sufficient intuition to restore the automatic voice's downstream flow, guiding ourselves after the grouse's call…

The erosion of language participates in the simultaneous erosion of the feeble mythological power accorded by the reality principle (or rather the performance principle, in Marcuse's correction) to its psycho-social definitions. All the figures of the sacred that have been, if imperfectly, put to sleep throughout this past century (the ideas of god, man, art) are, alas, in a hurry to be reborn in the corpses whose stench will not get lost by the holes in the ozone layer. Here come again the religions, the homelands, the families and the strumpot of Père Ubu… As long as the figures of the sacred are not named save via the voice of identitarian logic, one cannot grasp their organic link with the postures of mental erotics. On the contrary, surrealist automatism managed to recognize erogenous zones in the spirit, which the metaphysical interdictions of civilization name soul. It is from this mental place, not yielding to idealist undergrowth, that surrealism bets on a dialectics between the pleasure principle and what we must foresee as the surreality principle. This we must, pressed by the desire of revolution understood as the collective sublimation of all the unachieved desires. Already this desire is expected to elaborate on the level of an interaction the spontaneous dynamics of the imaginary, and the latter's transmission into a critical thought which reflects what is imaginable and no more perpetually conceivable. The ballast that this will have disposed in the depths of this era's consciousness, who would not be surprised to see it one day, raised amid the gigantic upheaval of a shared reverie, on the point of the best-formulated desires? I imagine, for the moment, an object ridding itself of a lamentable frozen plush, to exult the thousand solstices of a coral lip, as if in the slow cooking of anxious centuries memory hurried, slowly, to become a crystallized orgasm, the emerald where the seaweeds of voluptuousness and the live embers of utopia meet.

This text first appeared in *L'Ombre et la demande, projections surréalistes*, éd. A.C.L., 2005. Translated by Nikos Stabakis

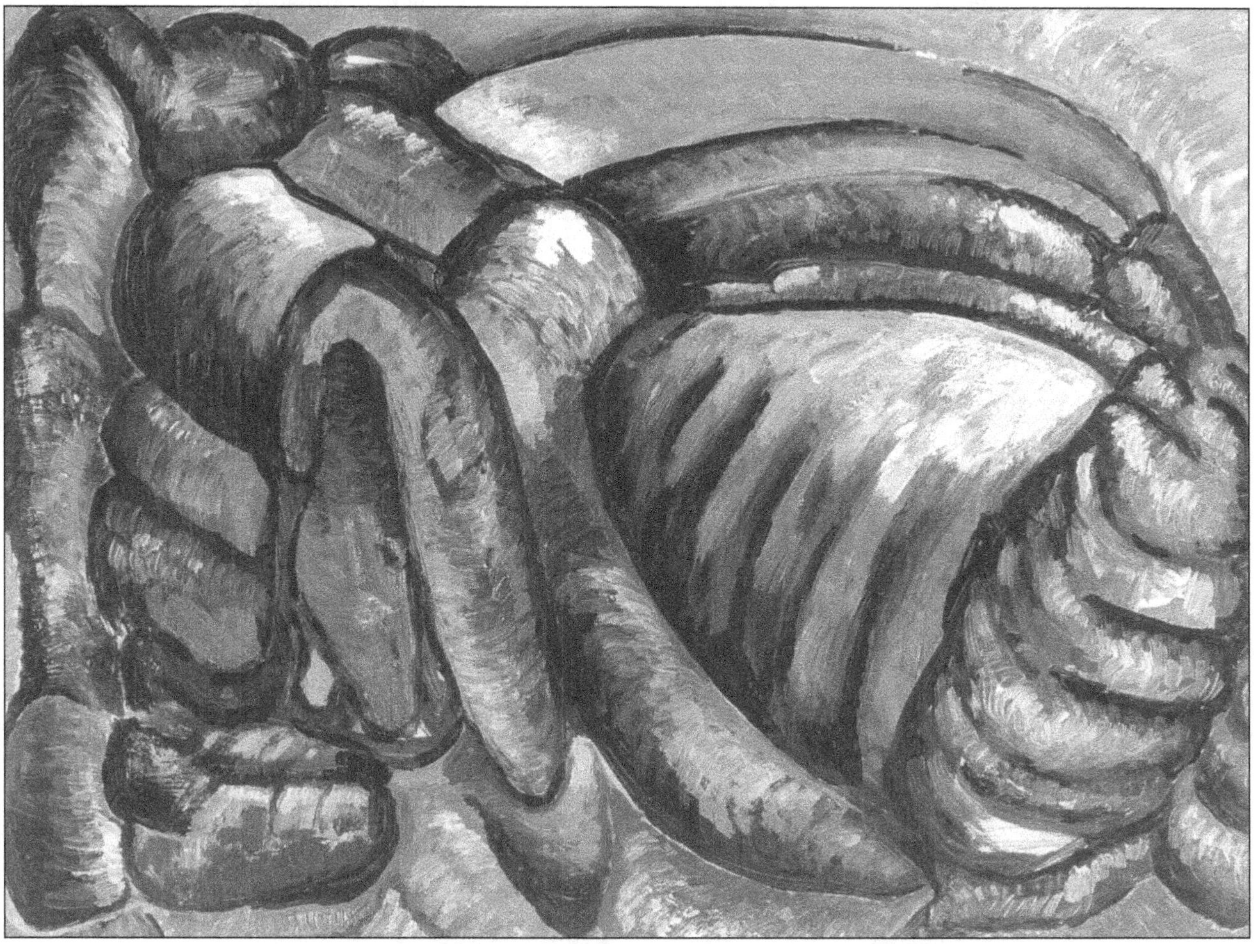

Night of Passed Fields, painting by John Welson

Letter to Mrs.

Josie Malinowski

We had to wade through the shallows to get to the ship, and I knew as soon as we were in the water that there was something terribly wrong with this place. A man was standing waist-deep in the sea, naked as the day he was born. When the waves crashed onto the beach, he looked like a normal swimmer, standing in the water. But when the tide drew out, we could see him for what he really was. He had an octopus stuck fast to his crotch, its tentacles wrapped lovingly around his body, and he was fucking it slowly. At first I thought the animal was dead, but then I realised that not only was it alive, but it too was getting a kick from being fucked by a human, and it was then that I knew this place had gone wrong, very wrong.

When we got onto the ship we found it utterly deserted, devoid of human inhabitants, but it was all wet like it had been flooded. Each door we tried led into another empty room, dripping wet. Eventually we came to a room that wasn't empty, but by God we wished it had been, or that we could have been blinded at birth to stop us seeing what was in there. A naked woman hung from the ceiling, a thick leather strap bound around her stomach, which was attached by rope to the ceiling, and left her body suspended, face down, in the middle of the room. By her head was a huge squid, calmly watching her. By her end was another octopus, which was gently reaching up to her buttocks with one of its tentacles and penetrating her with it. Some of our group looked away, nauseous, immediately, while others instinctively shot the depraved beasts dead and took down the girl, who was practically unconscious. Me, I simply looked on, unable to avert my gaze, at the incredible scene. I found myself being pulled away by a colleague who slapped me and told me I was in shock.

Upstairs I found no more signs of life but for a book, packed with notes, written by a human hand. Instead of handing it to my superior, as I knew I should, I found myself slipping it into my jacket and taking it home with me that night. Whatever happened to the octopus-fucking humans, I never found out, could never find anyone who'd tell me; but I did find out what happened on that ship.

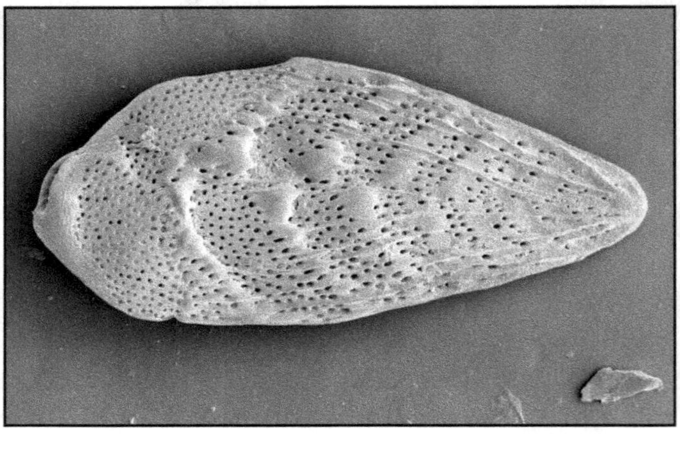

Surrealist Documents

Some Recent Political Tracts and Declarations

Breaking the leash:

a Surrealist Statement Against Torturocracy
on the Occasion of the Imperial Coronation
of George W. Bush, 2004

> Of the dungeons there had been strange things narrated—fables, I had always deemed them—but yet strange, and too ghastly to repeat, save in a whisper.
>
> —Edgar Allan Poe, "The Pit and the Pendulum"

In general, surrealists tend to ignore the hubris, ignorance, and narcissism of the electioneering so adored by the war-ad-dicted Democratic-Republican axis of elites. Yet, in the 1947 tract Freedom is a Vietnamese Word (later republished in the pages of the anarchist newspaper Le Libertaire), surrealists in Paris singled out a specific French governmental cabinet's newly-minted colonial war in southeast Asia: "Surrealism can only be against a regime whose members stand together behind a blood-stained disgrace as though it represents a joyful awakening." All governments are equally reprehensible, but any one that can so easily "collapse into the mire of compromise and extortion can be nothing but the calculated prelude to the establishment of a new totalitarianism," the tract explained. We were reminded of this when the Democratic Party convened in Boston in July, and again as the Republican Party bosses, their underlings, and their henchmen gather in New York City. In both instances, the party apparatuses happily stand together behind the bloody crimes of mass murder and torture in US-controlled Afghanistan and Iraq. We shudder to think about their next petro-imperialist crimewave against humanity which will be shrouded in the red, white and blue banners of this racist Christian civilization.

Systematic torture and the full-scale degradation of victims by the forces of law-'n'-order in Iraq is a symptom of the logic of the State and its inherent racist, colonialist configurations (tellingly, many of the soldiers directly responsible for meting out this abuse have worked as prison guards in the US). The awful humiliation and excruciating torment in US military prisons are not used solely to force prisoners into revealing vital information about the guerrilla war or into betraying their friends and family who may be taking up arms against the occupation and its quislings. Torture is also a coercive political technology deployed to terrorize and to demoralize an insubordinate population and to suppress the bitter truths about the rancid excesses of capitalism and the colossal failures of its wars.

Although the roads to the Abu Ghraib dungeon and the Guantánamo Bay concentration camp all intersect at the center stage podium of Madison Square Garden this week, none of us are naïve enough to think that these are exceptional phenomena isolated to only one group of politicians. The spokes of torturocratic ideologies radiate out far from the helpless individual whose body and will are being broken on its wheel. Torture is a routine activity happening every day in any number of countries throughout the world as an integral part of security operations, law enforcement systems, and State authority. Any consolidated power, not just that of the Bush-Cheney regime but the entire apparatus of the State itself, passes on its surplus of accumulated violence to the next coterie of corporate executives, military officers, and civil bureaucrats regardless of political party affiliation. This power is disguised as "national security" and "public safety," but it is nothing more than statist and capitalist self-interest. Therefore, police and military torture cannot be eliminated through well-intentioned legal-aid groups and human-rights reform movements—it can only be curtailed by the sustained dismantling of the State, its pretensions to moral and civil authority, and its jealously-guarded monopoly on violence.

It is for these reasons that we feel obligated to reassert surrealism against this ghoulish and self-congratulatory revival meeting in New York City this week. As the Republicans righteously speechify about this most terroristic war on terrorism, and as they swagger throughout the city attempting to sate their sanctimonious gluttony, we will be thinking of the lives that they so carelessly have helped to destroy in the last four years. Every time one of them spouts some twisted balderdash about "freedom," we ask that you remember their feverish efforts to build a prison planet, a sprawling carceral archipelago of violence, rape and fear stretching from Guantánamo Bay to Kabul, and from Baghdad to places like the infamous women's High Security Control Unit in Lexington, Kentucky, and the jails being used by the NYPD to cage our friends for speaking out against the RNC.

We denounce the snowballing totalitarianism practiced domestically and internationally by the Bush-

Cheney regime that is being applauded and honored at the Republican National Convention. Out of solidarity with the elegant wildfires of liberty, imagination, spontaneity, and sensitivity, we stand united and resolved against war, occupation, and murderous humanitarianism.

Freedom now, against jailers and police everywhere! Open the prisons! Disband the army!

SURREALISTS INTERNATIONAL

To have done with the spectre of god

a statement issued by
the Paris Group of the Surrealist Movement,
December 25, 2006

After the Second World War, throughout the economically developed world, religion, especially Roman Catholicism, had to abate its centuries-old claim to direct people's inner lives, their sexuality, their social and moral existence. A large portion of humanity thus reaped the fruits of the long anti-Christian struggles of the eighteenth century, initiated by the bourgeoisie and pursued even more vigorously by the labour movement, one of whose most valuable legacies was secularisation and the relegation of religion to the private sphere. The air we breathed was all the healthier, in that the age-old messianic strain that had permeated Christianity, having completely deserted the churches and abandoned transcendence, nourished all the utopian currents of the 1960s, hated so fiercely today by those who wield hegemonic power. In addition, the device of recruiting the imaginary, which for over a thousand years had been the monopoly of Christianity, was largely overtaken in its means and methods by the society of the spectacle that was coming into being. To some extent, the spectacle, which is essentially the profane realization of religion, took great care not to finish off its work of overtaking the religious; rather than doing away with religion, it kept it in its repertoire in the form of historical drama. It is this drama that it is presenting again today.

With the fall of Stalinist bureaucracies in Eastern Europe and the collapse of revolutionary ideologies that had been so useful in keeping the social system in equilibrium, capitalism ended up in a blind-alley of its own success, facing only itself. The more it unifies the planet through the relentless penetration of the commodity, the more it relies on false divisions to divert from their attempts directly to confront it those whom it exploits and whose lives it destroys. Of course, it does not create these divisions from scratch, and no conspiracy theory is needed to explain this process; it is its own historical movement – including its false trails (such as strengthening radical Islamism in order to weaken Soviet state capitalism) – that employs and amplifies pre-existing racial, ethical, sexual, religious and social divisions. That is why today we are witnessing the artificial resurgence of historic antagonisms between Christianity and Islam; of their old power only the ideological core of the religion survives, together with some set rituals that ensure the greater or lesser subservience of minds and bodies, especially where the religious can lean on the secular arm for support. Some people think they have discovered a clash of civilisations, whereas in today's world there is only the single barbarism of the hamburger and the mobile phone. Others (representatives of a frustrated Muslim bourgeoisie that would like to enjoy its share of the capitalist pie) think they're experiencing a re-run of the Crusades. And superimposed on this deadly mug's game is the reactivated confrontation between Western democracy and totalitarianism that had made the system work so well for more than half a century. Let us add, however, that in emphasising all these false oppositions, we are not over-stepping the mark by creating an equivalence between perceived everyday situations that cannot be compared. Just as during the Cold War it was preferable for everyone, proletarians included, to live in the so-called free world rather than in the so-called Communist world, one would have to be in particularly bad faith if one did not admit that in an Islamic society people's lives are even worse than just about anywhere else, even if they are not women, homosexuals or atheists, simply because they have to conform to the outrageous prohibitions and prescriptions of public morality.

In this equally tragic replay, the same situations are producing the same resort to nauseating tactical alliances; just as in the era of triumphant Stalinism appalling agreements such as the Molotov-Ribbentrop pact between Stalin's Russia and Hitler's Germany were made against what was even then called liberalism, today similar alliances are formed between the licensed critics of a liberalism once again wrongly described as extreme, and the worst Islamist regimes or organisations. What is in play when these deals are struck is still the abandonment of any kind of moral scruple, leading to the worst of confusions. Let us then spit on the inept Chávez, who shows no hesitation in supporting the criminal Ahmadinejad while at the same time taking himself for the executor of the will of God; let's spit on those European leftists who, confusing, as is their wont, an oppressed population and its alienated representation, offer their ridiculous support to the ultra-reactionaries of Hamas; let's spit on those British Trotskyists who make common cause with Islamo-fascists at local elections; let's spit on all those who, under the pretext of fighting imperialism, appear not to feel in their bones everything that is repugnant and unworthy in offering their hand to some proponent or other of religious dogmatism.

Our atheism is not a philosophical or logical position. It is, like the atheism of de Sade, the tone of a way of life, the palpable fluid in which we can breathe and in which our imaginary can enjoy its powers. The atheism of the positivists and other anti-clericals who pile up proofs of the non-existence of God appear to us like a fruit incompletely detached from the tree of a monotheism finally transformed into a simple ideology of transcendence. Our atheism is rather the radiant, joyful atheism of the Cyrenaics or of Lucretius, and, on the tangible level, it expresses the position of universal immanence that one finds among all animist peoples, for whom the sacred is none other than the sense of nature's presence. This is why the idea of a single omnipotent god appears to us so ridiculous and so tedious. And we cannot forget that this god, created in the worst image of man – an old, somewhat obsessive male – has always been used to justify the mental poverty of anthropocentrism and its voracious stranglehold on the wonder of the world. Should the imagination, drawn par excellence towards the excesses of poetic invention, be satisfied with such a sad figure on the horizon of its questioning?

The alleged return of the religious that the spectacle keeps trotting out for our benefit will in no way alter a fundamental fact: God died, and died definitively, more than a century ago; he was replaced by the religion of Capital, whose prophet is money, a prophet who, as we see in China today, unleashes passions all the more since it does not have to encumber itself at the same time with religious transcendence. But for peoples long subjugated by monotheism, whatever that may be, the ghost of God still prowls about, like an empty wineskin that is filled with the illusory answer to all the frustrations, rancours and oppressions ceaselessly generated by the economy and the class that reaps the benefit from them. And, like a lowering threat, this spectre weighs on the collective imaginary, polluting its language, purloining its hopes and curbing its impulses. To free oneself from this threat is to risk the only worthwhile adventure, that of freedom. So let us affirm once again the intrinsically blasphemous, anti-religious, and thus liberating character of poetic language, and our visceral disrespect for any submission to the empty bluster of the divine.

Translation by Kenneth Cox and Joël Gayraud, first published in *Prehensile Tail* No 4, [an occasional newsletter issued by Leeds Surrealist Group, England, March 2007].

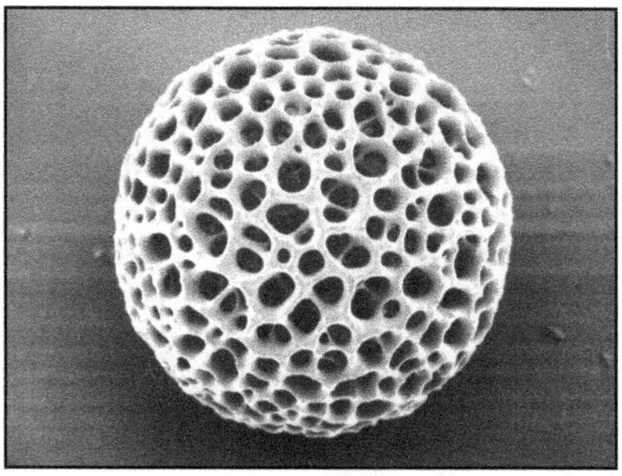

Contagious Fire

a statement issued by SLAG (Surrealist London Action Group), October 15, 2008

The collapse of the international banking system will have come as no surprise to anyone with a basic understanding of the workings of capitalism. It therefore came as a complete surprise to the bankers, whose knowledge of the world is limited to the figures flashing across their desks, and who judge their success by the number of other people's promissory notes they can cram into their pockets. Every one of the IOUs and unlimited credit notes they have used to enrich themselves constitutes a claim against future value. It was fictitious capital when they were bloating themselves on it – but now it has to be paid for with real money, out of our pockets, as governments fight to prop up an economic system. They can imagine no alternative, despite the fact that the system clearly doesn't work

Surrealists can only welcome the prospect of revolutionary upheaval. But we also need to prepare for it by weighing our courses of action carefully. What will happen next, and how might Surrealists respond most effectively? There are, of course, precedents, notably the Great Depression of the 1930s. What can we learn from the past? What are the similarities between now and the 1930s, and what are the differences?

When the 1929 crash took place, the European empires were in decline and the US was emerging as the world's largest economy. The vicious nature of the reaction that followed during the 1930s is well known: the eruption of fascism across Europe, the growth of nationalism and, ultimately, the devastation of the Second World War. The decade also saw the rise of Popular Front movement in France and Spain, which promised left-wing "unity" but instead delivered only disappointment and outright betrayal. Rather than hastening the overthrow of capitalism, the Popular Front sought merely to soften its worst crises, diverting the revolutionary energies of the Left into "unity" not just with non-revolutionary forces but even with sections of the ruling class itself.

The situation today is both similar and different to that of 1929. This crisis is unfolding against the background of the decline in US imperialism and the emergence of China and India as new imperialist powers. Capitalism was already global in the 1930s, but today it has reached unprecedented levels of international integration. Toxic debts have been packaged up, sold, and hidden in every corner of the international financial market. Thus the current economic collapse will take the world in the same reactionary direction as the 1930s, but in doing so will pose an even greater threat to humanity. The wars of Afghanistan and Iraq – scenes of US imperialism's desperate fight for survival – are only the beginning. Meanwhile, in the face of the threat to capitalism, Britain's erstwhile Labour "rebels" and the US's Democrats alike have been only too quick to fall into line in the name of unity. And just as in the 1930s, we can expect to see increasing efforts to "unite" different class and political tendencies into a popular front movement to stave off any revolutionary hastening of the collapse of capitalism. The failures of the Popular Front in the 1930s should stand as a stark warning to those on the Left who are trying to revive it today. It is truly alarming to see just how many so-called radical movements – the SWP in Britain, the LCR in France, the Links Partei in Germany, Rifondazione Communista in Italy – are already cheerleading that revival in Europe. Many of them actively support and take inspiration from Chávez and his allies in Latin America, who are already far advanced in their push to divert the popular desire for revolution into support for Latin American nationalism and capitalist reforms.

So how might we as Surrealists make sense of this situation? We have unshakeable confidence in Surrealism's ability to attract serious revolutionary enthusiasm everywhere. For that reason it is now more important than ever for us to be clear about our political choices. In particular, we must never forget the political implications of Surrealism's *internationalism*, and remain implacably opposed to all forms of nationalism, including those forms which make false promises to ameliorate recession, protect jobs, or even oppose globalisation. Our enemies are at home, and we must beware of being co-opted into their ideological offensives, whether it's acquiescing to the bank bail-out, supporting Obama, or invoking the chimera of "Islamo-fascism".

One thing we can know for certain: there are more shocks and crises of capitalism to come. We can anticipate those crises, and the revolutionary flashpoints and opportunities to which they will lead. If we are serious about our Surrealism, and about revolution – *and we are* – we will seize on the potential of every moment, will seek out and build on every opportunity to change the world, with all of the means at our disposal. Our politics must burn no less passionately, or urgently, than our poetry.

Burn the money and dance!

A statement issued by
the Surrealist Group of Madrid,
November, 2008

A group of about 40 people joined the gathering in Madrid against the G-20 summit in Washington on Saturday, the 15 of November, with the intention of telling capitalism to fuck off, criticizing through action the cornerstone of its filthy artifice: money, that bloody trash which won't survive the fall of the system and of which it is its totem and taboo. Therefore we burn it in advance of future bonfires that will sooner or later purify the old world, and we distribute the following leaflet in order to contribute as best we can to starting that fire.

Burn the money and dance!

Now they tell us that there is a crisis and *they lie to us,* just like when they announced prosperity from mutant cows fattened with transgenics, chemicals and plastic. Because economic recession and expansion *are a farce,* these two movements of growth and contraction of the same wave of servility, exploitation and fear which knocks you over and strangles you, me, us, wage-slaves, who live a crisis that is eternal, as to live means to pay for every realized act and for every nurtured dream, and from this we must dare to desire and act outside and against the market.

Now they will tell us that the crisis has a concrete and reasonable cause, that only one part of the system failed, that greed broke the bank and that to err is human, but it doesn't matter because the biblical wiseman Balthazar has arrived with his bag full of promises in order to reforge capitalism and repaint the bricks that lead to the Emerald City; and then Oz and its spectacle must continue, and this is entertainment. And they will continue to lie to us because *there is no cure* for capitalism: it is the crisis that reproduces itself, destroying men, women, cultures and continents until the ultimate consumption of the planet.

Thus it is necessary to destroy once and for all this recession, the prosperity and the economy that preoccupy certain people to such an extent. Therefore we burn money, totem and taboo, heart and blood, capitalism's ultimate abstraction and reality: so as to accelerate the crisis that destroys the wealth of *their* nations, so that the recession *recedes* until it suffocates in its own financial vomit, so that the economy dissolves and that life reappears. Because the currency that is so highly worshipped is just as false as everything else – a pestilential cloud that we will have to dispel until the daylight returns.

Maybe it will be said that this money doesn't belong to us, that it is part of the gross interior product of the national income and of the state treasury, those cursed monstrosities that overshadow what were once human relationships of collective production, of exchange and of gifts. But haven't we perhaps earned it from the sweat on our brow? Isn't it ours in exchange for the work and the time that we have sold for cheap? Therefore we would like to grant ourselves the happy luxury of destroying it, a luxury, however, that is within reach of any pocket because it is only a matter of getting fed up and *of daring*. And if we grant ourselves the *free* caprice of destroying it, it is simply because we haven't found a better use for it or that it is worth the trouble, and everything that could be done with that money, saving or investing it in order to make it grow and multiply as if it were a virus, or spending it in order to buy state of the art trash, consuming insipid distractions, earning laughable pensions, paying blood-sucking mortgages or financing campaigns in order to demand lamentable reforms are just so many other excuses that tie us to the economy and strengthen it at the same time. The time has come to cut such an umbilical cord: *we deny capitalism* and therefore we *reject its money*.

Thus we burn it, casually incinerating the economic train together with the pieces of paper that form its freightcars, and all its commerce. And we take leave remembering, as if there were any remaining doubt, that *there will be dancing but not money* in the world that we always keep within our hearts.

Crisis! More crisis!

1929... 1973... 2008... the third time's a charm!

Burn the money and dance!

The Chronic Critics

Translated by Eric Bragg and Bruno Jacobs

Nice Ride, collage by Diamantis Karavolas

The Phantom of Liberty Always Comes with a Knife between the Teeth

A statement issued by
Athens Surrealist Group
December 2008

The *ne plus ultra* of social oppression is being shot at in cold blood.

All the stones, torn from the pavement and thrown at the shields of cops or at the façades of commercial temples, all the flaming bottles that traced their orbits in the night sky, all the barricades erected on city streets, dividing our areas from theirs, all the bins of consumer trash which, thanks to the fire of revolt, came to be Something out of Nothing, all the fists raised under the moon, are the arms giving flesh, as well as true power, not only to resistance but also to freedom. And it is precisely the feeling of freedom that, in those moments, remains the sole thing worth betting on: that feeling of forgotten childhood mornings, when everything may happen, for it is ourselves, as creative humans, who have awoken – not those future productive human machines known as "obedient subject," "student," "alienated worker," "owner," "family wo/man." The feeling of facing the enemies of freedom – of no longer fearing them.

It is thus for good reason that those who wish to get on with their business as if nothing happens, as if nothing has ever happened, are worried. The phantom of liberty always comes with the knife between the teeth, with the violent will to break the chains, all those chains that turn life into a miserable repetition, serving to reproduce the dominant social relations. Yet from Saturday, December 6, the cities of this country are not functioning properly: no shopping therapy, no open roads leading us to work, no news on the government's forthcoming recovery initiatives, no carefree switching from one lifestyle TV show to another, no evening drives around Syntagma Square, etc., etc., etc.

These days and nights do not belong to merchants, TV commentators, ministers and cops: These days and nights belong to Alexis!

As surrealists we were on the streets from the start, along with thousands of others, in revolt and solidarity; for surrealism was born with the breath of the street, and does not intend to ever abandon it. After the mass resistance before the State murderers, the breath of the street has become even warmer, even more hospitable and creative than before. It is not in our competence to propose a general line to this movement. Yet we do assume our responsibility in the common struggle, as it is a struggle for freedom. Without having to agree with all aspects of such a mass phenomenon, without being partisans of blind hatred and of violence for its own sake, we accept that this phenomenon exists for a reason.

Let's not allow this flaming breath of poetry to loosen or die out.

Let's turn it into a concrete utopia: to transform the world and to transform life!

No peace with cops and their masters!

All in the streets!

Those who cannot feel the rage may as well shut their traps!

Nice Ride, collage by Diamantis Karavolas

Target For Spit

When nations grow old
the Arts grow cold
And Commerce settles on every tree
—William Blake

Those who work their lives away should have little reason to celebrate the pillar at the southwest entrance to the Lloyd Center Mall. This insidious column of giant coins inscribed with capitalist proverbs, pompously titled "Capitalism" as if we didn't already get it, appears more like a snide parody of the totem pole than an invention of the creative imagination.

It is indeed capitalism—atomizing us through forced labor—that is at the center of today's social order. A web of blood and sweat founded on empty promises, capitalism deceitfully veils the suffering it churns with ideas of prosperity and consumption, encoding us with delusions of potential grandeur. No amount of shopping can save you from the misery it produces. No quantity of property will make your life or your neighbor's any more complete. For what is capitalism but a huge lethal diversion from our real desires, our real lives?

Obviously a product of official art, this pillar of coins pays homage to the misery of the people. It is a symbolic representation of the neurotic, expansionist, war-mongering, class-based character of the American dream. In disgust, we, surrealists, cordially invite each and every insurgent worker and dispossessed to convene on this stick in the mud, and utilize it—until further notice—for a more appropriate purpose: as a target for spit!

The exploitive social relationship it praises relies solely on our cooperative subordination. Its destruction will depend on our joint insubordination! In honor of the material hammers of the imagination we call for a jailbreak out of this open-air prison of work and grief, and into a society of poetry, laziness, and love!

The Portland Surrealist Group
May Day 2004

Contributors to HYDROLITH

Will Alexander LOS ANGELES
John Andersson STOCKHOLM
Frank Antonsen COPENHAGEN
Apio OAKLAND
Rafet Arslan IZMIR
Michèle Bachelet PARIS
Marie Baudet PARIS
Johannes Bergmark STOCKHOLM/SZCZECIN
J.K. Bogartte MILWAUKEE
Erik Bohman STOCKHOLM
Daniel C. Boyer MICHIGAN
Eric Bragg BERKELEY
F.N. Brill PORTLAND
Ronnie Burk SAN FRANCISCO
Richard Burke ST LOUIS
Susan Burke ST LOUIS
Miguel de Carvalho COIMBRA
Eugenio Castro MADRID
Paul Cowdell LONDON
Mair Davies LONDON
Nacho Díaz LONDON
Schlechter Duvall INDONESIA
Alexandre Fatta QUEBEC CITY
Kristoffer Flammarion STOCKHOLM
Merl Fluin LONDON
Kathleen Fox ENGLAND
Mattias Forshage STOCKHOLM
Sarah Frances PORTLAND
Brandon Freels PORTLAND
Jesús García Rodríguez MADRID
Joël Gayraud PARIS
Guy Girard PARIS
Allan Graubard NEW YORK CITY
Robert Green CALIFORNIA
Vicente Gutiérrez Escudero MADRID
Stefan Hammarén FINLAND
Raúl Henao COLOMBIA
Patrick Hourihan LONDON
Dale Houstman MINNEAPOLIS
Bill Howe LEEDS
Bruno Jacobs STOCKHOLM
Diamantis Karavolas ATHENS
Vangelis Koutalis ATHENS
Cinns [Çağrı Küçüksayraç] ISTANBUL
Don LaCoss WISCONSIN
Sotiris Liontos ATHENS
Michael Löwy PARIS
Emma Lundenmark STOCKHOLM
Josie Malinowski LONDON
Lurdes Martínez MADRID
Marie-Dominique Massoni PARIS
Desmond Morris LONDON
David Nadeau QUEBEC CITY
Luís Navarro MADRID
Niklas Nenzén STOCKHOLM
Novadawn PORTLAND
Noé Ortega Quijano MADRID
Juan Carlos Otaño BUENOS AIRES
Ayşe Özkan ISTANBUL
Dominique Paul PARIS
Katerina Piňosovà PRAGUE
Ribitch BERKELEY
Rad [Rıdvan] ISTANBUL
Franklin Rosemont CHICAGO
Matt Rounsville TEXAS
Ron Sakolsky, VANCOUVER
Emilio Santiago MADRID
Bertrand Schmitt PARIS/PRAGUE
Shibek PORTLAND
Lisa Simmonson BERKELEY
Nikos Stabakis ATHENS
Dan Stanciu BUCHAREST
Wedgwood Steventon ENGLAND
Theoni Tambaki ATHENS
Iulian Tănase BUCHAREST
Debra Taub CALIFORNIA
Dominic Tétrault MONTREAL
Andrew Torch ST LOUIS
Sasha Vlad SAN FRANCISCO
Richard Waara SAN FRANCISCO
John Welson WALES
Onston [Can Yeşiloğlu] IZMIR
Michel Zimbacca PARIS

www.ingramcontent.com/pod-product-compliance
Lightning Source LLC
Chambersburg PA
CBHW080243170426
43192CB00014BA/2547
9780578050393